Projects in
Linguistics and
Language Studies

Third edition

Projects in Linguistics and Language Studies

A Practical Guide to Researching Language

me:
Alison Wray
Cardiff University

and

Aileen Bloomer
York St John University

Routledge
Taylor & Francis Group

LONDON AND NEW YORK

First published 1998 by Hodder Arnold
Second edition published 2006 by Hodder Education

This edition published 2013 by Routledge
2 Park Square, Milton Park, Abingdon, Oxon OX14 4RN
711 Third Avenue, New York, NY, 10017, USA

Routledge is an imprint of the Taylor & Francis Group, an informa business

The advice and information in this book are believed to be true and
accurate at the date of going to press, but neither the authors nor the publisher
can accept any legal responsibility or liability for any errors or omissions.

British Library Cataloguing-in-Publication Data
A catalogue record for this book is available from the British Library.

Library of Congress Cataloging-in-Publication Data
A catalog record for this book is available from the Library of Congress.

ISBN: 978-1-444-14536-6

Typeset by Datapage India Pvt Ltd

Contents

Preface to the third edition ix
Why we wrote this book ix
Who the book is for ix
What the book does ix
What the book doesn't do x
The second edition x
The third edition x

Acknowledgments xi

International Phonetic Alphabet xii

1 Introduction: starting on the
   right foot 1
   Choosing an area 1
   Getting organized 3
   Using resources 5
   Being a researcher 8
   Theory-only projects 10
   Setting up data-based research 11
   Being streetwise: keeping on the
     right side of your assessor.................. 14

Part I Areas of Study and Project Ideas

2 Psycholinguistics 17
   Textbooks and major journals................ 17
   Central themes and project ideas...........18
     How psycholinguists conceptualize
       language....................................... 19
     How we understand language 20
     Psycholinguistics and
       grammatical theory........................ 21
     Lexical and structural ambiguity 22
     How we produce spoken language 23
     How we produce writing................... 26
     Language and thought..................... 27

3 First-language acquisition and
   development 30
   Approaches to research........................ 30
   Terminology 31
   Textbooks and major journals................ 31
   The CHILDES database......................... 32
   Things to think about.......................... 32
   Central themes and project ideas...........34

Longitudinal case studies................. 34
Prelinguistic development................. 35
Over- and under-extension: lexical
  and semantic development 35
Children's morphology................... 36
Development of phonology and
  intonation 36
Comprehension of complex
  grammatical structures................. 37
Children's metalinguistic
  awareness 37
Colour terms 38
Carer language (or child-directed
  speech)....................................... 39
Conversational development............ 40
Sources of variation in
  child language 40
Literacy development 41
Developmental problems................. 42
Later language acquisition.............. 43

4 Second-language acquisition 45
   Terminology 45
   Textbooks and major journals................ 47
   Things to think about........................... 48
   Central themes and project ideas...........48
     Developmental sequences and the
       process of acquisition 48
     Comparison of L1 and
       L2 acquisition.............................. 49
     Language-learning targets 49
     Motivation 50
     Grammar-based and communication-
       based teaching............................ 50
     Vocabulary acquisition 52
     Different concepts expressed in
       different languages........................ 53
     The learner's approach and
       experience 53
     Interlanguage, error analysis, and
       contrastive analysis....................... 54
     Language assessment and testing....55
     Bilinguals, multilinguals,
       and polyglots............................ 55
     Language teaching policies.............. 56

Effect of the year abroad 58
Role of the social and political status
    of English as L2 59

5 Structure and meaning **61**
Textbooks and major journals 61
Central themes and project ideas 62
    Pragmatics 62
    Metaphor 64
    Sentence structure 65
    Words in isolation and in
        combination 67
    Morphology and etymology 70
    Punctuation 71
    'Correct' grammar 72

6 Style in spoken and written texts ... **76**
Textbooks and major journals 77
Central themes and project ideas 78
    Sound patterns within texts 79
    Lexical choice within texts 80
    Grammatical structure within texts 81
    Interpersonal function of texts 83
    Formality and informality 85
    Ideology and power 86
    Authorship 88
    Oral texts 88

7 Sociolinguistics **92**
Terminology and central concepts 93
Textbooks and major journals 94
Central themes and project ideas 95
    Quantitative approaches 95
    Social networks 96
    Qualitative approaches 97

8 Language and gender **101**
Terminology 101
Textbooks and major journals 102
Central themes and project ideas 102
    The gender variable in linguistic
        research 102
    Attitudes towards male and
        female language 103
    Gender differences in accent
        and dialect 104
    Differences in conversation and
        style of language use 105
    Gay language 106

Explanations of difference 107
Language and sexism 108
Gender-differentiated language in
    first-language acquisition 108
Language, gender, and education ... 109

9 Accents and dialects of English ... **111**
Terminology 112
Textbooks, reference sources, and
    major journals 112
Which accent/dialect to choose 114
Obtaining data 115
What to look for in an accent 115
What to look for in a dialect 115
Possible angles and project ideas 117
    Comparing the speech of three
        generations 117
    Comparing the accents of different
        non-native speakers 118
    Explaining why a variety has
        come about 119
    The political dimension of
        a variety 119
    Accent and dialect in literature 120
    Update study 121
    Comparison of two varieties 121
Things to think about 122

10 History of English **124**
Textbooks, reference sources, and
    major journals 125
Central themes and project ideas 126
    Researching words and names 126
    Pronunciation and spelling 129
    History of English dialects 131
    The profile of a feature of English
        across time 131
    Sociopolitical trends and influences
        on English 131
    English as a world language 132
    The influence of literacy
        on language 133
Things to think about 134

**11 Computer-mediated
    communication** **135**
Terminology 136
Textbooks and major journals 136

Central themes and project ideas.........137
    Impoverished language 137
    Changes in vocabulary 138
    Linguistic variation 139
    Discourse structure 140
    Semantics and pragmatics.............140
    Language production.....................141
    Interpersonal communication 142
    Identity and anonymity 143
    Technology and information............145
    Multilingualism and
      minority languages......................147
Things to think about..........................149

Part II Techniques for Collecting Data

12 Audio- and video-recorded data ... 153
Places to get data 153
Audio or video? 153
Naturalistic data.................................153
Ethics and legality 154
Quality..154
How much data do you need? 154
Practicalities.......................................155
What to submit....................................156
Things to think about...........................156

13 Experiments 157
What does experimentation involve?.....157
Designing an experiment.....................159
Things to think about...........................161
Advantages of experimental research ...163
Disadvantages of experimental
    research...163

14 Questionnaires, interviews, and focus groups 164
Deciding if you need a questionnaire,
    interview, or focus group..................164
Common uses of interviews, focus
    groups, and questionnaires 165
Logistics...165
Things to think about...........................170
Questionnaires....................................170
Interviews 173
Focus groups 177

15 Observation and case studies........179
Observation studies 179
Case studies.......................................181

16 Ethical considerations in research projects 184
Ethics policies and guidelines 184
The difference between confidentiality
    and anonymity 185
Data Protection Laws...........................186

Part III Tools for Data Analysis

17 Transcribing speech phonetically and phonemically........................... 189
The difference between phonetic and
    phonemic transcription 189
A few notes on phonemes...................190
Phonetic and phonemic symbols
    in word-processing 191
Hints on writing about pronunciation.....192
Checklist of phonemes 193

18 Transcribing speech orthographically 195
How to organize the presentation
    of a transcription..............................195
Turn taking..197
Silence and non-verbal
    communication in conversation..........198
Dealing with unusual pronunciations.....199
Transcribing unclear utterances............200
Marking pitch, emphasis, volume, and
    speed...201
External events 203
Presenting the transcription 203
Presenting the audio data itself...........204

19 Using computers to study texts 205
What is a corpus? 205
Why is a corpus useful?.......................205
How do corpus searches operate?........206
How do you find a corpus? 209
What are the main text analysis
    tools?...211
Making sense of corpus annotation......211
Using corpora effectively in your work ...212

Compiling your own corpus: potential
   problems 212
Limitations of corpora 213
Further reading 213

20 Statistics and your project 214
Do you need graphs and calculations
   in your project? 214
Descriptive statistics and basic
   calculations 215
Using statistical analyses 221
Textbooks 225
Help for the mathematically insecure 226
Key to the most common algebraic
   symbols used in basic statistics 228

Part IV Presenting Your Work

21 How to reference 233
What is the purpose of referencing? 233
General tips 233
What does a basic reference
   look like? 234
What is the difference between a
   'references' list and a 'bibliography'? 234
Basics of referencing 234
Details of the Harvard system
   conventions 237
Details of the Humane system
   conventions 245

22 Plagiarism and how to avoid it 247
What is plagiarism? 247
Will you get found out? 248

How to avoid accidental plagiarism:
   some strategies 248
     Referencing 248
     Taking notes 249
     Skilled writing 249
     Finding your voice 250

**23 Handy hints on writing good
academic English 261**
Before you start to write 261
As you are writing 262
After you have written 263
The uses of apostrophes 263
Using punctuation 264
Other common problems 265

**24 Hints on giving a good oral
presentation 267**
Some general points 267
Time management 268
Talk, don't read 269
Content 269
Slides (e.g. PowerPoint) 270
Handouts 272
Self-presentation 272
Rehearsing 272
On the day 273
Questions and answers 275

References 277

Index 301

Preface to the third edition

Why we wrote this book

We wrote this book because you can't learn how to write good essays and research projects just by reading the subject textbooks. There is a lot of knowledge that a student is expected to somehow 'pick up': what good research looks like; how researchers express themselves; where to start. Alert students will gather some of this information piecemeal from tutorials, feedback on their work, talking to other students, and so on, but there is usually no way of being sure that you have done all the right things until the work comes back marked.

From the marker's point of view, there are certain features that a piece of work can contain that will make it look credible. Many of the things that make the difference between a high mark and a low one are to do with having the knack of how to plan and present (whether orally or in writing) research effectively.

Who the book is for

The book is intended, primarily, for undergraduates taking linguistics or language studies as part or all of their degree programme, and who are expected to engage in research-type project work. However, those embarking on postgraduate research, particularly if they have not previously done data analysis in linguistics, will find the book a useful source of basic procedural information and references to key texts. Secondary- and high-school students engaged in project work should also find it approachable, even if it sometimes assumes more technical knowledge than they yet have.

What the book does

The book is arranged in four parts. Part I is divided into chapters covering some of the major sub-disciplines most commonly chosen by students for their projects. They do not always map onto a single undergraduate module or conventional sub-area of linguistics, because, in our experience, projects don't do this either. But it should not be too difficult to make the connections back to introductory textbooks or class notes. Within each of these chapters there is a brief review of introductory texts, a list of major journals and a brief account of the major research areas. **Key terms** in **bold font** can be used to find information in printed book indexes and glossaries, in dictionaries of linguistic terms or via electronic search engines. There are also over 350 practical suggestions for projects. These are specifically aimed at the needs of the student who is required to engage with data of some kind, but who is not expecting to make an original contribution to the field (though some of the projects undoubtedly could lead to this if handled well).

Part II contains chapters on methodology, which provide techniques and guidance on how to set up and run research. Part III contains tools: guidance in practical procedures, and specific information that is often needed but not always easy to find. The final part contains guidance on presenting your project in the required format, whether oral or written, and guidance on referencing and on how to avoid plagiarism.

But, before all that, there is an introductory chapter intended to set the scene and help the reader orientate him-/herself. We strongly recommend that this chapter is read before anything else.

What the book doesn't do

Although each of the project chapters contains an overview of the research that has been done in the area, this book is not intended to provide a full introduction to those areas. Rather than giving a great deal of primary information, already available in dedicated textbooks, we refer the reader to such books. In this way, we not only keep this book focused on its primary function but also provide the reader with the beginnings of a bibliography. Because the book is about practical projects, there are several areas of linguistics that are not covered at all. Furthermore, many of the projects that are proposed would not be suitable for a more rigorous (i.e. postgraduate or professional) research context. Rather, we have directed our attention unashamedly towards generating ideas that students will find inspiring and encouraging, and we have exploited the freedom from narrower research constraints that can still be enjoyed at this exploratory level.

The second edition

In the second edition, we introduced a chapter on ethical considerations, to replace the previous narrower coverage of the British Data Protection Act, and expanded the chapters on statistics and plagiarism. Throughout, we updated not only the references but also aspects of the content to reflect new technologies that were barely worth a mention when we were preparing the first edition. For instance, we offered guidance on the use of the Internet as a resource, including how to reference electronic material.

The third edition

In this third edition, we have responded to user feedback in two major ways: by adding a chapter on how to research computer-mediated communication and by providing guidance on how to present work orally, as many students are now required to do. We have updated all the other chapters as necessary and we offer yet more suggestions for possible projects. As in the second edition, our aim in making the changes has been to enhance the usefulness of the book to its student and staff users, without risking the integrity of the underlying concept, which the user feedback has indicated to be unique and valuable as it stands.

Acknowledgments

The key influence on us in creating this third edition was the feedback that we received in response to a users' questionnaire issued by our commissioning editor, Bianca Knights. We are grateful to her and to those who provided the uniformly helpful observations and suggestions, and we thank them also for their overwhelmingly positive comments on the previous editions. In reworking the text for a second time, we continued to rely heavily on the original material written by Kate Trott, Shirley Reay, and Chris Butler for the first edition, and we should like to thank them for allowing us to continue to use it.

We are particularly grateful to Lise Fontaine for her practical help with the drafting of the new chapter on computer-mediated communication. For feedback on drafts, specific observations, providing vital information, and other support for this or a previous edition, we wish to thank: Pauline Aldous, Margaret Atherden, Chris Butler, Louise Cooper, Tom Dawkes, Lise Fontaine, Geoffrey Leech, Andrew Merrison, Paul Rayson, Gordon Tucker and Mike Wallace.

Last but not least, we once more thank our past students at York St John University and Cardiff University. The cohorts that inspired the original concept of the book have been succeeded by others who have continued to show us, in their writing, speaking and questioning, just how much creativity and insight a good project can unleash.

Alison Wray
Cardiff University

Aileen Bloomer
York St John University

September 2011

International Phonetic Alphabet

THE INTERNATIONAL PHONETIC ALPHABET (revised to 2005)

CONSONANTS (PULMONIC) © 2005 IPA

	Bilabial	Labiodental	Dental	Alveolar	Post alveolar	Retroflex	Palatal	Velar	Uvular	Pharyngeal	Glottal
Plosive	p b			t d		ʈ ɖ	c ɟ	k ɡ	q ɢ		ʔ
Nasal	m	ɱ		n		ɳ	ɲ	ŋ	N		
Trill	ʙ			r					ʀ		
Tap or Flap		ⱱ		ɾ		ɽ					
Fricative	ɸ β	f v	θ ð	s z	ʃ ʒ	ʂ ʐ	ç ʝ	x ɣ	χ ʁ	ħ ʕ	h ɦ
Lateral fricative				ɬ ɮ							
Approximant		ʋ		ɹ		ɻ	j	ɰ			
Lateral approximant				l		ɭ	ʎ	ʟ			

Where symbols appear in pairs, the one to the right represents a voiced consonant. Shaded areas denote articulations judged impossible.

CONSONANTS (NON-PULMONIC)

Clicks		Voiced implosives		Ejectives	
ʘ	Bilabial	ɓ	Bilabial	ʼ	Examples:
ǀ	Dental	ɗ	Dental/alveolar	pʼ	Bilabial
ǃ	(Post)alveolar	ʄ	Palatal	tʼ	Dental/alveolar
ǂ	Palatoalveolar	ɠ	Velar	kʼ	Velar
ǁ	Alveolar lateral	ʛ	Uvular	sʼ	Alveolar fricative

OTHER SYMBOLS

ʍ	Voiceless labial-velar fricative	ɕ ʑ	Alveolo-palatal fricatives
w	Voiced labial-velar approximant	ɺ	Voiced alveolar lateral flap
ɥ	Voiced labial-palatal approximant	ɧ	Simultaneous ʃ and x
ʜ	Voiceless epiglottal fricative		
ʢ	Voiced epiglottal fricative	Affricates and double articulations can be represented by two symbols joined by a tie bar if necessary.	k͡p t͡s
ʡ	Epiglottal plosive		

VOWELS

Front Central Back
Close: i y — ɨ ʉ — ɯ u
ɪ ʏ / ʊ
Close-mid: e ø — ɘ ɵ — ɤ o
ə
Open-mid: ɛ œ — ɜ ɞ — ʌ ɔ
æ / ɐ
Open: a ɶ — ɑ ɒ

Where symbols appear in pairs, the one to the right represents a rounded vowel.

SUPRASEGMENTALS

ˈ	Primary stress
ˌ	Secondary stress
	ˌfoʊnəˈtɪʃən
ː	Long eː
ˑ	Half-long eˑ
̆	Extra-short ĕ
|	Minor (foot) group
‖	Major (intonation) group
.	Syllable break ɹi.ækt
‿	Linking (absence of a break)

DIACRITICS   Diacritics may be placed above a symbol with a descender, e.g. ŋ̊

̥	Voiceless	n̥ d̥	̤ Breathy voiced b̤ a̤	̪ Dental	t̪ d̪
̬	Voiced	s̬ t̬	̰ Creaky voiced b̰ a̰	̺ Apical	t̺ d̺
ʰ	Aspirated	tʰ dʰ	̼ Linguolabial t̼ d̼	̻ Laminal	t̻ d̻
̹	More rounded	ɔ̹	ʷ Labialized tʷ dʷ	̃ Nasalized	ẽ
̜	Less rounded	ɔ̜	ʲ Palatalized tʲ dʲ	ⁿ Nasal release	dⁿ
̟	Advanced	u̟	ˠ Velarized tˠ dˠ	ˡ Lateral release	dˡ
̠	Retracted	e̠	ˤ Pharyngealized tˤ dˤ	̚ No audible release	d̚
̈	Centralized	ë	̴ Velarized or pharyngealized ɫ		
̽	Mid-centralized	e̽	̝ Raised e̝ (ɹ̝ = voiced alveolar fricative)		
̩	Syllabic	n̩	̞ Lowered e̞ (β̞ = voiced bilabial approximant)		
̯	Non-syllabic	e̯	̘ Advanced Tongue Root e̘		
˞	Rhoticity	ɚ a˞	̙ Retracted Tongue Root e̙		

TONES AND WORD ACCENTS

LEVEL			CONTOUR		
e̋ or	˥	Extra high	ě or	ˇ	Rising
é	˦	High	ê	ˆ	Falling
ē	˧	Mid	e᷄		High rising
è	˨	Low	e᷅		Low rising
ȅ	˩	Extra low	e᷈		Rising-falling
↓		Downstep	↗		Global rise
↑		Upstep	↘		Global fall

1

Introduction: starting on the right foot

Choosing an area

In this book we are assuming that you are about to embark upon a data-based, dissertation-length project in an area of your choice. However, even if you are preparing an essay for a specific module, there is plenty here to help you. The secret of good research is to know what it is practical to do and what it is wise to do, so here are some questions you can usefully ask yourself.

What can be researched?

There are many questions that we can ask about language, but not all of them are suitable for a research project. Some questions cannot be answered for practical reasons, such as *How many words are there in all the languages in all the world?* Even if you could settle on an adequate definition of 'word' and 'language', you could never discover that information. A good research question is one that you can envisage finding an answer to. So, never just ask the question. Always imagine the possible answers and how you would find them out.

A good project is something that is doable within the bounds of the available facilities. To ensure that it is, plan through the stages very carefully, listing what you will need. For many students, it is a problem even getting access to a quiet room, let alone to a patient during brain surgery!

What area should I choose?

Remember you will have to eat, sleep, and breathe this project, perhaps for several months, so do yourself the favour of choosing something that you can live with, enjoy, and know that you are doing well. It makes sense to work on aspects of language that you have already found rewarding and gained good marks in. If you cannot think of a subject, this book has hundreds of project ideas. Alternatively, take half an hour with a cup of coffee and your old files and textbooks, and simply remind yourself of the aspects of language that you have found most interesting. Try to remember what it was about language that fired your enthusiasm in the first place. Maybe your studies so far have not given you an opportunity to pursue some of the interests that you brought with you, and now might be your chance to follow them up.

- If you have other projects coming up over the next year or two, prepare the ground now. As you read, think, chat, and write other pieces of work, jot down any thoughts, references, etc., in a book or file marked 'Project Ideas'. Then, when it comes to it, you will have plenty of ideas to choose from.
- In looking for ideas, try to use sources that are as up to date as possible, because ideas and techniques change as more is learned about the field of investigation. It is a good idea to base your work on something that someone else has done, either replicating the original study or changing one **variable** (see Chapter 20), such as the age or gender of the participants.

Who will supervise me?

Supervising student projects can be one of the most rewarding things that a university teacher has to do. You will get most out of a supervisor who shares your interest in the subject, especially if they are personally research-active in it. Don't just base your judgement on what someone has taught you in modules, as staff don't always get to teach their favourite subjects, especially in relatively small departments. Find out from the department's list of staff research interests who works in areas that interest you, and then arrange to see them. Most people love talking about their own research and will be delighted to have you take an interest.

What am I expected to do?

There are in-house rules for project writing and presentation: they may be uniform across the whole institution or department-specific. Check any instructions you have been issued with, or your module handbook, for guidelines. In-house rules include things such as:

- What the word limit is and how you calculate it. Do quotes, appendices, and summary tables count? Are you allowed to go over or under the limit and, if so, by how much? What happens if you don't stick to the limit?
- What happens if you submit your work late?
- What is the presentation format? Is it compulsory to word-process? Do you have to submit work in hard copy, electronically, or both?
  - If you are handing in hard copy, do you need to leave a right-hand as well as a lefthand margin? Should you write/print on one side of the paper or both, and in single, 1.5, or double spacing? How many copies are you to submit? Does the work have to be bound, or in a certain type of folder? Should your name be on every page, or is your work marked anonymously? Even if there are no specific rules, put yourself in the place of the person marking not just your project but numerous others like it (possibly at 2 o'clock in the morning), and think about the following points. If comments are to be made on your work, it is not helpful to put each sheet in a separate plastic envelope. In some kinds of presentation files, the words at the right-hand edge of the reverse side of the paper cannot be read because of the file-grip mechanism, so you need to leave a margin. As a general rule, the smaller the package your work comes in the better – walking home with 40 ring binders is actually a physical impossibility. See also 'Presenting symbols and numbers' near the end of this chapter.
  - If you are submitting your work electronically, what format should you save it in (e.g. Word version, pdf)? How should you submit any audio or visual material, including anything you only have in hard copy, such as magazine articles? Are you to email the work or provide it on a disk? If it is to be marked anonymously, do you have to

remove the 'signature' on the file that identifies you as the author? Will your work be put through plagiarism-detection software, and if so, what are the implications for how you prepare your work? For more on plagiarism see Chapter 22.

- What is the preferred **referencing system**? A full description of the two most common ones (the **Harvard** and the **Humane**) can be found in Chapter 21.

Getting organized

How do I organize my time?

You have only limited time to achieve your goal. You want your work to be as good as possible, which means not rushing it, but also not wearing yourself out. You need to use your time well and know when to stop. You will have other things to do at the same time as the project, including, quite possibly, other deadlines to accommodate. Only by planning can you really identify what needs doing, in what order, and how long it will take. If you don't have some idea of this, you are leaving a great deal to chance. One way to schedule things is to work backwards (Table 1.1).

Table 1.1 Working backwards from the deadline

Date	Task
16th	DEADLINE
15th	Print final version (NB: *never* leave printing to the last day. You *know* why!!). Add any handwritten bits (symbols, diagrams, etc.); photocopy; take to the binder. (Note that while some types of binding can be done while you wait, others take longer. Check in advance, so that you can make allowances in your schedule.)
13th	Draft-print 'final version' and read it *slowly* for typing errors, style, expression, accuracy in referencing and general sense; make any alterations
12th	Write conclusion and final version of introduction
11th	Finish chapter/section X
6th	Finish chapter/section Y

It is important to honour your timetable. When you have achieved your goal, stop and rest. Getting ahead of your own schedule can be a good psychological step, but only if you don't slow down so much that you waste the time you gained. If you get wildly outside your timetable, rewrite it, taking into account any factors you overlooked last time, and making any necessary adjustments in what you hope to include.

Should I make a plan?

Yes. From the start, have a clear idea of what you hope to include and what you don't. Write a list of chapter and/or section headings, and decide what will go in each (see below). Whenever you come across a useful idea or reference, note it in the appropriate place on your plan, so that you can find it when you need it. You can always change your plan later, but it's better to have one. It saves you doing all sorts of unnecessary work for chapters or sections that you haven't realized you won't need to write. Also, read the 'Before you start to write' section of Chapter 23.

How should I structure my work?

In linguistics, and especially in 'scientific' linguistics, it is a good idea to write under headings: this helps to keep everything in its place, saves words, and makes the work much easier to read. There are various possible structures and no single way is correct (but do check what you are required to do). Typically, however, the following components will need to be included (see also 'What research looks like', below):

- *Title*: Make it informative about what you are finding out.
- *Abstract*: A short description (often only one paragraph) that summarizes your study, including what you found out. It is *not* the same as an introduction. Write the abstract last, when you have the full picture of what you have achieved.
- *Introduction*: A short contextualization of your topic, introducing your topic, and indicating why it is important to address it. A brief outline of how the rest of your write-up is structured.
- *Literature review*: Brief, succinct critical evaluations of how existing research contributes to answering your focal question. See below for more on how to write such a literature review. Conclude the review by identifying one or more **research questions** that the existing research leaves unanswered, and that you aim to answer in your own study. Where possible, include predictions or hypotheses about what you will find.
- *Methodology*: A description of your data: e.g. the source of your texts, who your informants are, how you have designed and administered your research tools (questionnaire, experiment, etc.). You may want to include a brief rationale for your chosen approach, based on the literature.
- *Data* or *Results*: A straight description of the data you have gathered.
- *Analysis*: Organized according to the research questions that you identified as needing answers or predictions/hypotheses that needed testing; compare, contrast and/or evaluate patterns in your data, using graphs and statistical analyses if possible and appropriate.
- *Discussion*: Take your analyses back to the literature, comparing what you have found with what you discussed in the literature review, and commenting on what it means. As appropriate, consider how your findings may have been affected by limitations in the design of your work or problems with how you carried it out. But leave your reader with a sense that you have nevertheless achieved something worthwhile: present your work in a positive light where you can.
- *Conclusion*: Explain how the outcomes of your Discussion section help to locate your findings within the topic field. Identify any remaining questions and suggest what could be done in the future, and how, to find answers to them.

You can choose different headings for your chapters or sections from those given above, but always keep a clear sense of the purpose of each component of your account.

Using the word limit imposed for your work, calculate how many words you have for each of the above components. If you find you need more words in a section, take them from another, in order to stay inside the word limit. By identifying subsections, you can subdivide the word counts further, until you never have more than a few hundred words to write under a given heading. This will help you maintain discipline and focus, and give you clear warning when you have too much or too little to say (so that you can restructure the plan to accommodate it). It will also encourage you, since you will always know exactly how much of your project you have written up and how much you still have to do.

Using resources

Books and journals

Although *textbooks* are a good place to start, in research it is poor practice to rely heavily on them. Rather, use them as a gateway to the original literature that you need to track down and read for yourself. In each chapter in Part I, we recommend relevant textbooks. However, ones that cover a wider range (such Fromkin *et al.* 2010; Hall *et al.* 2011; Merrison *et al.* forthcoming; Thomas and Wareing 2003) might also be useful when you are trying to decide where to start. *Readers* can be an excellent way to access classic papers in an area of enquiry: scan the editors' introduction for a justification of why a paper was selected. Many are focused on specific areas (e.g. Coates and Pichler 2011; Coupland and Jaworski 2009; Trott *et al.* 2003). Griffiths *et al.* (2010) select original papers on a wide range of linguistic topics – a fact that might help you see useful links between different topics. *Edited collections* feature chapters by many different writers on the same theme. Some collections are more principled than others, however: some are simply papers presented at a certain conference and may not be ground-breaking. *Monographs* are complete books written by one author (or by co-authors, with no indication of who wrote what). They can be difficult to differentiate from textbooks, but normally will focus on a narrow theme and argue a particular point of view. Reading entire books is time-consuming, so use the blurb on the back, the Introduction and the Conclusion to find out what the author is claiming. Then use the index and/or the table of contents to identify the most relevant topics for your interests. *Journal articles* can be technical, but tend to be succinct and in a format not dissimilar to your own project. If you find a journal article difficult to understand, whether because of its style or because of the previous knowledge that it assumes, start by reading the abstract, the Introduction, and the Conclusion, to get the main points and orientate yourself. Then go back and read the rest of the article if you judge that it is relevant enough to your needs. Use the reference lists in journal articles as a quick way of finding other relevant material. Specialist *encyclopaedias* (especially Brown 2006; Crystal 2003b, 2010; Malmkjaer 2010) and *handbooks* (e.g. Aarts and McMahon 2006; Aronoff and Rees-Miller 2001; Davies and Elder 2003; Kaplan 2010) are an excellent resource, because the top people have been asked to summarize the issues in their specialist field. You can also use *abstracting databases* (see later), *bibliographies* (these tell you who has written what in a given subject area), unpublished *MA dissertations* and *PhD theses*, and archives of past undergraduate *projects* (though remember that work by students is not usually of the same quality as published research!).

Where to look in libraries

Most libraries keep the latest issues of journals in one place, and then bind several issues together and put them on the stacks (shelves). For books, remember to check other sections than just linguistics (e.g. education, sociology, philosophy, psychology) that may have relevant books. Besides your own and any other local university or college libraries, remember to consider hospital and other institutional libraries and local archives. The local city or county library may also have useful books and, if you need inter-library loans (see below), you may be charged less there than in your own institution. Major university libraries and public libraries in large cities may not let you borrow books, but you can arrange in advance to gain read-only access. National libraries, such as the British Library in London, normally require a special ticket, and you may need a letter of introduction from your institution confirming that you are engaged in research.

Libraries in most countries operate a system of *inter-library loans*, whereby a book or journal article not available locally can be obtained from elsewhere. There is normally a charge for this service, but it may be subsidized by your department or, at a civic library, by the local government.

Electronic resources

Libraries now carry a great deal of information in electronic form: usually on networked databases, or through institutional subscriptions to Internet services. You may be able to access your university's materials remotely (via the Internet from your home computer) using a password. Enquire with a librarian about what is available. If there are training sessions on how to use the resources, take advantage of them. Many printed journals are now also available electronically, and you can search for what you want, and then download and print out (via PDF) a copy identical to the printed one. A great many journal papers and other resources that are otherwise not available can be obtained through the ERIC clearing house, http://www.eric.ed.gov/.

There are several ways of saving time by knowing how to use search tools, particularly those that look for journal articles and books on a particular topic. Particularly useful are Linguistics and Language Behavior Abstracts and the Web of Knowledge, both available through subscription, and Google Scholar (http://scholar.google.com), free on the Internet. All of these include an abstracts database. Abstracts databases are important because few people have the time to check every journal as it comes out, and there is therefore a danger of missing things relevant to their work. The databases carry abstracts of all the papers in the various publications that they cover, updated on a regular basis. The entries are searchable by author, keyword, and text. The idea is that you can find many entries that may be relevant to your needs and, on the basis of the abstract, decide whether or not to obtain and read the full paper. Remember: reading the abstract is *not* a substitute for reading the article itself if you are intending to refer to the research. A brief summary cannot give you sufficient detail for your purposes, so you must read the full account in context.

The Internet as a source of information

A huge amount of information is available via the Internet. There is no quality control, however, so it can be inaccurate or even positively (and deliberately) misleading. For this reason, it is a good idea to operate with caution: use what you find as a stepping stone to your goal, rather than as a goal in itself. That is, if you find on a website a claim that something is the case, don't simply accept it and quote it. Rather, look for references that back the claim up, and then track them down for yourself. Don't be satisfied until you have found evidence that is reliable (see 'Reviewing the literature' below). Where you do want to use information from websites, prefer those belonging to official organizations or to people whose credentials you can check. Students often ask specifically about the status of Wikipedia, http://en.wikipedia.org/wiki/Main_Page, a free encyclopaedia that is written by, and constantly updated by, its users (that is, anyone). Although Wikipedia is vulnerable to the obvious limitations of being compiled in this way, the intention is to create a reliable database by allowing its readers directly to edit existing pages, so that they, in effect, review the quality of the account, and remove any inaccuracies. Inevitably, the issue comes down to how 'accurate' and 'inaccurate' are defined, particularly when it comes to topics that are not subject to hard scientific facts. Our advice is to treat Wikipedia like any other Internet source: possibly accurate but not necessarily, and therefore a great place to orientate yourself and get ideas, but not the end of the line. Take what you discover, and check it in other sources. If you cannot find any supporting evidence for a claim, then maybe that claim is unreliable and should not be used. Having said that, the changing text in Wikipedia, along with the *talk* page for each article (see http://en.wikipedia.org/wiki/Help:Using_talk_pages), have the potential to underpin a fascinating research project about the way that meaning is negotiated (see Project 165). For guidance on how to reference material from the Internet, see Chapter 21.

Online viewing of books

Books are expensive to buy and take time to obtain through the library. Many books are now viewable, albeit only in part, through the Look Inside facility in Amazon, on the publishers' website, or via Google Books (http://books.google.com). The former two points of access are often best for recent publications. Usually you can read the first chapter, and view the contents list and index. You may be able to access other parts of the book using the 'search' facility in Look Inside. It can be tantalising to have some but not all of the information you need from a book, but sometimes it is enough to get you on your way, particularly if a search provides you with references that you can follow up elsewhere. Google Books carries the complete text of books that are out of copyright and selected pages of other books. Sometimes, you can read an entire chapter, though often you will find that the key page you need is not available. As a result, you cannot rely on these methods to access all your reading, but they can certainly help you check for information.

People

There are lots of people in the world who know things that you don't, so ask them. The golden rule is to ask sensible questions, so that you don't annoy people or waste their time. If you do your homework first, most people will be pleased to give you time and information.

Databases

Databases are resources that offer you linguistic material for research that you could not possibly gather for yourself. They include general corpora of English and other languages (see Chapter 19), and specific corpora such as the CHILDES database of child language (see Chapter 3).

Dictionaries and glossaries

If you are unsure what a word or a technical term means, then look it up. Apart from general English-language dictionaries, there are a number of specialist linguistics dictionaries, including Crystal (2008), Trask (1993, 1995), Trask and Stockwell (2007) and Richards and Schmidt (2010). Glossaries include Leech (2006) for grammar, Carr (2008) for phonology, Cruse (2006) for semantics and pragmatics, Aitchison (2003) and Field (2004) for psycholinguistics, Davies (2005) for applied linguistics, Macaro, Vanderplank and Murphy (2010) for second language acquisition, and Baker, Hardie and McEnery (2006) for corpus linguistics. In addition, many linguistics textbooks (e.g. Merrison *et al.* forthcoming) have glossaries at the back.

Being a researcher

There are certain hallmarks of being a researcher, certain assumptions that are made, and ways in which the work is approached. Here are a few pointers.

What research looks like

Most research engages with one or more **research questions** – that is, questions that you will answer through an investigation, rather than just by reading. However, the research questions are derived from what you have read, and existing **theory** creates the best foundation for asking something new, or for applying an old question to your particular data. Some kinds of theory make it possible to make a prediction about what you will find, often framed as a **hypothesis**. An experimental hypothesis makes predictions about the outcome of specific controlled events, and the outcomes actually achieved enable you to confirm or fail to confirm the hypothesis (see Chapter 13). Hypotheses and predictions can also be used in non-experimental research. They enable you to identify in advance what contrasts or features you are likely to find (and therefore should look for) in your data. For example, in an observation study, your hypothesis might be that a child will interact differently with adults from the way it does with other children. This gives you a focused goal, and reminds you to avoid introducing other differences between the two situations, such as what activities the child is engaged in. If your research is not built upon a hypothesis, there is a serious danger that you will not be able to explain what you have found out.

Much legitimate research involves rerunning experiments and analyses done by others, challenging established theories with new data, and so on. Because linguistics spans the sciences and the humanities, it deals with strikingly different kinds of intellectual material:

- quantitative data, on which statistical tests can be done: experimental results, word counts, etc.;
- qualitative data: judgements, perceptions, insights, etc.;
- pure theory: models of internal processes which, though testable in terms of what language is like, are in essence non-experimental.

Reviewing the literature

In an essay, project, or dissertation, you will normally be expected to have a literature review. It is easy for this requirement to seem overwhelming and/or to get out of hand.

Simply, there is too much out there for you to read it all and it can be unclear how you should decide what to read, how carefully to read it, and how much detail to report. The following guidelines may help:

- Draw up a skeleton plan (e.g. contents page) of your entire project (see earlier), and work out how many words you can afford to give to your literature review. Once you have decided what issues to cover (see below), further subdivide by theme until you establish that you have an average of, say, just 350 words to cover each topic within the review. By knowing the word limits from early on, you can easily see when it will be pointless to read any more.

- Don't conceive of the literature review as being a description of as many different ideas in the general area of your project as you can find. If you do, you won't know what to choose nor be able to say anything interesting about it. We offer guidance on the literature review below.

- Drive your literature review by *topic*, not publication. Specifically, begin with the precise focus of your project, and derive interesting questions from that, which you can ask of the literature. By asking questions you will find it easy to *harvest* books and journal articles for what they say that is *relevant*, rather than simply reporting everything they contain. You will also find it easier to compare and contrast different claims. In a project examining the differences between the language of a 4-year-old twin brother and sister, obvious questions to ask of the literature might include: How would the language of a 4-year-old non-twin girl normally compare with that of a boy of the same age? Is development of language in twins usually different from non-twins? What sorts of features are likely to be most interesting (e.g. phonology, grammar, vocabulary, social interaction)?

- Some of your literature review might be about methodology, focused around a question like: What methods have been successfully used by others to study the language of young children? You may choose to introduce such a topic when you reach the methodology part of your account. In fact, don't conceive of the literature review as a single lump of text (e.g. a chapter) if it makes more sense for your story to introduce it in parts, according to the questions you are asking at different stages of your account.

- View the literature review as a boxing ring, not a display cabinet – that is, use what you read to identify disagreements and paradoxes. You can then act as referee, commenting on who you think has the stronger argument and why. Disagreements are difficult to see if you simply describe first one author's work and then another's, but, if you are using the resources to answer *your* questions, then you will naturally want to report similar (or contrasting) claims together, giving you the opportunity to comment on how they relate. See Chapter 22 for more guidance on how to achieve this.

- Expect to evaluate what you read, not just report it. Not every claim in print is reliable or well justified by evidence. For guidance on how to evaluate the literature and write a critical literature review, see Wallace and Wray (2011).

How to read and how to make notes

Avoid just reading things that might be relevant in some general way. Always know why you are reading something and what you hope to find out, and don't make notes that are not specific to your work. Rather than ending up with separate pages of notes for each book or article you read, make the notes under the headings for which they are appropriate, so any page of your notes will contain references to several different works. This means that you are more likely to notice when two authors disagree. It also means that writing up can be done without wading through all the notes again. Always label a note or quote with the author's name, date of publication, and page number, so you know where to find it again. If what you have written down is a quote, put it in inverted commas, otherwise you may later think that it is in your own words. To present someone else's words as your own is plagiarism (see Chapter 22). Copy accurately, especially spelling and punctuation.

Theory-only projects

In some circumstances, it may be possible to focus entirely on the critical evaluation or the development of a theory or model without collecting any data of your own. There are two basic reasons why you might embark on a theory-only project. First, you may want to write about an aspect of language that either is not amenable to testing or cannot usefully be investigated via data collection (though, either way, it should still be possible to illustrate your points with linguistic examples). Areas of linguistic study where these criteria might apply in some circumstances include the evolution or origin of language, philosophy of language, or syntactic theory. Second, it may not be feasible to collect the sort of data that you require. In this case, you will be referring to data-based research, but it will be the published material of other researchers. Into this category might fall projects focusing on clinical linguistics, exotic languages, historical linguistics, and so on. Do not see theory-only projects as an escape route from empirical research – they are difficult to do well. In addition, check that a non-empirical project is acceptable for your assessment.

If you are writing a theory-only project, begin with a clear overview of the literature. You should read around the area that interests you as extensively as is practical, because otherwise your arguments will be unsubstantiated. Identify a theory that interests you and which you feel is open for debate and then try to find an angle on it that will create an interesting discussion. One way is to apply it to a new issue. For example, an existing model of lexical retrieval for monolinguals could be discussed in the light of the needs and practices of multilinguals. Can the model cope with additional languages easily or does it need reorganizing? A model that represents the transition from thought to utterance could be explored from the viewpoint of human evolution: does it lend itself to there being a survival advantage at every stage of man's evolution? Or, if someone has proposed a model that accounts for the production of speech, how easily can it be applied to writing? Can it simply be reversed to account for comprehension? If it is a model of adult language, does it apply equally to children?

Draw diagrams to demonstrate how your model works. Diagrams should be explicit and should adequately illustrate the sequence of events that will produce the envisaged outcome. It should be possible to explain the predicted results if the structures are subject to breakdown or malfunction at any stage. Explain the ways in which your model differs in construction, process, and outcome from others.

Setting up data-based research

Chapters 2–11 in this book explore the types of projects that you may be able to undertake. Different areas of research require different techniques, and these are described in Chapters 12–16. But, before you start, there are many general considerations, which we will look at now. It is very important that you read the next few pages, and that you remember to reread them as you plan and carry out your project. What is said below is, of course, subject to modification in the light of what your own course requirements are, so don't forget to check with your own supervisor or tutor what you are expected to achieve, what methods or approaches are preferred, and what equipment is available.

Making sure you know enough

Although it is best to choose a project that uses skills that you already have, this may not be entirely possible. If you need additional skills, check whether there are tutors who can help, either directly or through recommending self-study texts or other sources of assistance. Ask a tutor to give you an honest answer to the question 'Am I up to it?'. See if there are modules you can opt for or specific lectures you can attend that could help. If you know well in advance what your project will be on, plan your modules to prepare you for it. Lecturers often remark that students could help themselves more during project work by looking back carefully at modules that they have previously taken, perhaps digging out old lecture notes and reading lists and generally making use of established resources.

Getting participants and informants

Studying human language normally requires access to people. You may want to work with one person in some detail or you may need to get a number of people to perform some task, either individually or as a group. Either way, you must be sure that appropriate people will be available. How will you persuade your participants to give up their time? What will you tell them about the purpose of your study? If you want to compare males with females, say, are you easily going to recruit the same number of each? If you are collecting your data in the vacation, whom will you use? If you recruit willing members of your family, what will be the effect of their differences in age, education, and so on?

Remember that your participants are doing you a favour by participating. It is in your interests to keep them sweet, so be as efficient as you can in making arrangements, keeping to appointments, and clearly explaining what you want them to do. Remember to thank them afterwards. Participants may be interested to know, at a later date, how the study turned out.

Accessing and using equipment

Establish what you need and whether it is available. Do ask for help and advice from the technicians or others (e.g. postgraduates) who know about the equipment you need. If your own department does not have what you need, another one may. If you have a clear idea of what a piece of equipment does, then you may be able to think of an alternative (cheaper, simpler, low-tech) way of achieving the same result. If you need special computer software, is there a fellow-student who can help you write it?

Safety and ethics

If you are at all unsure about the safety aspect of your data collection, get advice. You will not be very popular if you kill one participant in three, and you should really aim to avoid even sending them away with a headache. (The headaches that you get are, however, par for the course.) As for ethical matters, check if there are procedures in your department that you need to follow (see Chapter 16 for more information).

Reducing the risk of it going wrong

Research that involves other people is sure to present all sorts of problems you haven't foreseen. If your questionnaire is ambiguous, your experimental stimuli are inappropriate, or your audio recorder battery runs out, you can end up with data that is useless or no data at all! Beware of the **observer's paradox**: your participants' awareness that you are studying them may have an effect on their linguistic behaviour, so that the data are not representative of what would happen if no observation were taking place. There are techniques for minimizing the problem (see Chapters 12–16), but often it is sufficient simply to acknowledge that there may have been such an effect, and not worry too much about it.

By running a **pilot study** (experiments and questionnaires) or a rehearsal (recordings and interviews), you can identify many problems and fix them before you start. A pilot study is a trial run using a small number of people similar to those you will use as participants. Even if you are doing an observational study, a case study, or a text analysis, you can have a dummy run by taking a small piece of suitable data and working through it to check that you will be able to achieve your objectives. Try to make the pilot as representative as possible by taking it seriously. Gather the results and practise processing them, whether through the tables and statistics (invent additional figures if that helps the number crunching) or through some process of interpretation. Ask the people who took part in the pilot or rehearsal to help you modify the procedures so that they will work better (Would two short sessions be better than one long one? Were the instructions clear?). If it is an interview study, ask your pilot participants to help you frame the questions or procedures better. Because of their advance knowledge of the procedures and stimuli or questions, it is usually inappropriate to use pilot participants again in the main study.

Ending up with manageable results

The biggest single error made by inexperienced researchers is not thinking about what the results will look like until they have them. It may seem as if the difficult part of the work is getting the data, but it isn't! There is nothing worse than sitting down with 40 hours of video data or 300 pieces of paper and thinking, 'What do I do with this lot?' Here are some tips:

- If you won't have time to listen to an hour's recorded data from each participant, don't collect so much.

- If you are designing a questionnaire, make sure you know how to collate the full range of answers you may get (see Chapter 14).
- Decide in advance what to do with a rogue result or an unhelpful respondent – can you identify in advance clear grounds for excluding such a case and no others? Do you need a couple of extra participants as back-ups, in case you can't use someone's results?
- Check whether you are expected, as part of your assessment, to perform statistical tests on your results. If you are, or if you feel that it is appropriate to do so, work out in advance which test(s) you will use, and have a clear idea of how you will generate the values that go into them. Chapter 20 will help you.

Handling data and knowing how to interpret your results

Summarizing data (especially scores) into formats that are easy to digest and compare is essential if both you and your assessors are to make sense of them (see Chapter 20). Clearly thought-out and labelled tables can save space. You needn't restate in prose what is in them but you must to refer to them and interpret them. Give worked examples of some of your results, plus detailed general discussion, before drawing broader conclusions.

Numerical data may appear straightforward, but you can easily end up not knowing what the numbers actually mean. Before you start, make sure you are able to state clearly what it will mean if result A is bigger than B, B is bigger than A, A and B are the same, and so on. Know where every figure will go in a table and which ones you will want to compare with which. Use Chapter 20 on statistics before you design your study, to ensure that you will have results you can process.

Non-numerical datasets are often much messier and much more difficult to draw firm conclusions from. You may know that a speaker tends to put up more resistance to an interruption by person A than by person B, but how can you back that claim up adequately? Look for clear examples and ask yourself often 'Does the evidence really demonstrate what I think it does?' If you cannot find examples, then maybe it does not!

Discussion and drawing conclusions

If you did not find the patterns you expected in your data, you still have a result. Consider why it has happened. Could the reason lie in your experimental design? Be prepared to evaluate your work critically and state how it could have been improved. This needn't be done in a self-deprecatory manner. Remember that one major purpose of research is to identify what to investigate next and how, so an unexpected result can be useful.

Aim to draw some conclusion about an aspect of how language works or how people use or process language. At the very least, you should be able to provide some speculations, on the basis of your data, about what the phenomena that you have observed are and how they can be explained. There is nothing wrong with reasoning through various possible arguments and visibly discarding one model in favour of another: it gives the assessor a much clearer idea of how you have reached your final conclusion. Make sure that any questions you have asked in your account have been answered and that you bring the reader back to your starting point: how your study fits into the broader frame of the topic area.

Presenting symbols and numbers

- If you want to present phonetic symbols in your work, you need to locate a reliable font: see Chapter 17.
- Spell the numbers one to ten as words (except in dates). Larger numbers can be written as figures (e.g. 24). However, avoid starting a sentence with a number, so write: *Twenty-four informants took part in the study.*

Avoiding plagiarism

The threat of plagiarism is a source of great anxiety to lots of students who never have and never will plagiarize. On the other hand, unless care is taken with the way you write, you may inadvertently plagiarize. A definition of plagiarism and guidance on practical ways to avoid it, with a worked example, can be found in Chapter 22.

Being streetwise: keeping on the right side of your assessor

It pays to understand the psychology of your assessor. It is in your interests to maximize the chance that there is a smile on his/her face from the moment your project reaches the top of the pile to the moment that the grade is put onto the mark sheet. The best way to achieve this is by writing outstanding work, but there are a few other tactics as well, that will make an assessor feel that you have taken care to make your work easy to read.

- Obey the house rules for presentation, word counting, and deadlines.
- Express yourself with care (see Chapter 23).
- Label your work clearly and, if there is any danger of odd pages coming loose, label every page. Use page numbers.
- With audio, video, or other supplementary data, make sure it is obvious what it is, and how to navigate it (see Chapter 12).
- Indicate clearly the structure of your work, so that the assessor knows at every point what you are doing and why.
- Word-process. If you have to write things in by hand (e.g. phonetic symbols), then remember to do it, and make them neat and legible. If your writing is terrible, get a friend to write them in for you.
- When you think your work is ready to hand in, pretend to be the assessor picking it up and opening it. Will it give the impression you want? If not, fix the problems.

There is a lot to think about – perhaps more than you had realized when you decided to do a project – but much of what we have identified in this chapter can be applied quite naturally as you proceed. The key thing is to enjoy the opportunity of researching your chosen linguistic topic in depth. It will be a lot of work but there is a very good chance that your project will be the piece of work that you are ultimately most proud of.

Part I

AREAS OF STUDY AND PROJECT IDEAS

2

Psycholinguistics

Psycholinguists ask questions such as the following:

- How does our brain organize the words that it stores?
- How does it access them so quickly and efficiently?
- What causes the *tip-of-the-tongue* phenomenon, when a word just won't come to mind?
- Why are we more likely to mishear something that is out of context?
- How do we know how to finish off a sentence that someone else starts?
- How similar are the processes of listening and reading?
- When the brain encounters a sentence it has never seen or heard before, does it have to look everything up in some vast dictionary and grammar store, or are there shortcuts that it can take to work out what it means?
- Does the brain process the words in the order in which it hears or sees them, or does it store up strings of words and then process them all at once?
- Why don't we take idioms like *He's one sandwich short of a picnic* literally?
- How do we know when someone has made a mistake in what they have said?
- What mechanisms operate during speech production to ensure that all the words come out in the right order and with the right intonation?
- What can the language of brain-damaged people tell us about how language-processing occurs?

Just imagine trying to teach a computer to speak and understand a language exactly like a human, and it becomes clear why we shouldn't take the answers to questions like these for granted.

Textbooks and major journals

Psycholinguistics is a sub-discipline of both psychology and linguistics, and the slant within textbooks varies accordingly, so you are likely to encounter some rather different viewpoints and approaches. Aim for recent publications when you are trying to get an overview of what the current issues are. Useful introductory texts include Aitchison (2011, 2012), Field (2003), Steinberg and Sciarini (2006), Carroll (2008), Harley (2010) and the more detailed Steinberg, Nagata, and Aline (2001). Also check handbooks (e.g. Gaskell 2009 and Traxler and Gernsbacher 2006, plus Kroll and De Groot 2005 on psycholinguistic approaches to bilingualism, and Guendouzi, Loncke and Williams 2011 for a focus on communication disorders) and various entries in linguistics encyclopaedias (especially Brown 2006). Harley's (2011) six-volume set of state-of-the-art overviews of issues in psycholinguistics is a treasure trove, if your library has a copy. Psychology textbooks that focus on language include Harley (2007) and there are chapters on language in Eysenck and Keane (2010) and Pinel (2011). For project ideas, Field (2005) and Prideaux (1990) are good sources, and Clark and Clark (1977) remains a classic. Aitchison (2003) and Field (2004) provide information on key concepts in psycholinguistics.

Journals in the field of psycholinguistics can be rather daunting, because many of them build on complex theory and methodology. You may not be able to fully replicate anything published in a journal, but you may get some ideas about what questions are interesting and why. Useful journals for projects in psycholinguistics include the following:

JOURNALS

Applied Psycholinguistics

Brain and Language

Cognition

Cognitive Linguistics

Communication Disorders Quarterly

International Journal of Language and Communication Disorders

Journal of Communication Disorders

Journal of Experimental Psychology: Learning, Memory, and Cognition

Journal of Memory and Language

Journal of Psycholinguistic Research

Journal of Research in Reading

Language and Cognitive Processes

Language and Cognition

Language and Communication

Language and Speech

Memory and Cognition

Mind and Language

Quarterly Journal of Experimental Psychology

Reading and Writing

The Mental Lexicon

Written Communication

Written Language and Literacy

Central themes and project ideas

There are two levels at which a project in psycholinguistics can operate:

- If you have some experience of experimental research and have access to specialist equipment and supervision, you can plan to replicate or adapt a published experiment. Find references to such experiments by reading overviews, and go from there back to the original account, normally in a journal. Only the original paper will give you sufficient detail of the procedures and analyses to plan your own work. Get advice at an early stage from your supervisor, and ensure that you leave plenty of time. General guidance on experimental work can be found in Chapter 13.

• If you are not experienced, if you have little call on equipment, and/or if your supervisor has insufficient time or specialist knowledge to support you, you are not in a position to conduct research that is compatible with the complex procedures of the published work. However, there are plenty of projects that require less technical skill but which can still be used to shed light on the psychological processes of language. It is mostly projects of this sort that are suggested in the following sections.

How psycholinguists conceptualize language

Following Fodor (1983), most psychologists believe that human cognition is modular. This means that it consists of a number of independent processors. If processors operate independently, then it should be possible to find people who have impairment of one, while the others function normally. As far as language is concerned, interest lies in establishing whether the processes responsible for the production and comprehension of speech and writing are four independent ones or not. For example, clinical psycholinguists want to know whether losing the ability to process *spoken* input will affect the processing of *written* input as well: does what we see on the page have to be turned into 'speech' before it can be decoded?

PROJECTS

1   Investigate the hypothesis that some types of extraneous sound are more distracting to linguistic processing than others. Give a difficult linguistic task to three groups of participants, one with speech played in the background, one with non-vocal music and one, control, group with no sound. Use the literature to make a prediction about which condition will prove most distracting.

2   Compare memory for objects with memory for words. Give one group of participants a set of household objects to memorize. Give a second group just a list of the names of the same objects to memorize. Use the literature to decide on your hypothesis, e.g. it is easier to remember the names of objects than it is to remember the objects themselves. Consider how your experiment might help establish whether the process of memorizing an object involves naming it. What sort of processing model is most consistent with your results?

3   In order to find out if training on one linguistic task is transferable to another task, give one group of participants training in strategies for memorizing random lists of words, give a second group no training, and then ask both groups to memorize long lists of words and recall them. In a second test, give them long lists of numbers to recall. Use the literature to decide on the most robust hypotheses to test, e.g. the trained group will perform better in the words list than the untrained group; the memorization of words and numbers require different skills, so training in one task will not be an advantage in another. Consider the significance of an outcome where the untrained group performed better on: the word test; the number test; both.

How we understand language

Speech comprehension

Research into the comprehension of spoken language has focused on research questions like the following: How do we deduce meaning so efficiently when the quality of the acoustic input is so variable? How do we work out so quickly what a word is – often after only the first two phonemes? One theory that offers an answer is the *cohort model* (Marslen-Wilson and Tyler 1980): as soon as we hear a word begin, we 'flag up' all the words we know which have that sound at the beginning, creating a **word-initial cohort**. We then disqualify those that no longer fit when the next sound is heard, or which are unlikely because of the context. The cohort model is described in most introductory books on psycholinguistics.

PROJECT

4   Ask as many friends and relatives as you can to jot down examples of slips of the ear (e.g. *Hormone treatment should be available for postmen or pausal women:* post-menopausal women), that is, when they mishear something (collect your own examples too). Give them as much time as possible – at least several weeks – and make sure they remember to make a note of things at the time. A taxonomy can be found in Garman (1990: 162–4). Use the examples to assess models of lexical processing. What characteristics do misheard items share with the items they are mistaken for? Are there any examples of mishearings that do not begin with the same sounds? If so, how can the standard models of processing account for them?

Reading

Reading is a secondary linguistic skill. Whereas a child develops naturally the facility to speak and to understand speech, reading and writing are learned. They are an extremely recent innovation in mankind's development and still have little or no role in many parts of the world. Therefore, we should expect that the processes of reading and writing are overlaid on the much older processes of understanding and producing speech. However, evidence from some kinds of brain-damaged patients suggests that, when we read, we do not always simply translate the words on the page into a phonological representation and access the meaning that way: rather, there appear to be shortcuts that do not involve the mediation of speech processes.

For comprehensive coverage of the psychology of reading, Rayner *et al.* (2011) is a good source. For models of reading, see Coltheart (2005), Hillis (2002) and Eysenck and Keane (2010). Questions of particular interest include: Is the recognition of a word aided by the preceding context? Do we identify words by recognizing the component letters or by overall word shape? Models that aim to account for reading processes include the *logogen model*. Each word has a threshold of activation, which, when reached, triggers its recognition. Activation towards the trigger is caused by seeing the letters of the word, by context, by the general frequency of the word, and by its recent use. The logogen model is described in most introductory textbooks.

PROJECTS

5   Investigate whether reading is mediated by phonological processing. Present on a
computer screen sentences that are (a) acceptable (e.g. *Chess appeals to clever boys*);
(b) nonsense (e.g. *Trees blossom during knives*); and (c) nonsense, but sound identical
to acceptable ones (e.g. *Wardrobes and dressers differ in sighs*). Time your participants
pressing one or other of two keys, according to whether the sentence makes sense
or not. Hypothesis: sentences in set (c) will take longer to judge as nonsense than
those in set (b) because the phonological form will compete with the visual one.
Alternative hypothesis: there is no phonological involvement in silent reading, so (b)
and (c) will take the same amount of time to decode and respond to. To counter
the problem of some sentences simply being intrinsically harder than others, use
two groups of participants, each of which has homophones where the other has
the correct spelling (so the second group would have *Wardrobes and dressers
differ in size* in set (a) and *Chess appeals to clever buoys* in (c). In constructing the
stimuli, remember that the position in the sentence of the homophone may make
a difference to the speed of processing because, if the first three words are already
nonsense, you don't have to look any further. Compare your results with those of
Baron (1973).

6   Base an experiment around that of Van Orden (1987): measure reaction times to
questions such as: *is BREAD a FOOD?; is MELT a FOOD?; is MEET a FOOD?* Van Orden's
hypothesis was that the decision for 'meet' would be affected by the fact that it
sounds identical to 'meat'.

Psycholinguistics and grammatical theory

Research in both syntax and psycholinguistics has offered models of how sentence parsing
(decoding) is achieved. Clifton and Ferreira (1989: 79) provide a useful list of sentence types
predicted to take longer to parse according to *their* model. Parsing models by Bever, Kimball,
and Frazier and Fodor are described in Garnham (1985: 77–87). For a comprehensive
description of model types, see Garman (1990, Ch. 6).

The idea that language is managed using large strings and templates is fundamental
to the notion of **formulaic language**. A number of researchers, including Pawley
and Syder (1983), Sinclair (1991), and Wray (2002, 2008) have suggested that language
comprehension and production can be at least partially achieved using 'a large
number of semi-preconstructed phrases that constitute single choices, even though
they appear to be analysable into sections' (Sinclair 1991: 110). Among those noted
by Pawley and Syder is: *NP be-TENSE sorry to keep-TENSE you waiting*, which generates
many sentences all to the same pattern, including: *I'm sorry to keep you waiting; I'm so
sorry to have kept you waiting; Mr X is sorry to keep you waiting all this time* (Pawley
and Syder 1983: 210). These constructions, and others that are more fixed, such as
What in the world and *The thing is*, are variously called **sentence frames, (routine)
formulae, chunks, schemata, templates, sentence builders**, and **lexical
phrases**. They may be advantageous as regards processing resources (Wray 2002, 2008)

and/or language learning (Nattinger and DeCarrico 1992). If quite lengthy phrases or clauses can be stored and accessed like single lexical items, there are important implications for models of how we process sentences, and certain predictions can be made about patterns in speech errors.

PROJECT

7   Record someone recounting the same experience several times to different people (and maybe several weeks apart) to see if the same structures and expressions are used to describe the same events on separate occasions. Consider the implications of 'preferred' ways of saying things, for a standard model of language processing.

Lexical and structural ambiguity

There are potential lexical ambiguities in much of what we hear. Why do we not normally notice that, for example, *Have you got enough time for this?* could equally well be *Have you got enough thyme for this?* Researchers have wanted to establish whether all the possible interpretations of a phonetic string are available at first, and then eliminated, or whether one interpretation is assumed (possibly the most frequent) and the others remain unretrieved unless there is a problem making the chosen one fit the context. There are accounts of research into lexical ambiguity in Garnham (1985: 62–7), Aitchison (2012) and Harley (2007).

Ambiguity also occurs at the syntactic level. It entails two or more possible interpretations of the structure of a clause, as in *Hubert saw his grandmother with a telescope*. Syntactic ambiguity is of interest because it can tell us how our grammatical and semantic processing interact. If we decode a whole clause grammatically before we try to interpret it, then we should not expect to find any evidence of the semantic context having resolved the disambiguation before the clause has ended. Evidence from experiments such as those of Tyler and Marslen-Wilson (1977) suggests that we do use semantic information to help us resolve syntactic ambiguity. For further information, see Harley (2007, Ch. 10).

Garden-path sentences

Garden-path sentences (GPSs) are so called because they *lead us up the garden path* by misleading us about their construction. A popular type of example uses the coincidence of the simple past tense and the past-participle forms of certain English verbs, e.g. *The ball bounced past the window burst*, in which the verb is read as simple past but is only comprehensible as a past participle (*The ball that was bounced past the window burst*). GPSs are significant because our problems in interpreting them as grammatical appear to depend on our decoding strategy: we seem to decide on the form of the verb before we get to the end of the sentence. For a fuller description, see Quinlan and Dyson (2008: 526ff) or many other introductory psycholinguistics books. A useful account of much other research into the processing of sentences is given in Eysenck and Keane (2010, Ch. 10) and Harley (2007: Ch. 10).

PROJECTS

8   In many cases, one reading of a lexically or structurally ambiguous sentence makes more sense in the context than the other reading, but there are also cases where context does not disambiguate them. Do informants still tend to think of one of the two available readings first, even when both are equally plausible? If so, do they all think of the same one? One theory suggests that the more frequent meaning will be accessed first (see Garman 1990: 255–7, Harley 2007, Ch. 10). Construct sentences that contain ambiguity, but where the two readings seem equally likely (e.g. lexical: *Everyone enjoyed the port*; structural: *Marmaduke had a conversation with a postman riding on a horse*). Randomize the order of the sentences and audio-record them, ensuring that the way they are read does not favour one interpretation over the other. Interview informants individually. Tell them that the stimuli are ambiguous, then play them one sentence at a time, and ask them which interpretation they registered first. Use the literature to decide whether your hypothesis should be that all your informants will tend to think of the same reading first, or that either reading is as likely to be recognized first, if there is no context to aid the interpretation.

9   Do 'complex' sentences take longer to process than 'simple' ones? Write active and passive versions of each question and divide them equally between two sets. Present a passage on computer screen, and then pose true/false comprehension questions, giving each set to a different group of participants. Time participants' responses to the questions (have them press one computer key for 'true' and another for 'false'). Hypothesis: passive questions will take longer to respond to than their corresponding active. Because any given question is framed in the passive to one group and the active to the other, you are controlling for some questions being inherently more difficult than others. Remember that some passive sentences are easier to identify than others, because pragmatics precludes the possibility of seeing the grammatical subject as the actor (e.g. *The walls were painted by the handyman*). A low-tech alternative is to audio-record the questions and time the participants' verbal 'true/false' responses. Do this by recording the entire question–answer session so that you can measure the time accurately later.

10 Sachs (1967) asked participants whether or not they had heard certain sentences in a passage: some sentences had been there and, of those that had not, some were paraphrases of what had been there (e.g. passive where the original was active), while others were different in meaning. Her results indicated that we discard the information about form after decoding it but remember the meaning. Replicate her experiment, perhaps with some modifications, and see if your results agree with hers.

How we produce spoken language

In order to speak a word, we have to access a store of words, find and retrieve a match for the idea, activate the instructions about how to pronounce it, and pass those instructions to the articulators (tongue, larynx, and so on). To produce a whole utterance, there must be forward planning to ensure the words are articulated in the right order, with the correct intonation, and so on. Sometimes things go wrong.

Speech errors and tip of the tongue

Inadvertent errors in the speech of normal people can provide indications of how we access individual words and how we plan the larger units of our utterances. Garrett (e.g. 1976) studied speech errors in some depth (see Caplan 1987: 273–4), and found:

- more errors with content words than other words, including semantic substitutions, words swapping places (e.g. *he is planting the garden in the flowers*), and the transposition of sounds between words (e.g. *shinking sips* for *sinking ships*). Where an affix gets separated from its root (e.g. *He is schooling to go* for *He is going to school*), it is the affix that stays in place and the content word that moves.
- Prepositions occasionally undergo semantic substitution.
- There is always a phrase boundary between the two words in a word swap.
- There is rarely a phrase boundary between the two words in a sound swap.

For an examination of a whole range of speech errors, see Garman (1990: 151–62). Fromkin (1973) provides an easy introduction to slips of the tongue and Cutler (1982) investigates them in more depth. A short assessment of the processes involved is given in Eysenck and Keane (2010, Ch. 11). For some examples, see Crystal (2010, Ch. 45). Jaeger (2005) lays out a methodology for collecting slips of the tongue, and her adult speaker data can be downloaded from http://linguistics.buffalo.edu/people/faculty/jaeger/AdultData.pdf.

General accounts of the tip-of-the-tongue phenomenon can be found in Aitchison (2012) and Garman (1990: 170–1), and more detail is provided by Brown (2008). An experiment designed to elicit the tip-of-the-tongue phenomenon in controlled conditions is reported in Brown and McNeill (1966). The experiment is briefly described in Harley (2007, Ch. 13), Garman (1990: 170), and other introductory texts.

Aphasia

Many descriptions exist of speech errors and word-finding difficulties in people with **aphasia** (language disturbance after brain damage) and, clearly, models of normal processing need to be able to account for the phenomenon. Among the word-level symptoms that manifest themselves in various forms of aphasia are:

- an inability to access content words: this is like an extreme form of the tip-of-the-tongue phenomenon;
- making up non-existent words (**neologisms**);
- semantic errors: substitution of a word with a similar or associated meaning;
- phonological errors: problems with sequencing the sounds, or the persistent use of a wrong sound over several attempts;
- more problems with verbs than nouns;
- memorized texts (prayers, poems, etc.) are produced more easily than novel sentences.

Broca's aphasia features agrammatism: problems assembling words into sentences and with the elements that carry the grammatical structure, such as function words (e.g. prepositions) and word endings. People with Wernicke's aphasia produce long strings that are incomprehensible, displaying better access to the grammatical words than to content words. Information about the major symptoms of aphasia can be found in most introductory textbooks on psycholinguistics and in all of those on language disorders (e.g. Guendouzi,

Loncke and Williams 2011, part 3). A general consideration of how aphasia contributes to research into normal processing, and many examples of aphasic speech, can be found in Aitchison (2012). For a detailed introduction to aphasia, see Pratt and Whitaker (2006).

PROJECTS

11   The Brown and McNeill (1966) tip-of-the-tongue experiment is reasonably easy to replicate. You may want to modify it in various ways. Reading their account may give you ideas for an experiment of a different design that elicits the same phenomenon.

12   Write a case history of a person with aphasia, include examples of spontaneous speech, recitations of well-known rhymes or lists (e.g. days of the week), specific naming tasks, and so on. If you have the opportunity to conduct a longitudinal study, log the person's improvement or deterioration. What strategies does he/she have for coping with the problems? How do carers and others approach communication? Does teaching or therapy have any long-term effect?

13   Challenge one or more models of language processing (in general) or lexical retrieval (in particular) to adequately explain the patterns of word-loss described in the aphasia literature. Use a resource like Eysenck and Keane (2010) or Harley (2007) to find a suitable model.

14   Find a person with word-finding difficulties and catalogue: words consistently accessible; words occasionally accessible; words never accessible, and words said in error for other words. Look for semantic and syntactic patterns to these sets and use this to test hypotheses such as: concrete nouns are more easily accessed than abstract ones; function words (*and, by, of, yet*, etc.) are very difficult to access; word substitutions are always in the same word class (noun for noun, verb for verb, etc.); personal names are more difficult to access than generic nouns (e.g. *John* is harder to access than *boy*). Are whole sets of semantically linked words lost? Each case is different and the patterns you find will depend on the precise symptoms of the individual, so don't prejudge. Use the information to examine one or more models of lexical storage and access.

15   Elicit speech errors by recording participants when tired or drunk, or when reading a technical passage aloud. Sort the errors into types and use them to evaluate a model of reading and/or speech production.

16   Collect speech errors over a long period of time or use commercially available audio- or videotaped compilations of outtakes from TV or radio. Rather than just listing your examples, use them to challenge or support models of speech production. In categorizing and analysing your data, consider questions such as: What was said? What was intended? How soon did the speaker spot the problem? Why at that particular point? Did the listener spot the problem? Why/how? What did the speaker do? What did the listener do? Was there an actual, or potential, breakdown in communication? What is the phonetic/articulatory relationship between what was said and what was intended, and what happened in the phonological environment, e.g. did any assimilation match the intended or the actual output?

How we produce writing

In order to write a word, we need to first select it from the mental lexicon and then access information about how it is spelled. Interesting questions arise about whether speakers of different languages have different processing systems, because in languages with a good grapheme-phoneme correspondence, such as Spanish, it is possible to move between pronunciation and spelling via simple 'rules', whereas English has many words that are not pronounced as they are spelled (e.g. *knight*; *Leicester*).

Slips of the pen

As we might expect if our model of writing parallels that for reading, there is evidence that errors in writing can occur at letter-part, whole-letter, and word level. Garman (1990: 165–7) describes slips at all these levels. For many more examples, and a fuller examination of what they can tell us, see Hotopf (1983). There has been little research on errors in the writing of longer units, perhaps because we are more likely to spot them as they are happening and to repair them at an early stage. However, Hotopf examines a sizable collection of data.

PROJECTS

17　Adapt the Sachs experiment (see above) for written input. Use one of the current models of processing (such as those reviewed in Eysenck and Keane 2010) to predict in what ways changing the medium may change the outcome of the experiment. Are your predictions borne out?

18　Replicate the experiment reported by Kaufer *et al.* (1986), in which writers were asked to think aloud as they composed text and the location of their pauses was noted. It was found that experienced writers operated in larger units than inexperienced ones.

19　Get participants to type a passage as fast as possible onto a computer without being able to see the screen (it is best if they are fairly fast typists). As they can't see what they've put in, they will be unable to go back and correct. Analyse the errors, first separating out those that are to do with adjacent keys. Are there transpositions across words, across phrase boundaries, etc.? Relate your findings to those from research into slips of the pen and dysgraphia (see below).

20　Replicate or adapt Griffiths's (1986) experiment where participants copied a written passage while observers noted where they paused to look back to the original. He found that pausing was not random, but tended to happen at syntactic (constituent) boundaries. The methodology could be adapted for copying onto a computer.

Dyslexia and dysgraphia

Dyslexia, in common parlance, actually refers to **developmental dyslexia** and **developmental dysgraphia**: difficulties that some children of normal intelligence have in learning to read and write, and which can persist into adulthood if not remedied. There are several reasons why developmental dyslexia and dysgraphia are still not understood:

• Until recently, children with severe dyslexia were misdiagnosed as stupid or lazy.
• Bright, resourceful, and/or highly motivated dyslexics often find ways of compensating for their difficulties, and indeed may not always realize that they are dyslexic.

- The terms 'dyslexia' and 'dysgraphia' do not describe single phenomena. They are used of an array of symptoms and a given individual may have only some of them. These symptoms may indicate different levels of severity in a single brain dysfunction, or may be caused by different things.

To find out more about developmental dyslexia and dysgraphia, see Reid and Wearmouth (2002) and Molfese *et al.* (2006).

Acquired dyslexia and **dysgraphia** also exist. These conditions affect individuals previously able to read and write but who have lost some or all of that ability after a brain injury. Acquired dyslexia can take different forms, suggesting breakdowns at different stages of the reading process. See Luzzatti and Whitaker (2006) for an overview that includes theoretical models.

PROJECT

21 Analyse data from a dyslexic child (or adult) before, during, and after remedial help. Gauge the extent to which the problem has been solved, poor skills have been directly improved, and/or alternative strategies have been developed to compensate for an immutable deficit. Incorporate your assessment into a model of reading, to explain what differences in the processing procedures appear to have been achieved in order to improve the outcome.

Language and thought

Since the work of Sapir and Whorf, there has been much interest in the question of whether we 'simply' express thoughts through our language, or whether the way our language operates has an effect upon the way we think. Out of this have come two hypotheses, the stronger **linguistic determinism** – the way we think is determined by our language so that we are, as Sapir put it, 'at the mercy of our language' – and the weaker **linguistic relativity**: we are more likely to interpret the world in a certain way because of our 'language habits'. The theme was taken up by George Orwell who, in an essay at the back of his novel *Nineteen Eighty-Four*, explains how a new version of English, 'Newspeak', will prevent subversive thought by containing no words capable of expressing it. For direct access to Whorf's ideas, see Carroll (1956/2011). For one critical appraisal of the debate, see Pinker (1994, Ch. 3); Pinker concludes that the Sapir–Whorf position is unsustainable, and that thought is independent of language. However, Deutscher (2010) concludes the opposite.

PROJECTS

22 A counsellor was recently heard to say in a radio interview, 'Before we talked about problems we didn't think about them.' This might imply that if there was no counselling culture, many of the problems it deals with would not exist. Survey the views of counsellors, clients, and people who have never used a counsellor to explore the hypotheses that talking about something (a) changes the way you perceive it; (b) can create a problem in your mind that didn't exist before; and/or (c) gives you words to express thoughts and feelings you already have. Link this to the Sapir–Whorf hypotheses of linguistic determinism and linguistic relativity.

23   Someone who does not eat meat is called a *vegetarian*, someone who eats no animal products at all is called a *vegan*, and someone allergic to gluten is referred to as a *coeliac*, but there is no commonly used term for a person who avoids just red meat or just dairy products and no clear way to differentiate between vegetarians who do and do not eat fish. Compile a list of common dietary preferences and conduct a survey to find out how people commonly refer to them. What level of consistency is there? Does it matter if there is no agreed terminology for things, provided we can find some way of talking about them? Would there be any advantage for our ability to conceptualize and communicate if there were agreed words for all of these different preferences and conditions?

OTHER PROJECT IDEAS

24   Design your own model to show how different components of language processing interact. Are the words selected first and then made into a sentence or is the sentence planned first and then words slotted into it? At what point are the sounds selected? Are they selected as *phonemes* and then given an allophonic identity at a later stage or is all the phonetic information selected at once? Evaluate the model against published data or other models.

25   Take a psycholinguistic perspective on some other area of linguistics that you know well, such as phonetic sequencing, the production and/or comprehension of intonation, the construction and/or comprehension of sentences, functional approaches to language production/comprehension, the storage of idioms, and so on. Draw up a model or use one from the literature and then take a detailed look at what the model needs to deal with in the course of constructing or understanding an utterance. Remember that it will be your detailed knowledge of this other area of linguistic theory that will justify the model you produce.

26   Investigate experimentally the hypothesis that science students will perform less well on a difficult linguistic task than humanities students. Justifications for this hypothesis might be, for example, that: any individual is either mathematical or linguistic, and people select careers that reflect their strengths; scientists do not get as much practice in language tasks; scientists are less confident in language tasks. If the results do not support the hypothesis, suggest reasons why.

27   Run an experiment separately on two groups. In both cases, tell them to write down as many words beginning with, say, 'm' as they can think of in two minutes (you can make this harder by specifying that they must be nouns and/or more than three letters long). Then go through the same procedure again (using a different letter) but, before they start, tell one group that an average score on this test is ten words and tell the other group that it is 35 words. Use the literature to decide which of the following hypotheses to favour: (a) when people feel pressured into attaining high standards, they will perform less well; (b) when people feel pressured into attaining high standards. they will perform better; or (c) putting pressure on people does not

significantly reduce or increase their ability to access items in the lexicon. Use the results of the first task as a control (see Chapter 13), to check that the two groups are capable of performing to similar levels in identical conditions. Then you can have confidence that any differences in the second task are relevant to your hypotheses.

28   Monitor the progress of two individuals with aphasia who are considered by the experts to have broadly similar symptoms and prognoses, but one of whom gets more help (speech therapy, family involvement, and so on) than the other. Use this to examine the role of practice, motivation, and the need to communicate in the recovery of speech.

For further project ideas, see Prideaux (1990), Clark and Clark (1977), Greene and Coulson (1995), and Field (2003).

3

First-language acquisition and development

Research in first-language acquisition and development addresses the central question of why and how children succeed in acquiring language. Questions of current interest include:

- What do children bring to the process of acquisition?
- Are there general patterns (universals) for the acquisition of all human languages?
- How crucial is the role of the language the child hears around it, both from carers and from other children?
- To what extent do children vary in their language acquisition and usage and why?
- How long does language acquisition take?
- Is there a 'critical period', or finite age range, within which acquisition must take place, if it is to occur at all?
- To what extent should the acquisition of literacy be seen as part of the language acquisition and development process?
- In what respects are the processes of oral and written language acquisition similar?
- How does literature written for children reflect their developing knowledge of language?
- How does language acquisition proceed in bilingual or multilingual children?
- Do the processes at work in second- or foreign-language acquisition in adults resemble the processes of first-language acquisition?

Approaches to research

Many of the above questions are addressed by studying the structure and meaning of the language produced by children at different ages or stages of development. This has made it possible to construct a generalized profile of the stages of language acquisition, and to make detailed comparisons of the child's language and the adult model. Study of the variation between children focuses on the *rate* at which features of language are acquired and the *route* of development – that is, the order in which language rules are acquired and the strategies used to acquire them. Researchers are also interested in how language comes to be used in ways appropriate to social context, gender, and social group, and this entails an examination of the mechanisms by which situation-sensitive usage is acquired, and the relevance of adult role models. Cross-linguistic and cross-cultural comparisons of the acquisition process provide a broader baseline for hypotheses about innate language abilities and universals. Studies of different types of language disability and abnormal delay in acquisition, whether due to internal or external causes, tell us about normal processes by indicating what it looks like when various individual components go wrong.

Terminology

Acquisition is often used to refer to the learning of language structures or rules, especially those of grammar, phonology, and so on. (Note that within the context of second-language acquisition research, the term 'acquisition' can have a slightly different meaning, see Chapter 4.) **Development** often refers to the child's *use* of the acquired language rules and structures in a widening variety of language contexts.

Textbooks and major journals

There are many excellent books on language acquisition, so take a look on the relevant shelves in your university library. Lieven (2006a, b), MacWhinney (2003), Steinberg *et al.* (2001, Ch. 1), Rowe and Levine (2011, Ch. 8) and Fromkin *et al.* (2010, Ch. 8) provide excellent short general overviews. Less detailed overviews can be found in Crystal (2003b, Section 24), and Crystal (2010, Part VII). Useful introductory books include Foley and Thompson (2003), O'Grady (2005), Clark (2009), Hoff (2009) and Saxton (2010), and an excellent reader is Trott, Dobbinson, and Griffiths (2003). Detailed accounts of key issues in first language acquisition can be found in the various papers in Tomasello and Bates (2001) and in Ritchie and Bhatia (1999), where there is also a chapter on methodology. A good starting point for information on literacy learning is Garton and Pratt (1998) or Hall *et al.* (2011, Part II). For an account of learning to read, see Oakhill and Cain (2006), and also Kress (1997) on early literacy and Kress (2000) on children's spelling. The latter stages of language acquisition, including pragmatic development in adolescents, can provide an interesting focus – see Nippold (2006) for an overview. Hoff (2011) is dedicated to the practicalities of researching child language. For project ideas, try Peccei (2005). Useful journals for projects in first-language acquisition include the following:

JOURNALS

Annals of Dyslexia

Applied Psycholinguistics

British Journal of Developmental Psychology

Child Development

Child Language Teaching and Therapy

Cognition

Developmental Psychology

First Language

Journal of Child Language

Journal of Educational Psychology

Journal of Experimental Child Psychology

Journal of Memory and Language

Journal of Psycholinguistic Research

Journal of Reading Behaviour

Journal of Speech and Hearing Research

Language Acquisition

Language Learning

Merrill-Palmer Quarterly

Psychological Review

The CHILDES database

The Child Language Data Exchange System (CHILDES) is a computer-based collection of child language data accumulated by individuals and groups of researchers, and available on the Internet at http://childes.psy.cmu.edu/. It is briefly described in Crystal (2003b, 2010). If you want good-quality data and have not got the resources to collect it yourself, you can use data from CHILDES instead, though you will have to understand the notations that are used. Data collected for one type of analysis can often be used for a quite different one, provided that the transcription has included sufficient detail.

Things to think about

- Focus on an aspect of child language that enables you to capitalize on the core skills and knowledge that you are most competent and interested in.
- Make sure you have a general overview of the main stages of language acquisition and development, so that you know roughly what to expect and look out for, and where it fits into the broader picture.
- Engaging in an analysis of your data from within an established theoretical framework, drawn from such areas as syntax, semantics, or phonology, is important in assuring that you avoid simply listing examples; you should be identifying patterns and commenting on their significance.
- Children do not possess adult competence in language use. Child language has its own rules, which may not closely resemble those of adult language, so be careful in identifying things as 'wrong' or 'ungrammatical' – in the child's system they may be correct.
- Remember that child language can include writing, which may be studied in its own right or compared with the spoken language of children.
- Although the preschool years manifest most development, some structures and skills of oral language, such as passives and relative clauses, do not appear in this period. Intonation patterns are also still developing and broader aspects of communicative competence can also provide a rewarding focus with older children.

Accessing children

Recent legal changes offer greater protection for children, so it is no longer as easy as it once was to get access to child participants at school or through youth organizations. The new restrictions may be reflected in your university's own ethics policies – you may need to get clearance for working with anyone under 16 – and almost certainly they will determine the way that a school or other organization handles your approach. You will fare best if you use personal contacts. Otherwise, you could approach the school that you attended yourself, or ask current parents, if you know some, to introduce you. Certain procedures, which might include police checks, will still be required, so leave plenty of time for them. Despite the potential complications, approaching a school remains a good way of contacting a large number of children from a wide variety of backgrounds and ages.

Write formally to the head teacher, stating clearly what your work will involve. Explain how the children might benefit, given that you will be intruding on their school time. Indicate what extra work, if any, may be involved for staff. Look for ways of linking your work to an ongoing class project. If you can afford to help out during your visits this may help to make your involvement more welcome. The head teacher will almost certainly require you to seek parental approval, as, in the eyes of the law, children are not old enough to decide what is in their best interests.

Working with children

- Children do not necessarily behave in a similar way to adult participants. Children you know already could find it difficult to adjust to the formal procedures in your investigation, if they have previously seen you only in informal contexts.
- When planning activities, remember that children have a shorter attention span than adults. Show your planned activities to teachers or parents in advance, to check that the materials are pitched at an appropriate level.
- If using pictures or other types of stimulus to generate language use, a pilot run will help you check that the children can make sense of the images. Drawn images with unusual shading, for example, can distract children into irrelevant questions and comments.
- To avoid having some children feeling left out and to ensure good relations with the school, you may have to include children whose data you do not plan to use.
- Children are often far more curious than adults about recording equipment. Not only may they be distracted or inhibited by it, they may want to play with it while you are collecting data.
- Children tend to move about far more than adult participants. Can you set up your audio- or video-recording equipment to cope with this?
- Parents and teachers may be keen that the children cannot be identified from your recording. Protecting identity is obviously much more difficult with video than audio data. Be sensitive to the justifiable concerns of adult carers about the potential for video material to fall into the wrong hands. Also be aware that some teachers may be nervous of their teaching being videoed.

- School environments can be very noisy and prone to unexpected disruption. The time available may prove rather shorter than you expect.
- It can be very hard to distinguish between different child voices in audio recordings, even when you know the children quite well. This is especially true when several are interacting. It can even be difficult to differentiate girls from boys. Using a video recorder and getting children to introduce themselves on audio recordings at the start of activities are two ways of reducing the risk of later problems, but most importantly, keep careful notes at the time.
- If your work involves an assessment of children's social class or background, be aware that children are not always able to supply reliable information themselves, school records are not always very up to date and schools and parents might be cautious about releasing such data. Furthermore, socio-economic categorizations based on parental occupations are not always appropriate or accurate.

Central themes and project ideas

There is a huge range of possible project areas within the field of child language, because many aspects of language can be studied at different stages of development. What is provided below is a selection of areas and ideas taken from some of the main branches of research within child language, including studies of prelinguistic development; the development of core structures, such as grammar and phonology; broader aspects of communicative competence, such as conversation and joke-telling; literacy development; and variation in child language.

Longitudinal case studies

Many linguists have undertaken and published case studies of their own children or of a few specially selected children. The emphasis for most has been on finding out more about 'normative' development. Roger Brown conducted a longitudinal study of three children, Adam, Eve, and Sarah (Brown 1973). This work is a primary source of information on analyses and indices of development, such as a child's Mean Length of Utterance (MLU) and stages of grammatical morpheme development. Paul Fletcher studied his daughter, Sophie (Fletcher 1985), providing a 'profile' of her development in areas including syntax and phonology at strategic points in her early life. Michael Halliday studied his son Nigel's early vocalizations and transition into early multiword utterances from a functional perspective (Halliday 1975). His proposed 'developmental functions of language' provide one key framework for the analysis of early utterance meaning. More recently, Deb Roy attempted to record as much of his son's language development as possible, by collecting data for 10 hours per day every day (see http://www.media.mit.edu/cogmac/projects/hsp.html).

Conducting a longitudinal case study requires commitment over a considerable period, not just from you but also from the child and its family. If you know you have a project coming up, and you think you might want to write a study of this sort, talk to a potential supervisor early on about starting to collect the data. It is better to collect something you end up not using than to wish later that you had planned ahead.

PROJECTS

29 Follow the language development of two children of the same age, one of whom is an only child and one of whom is the youngest in a larger family. Do language features appear at the same rate and in the same order? How might their profiles of development be determined by differences in their everyday communication needs? Use children from a similar background and of the same gender to minimize other sources of variation.

30 Record a child every few weeks as he/she learns to read. Do the skills develop gradually and/or is there a sudden transition from being a non-reader to being a reader? Ask the child for his/her own thoughts on what reading is, what it is for, and how it is achieved.

Prelinguistic development

Are children working on their language development before they can produce their first word? In recent years many researchers have addressed this question, examining aspects of prelinguistic (i.e. birth to one-word) development. Halliday (1975) looked for evidence of the same sound strings or 'proto-words' being used consistently to refer to the same things. Other researchers, such as Stark (1986), have focused on how prelinguistic sound-making, such as cooing and babbling, lays the foundation for phonological and intonational development. Useful examples of research can be found in Tomasello and Bates (2001).

PROJECT

31 Video a prelinguistic child with its mother. Show the recording to the mother and ask her which of the baby's noises and gestures she believes are intentional communication. Analyse these, looking for patterns and for indications that they are the precursors of language. Include a commentary on any difficulties you encounter with this. Remember to relate your findings to those of other studies, and/or to profiles of normative ages and stages of development.

Over- and under-extension: lexical and semantic development

Young children often use words in a way that suggests they understand them differently from adults. They may use a word to refer to too wide a category of things, such as 'apple' for any round fruit: this is known as **over-extension**. Conversely, they may use a word to refer to too small a category of things, such as 'dog' only for the family's pet dog and not for the next-door neighbour's (termed **under-extension**). This is a rich field for possible projects, since nearly all children, irrespective of their native language, go through periods of apparent over-extension of words (under-extension is less well documented). Several researchers have proposed explanations for this behaviour. One key contributor is Eve Clark, whose early proposal, the **Semantic Feature Hypothesis**, is still perhaps the most influential of all (see Clark and Clark 1977).

PROJECT

32 Collect examples of over-extension in a child's speech, taking care to keep notes of precisely what was being referred to. How easy is it to identify the perceptual boundaries that the child might be operating with, when it assigns the same name to several things? What support is there for the hypothesis that the child's view is the same as the adult's, but it just doesn't have enough words for everything it wants to talk about? (You could get insight into this by seeing how easily the child adopts a new word that breaks up the set.) Aitchison (2012) will give you some preliminary pointers to what over-extension may entail.

Children's morphology

One of the best-known studies in this area is Jean Berko-Gleason's 'wug' experiment, of which simple summaries are given in Aitchison (2011, pp. 112ff.) and Fromkin *et al.* (2010, Ch. 8). The study demonstrated that children have an internalized rule for the plural, because they were able to give the correct phonological form for made-up words. Children often make apparent errors in the way they form past tenses, comparative adjectives, and plurals, going though a phase of using a regular ending where the adult form is irregular. Since this is a very common phenomenon, it makes it an accessible and popular project area.

PROJECT

33 Draw up an inventory of morphological 'errors' in a child's language production. Categorize each according to whether it is an irregular form for a regular one, a regular form for an irregular one, or an irregular form for a different irregular one. Also ascertain which word classes the errors occur in: verbs (are all tenses represented?), nouns, adjectives (e.g. *the bestest* for *the best*), etc. If the balance is unequal, look for reasons, both within child language development and within the target language that the child is aiming for. Compare your findings with those reported in the published literature.

Development of phonology and intonation

One very productive approach to the language of under-fives especially is to study apparent 'mispronunciations'. These can appear to be idiosyncratic mistakes but, as with inflectional errors, many children display similar patterns, and they are considered to be part of normative development unless they persist for too long. Excellent summaries of the patterns of mispronunciation, which make useful analytical frameworks, can be found in the classics Clark and Clark (1977, Ch. 10) and de Villiers and de Villiers (1978). Smith (1973) is acknowledged as a key source study. For a recent overview, see Stoel-Gammon (2006).

On intonation, Cruttenden (1974) is still a useful study. He used recordings of the football results, studying children's ability to predict the second part of the result on the basis of the intonation used in the first. Seven-year-olds were found to be poor at predicting whether the second part of the score was higher, lower, or a draw, whereas, by ten, children were generally far more skilled. Adults usually have few problems with such predictions. Such work suggests that, while intonation is one of the first aspects of language that children focus on and start to master, it is also one of the last to be 'perfected'.

PROJECTS

34   Replicate Cruttenden's study and compare your results with his. If there are differences, what might account for them?

35   Analyse the consistent 'mispronunciations' in words that you elicit from a 2-year-old or 3-year-old child. Identify the phonological processes (substitution, assimilation, syllabic structure) that characterize these mispronunciations (see Clark and Clark 1977 and de Villiers and de Villiers 1978, for systematic coverage of these). Look at the articulations of particular developing phonemes in different phonotactic contexts (word initial, word medial, word final, connected speech, etc.) and compare the patterns of consonants with those given in Crystal (2010, Ch. 40). As Crystal's caption indicates, there is substantial variation in the speed of the acquisition of consonants. There can also, however, be some difficulty in knowing whether the child has or has not fully mastered a consonant. Drawing on the experience gained from your analysis, explore various possible reasons why this problem might be encountered by linguists.

Comprehension of complex grammatical structures

Carol Chomsky probed children's comprehension of structures such as active and passive sentences by asking them to perform actions with puppets. Her study also investigated other structures, such as the use of the verbs 'ask', 'tell', and 'promise', in an attempt to shed light on why these features are acquired later than other aspects of language. See Chomsky (1969; also summarized in Hoff 2009, p. 249). For a general overview of how syntax develops in children, see Bavin (2006).

PROJECT

36   Taking careful note of Chomsky's procedures and stimuli, devise an experiment of your own along similar lines. Make it close enough for your results to be compared with hers. How do you account for any differences? Write also about the procedural difficulties inherent in this kind of experiment.

Children's metalinguistic awareness

Research in this area has focused on:

- children's awareness of what a word, sound, and sentence, etc. is, and at what age or stage of awareness each type of structure emerges.
- the role of language games and nursery rhymes in promoting metalinguistic awareness.
- the link between metalinguistic awareness and the development of literacy. See Garton and Pratt (1998, Ch. 7) for summaries of example studies and further references.

- children's appreciation of verbal jokes and puns. This skill is very much part of a child's broader developing communicative competence, and can be an entertaining area in which to run projects. For children to understand jokes and puns, they often need to understand **sense relations** such as synonymy and polysemy. This may also be linked to a milestone in cognitive development that Piaget proposed that children reach at about the age of 7.

PROJECT

37   Following established research practice, test children's surface and deep understanding of humour by telling them jokes, monitoring the reaction, and then asking the children to explain why the joke was funny or why it was a joke. Crystal (1989: 185 ff.) provides very introductory information on this 'playing with language' and Trott (1996) gives a more detailed overview. Some source studies include Fowles and Glanz (1977) and Shultz and Horibe (1974).

Colour terms

This is an interesting and relatively little-studied aspect of child language development. It can be studied as part of overall lexical and semantic development. For introductory information, see Crystal (1989: 99 ff.) and, for a fuller summary, Trott (1996: 26–30).

PROJECTS

38   Keep a note of the order in which a child acquires colour terms and what objects the child labels with them. Compare your results with the findings of Berlin and Kay (1969), regarding the order in which languages add colour terms to their inventory (for a brief summary of this, see Crystal 2010, Ch. 17).

39   Some children go through a stage of using colour terms liberally but apparently quite haphazardly. If you know such a child, make a careful study of this phenomenon: does the child simply not know which colour name is which, is it operating 'over-extension' (see earlier) of the colour names it knows, or has it failed to grasp the notion of colour-naming at all, so that it doesn't realize what property of an object is being referred to when it is called *red*?

40   If you have access to a child who is bilingual, compare the order in which the colours are correctly learned and used in each language. To do this, you will need to understand both languages yourself or have help from someone who does. It does not matter if the colour terms develop in one language before the other, but include in your account a consideration of what effect knowing (some) colour names in one language might have on learning the colour terminology of the other.

41   Compare colour-term acquisition in two monolingual children acquiring different languages. Use children of the same gender, and whose background and day-to-day experience are as similar as possible. As in Project 40, make suitable provision if you do not know both languages yourself. Compare your results with normative

development as reported in the literature. Are there any linguistic or social reasons that you can identify to account for any differences between your two participants, or your participants and the reports in the literature?

42 Test a small number of children who have not yet mastered their colour names by playing a sorting game with them, in which they have to put like colours together. Do they choose to put together different shades of blue, separately from shades of green, etc.? Use your findings to address the question of whether children have the colour concepts *before* the words appear (cf. Berlin and Kay 1969, but also Pinker 1994: 62 and 65–6) or whether, as with most words, they have to learn the boundaries of meaning by experience (see 'under-' and 'over-extension' above).

43 Are there differences between males' and females' uses of colour terminology? Use a paint chart with the names of the colours removed, and ask, say, three boys and three girls aged about eight or nine to give each colour an appropriate name. Do both sexes find this task equally easy? What sort of wider vocabulary (e.g. names for things in the physical world) is drawn upon to meet the shortfall in established colour names? Do girls know more of the secondary colour names (such as *vermilion, maroon,* and *ochre*) than boys? Warning: be sensitive to the possibility that children may become confused and/or bored if they are bombarded with too many colours for which they do not have names.

Carer language (or child-directed speech)

The role of carer language, or **child-directed speech**, has been a hotly debated issue in child language ever since Noam Chomsky declared adult language to be a 'degenerate' model from which children could never learn all the rules of their language. A key researcher has been Catherine Snow (e.g. Snow 1986). Of interest are the properties of carer language and the extent to which it is necessary, or at least beneficial, to the child's language development. However, it is not easy to establish such a causal link. One approach has been to compare language acquisition in cultures where carers use no special language register with that in cultures where such a register has been identified. Famous studies of this nature are by Ochs in Western Samoa and Schieffelin in Papua New Guinea (see Romaine 1984, Ch. 6 for a description of these).

PROJECTS

44 If you are fluent in two languages associated with different cultures, observe the carer talk used with a child from each. Look for special vocabulary, intonation features, repetition, simplified structures (e.g. short sentences), and the overall amount of verbal communication offered by the carer. You may find Heath (1983) useful, a study of middle-class white and lower-class black and white communities in the United States, showing how children are socialized, through the influence of adults, into particular expectations and norms of language usage.

45   Do fathers as well as mothers use the special features of carer language? Using Berko-Gleason (1975) as a starting point, gather your own data from a family where you can record both parents in one-to-one interaction with the child. If feasible and appropriate, extend this to study the carer talk of an older sibling. As carers may be inhibited from behaving normally when someone else is listening, be prepared to record for quite a long time. Alternatively, explore the possibility of leaving the machine on while you leave or even using a baby intercom to listen in during your absence.

46   Observe one or more young children playing with dolls. Do they use features of carer language? See Romaine (1984, Ch. 6) for studies.

47   If you can find a pair of mixed-sex twins, record the carer talk that goes on with each individually, and the two together. Wells' Bristol Survey found evidence that parents talked more to boys during some activities and more to girls during others (see, for example, Wells 1986b).

Conversational development

This field tends to overlap with that of the role of carer language (see above), since it is generally acknowledged that children first learn from carers how to participate in conversations. McTear (1985) and Foster (1990) provide coverage of conversational development. Garton and Pratt (1998, Ch. 6) summarize some research (largely from the Bristol Survey) into the differences in conversation that children encounter when making the transition from home to school.

PROJECT

48   Compare the conversational skills of two or more children either of different ages or of the same age but different gender, social background, or family size, etc. Are there indications that any differences you find are genuinely to do with the *development* of conversation skills, as opposed to more permanent differences in style and/or personality? One type of data that might be particularly interesting is children's telephone conversation skills.

Sources of variation in child language

Since the early 1980s, there has been growing interest in the variation between children in their rate and route of acquisition. This has developed in part as a reaction to the tendency for child-language researchers to focus on the 'average' or 'normal' child, as though all children develop identically. Researchers have started to consider a range of sources of variation in terms of how they might influence children's long-term language development and how they could affect the way that children behave as participants in fieldwork projects. A considerable amount of key research on sources of variation stems from the Bristol Language Survey (see Wells 1986a, b). A useful introduction is provided by Wells (1986b). Romaine (1984, especially Chs 4 and 6) provides coverage on social class, gender, peer group, school, and family. Coates (2004, Ch. 9) and Swann (1992) also give excellent coverage on gender.

PROJECT

49 Using a detailed child's picture book (e.g. from the *First Thousand Words* series), test children of the same age, who contrast on one of the variation criteria listed above, on their range of vocabulary. For example, you could test a boy and girl, or two girls from different backgrounds, or two boys, one of whom is in full-time preschool education while the other is not. How easy is it to gain a clear picture of any differences? You could also write about any limitations that you consider intrinsic to collecting data in this way.

Literacy development

For introductory coverage, see the textbook review earlier in this chapter. Read more specifically about research in this area in Garton and Pratt (1998, Chs 7–10), Steinberg *et al.* (2001, Ch. 3), Perera (1979, 1984, 1986), and Smith (1986). For information on dyslexia, see Chapter 2 of this book.

PROJECTS

50 Interview children, teachers, and parents about the impact that they consider the *Harry Potter* books to have had on the children's enthusiasm for reading, their concentration and their linguistic development. Do adults and children agree about what it is that makes these books special? To what extent are the benefits of reading them viewed as spilling into a more general enjoyment of reading?

51 Focusing on a child who is still reading short texts in large print, make a list of all the vocabulary in every book that the child reads over the course of a month (or longer if you can). Sort the words according to the frequency of their occurrence in the texts you are studying. Type out sample words and ask the child to read them to you and explain their meaning. What relationship do you find between the child's knowledge of a word and the frequency with which he/she has encountered it?

52 Investigate the relationship between a child's ability in reading and spelling. Find examples of words that the child spells incorrectly or inconsistently, and find out whether he/she also struggles to read them. Are there any words that the child can spell correctly but finds difficulty in reading aloud and/or understanding? Use a psycholinguistic model of the relationship between reading and writing (see Chapter 2) to help explain the patterns you find. Warning: some word meanings (including many very common words, e.g. *the*) are very difficult even for an adult to explain: don't expect your child participants to do anything that you would struggle to do yourself.

53   Select some reading books aimed at children of different ages and analyse the grammatical complexity of the sentences, using Nippold's (2006: 317) examples as a guide. Are the structures uniformly more complex as the target reading age increases or do other factors come into play as well, such as the subject matter of the book?

54   Interview some authors of children's fiction. What do they consider to be the most important considerations when writing a book for a certain age of reader? How do they successfully operate within these constraints? Show some of their works to children of the intended age, in order to evaluate how effective the author is in achieving his/her objectives.

55   Go into local libraries and bookshops and ask to be shown books suitable for a boy aged 7, a girl aged 10, and so on. Whenever you find helpful assistants, ask them to explain to you how they can look at a book and know who it is suitable for. In particular, try to get them to tell you what features of the language they look for. In this way, identify the various features that adults appear to use in deciding what is suitable for a child of a particular age and compare them to the features that children themselves identify when browsing through books.

Developmental problems

A number of conditions are either characterized by, or else can lead to, a delay or overall reduction in the scope of language acquisition. They include autism, blindness, deafness, dyslexia, specific language impairment (SLI), and Down's Syndrome. Usually, you will only take on a study of someone with such a condition if you already know them, and you need to maintain particular sensitivity towards the participant and his/her family during your investigation, remembering always that the standard expectations of a child of that age may not be appropriate.

PROJECTS

56   Conduct a case study of a child with a particular disability affecting language (such as a hearing impairment, stuttering, or autism). Can you establish what, exactly, the difficulties are, and which aspects of language are not causing any difficulties at all? You will need to read up about the disability in question before you start the case study, and be warned: you may find that relevant books on the subject are quite technical or that the approach to language is different from the one you are familiar with from your previous studies.

57   Find a child with very poor speech production, and research what carers say to the child. Does the fact that the child's speech is difficult to understand affect the quality of the input that he/she receives? Using published studies of the way in which language acquisition proceeds, consider the potential long-term effects on the child of not receiving the same kind of input as other children.

Later language acquisition

Language acquisition continues into adulthood. According to Nippold (2006), 6-year-old children have less than one-third of the vocabulary that they will know by the end of their teenage years and create sentences that are only 60 per cent the length of those of adults and less structurally complex. The ability to understand and use metaphors, idioms, and proverbs also develops late, as does the capacity to appreciate the subtleties of pragmatics and to develop an argument. The way that narratives are constructed also changes over time (Pearson and de Villiers 2006). By focusing your research on older children or young adults, you can avoid some of the basic procedural complications that often arise with the very young.

PROJECTS

58   Find a dictionary of proverbs and select examples that are particularly graphic and metaphorical. Show them to 12-year-olds and ask them to guess what they mean and how they might be used. Examine the responses you get: how similar are they and what do they reflect about the world-view and experiences of that age group? For comparison, give the same proverbs to some informants in their sixties – how do you account for the similarities and differences you find?

59   Ask children of different ages, and also adults, to look through a joke book and select the three jokes that they think are funniest (use a book that has a variety of different types of joke). Are there any patterns regarding the kinds of jokes that are considered funny at different ages? Aim to explain the patterns in terms of the development of pragmatic understanding.

60   Show a silent cartoon film to children of different ages and then record them telling the story back to you. Use a story they have not come across before, as children are very good memorizers! Analyse the sophistication of the child's narrative of the story and how the events are connected. See Pearson and de Villiers (2006: 691) for a useful framework.

OTHER PROJECT IDEAS

61   Conduct an observation study of how children interact with each other when they are engaged in activities at home or at school. Example: how they use language co-operatively in playing a game or undertaking a classroom task.

62   Observe the differences between parental and teacher strategies in telling stories with children or in controlling children.

63   Make a study of children's command of language **register**: how does the way that they talk to each other differ from the way they talk to the teacher?

64   Do a cross-sectional study of children at different stages of their development, aimed at creating a general picture of sequences of development. (Note that this entails the assumption that child A will behave like child B when it is child B's age, so no account is taken of variation between individuals.)

65   Run an experimental study of comprehension, perhaps repeated over a period
      of time. For example, you could test participants' comprehension of dimensional
      adjectives by showing them a set of five illustrated cards and asking them *show me
      the picture where the fence is taller than the tree.* (See Cruttenden 1979, Section 4.5.1,
      for a summary of, and references to, studies on dimensional adjectives.)

66   Ask a child to identify a much-loved story book and then ask him/her to tell you the
      story without reading the text. How much of the text does the child reproduce word
      for word? What sorts of words, phrases, and sentences seem to be most likely to have
      been memorized in the course of reading, and why?

4

Second-language acquisition

There is considerable interest in the processes by which we succeed or fail in learning a second (or third, fourth, etc.) language. The insights we can gain from research into this area can tell us much about the nature of language, how the brain stores language, and how language learning takes place. Research into second-language acquisition asks questions such as:

- Is classroom learning a valid way to gain communicative language skills?
- Is there a fundamental difference between being taught a language and picking it up from the environment?
- Which language-teaching methods work best?
- Is second-language acquisition intrinsically the same as or different from first-language acquisition?
- How does the brain organize the storage and accessing of more than one language?
- Why are some adults more successful at language learning than others?
- Are children inherently better at language learning and, if so, why?
- Does residence abroad make a qualitative difference to language skills?
- How can we accurately gauge the linguistic knowledge of learners?
- Are there any consistent patterns in the order in which learners master language features?
- How effective are immersion programmes, self-teach courses, and other specialized approaches?

Terminology

In your reading on this area, you need to be aware that the same terms might be used with slightly different meanings by different authors. Here is some of the most common terminology. **The mother tongue (MT)** is the language acquired in early childhood from parents and spoken in the home environment; it is normally synonymous with **first language (L1)**. Although these terms may seem easy to define at first glance, there are many situations in which it might be difficult to identify which language deserves either or both of these labels: for example, when each parent speaks a different language, when two or more languages are commonly used in the family or immediate community, when the child is regularly exposed to a second language outside the home, or when the child (or adult) is more comfortable with and fluent in a language learned later and/or has forgotten his/her earliest acquired language. Such situations are by no means uncommon – in world terms, monolingualism is not the norm. **Bilingualism** and **multilingualism** are also difficult to define, because there are so many different situations and possible states of knowledge. Even if individuals know two languages (bilingualism) or more than two (multilingualism), they may have equal fluency and ability in them, or some (however minimal) ability in one language together with fluency in one or more others. They may have the ability to switch easily between languages in speech, or may be able to understand but not speak some of them. Li Wei (2006a) and Edwards (2004) both provide useful information. Weber and Horner (2012) and Chapter 8 of Pavlenko's (2011) edited collection give overviews of the latest research and theory about how people think and speak in two languages.

Foreign-language (FL) learning occurs when the language is taught in the L1 environment, often through the medium of the L1, such as when French children learn English at school in France, through the medium of French. A **foreign language** 'plays no major role in the community' (Ellis 2008: 6). **Second-language learning** occurs where the language being taught is that of the host community, such as in the case of Chileans arriving in Britain and learning English either informally or in classes. The term **second language (L2)** is also used in a more general way, as a cover term for second and foreign language, and it may also be used to refer to a third or fourth language. The term **second-language acquisition** is used to refer to both acquisition and learning (in Krashen's sense – see below), and you will find this abbreviated to **SLA, 2LA**, and **L2A**. There are many situations in the world where the distinction between **foreign-** and **second-language** learning is not so clear-cut, especially where the language being learned has some sort of special political or social status or significance, as with English in India or South Africa, for example, **EFL** and **ESL** refer to English as a Foreign and as a Second Language, respectively. The terms **TEFL** (Teaching EFL) and **TESL** (Teaching ESL) have largely been replaced by the term **TESOL** (Teaching English to Speakers of Other Languages).

Acquisition *vs* **learning** is a distinction made by Stephen Krashen at the beginning of the 1980s in relation to his 'Input Hypothesis'. In Krashen's terms, **acquisition** is the subconscious assimilation of the language without any awareness of knowing rules. This is how the child gains its first language, and what children and adults may be capable of achieving for a second language, if exposed to it in a natural way and enabled to pick it up subconsciously. **Learning** is a conscious process, achieved particularly through formal study, and resulting in an explicit knowledge of rules. Although Krashen's ideas have become well-anchored in some areas of L2 study, there has been extensive criticism of his model, and it is worth reading about why, if you plan to research in this area. For one overview, see Ellis (2008: 246–52).

Language skills are normally defined as the skills of listening, speaking, reading, and writing. Some formal classroom activities will encourage the learner to focus on one or two of the skills, others focus on integrating the skills within a communication activity. For insights into the differences between these skills in the teaching and learning process, see Nation (2009) and Nation and Newton (2009).

Textbooks and major journals

Ellis (2008) and Macaro, Vanderplank and Murphy (2010) have an extensive glossary of terms. Useful starting points for information on second-language acquisition are handbooks and readers (for example, Bhatia and Ritchie 2012; Carter and Nunan 2001; Davies and Elder 2003; Doughty and Long 2003; Gass and Mackey 2011; Kaplan 2010; Li Wei 2006b; Lowie *et al.* 2005). Another useful resource is Macaro (2010). Kachru *et al.* (2009) links into relevant global issues, as does Block and Cameron (2002). Guidance on carrying out research in second-language acquisition can be found in Brown and Rodgers (2002), Ellis and Barkhuizen (2006), Mackey and Gass (2011) and Li Wei and Moyer (2008). Dörnyei (2009) offers specific information on using questionnaires in 2LA research and Dörnyei and Ushioda (2010) covers research on motivation. Useful journals for projects in second-language acquisition include the following.

JOURNALS

AILA Review[1]

Applied Linguistics

Applied Linguistics Review

Applied Psycholinguistics

Computer Assisted Language Learning

ELT Journal

International Review of Applied Linguistics in Language Teaching (IRAL)

Journal of Applied Linguistics

Journal of Second Language Writing

Language Learning

Language Learning in Higher Education

Language Teaching

Language Teaching Research

Modern English Teacher

ReCALL

Second Language Research

Studies in Second Language Acquisition

System

TESOL Quarterly

[1] Issues of AILA from 1993–2001 can be downloaded from: http://www.aila.info/publications/ailapublications/ aila-review/downloads.html. For later issues, check the contents lists on http://www.benjamins.com/cgi-bin/t_ seriesview.cgi?series=AILA and then ask your lecturers if anyone has a copy of what you need, as this journal comes free with a subscription to some professional organizations for Applied Linguistics.

Things to think about

- Overall, language learning is a slow process, and you may not have a long enough time period to conduct a study that involves steady progress. However, you can certainly observe specific learning events, and if you introduce new material to learners, you can track their knowledge of it.
- 'Think-aloud reporting' is a technique whereby the researcher asks learners to verbalize their thinking processes as they complete a task. You can find out more about this in Tirkkonen-Condit (2006).
- Think carefully about which language you will use in your dealings with participants. Tempting as it is to use the language you know best, bear in mind that this may cause difficulties for non-native speakers. If using a questionnaire it may be better, in some circumstances, to use the native language of the participants. However, be careful not to make assumptions about what language that is, or their level of literacy in it.
- For more guidance on practicalities, see Mackey and Gass (2011).

Central themes and project ideas

Developmental sequences and the process of acquisition

Is there a fundamental difference between the processes of first- and second-language acquisition? It is well documented that children acquire certain morphological features of L1 (such as verb endings, and plural and possessive forms) in a fairly consistent order (e.g. Brown 1973; de Villiers and de Villiers 1973). Many studies have looked for a similar order of acquisition in the second language. For an overview of this research, see Ellis (2008, Ch. 3), Lightbown and Spada (2006), and most other introductory texts.

PROJECTS

67 Ask for access to the work of some language learners over, say, the past two years. Look for evidence of the successful and unsuccessful incorporation of, say, verb forms into their free writing (a) immediately after the form has been taught; (b) several weeks after; and (c) several months after. If they are learning English, compare the order of acquisition with that given by Ellis (2008), Lightbown and Spada (2006), or some other authoritative source. If they are learning another language, find out if similar sequences have been identified (there are references to work on German in Ellis 2008: 96ff.). Remember that a single example of a form being used correctly is not necessarily evidence that the learner has mastered it. You could base this project on oral and written data to compare the same students' acquisition of the same feature in speech and writing.

68 Interview one or more teachers about their approach to teaching, say, verb forms, the plural, or the possessive. Are they aware of the research into the order of acquisition? Use their responses and your reading to explore whether SLA research is of no, of some, or of paramount importance for the teachers' practices in the classroom, and why. For help, look at Alderson (1997) or Doughty and Long (2003).

69   Compare the sequence of presentation of language forms in one (or more) TESOL textbook(s) with the acquisition sequences reported by Ellis (2008, Ch. 3). See also Hawkins and Lozano (2006) for an overview of developmental sequences in 2LA.

Comparison of L1 and L2 acquisition

Research into the similarities and differences between L1 and L2 acquisition goes further than just the developmental sequences described above. Much has been written about the learning environment, the quantity and quality of the input, the expectations and the actual output, the attitude and tolerance level of the listener to errors and dysfluency, the time period over which the language is learned, and so on. A number of ideas could be developed from reading about **universal grammar** in more detail in, for example, White (2003), Cook (2008, Ch. 12) or Doughty and Long (2003).

PROJECT

70   Compare carer-talk (**motherese**) addressed to an L1 learner, with foreigner-talk. What are the similarities and what are the differences? Compare them for: range of vocabulary, use of any special words, the complexity (or absence of it) of the grammar, any non-adult or non-standard grammatical forms, pronunciation, intonation, volume range, and so on.

Language-learning targets

Many people leave school saying that they 'know' another language, meaning that they can just about buy a postcard or a cup of coffee using it. For others, knowing another language would mean that they could speak and write fluently about a wide range of subjects and could follow the speech and writing of others with no difficulty. In other contexts, it might mean being able to discuss the rules of grammar in great detail, whether or not that knowledge could be applied in comprehension or production. If we want to include all native speakers within the group who do 'know' the language, what constraints does that put upon the definition? What sorts of targets or goals do learners have?

PROJECTS

71   Use evidence from errors in the speech or writing of advanced non-native speakers to identify some of the more subtle aspects of full competence in a language. Pawley and Syder (1983) may give you some ideas.

72   Compare the views of some learners and their teacher (interviewed separately), about what 'knowing' a language means. If the responses do not fully correspond, consider what implications this might have for the success of the teaching and learning process in that class. Remember to consider the effect on some people of consistently failing to meet the goal they have set themselves.

73   Monitor the range of input encountered by one or more intermediate learners, looking at (a) variation between native speakers (within a group or family, national, and international); and (b) contemporary change (for example, in the vocabulary and expressions of adolescents). How do learners handle such variation?

74   By careful observation of your own day, or by 'shadowing' a foreign student, compile guidelines for what English a foreign student most needs for successful communication in your college or university environment. Variations on this, if you have access to the appropriate environment, include: a nurse or doctor in a hospital, a businessman visiting another country in order to make a formal presentation about a product or service he hopes to sell, and so on. You may find it valuable to engage in some role play with a friend, to explore some of the finer points of these scenarios.

75   Carry out a survey of English-language teaching schools and units, to see how they go about testing the level of their students at entry. Are they satisfied with the accuracy of the tests (i.e. do they have to redistribute the students across ability levels a week later because the tests did not correctly sort them into groups)? See the later section in this chapter for more on testing and assessment.

Motivation

What role does motivation play in language learning and what will motivate someone to learn? What sort of control might a teacher have in supporting and increasing motivation in a class? These questions are of immense importance in studying second-language acquisition. For an overview of the issues and how to research them, see Dörnyei and Ushioda (2010).

PROJECT

76   Interview language learners from the top and bottom grades in a language class, and ask them what they like and don't like about learning the language and why. Ask them what would increase and decrease their motivation. Do you think that reduced motivation in learners results in lower performance levels or that lower performance levels result in reduced motivation? Draw up some recommendations for teachers and learners about practical ways to increase and sustain motivation.

Grammar-based and communication-based teaching

Some teachers work on the assumption that, without a thorough grounding in the grammar, semantics, and phonology of the target language of English, the student cannot be expected to know and use the language. Their lessons will therefore focus on teaching grammatical structures, introducing lists of new vocabulary and correcting the students' pronunciation. Such an approach to language learning is widespread in many countries and it contrasts with approaches that focus primarily on communication. In the latter, students are expected to use the language to interact (e.g. in role plays) and to share real information.

There will be fewer activities that involve the more mechanical manipulations of language forms that appear in a structurally based lesson. The Natural Approach (Stephen Krashen), Suggestopaedia (Georgi Lozanov), Community Language Learning (Charles A. Curran), Language from Within (Beverly Galyean), Total Physical Response (James Asher), and Task-Based Learning (Prabhu, Nunan, Willis) have all been developed as alternatives to 'formal' teaching, and each makes substantive claims for its own validity. You will find overviews of these approaches in most introductory textbooks.

PROJECTS

77 Cook (2008) considers explicit teaching and the learning of the formal components of the language and suggests comparing a range of textbooks to see the different ways in which the language can be made explicit. You could do this for English or for another language that you know, or you could look for variation across different languages within a single published series, such as Linguaphone, Hugo, Teach Yourself, one of the BBC series or online language learning materials.

78 Obtain several different beginners' courses for a language and persuade participants to spend a set number of hours over a week studying the language, using the course material you assign to them. At the end of the week, interview the participants as a group and individually, to find out, for example, how easy, interesting, or useful they found the approach, whether they think they learned anything, and whether they would feel motivated to carry on.

79 Make a single visit to each of several language classes (with different teachers) and assess each on a continuum for formal grammar instruction, communicative activities, the use of L1 to explain things, and so on. Supplement this information with interviews with the teacher and a couple of students from each class. Ask them what they felt the balance was in the lesson you observed, as a way of assessing the correspondence between their views and yours (consider the significance of a mismatch between views of teacher and student(s) in the same class). Check whether the teaching content and/or approach is laid down by the institution and, if so, whether it is what the teacher would use by choice. To what extent can this, or any teaching, be labelled as fully 'communicative' or 'grammar-driven' and why? Classroom observation is difficult to do well and you may find Spada and Fröhlich (1995) useful in developing your approach.

80 Make several visits to one language class where there is at least some explanation of grammatical detail given in L1. Make a note of all the sentences that contain technical terms (recording the lesson will make this easier). List a selection of the sentences (don't just list the words out of context, as that makes the test much more difficult) and ask members of the class to write down what each one means. Use the scores to assess the extent to which the students are successfully grasping the grammatical information and consider whether it is a prerequisite for learning a grammatical point that you understand all the techical terms used to describe it. Try to avoid implying that the teacher is somehow failing – explaining language is very difficult!

> **81**   Interview a group of learners about their goals in studying the language (such as
> what they will use it for). Widen this into a discussion of whether teachers need to
> be aware of what the learner expects or dreams of, and what they can do about it
> if they do. In a separate interview with the teacher, find out what he/she *thinks* the
> learners want the language for. Assess the extent to which the learners' goals map
> onto the style and approach of the teaching they are receiving and the sort of work
> they are being asked to produce.

Vocabulary acquisition

A wide range of studies has been carried out on the processes and the significance for
overall learning of vocabulary acquisition. Among the questions that have been addressed
are: Does it help or hinder learning if you present vocabulary out of context? Does it help
learning if you teach the key vocabulary *before* you read a new passage, or should you let
the learners read it first, and then have the new words explained? How many words do
you need to know in order to function adequately in a language (for example, to hold a
conversation, read a newspaper, or follow a TV drama)? Should you teach or learn words
with related meanings together (such as opposites, synonyms, members of a set) or is that
confusing? When can you say that you 'know' a word? What is the best way to memorize
words? How can you test how many words a learner knows? Does it matter which words
you learn first? How can you tell how difficult a passage is going to be for a learner to
read? Answers to these, and other related questions, are considered in Nation's (1990,
2001) research.

PROJECTS

> **82**   Interview learners about their attitude and practical approach to vocabulary learning.
> Use this information to evaluate critically assumptions made in the research, and
> make suggestions for how teachers might help learners more.
>
> **83**   Using data from willing 'guinea pigs', write a critical evaluation of the Linkword
> learning system developed by Mike Gruneberg as the *Instant Recall* technique (e.g.
> Gruneberg 2002a, b). You can read more about the use of mnemonic techniques in
> vocabulary learning in Nation and Newton (2009: 132ff.).
>
> **84**   Get a class of language learners to memorize a set of words (and their translations)
> from a language they do not know. Test them and identify the most successful
> learners. Get them to tell the class what their techniques are. Go through the same
> process again with a new set of words, telling the poorer performers to try one of
> the successful techniques. Compare the performances across the two tests to see if
> adopting the 'successful' techniques has had an effect. Widen this into a discussion of
> the usefulness of teaching learning *techniques* as well as the language itself.
>
> **85**   Use one of the tests at the back of Nation (1990) as the basis for your own
> investigation. Alternatively, if you have very high competence in another language,
> try producing one or more of the tests in that language and chronicle the problems
> you encounter.

Different concepts expressed in different languages

German has two words that both translate into English as *but*. In translating the sentence *Jane went to the pictures but I stayed at home*, the German word *aber* would be used for *but*. However, in the sentence *Jane didn't go to the pictures but stayed at home*, the word *sondern* would be used. German, French and many other languages have two words for *yes* as well, depending on whether the speaker is agreeing or contradicting with what has been said before. In Welsh there is no single pair of words for *yes* and *no* – you need to know what the verb is, what tense it is in and where it comes in the sentence before you can choose the right word. Researchers have been interested in investigating whether such differences between languages make them more difficult to learn, or whether all humans share an underlying sensitivity to differences in meaning, even if not all languages show them.

PROJECT

86   With the help of a bilingual informant, identify words in one language that do not have simple corresponding translations (words relating to culture, religion, and food are often good candidates). Get a group of participants who do not know the foreign language to learn the words on this list, plus, interspersed, a balancing number of words that *do* have a direct translation. Compare their success in remembering the words: is it easier to learn a word that you can 'hook' directly onto an L1 word?

The learner's approach and experience

What makes a successful language learner? Ellis and Sinclair (1989) look at this question, and you can gain an overview of work in the field from Richards and Lockhart (1994: 63–6). Stevick (1989) presents seven case studies of language learners, each of whom has a different approach. Bailey and Nunan (1996) provide a collection of papers on teaching methodology, but from the perspective of the learners and teachers rather than the theorists. One of the most influential studies of the 1970s was that of the *Good Language Learner*, conducted by Naiman, Fröhlich, Stern and Todesco (1978/1995). A compilation of personal accounts by outstanding Chinese learners of English (*21st Century China Daily* 2005) gives fascinating insights into successful learning strategies for oral performance, especially text memorization – see also Ding (2007). In recent years, research into learners' strategies has come under the heading of 'individual differences'. For one extensive overview, see Ellis (2008, Ch. 13). Meanwhile, an insight into how learners operate as a group in the classroom can be gained from Dörnyei and Murphey (2003).

PROJECTS

87   Do a case study of a good language learner and see how easily (if at all) he/she fits into one of Stevick's or Naiman *et al.*'s categories, by carefully identifying and categorizing his or her approach to different aspects of the learning process.

88   Pre-test some willing language learners on the vocabulary in a passage that they have not seen and keep a note of the material that they do not know. Give them the text to memorize for recitation. Afterwards, record them reciting the text, and interview them regarding the difficulties they had. Test them on the words they did not know before they saw the passage – has memorizing it led them to learn the meanings of the words or have they bypassed that learning? You could compare the results of this experiment with those of a similar group who were simply introduced to the text, without having to memorize it. Do your findings suggest that memorization could be used as a learning tool?

89   Interview some language teachers about what differences between learners they feel are most challenging to handle in a classroom, and why. Compare their views to the features that researchers have identified as most significant for learning (see Ellis 2008, Ch. 13 for ideas).

Interlanguage, error analysis, and contrastive analysis

Interlanguage, a term coined by Selinker (1972), is used fairly loosely by many to mean, variously, what the learner can do at any given point after beginning L2 but before perfecting it, the total profile of all the learner's performance stages from beginning L2 to perfecting it, the underlying knowledge that produces the imperfect performance, and a system essentially the same for all learners, featuring rules and patterns consistently found at any given stage, irrespective of the L1 and the learning method (see also Ellis 2008, p. 968). In Selinker's original definition, interlanguage is the result of having to use a learning system that is not language-specific. For him, its features result from a combination of **language transfer** (elements of L1 are incorrectly imposed onto L2), **overgeneralization** (using an L2 rule in inappropriate conditions), **transfer of training** (an artefact of the teacher's style, creating an apparent rule where there is none), **learning strategies** (choices made by the learner to achieve short-term learning goals, such as simplifying the verb system), and **communication strategies** (a focus on getting the message across, even at the expense of total accuracy) (Cook 1993: 18–19). For an overview of interlanguage, see Tarone (2006).

    Error analysis was for many years the standard approach to identifying the features of an interlanguage. **Contrastive analysis** takes direct account of how the L1 and L2 differ in their expression of an idea or their construction of a grammatical relationship and predicts certain errors directly emanating from using the L1 patterns in L2. For an account of error analysis, see Ellis (2008, Ch. 2). Swan and Smith (2001) is useful for finding out what major types of interference can be expected from learners of English with different first languages.

PROJECTS

90   Compare the errors made in English by native speakers of two or more languages that you know in such areas as vocabulary use, grammatical forms, and pronunciation. Do they make substantially different errors? Are you able to account

for the errors in terms of features of the L1? Do the patterns correspond with those documented in Swan and Smith (2001)?

91   Collect and sort the corrections made by a teacher in class: which errors are allowed to pass? Interview the teacher to find out why and in what circumstances they choose to focus on certain errors and not others.

Language assessment and testing

There are almost as many forms of language test as there are approaches to language learning, because it would not be fair for students drilled in grammar and translation to be tested only on their communicative skills, and vice versa. In actual fact, it is often the examination tail that wags the teaching dog, and much classroom practice is determined by the testing methods used in the external examinations ('washback'). For information on testing and assessment, see Bachman and Palmer (2010), Brown and Abeywickrama (2010), Douglas (2009) and Fulcher (2010).

PROJECTS

92   Find two classes of equivalent level, working towards roughly equivalent exams for different examining boards or agencies. Is it possible to identify any strong patterns in the teaching that reflect the exam format? What effects might such restrictions have upon balanced learning? If you can, find out what motivates the different examining agencies to present their tests in the way they do (it may not be all to do with language-related considerations at all: perhaps, for example, some sorts of answers are quicker to mark than others).

93   Explore some of the formal and communicative tests of English for speakers of other languages (e.g. those produced by the University of Cambridge), asking how far they are genuine tests of language ability. Ask experienced teachers for their opinions on how easy it would be for a candidate to learn how to pass the exams while lacking aspects of the ability in that language that is assumed to go with such a performance.

94   Get hold of some tests for foreign learners of English (as above) and give them to native speakers to do. You could use people with different levels of education and of different ages, including children. How do they perform? What would the implications be of (a) consistently very high scores; and (b) a range of scores, some of which are below those of non-native speakers? What account should be taken of age and level of general education in *non*-native speakers?

Bilinguals, multilinguals, and polyglots

Bilingualism is an enormous area of research in its own right. As much of the work does not directly relate to the acquisition of the languages, we shall not cover it here. However, there does exist work on how already knowing more than one language affects your subsequent learning of languages. Many *polyglots* (speakers of several languages) say that language learning becomes easier the more languages you learn, because you get the hang of how to do it and can make generalizations and predictions based on your previous experience of what languages can be like. Yet many learners experience interference between their foreign languages. Why that happens is perhaps a question for the psycholinguist, but how it affects the learning experience is a question relevant to SLA research. For a general overview of bilingualism, see Li Wei (2006a) and Bhatia (2006), and for more on how bilinguals think, see Pavlenko (2011).

PROJECTS

95 Interview a group of polyglots and childhood bilinguals. Are their experiences of interference between the languages (in retrieving words, say) the same or different? Use your findings to construct a model of how the different people might store their languages in the brain and access them. Compare your models with those described by Li Wei (2006a: 2–6).

96 Devise an experiment that will elicit cross-language interference. For example, you might get participants to translate words alternately, and at speed, into their L2 and L3, and see how often they come out with the right word in the wrong language. How do your findings relate to the predictions that the models described in Li Wei (2006a: 2–6) would make?

Language teaching policies

Most countries have experimented with different foreign-language teaching policies over the years. In the UK, attempts to teach French to young children can be traced back to the 1960s. Burstall *et al.* (1974) report on why they were unsuccessful. Halsall (1968) compared French teaching in Holland, England, and Flemish-speaking Belgium. She concluded that 'there was ... on average, a real inferiority in the standards achieved for French in the English secondary modern school at the 3rd and 4th year levels' (p. 89). A useful source of insight into the factors that might account for this (such as motivation, amount, and type of input and attitudes at home) is Clark (1987, Ch. 5), which documents practice and attitudes towards foreign-language teaching and learning in Scottish schools, while Crichton and Templeton (2010) offer a more recent perspective on the same topic. A few UK schools experimented with teaching a curriculum subject such as history or geography through the medium of French or another language, with impressive results. For specific accounts of such attempts, see Hawkins and Perren (1978, Chs 2–5). For recent information, with practical ideas for teaching languages to primary-age children, see Hood and Tobutt (2009), Kirsch (2008) and Martin (2008).

More recently, the European Union has been maintaining its proactive position on language learning. *Promoting Language Learning and Linguistic Diversity*: *An Action Plan 2004–2006* (European Communities 2003) clearly states that, 'It is a priority for Member States to ensure that language learning in kindergarten and primary school is effective, for it is here that key attitudes towards other languages and cultures are formed, and the foundations for later language learning are laid.' The Action Plan continues, 'Member

States agree that pupils [in secondary schools] should master at least two foreign languages, with the emphasis on effective communicative ability: active skills rather than passive knowledge. "Native speaker" fluency is not the objective' and, as far as Higher Education is concerned, 'All students should study abroad, preferably in a foreign language, for at least one term, and should gain an accepted language qualification as part of their degree course.' In 2007 the Dearing Report proposed a new strategy for introducing languages in primary schools in England (see Primary Languages 2011).

PROJECTS

97 Interview a group of native English-speaking, and non-native overseas students about their language-learning experiences in school. How much time was given to the language? How much homework did they get? How much support did they get from home? What did they think they would use the language for? Make sure you are comparing like with like: visiting students are, by definition, motivated to try out their (above-average?) English, so at least compare them with home students who are studying a foreign language.

98 The Dearing Report recommended that all 7–11-year-olds in England must have the opportunity to learn a foreign language by 2010. Investigate, either directly or via media and other reports, the extent to which this proposal has become a reality, and the issues arising from it. If you have access to a school that is offering a foreign language to that age group, study the approach taken and assess its efficacy. How do the expectations of the teachers match up to what is known about children's inherent ability to learn languages effectively?

99 Interview school students and try to ascertain what motivates them to choose to study one or another foreign language. Have they dropped a language and, if so, why? What do their parents think of language learning? If you have access to individuals from more than one country, incorporate a comparison.

100 Hawkins (1987, Ch. 3) poses the question 'Why French?' and explores the complex issue of how French came to be, and has remained, the first foreign language offered in most British schools. Re-examine his arguments in the light of subsequent political change or consider which languages are most appropriately taught in multi-ethnic schools. Rees (1989: especially 85–91) is a valuable source of information about attitudes to, and the feasibility of, offering a wider range of languages in schools.

101 Develop a strategic plan for supplanting the customary first foreign language in schools in your country (e.g. French in England) with another language. You should consider the significance of the language you choose (should it be a language of commercial importance, such as German or Chinese, political importance, such as Arabic, cultural importance, such as Italian, or a language with a large worldwide population, such as Spanish?). Work through the practical implications, including what happens to all the teachers whose specialist language is no longer needed, where the new teachers will come from, the possible effects on culture and balances of power within and beyond your country, and so on.

102   Make a study of foreign-language teaching in the former Eastern bloc countries since the collapse of communism. Focus on the marginalization of Russian as the first foreign language (outside Russia) and of other East European languages (inside Russia), and the rapid introduction of English. How has this been achieved? Are the standards achieved in English comparable with those previously achieved for Russian or other languages? You could try making contact with teachers of English in these countries via the Internet, or via a TESOL unit that is involved in training overseas.

103   Investigate the history and current status of Welsh teaching in Wales, Irish in Ireland, Basque or Catalan in Spain, or the teaching of another indigenous minority language. If possible, visit some schools and interview teachers and pupils with the minority and the majority language as their mother tongue. If you cannot travel that far, write to them, or make Internet links.

Effect of the year abroad

Students who are sent abroad for a year's study expect, and are expected, to improve their language skills in the host language, but there has been surprisingly little research into the nature and amount of improvement achieved. Milton and Meara (1995) review some studies and report their own, in which the greatest improvement was made by those with the poorest skills at the outset. Students who were already competent benefited much less, if at all, linguistically.

PROJECTS

104   Record an interview with an overseas exchange student at the beginning of his/her visit and again some time later. In both interviews, talk about the same topic, so that it is easier to compare the two performances. Choose a topic about which he/she already has some knowledge at the time of the first interview. Analyse the language of the two interviews for fluency, breadth of vocabulary, variety of grammatical structures, length of conversational turn, idiomaticity, ability to make jokes and witticisms, and so on, and list the types of error and their frequency. Use this data to assess the general improvement of the student during the stay. You could also ask him/her in the second interview what he/she feels about the level of improvement and how it seems to have been achieved (for example, by socializing, studying, or watching TV). In the light of Milton and Meara's findings, this study may work best with an individual who is not highly competent on arrival.

105   How important is the year abroad for becoming fluent? If it were not possible to spend time abroad, would it matter? Read the article by Reisz (2011) and then interview language learners who have and have not spent time abroad to improve their language skills, to see if they feel it matters. For instance, you might look for some students from China, where it is often not possible to travel abroad until one is already fluent.

Role of the social and political status of English as L2

English occupies an extraordinary and complex position in the modern world. Its precise status varies in different places and is subject to constant change. It is not always easy to see who or what has elevated it to its position and what maintains it: culture, policy, or something else? Crystal (2003b) has a section entitled 'World English', in which he considers the different international varieties of English and asks whether the English language is under threat or is a threat to other languages. Crystal (2003a), Jenkins (2009), Kachru *et al.* (2009), Kirkpatrick (2010) and Melchers and Shaw (2011) are dedicated to this subject. Hartmann (1996) contains a range of papers on aspects of the role and status of English in the European Union, including its use as a *lingua franca*, the adoption of English loan words into other languages, and the phenomenon of bilingualism with English in different EU countries. You can search the Internet for policy documents and a range of views on the place of English and other languages in Europe. The same can be done for other languages in other countries, e.g. Spanish in the United States. For a history of English-language teaching, which indicates how the status of English has been reflected in the changing demand for it abroad, see Howatt and Widdowson (2004).

PROJECTS

106 How has the current language situation (including foreign-language provision and proficiency) arisen in a particular country of your choice? South Africa, India, and China would make interesting case studies. You need to think carefully about how you will gain the necessary information. A government office or embassy will give the official reasoning, but you may want to discuss the issues with citizens of that country as well.

107 Explore the reasons why English language is, or is not, on the school syllabus in a particular country. This type of project could simply take a historical perspective and explain how the country in question has reached the situation in which it now finds itself; or you could attempt to predict what language provision will be most appropriate for the country in the near future.

OTHER PROJECT IDEAS

108 Conduct some tests, or interview teachers, or both, to investigate whether girls are better at learning foreign languages than boys.

109 Through observation of non-native speakers in real interaction, analyse how the learner's social behaviour in the learning situation correlates with his/her overall achievement, fluency, and/or accuracy.

110 Consider, in a theory-based project, to what extent learning Orwell's Newspeak (described in an essay at the back of his novel *Nineteen Eighty-Four*) would be the same as, and different from, learning an L2.

111 Compare three beginners in a foreign language: one in a regular class, one working with an individual tutor (contact could be made via a local Home Tutor scheme) and one teaching himself/herself. Apart from monitoring and comparing their progress (remember to devise tests that do not favour one or the other's approach), consider what advantages and disadvantages each method of learning has, as regards changes in motivation, commitment, and interest, availability of feedback, accuracy of what is learned, number of hours put in and how regularly, and so on.

112 Use the various accounts of successful learning in Stevick (1989) as the basis for a critical appraisal of a model of how languages are learned.

113 Drawing on Wright, Betteridge and Buckby's (2006) *Games for Language Learning*, evaluate the potential for games to play a constructive role in L2 learning. For example, examine why they might work and what aspects of learning are *not* easily supported through games. If possible try out a few games on some volunteers and get their views on them, or invite some language teachers to talk to you about whether or not they use games and why.

For further inspiration, read Ellis (2008, Ch. 1), and follow up an idea that interests you by finding his more detailed account elsewhere in the book – or explore any of the issues raised in other books mentioned in this chapter.

5

Structure and meaning

In this chapter we look at research that might fall under the headings of pragmatics, syntax, semantics, morphology. Each of these areas extends considerably beyond what we cover, however, and you may want to seek further information in specialist textbooks, some of which are listed in the next section.

The sorts of questions that you might want to ask in a project on structure and meaning include:

- How does a speaker convey messages indirectly, i.e. ones that are not explicitly carried in the words themselves?
- How does a speaker express subtle differences in meaning by shifting elements of the sentence around, or by choosing one word rather than another?
- How do we express politeness through structure?
- What makes jokes funny?
- Why are some sentences ambiguous?
- What restrictions are there regarding which words can go with which others?
- What does a word mean and who decides?
- How do intonation and punctuation contribute to meaning?
- What is 'correct' grammar?
- How are words constructed?
- What role does the hearer play in making sure the speaker's utterance is correctly understood?
- How do languages (and varieties of a single language) vary in the way they express meaning through words and through strings of words?

Textbooks and major journals

Leech (2006) provides a glossary of grammar terms. Halliday and Matthiessen (2004) is a thorough introduction to Functional Grammar, an approach to analysis which many students and researchers find valuable in relating structure to meaning. Dixon (2005) explores meaning through grammar, and Hewings and Hewings (2005) has project ideas on grammar. Saeed (2009) provides a thorough introduction to semantics though if you have not studied semantics before, Kearns (2011) might be an easier initial resource. You can look up terms relating to semantics and pragmatics in Cruse (2006). A good introduction to metaphor is Knowles and Moon (2006), and for morphology try Booij (2005) or Carstairs-McCarthy (2002, 2010). For pragmatics, Huang (2006), Mey (2001) and O'Keeffe, Clancy and Adolphs (2011) provide comprehensive introductions, and Grundy (2008) gives useful guidance on executing projects. Carter *et al.* (2007) show how authentic everyday text can be analysed from a range of perspectives.

Journal articles on any of these areas can be quite difficult to read but they do indicate the questions that the experts want to answer and their questions may inspire similar questions for your project. Useful journals for projects on structure and meaning include the following:

JOURNALS

Corpus Linguistics and Linguistic Theory

English Language and Linguistics

English Today

Functions of Language

Humor

International Journal of Corpus Linguistics

Journal of Linguistics

Journal of Politeness Research

Journal of Pragmatics

Journal of Semantics

Language

Linguistic Inquiry

Linguistics and Philosophy

Linguistic Review

Pragmatics and Society

Yearbook of Phraseology

In addition, we recommend that you check the journals lists in other chapters in this book, if your interest in structure and meaning coincides with, say, language and gender, history of English, or language development. Research in such areas often deals with structure and meaning in a more accessible way than does the research that focuses directly on semantics, pragmatics, and syntax.

Central themes and project ideas

Pragmatics

Much of our verbal communication is expressed in rather indirect ways, creating a potential obstacle course for the hearer. For example, arriving at someone's house on a muddy day, we might be expected to interpret *I'll see if I can find my spare slippers* as an invitation to take our shoes off at the door. However, such indirect communication is risky for the speaker: we might genuinely not pick up the hidden message or we might deliberately choose to ignore it. In our day-to-day interaction, there is more than an exchange of words: there is a social dance, and we, as the listener, may choose to keep in step or clumsily to upset the rhythm of the communication by not listening to the music. Pragmatics deals with the hidden messages.

In **Speech Act Theory** (Austin 1961, 1962; Searle 1965, 1975, 1979), the way in which apparently straightforward utterances perform complex interactional tasks is revealed. For example, **performatives**, easily identified by the possibility of inserting the word *hereby*, have a permanent effect upon the state of the world (e.g. *I name this ship HMS Endurance*; *I bet you £5 he loses the match*; *I promise to return the book*). In an important application of Speech Act Theory, Shuy (1993) explores the forensic role of the linguist in ascertaining whether or not an individual has committed a crime that hinges on a performative speech act. The subtlety of such research lies in the fact that it is rare for an illegal offer such as a bribe to be made explicitly and, in the absence of a recording that contains the words 'I'm offering you a bribe', it is obviously difficult to be sure that the speech act (verbal agreement) was actually carried out.

Grice's (1975) theory of **Conversational Implicature** takes account of the need for the speaker and the hearer to enter into a pact regarding how things will be said and interpreted if communication is to be successful and efficient. Grice's four **maxims** characterize this co-operation: the hearer will assume that the speaker is only saying things that are relevant to the current state of the conversation, giving neither too little nor too much information, speaking truthfully and avoiding ambiguity and obscurity. The speaker may deliberately flout a maxim in order to deceive the hearer (e.g. by telling a lie), something that is made easier by the hearer's expectation of co-operation (i.e. assuming the truth will be told). Hearers or readers will work very hard to find relevance in an utterance, as can be seen from our ability to interpret an exchange such as: *A: Is there any more butter? B: I didn't leave work till seven*. Besides Grice's own (1975) paper, you can read about conversational implicature in Levinson (1983: 97–166), Thomas (1995), Mey (2001) and Grundy (2008).

Relevance Theory (Sperber and Wilson 1995) is based on the belief that humans pay attention to the information that they perceive to be relevant. Their account solves the problem of how communication succeeds even though speaker and hearer do not know how much information about the situation the other has. Relevance Theory is not easy to get to grips with. Rather than reading the whole book, try Sperber and Wilson's (1987) précis of it, Mey (2001, Ch. 4), Yus (2006) or Grundy (2008).

PROJECTS

114   Examine the text of a play for evidence of implicit messages, and consider what the playwright is deliberately conveying about the attitudes and personality of the characters.

115   Write two scripts for the same sequence of events, one that is totally explicit and one that expresses the same information by implication, shared assumptions, and so on. Get three people to judge each one for naturalness or plausibility, and to describe their reaction to the characters.

116   Examine one or more comedy TV sketches that rely on pragmatic manipulation for their humour (*The Two Ronnies* is particularly good for this).

117   Take a five-minute sequence from a TV comedy show and write a commentary, to run alongside the script, that describes what the audience is intended to understand, even though it is not explicitly stated. Use the script and commentary to identify how the language in the script, along with other signals such as glances and gestures, studio laughter, and music, variously signal information to the audience, and what this tells us about what you need to know about culture, language, and behaviour in order to find that comedy funny.

118   What we say when we want to get something done provides interesting paradigms, in which a decreasing scale of directness may reflect increasing levels of politeness. For example, all of the following could be used as a request for a book: *Give me that; Could I have that, please? Would you mind passing me that book? I haven't seen that book; That book looks interesting.* Examine data from, say, episodes of a soap opera, to evaluate how the level of directness reflects the relationships between the characters, as independently demonstrated by their behaviour and the content of their utterances (e.g. Do two people who dislike each other use more direct framings? Do two people of unequal status contrast in their politeness markers when talking to each other?).

119   Analyse different types of joke (puns, shaggy-dog stories, and so forth) for ways in which they flout Grice's maxims (e.g. consider what the person hearing a joke is expecting).

120   Record a group of people carrying out a particular task and compare that recording with a scene from a soap opera where the characters are accomplishing the same task (e.g. telling somebody what to do). Is the scripted exchange more direct than the authentic non-scripted?

121   Record a lesson and analyse how a teacher gets the class to do what he/she wants them to do. How directly are the instructions given and how do different modes of address impact on the reactions of the class?

Metaphor

While we are accustomed to seeing metaphor as a feature of literary language, it is clear that we also use it in everyday life. We talk about the *journey through life*, about *battling something out*, or about *sailing through an exam*. Financial reports talk about one currency *weakening* or *strengthening* in comparison to another. Research on metaphor obviously needs to do more than just list examples, so you need to find out about the major theoretical approaches to understanding it (see, e.g. Cameron and Low 1999). Among these is the **constructivist** approach, which you can read about first-hand in Lakoff and Johnson (1980). They propose that, rather than being an abstraction away from a more fundamental, literal way of seeing things, metaphor is the very basis of the way in which we make sense of the world, and, in effect, is what our 'reality' is based upon. A useful overview of theories can be found in Gibbs (2006). For concise definitions of **metaphor** and other devices, see Crystal (2003b: 421; 2010, Ch.12).

PROJECTS

122 Identify the metaphors in a passage from a novel and systematically replace each with a more literal equivalent. Show the new passage to informants and ask them to rate it for readability, interest, and style. Then show them the original and ask them to rate that. Is it possible to say that the use of metaphor always produces better prose?

123 Analyse how reports in the media use metaphor. Choose a particular event and identify the metaphors used. How do metaphors create particular images for the reader or hearer, and are these images sustained with associated metaphors, or simply used and then dropped?

124 If you are familiar with Old or Middle English, compare the metaphors used then with ones used in a similar (i.e. literary) context today. Crystal (2003b: 23) gives some examples of metaphors in Old English, including *hronrād* (*whale-road*) for sea, and *bānhūs* (*bone-house*) for *human body*. One way to test how similar our 'feel' for metaphors is to that of years ago is to see whether modern informants can make sense of a modernized version of the old ones. If the choice of metaphors then and now is essentially similar, what does that tell us? If old and modern metaphors seem quite different in kind, why might that be?

125 Consider the claim that 'most lexical items [are] dead metaphors' (Sadock 1979: 48) by conducting an etymological study of English vocabulary. For example, Partridge (2008) gives the origin of *lord* as Old English *hlāfweard* (*loaf-guardian*) and that of *lady* as *hlāfdīge* (*loaf-kneader*). To keep a focus, pick one sub-area of vocabulary for the study, such as words for people or tools. Remember to link your findings back into a theoretical discussion of the nature and function of metaphor.

126 Search through books about how to be a successful creative writer, for guidelines on the pros and cons of using metaphors and the advice on what to do and what to avoid. Do the books agree and are the examples convincing? Can you identify underlying common beliefs about what makes a metaphor effective and desirable? Where you can, do you view the beliefs to be built upon current fashion or more fundamental linguistic principles?

127 Lakoff (1992) outlines very clearly how metaphor was used to frame reports of the 1990–91 Gulf War. His observations include: *the State as a person, war as a competitive game, international politics as business*, and *war as medicine*. Using his framework, analyse the framing of a more recent conflict to evaluate the extent to which the metaphors are the same or different, and why that might be.

Sentence structure

The precise way in which words are strung together can subtly affect the meaning. For example, word order can change the topic (focus). Compare: *There's a tiger on the church roof, It's a tiger that's on the church roof,* and *It's the church roof that a tiger's on.* Omitting information can also have a marked effect on the slant of the message. Compare: *The soldier fired his gun at the protester at point-blank range; The gun was fired at the protester at point-blank range; The gun fired at the protester at point-blank range,* and *The protester was shot at point-blank range.* To understand this kind of variation, it helps to identify the **roles** of the different participants in the events. Here, the soldier is always the person firing the gun (**actor**), even when he is not mentioned and some other noun phrase is the subject of the sentence. The gun is always the **instrument**, irrespective of whether the phrase *the gun* is subject, object, object of a preposition, or not mentioned at all. The protester is always the **patient**, i.e. the one who is shot. A useful introduction to semantic roles is Bloor and Bloor (2004, Ch. 6). There are also some examples, with discussion, in Pinker (1994: 114). For some insight into the subtleties of our linguistic understanding compared to that of a logical machine, see Pinker (1994: 78–81).

Not all differences in meaning are explicit on the surface, however. Syntactic theory examines the structures that underpin sentences and attempts to account for a range of phenomena, such as unexpectedly ungrammatical sequences and ones that are apparently similar but where structural differences exist, like: *The pupils are usually easy to help* and *The pupils are usually eager to help.* Here, it seems as if there has been a straightforward replacement of one adjective with another, but this is not so, as we can see if we ask *who does the helping?*

Syntax also addresses issues of ambiguity, as in *Biting insects can be unpleasant.* You can learn a lot about the nature of English by trying to make up further examples of this kind. One particular type of ambiguity is the garden-path sentence, where there is, in fact, only one grammatical reading, but we are fooled by the sequence of words into looking for a different one (e.g. *The soup boiled vigorously spilt over; The ball bounced past the goalpost burst*). These are grammatical only if you read them as a (legitimately) shortened version of sentences with *that was* after the subject noun phrase. Again, trying to make up your own examples of garden-path sentences will soon indicate to you how they work. You can read about them in Pinker (1994: 212–17) and in Kess (1992: 129 ff.), where you will also find accounts of psycholinguistic experiments using them. They are also briefly mentioned in Chapter 2 of this book.

PROJECTS

128 Compare newspaper accounts of an event (something with strong political implications is best, such as a scandal at the heart of a political party), using publications that are likely to take sides. Look for different ways in which the same story can be told so that a different emphasis (e.g. about blame) is achieved. For guidelines on how to do this, see Freeborn *et al.* (1993, Ch. 9).

129 In newspapers that take opposing stances, compare the use of language in the editorial opinion in the leader columns. Choose editorials on emotive events about which contrasting views are possible, such as assisted suicide or immigration policy, rather than catastrophes or atrocities that everyone will condemn.

130 Examine the writing of a 9-year-old, an 11-year-old, and a 13-year-old for evidence of a developing ability to manipulate the structure of English for the purposes of subtle expression. You could achieve this by asking each of your participants to write on the same topic, and imposing certain conditions. For instance, can they tell the story of a day in the life of a person without giving away the person's gender, or the fact that he/she cannot speak the language, or is living on another planet?

131   For one or more other languages that you know, work out whether garden-path
      sentences can be made in the same way as they can in English, and if so, why?
      If not, why not? If they can, do native speakers have more or less trouble seeing
      the meaning than native speakers of English do with English ones? Can you find
      any types of structural ambiguity that do not operate in English but do in another
      language?

132   Collect grammatical slips of the tongue, such as *She doesn't do anything once she
      gets there, except be's there* and *That's a whole nother issue*, and account for them
      structurally. Begin by considering what was intended and how else it might have
      been said, and try swapping other words in (e.g. *stay(s)* in the first example and
      new in the second).

Words in isolation and in combination

Although one might think that a language would only have one word for each idea
and that words would fit together quite simply to express relationships, this is actually
not true. Words often have quite restricted usages, dictated by words with which they
collocate (co-occur). For example, we say that humans eat *food*, while farm animals eat
feed; you *melt* cheese and metal, but you *smelt* ore; you *pinpoint* a distant building, but you
sight a distant animal. Collocations can create some odd anomalies: why can we say *Merry
Christmas, Happy Christmas,* and *Happy New Year,* but not *Merry New Year*? You can find out
about many of the curiosities of collocation by looking at works derived from the Cobuild
project, such as Sinclair (1991) and Collins Cobuild (1991, 1996).

In specialist areas, vocabulary can be remarkably specific, as the terminology in Table
5.1 taken from Farb (1973), shows.

Table 5.1 Terms for animals

	Cattle	Horses	Sheep	Swine
female	cow	mare	ewe	sow
intact male	bull	stallion	ram	boar
castrated male	steer	gelding	wether	barrow
immature	heifer	colt/filly	lamb	shoat/gilt
newborn	calf	foal	yeanling	piglet

Source: Farb (1973)

Some specific subject areas have a vocabulary, even a grammar, that is incomprehensible
to the uninitiated. Heraldry is a particularly striking case, as this extract from Tim Lewis's
satirical novel *Pisspote's Progress* shows:

> *The shield was per bend sinister, or a witch's hat gules, sable a cat embowed sable on an
> increscent moon argent, and chief sable a crucible and crossed mortars or. Above it was the*

crest, a king's head sanguine in a cauldron sable above a royal crown on a gold helm with seven bars, a torse or and azure, mantelling azure turned or, with crossbone supporters argent above a compartment of magrobs or in a chest sable. (Lewis 1991: 331)

Another focus of interest is what a word 'means'. Does 'gay' *still* mean 'happy'? Does it *only* mean 'happy'? and so on. In *Alice Through the Looking Glass*, Humpty Dumpty tells Alice, 'When I use a word, it means just what I choose it to mean – neither more nor less' (Carroll 1865/1971: 114). Much has been written about this idea of meaning residing only in usage. In his play *Dogg's Our Pet* (1979), Tom Stoppard experiments with Wittgenstein's ideas by showing how it is the use of words that determines what they mean. On the other hand, there is evidence that word meanings are anchored in certain perceptual or cultural constants. According to Rosch's prototype theory (see Field 2003, Ch. C4), language users will consider some examples of a set to be more typical members than others. For instance, a sparrow is a more typical example of 'bird' than a penguin.

PROJECTS

133   Consider the following potential combinations: *good/strong/high* with *likelihood/ probability/possibility/chance*. Ask native speakers to give judgements about how acceptable they find each combination. How similar are the patterns for different informants? Now search a large corpus for each combination, to see what the distributions are in language use (see Chapter 19). Do these findings match your informants' judgements? If they do, consider how individuals could know so much without having read all of those texts. If they do not, consider what it means that individuals' intuitions contrast with the evidence from corpus measurements.

134   Pawley and Syder (1983) suggest that one of the ways in which even highly proficient non-native speakers can give themselves away is by their use of grammatical sequences of the language that are not idiomatic. Assess the extent to which the spoken or written language of one or more fluent non-native speakers does indeed mark itself out in this way. Consider who decides what is idiomatic, and under what circumstances non-native usage might come to be adopted more widely.

135   Choose an area that interests you (such as cookery or equestrianism) and identify specialist words and the words they collocate with. For example, in cooking, what can be *browned, griddled, poached, or sautéed*? (See Cook 1997: 98–9, for a brief exploration of cookery terminology.) If English had to reduce its vocabulary by one third, which words from this field could be discarded, and which others could expand to cover the gap they left? Is specialist vocabulary necessary or just the product of history? What effect would such simplification have on communication?

136   On p.1 of Collins Cobuild (1996) there is a list of **meaning groups** for verbs, including the words they collocate with. Take these meaning groups and try to account for how or why the English language divides things up this way (does it reflect the language itself? human perception? history? culture?). Is there a conscious aspect to these sets or do native speakers have no idea about them? Show some native speakers the lists and ask for their reactions.

137 Remove the terms from Table 5.1, and see how many of them native speakers can fill in. Are there patterns regarding what people know and don't know? Why might some terms be more central to our common vocabulary than others? Use a word frequency list (see Chapter 1) and/or a corpus search (see Chapter 19) to check whether it is the least-used words that are least well-known. If it is, consider whether infrequency causes unfamiliarity or the reverse.

138 Compare the frequency distributions of words in comparable texts from different dates in the twentieth century. You can conduct an electronic comparison using Nation's Range software (Nation 2001). Leech *et al.* (2001) also provide useful data as a starting point.

139 Construct a list of common collective nouns (e.g. *flock of sheep, pride of lions, shoal of fish*). How have they come about, and how long have they been in use? (Use the full *Oxford English Dictionary* or a good etymological dictionary – references are given in Chapter 10.) Why do we need such terms (if at all)? Under what circumstances might newly coined ones end up coming into common usage?

140 Compared with some other languages, English has very few kinship terms. What is the sociocultural significance of a lack of different words, for example, for *mother's sister* and *father's sister* in English? Make a comparison with other languages that you know and read more widely about languages that you don't know, to establish the motivation for the creation and retention of these terms. You could extend your research by asking informants to talk about their families, to establish how the practicalities of designation are handled. For instance, is it common for the maternal and paternal grandparents to be differently referred to, and if so, is there any pattern across families? Do people see any need to indicate, when referring to aunts, uncles, and cousins, which side of the family they are from?

141 Investigate the meaning that informants give to words such as *barely* in a sentence like *He barely has ten books on his shelf*. How many has he? More than ten, fewer, or exactly ten? Another interesting word is *orphan*. Precisely who counts as one? Can you cease to be one? If you were brought up by foster parents while your own parents were still alive, who would have to die for you to become an orphan? Use examples like this to explore the agreement, or lack of it, between native speakers about precise definitions, and to discuss whether or not it matters.

142 Explore the meaning of the word *edition*, carefully identifying its range of uses (including *special-edition* chocolate bars and cars). Ask informants what the word means (a) in isolation; and (b) in its different contexts. How easy is it to pin down a central core to its meaning, and how does that relate to the history of the word's use? Find other words used in an extended way, probably also in advertising or marketing, and investigate them similarly (e.g. *'fresh' orange juice/cream; light/lite; bio*). How effectively can these uses be explained using Rosch's prototype theory (described above)?

Morphology and etymology

The morpheme is the smallest unit of meaning. Some morphemes (**free morphemes**) stand alone, such as *dog, smile, black, from, also*. Others are **bound**, needing to combine with other morphemes, e.g. *-s* (plural), *un-*, *-ish*, *pseudo-*. You can find examples of the prefixes and suffixes of English in Crystal (2003b, Ch. 14). English is a particularly fascinating language to study, because its history of borrowing from other languages has left it with an enormous collection of morphemes, not all of which still have meanings that are recognizable without recourse to a dictionary. Because of this history, for English the studies of morphology (how we make up words today) and etymology (how words have come to have the form they do) are closely allied. For more information and suggestions for projects on etymology, see Chapter 10.

PROJECTS

143   Look through Facebook pages for words that are new to the language or interview some children about the current playground vocabulary, what it means, and how they use it. Investigate the way in which these words have been constructed and/ or where they have been borrowed from. If they are borrowed, have they had their meaning changed? When and how did they first appear? Do they express an idea for which there was previously no word? If not, what was wrong with the old word? Is there any way of telling which of the words will last, becoming fully established in mainstream English, and which will soon fall into disuse again?

144   Look through magazines from the 1950s or 1960s (these may be available electronically) and try to identify words that were new then. They are likely to be names for new products and devices. Divide them into two categories – those that have survived and those that have not – and look for reasons why each word may have undergone its fate.

145   Find out about the construction of vocabulary in a sign language used by deaf people. What happens when a new sign is needed? Who introduces it and under what circumstances? How does the sign language express things like past tense, plural, or the conditional? Interview signers who also know English about the way in which the two languages are the same and different.

146   Take a passage from a novel or a document and attempt to rewrite it using only monomorphemic words (i.e. words that cannot be broken down any further into meaning components). What problems arise with: availability of vocabulary, deciding whether a word is monomorphemic or not, style, and so on?

147   Anderson (1988: 185 ff.) explores the restrictions on English vocabulary formation, which outlaw *He sang *goodly; She stared in *amazion; The bruise began to blacken and *bluen. Jamie Oliver is a good *cooker* (the asterisk indicates that the word does not exist). Use this as a basis for an analysis of idiosyncratic vocabulary in the work of a poet such as Gerard Manley Hopkins or e. e. cummings. What determines whether words of this kind are seen as humorous on the one hand, or beautiful and creative coinages on the other?

148 Make a list of words that, if split, have a different meaning, such as *altogether/all together; into/in to; however/how ever; everyone/every one; layby/lay by*. Ask informants to pin down the differences in meaning. Research the history of the words, to find out whether the opposition has always existed. Pay attention to the syntactic classes of the words and the structures in which they appear. For further examples, see Greenbaum and Nelson (2009, Ch.9).

Punctuation

Punctuation plays various roles in clarifying meaning. Putting a word in inverted commas, for example, can indicate that the writer considers it unfamiliar, inappropriate, and so on. Commas are used to indicate the structure of the sentence, sometimes clarifying potential ambiguity, and, without punctuation, a string of words may be complete nonsense. One well-known example concerns what two students wrote in a translation exercise: *Jones, where Smith had had 'had', had had 'had had'. 'Had had' had had the teacher's approval.*

PROJECTS

149 Remove the punctuation from some texts and get informants to put it back. To what extent do they agree? Categorize the conventions into those that genuinely make the meaning clear and those that could be dispensed with. Do your informants have most difficulty with those aspects of punctuation that play the least role in clarifying the meaning? Survey their attitudes to and problems with 'correct' punctuation.

150 Truss (2009) provides examples where the meaning of a text can change completely, simply by changing the punctuation. One of her examples is *A woman, without her man, is nothing.* as opposed to *A woman: without her, man is nothing.* Track down and/or create similar examples and use them to work out which aspects of English vocabulary and structure are most vulnerable to this kind of potential ambiguity. Give your examples, with no punctuation in at all, to some informants and ask them to add punctuation. Does one of the two options tend to be more commonly selected than the other? If so, which, and why?

151 Research the history of punctuation in English, both in books about the history of the language and by looking at original texts from Old, Middle, and Modern English. Was there ever no punctuation at all? Which usages have existed longest? Has their scope of application changed?

152 The poet e.e. cummings makes very limited use of punctuation. Show some of his poems to informants and compare their reactions and their understanding of the meaning. Does the poet's approach permit subtle expressions of meaning that would be destroyed by using punctuation more conventionally, or is it just a gimmick?

153   Is the apostrophe disappearing from written English? Truss (2009: 37) claims (as
do many others) that 'it's on its last legs' and bemoans 'showbiz promoters [who]
stick apostrophes in names for purely decorative purposes'. Collect examples of the
use of apostrophes in a wide variety of texts (e.g. shop names, market-stall labels,
hoardings, menus) and decide where the apostrophe is being used meaningfully,
where decoratively, and where for some other reason.

'Correct' grammar

In order to understand the issue of **correctness** in grammar, it is necessary to differentiate
between *linguistic* and *social* judgements. A descriptive linguistic approach recognizes that
many of the features that are considered 'incorrect' in English are in fact simply *non-standard*
and, within their own variety, they are entirely grammatical and consistent. However, the
existence of a 'standard' English indicates that there is a variety of the language that is
socially and culturally more acceptable than the others. Forms that do not adhere to it are
often seen as 'incorrect'. See Freeborn (1995) for a review of the arguments regarding what
constitutes 'good' and 'correct' English and for examples of how actual text does not always
conform to the 'rules'. Freeborn *et al.* (1993, Ch. 1) and Crystal (2003b: 366–7) also discuss
the question of correctness, and Wray (1996) explores the conflicts between prescriptivism
and descriptivism that arise when academic linguists have to correct the work of their
students. Cameron (2012) gives a spirited account of the debate in her chapter 'Dr Syntax
and Mrs Grundy: the great grammar crusade'. On the other hand, Marenbon (1994: 20)
suggests that descriptivism and prescriptivism are mutually supportive: 'by describing how
a certain language is spoken or written, the grammarian prescribes usage for those who
wish to speak or write that language'.

PROJECTS

154   Compare the grammar of two strong dialects of English (such as Scots, Geordie,
Black English Vernacular, Indian English) or compare one of them with standard
English. What things can be expressed by one and not the other? For some ideas
on this, see Labov's paper on non-standard Black American English, originally
published as Labov (1969) but also available in many collections of classic papers
in sociolinguistics. Consider the implications for the expressive potential of an
individual if we accept or reject his/her variety as a legitimate form of English in
its own right.

155   Research the history of a prescriptive feature of English grammar, such as not splitting
infinitives, not ending sentences with a preposition or the use of apostrophes. Use
textbooks on the history of English (see Chapter 10) and original sources where
possible. Categorize a collection of conventions (along with some examples of them)
into two sets: those that reflect a long-standing convention and those that are a
recent imposition. Mix the two sets together and ask native and non-native speaker
informants for their views on how important it is to adhere to the rule and how long
they think it has applied to English. Do your results suggest that a rule has

more, or less, credibility if it is believed to (or actually does) reflect a long-standing tradition?

156 Do school pupils, teachers, school governors, and employers in business and in the public services share the same opinions on what good English is? Show the same stimuli to pupils and one of the other groups above and compare the responses. For example stimuli, see Freeborn *et al.* (1993: 11–12).

157 Examples such as *I would of done that* or *she was been silly* are often marked as errors in student essays. Find more examples and explain how the non-grammatical forms might have been produced. Interview teachers about the prevalence of such errors and ask them how they try to help their students not to produce them. Then tell the teachers that, according to some theories of language change, it is only a matter of time until these 'errors' become acceptable. Ask them to categorize the examples for the likelihood that they will be acceptable within the next 20, 50, and 100 years and ask them under what circumstances they believe that the drift towards acceptability might and might not occur. Compare their responses, to establish whether teachers hold common views about correctness and their role in promoting it.

158 Use a corpus search to discover the ways in which the reflexive pronouns (e.g. *myself, yourself*) are used. Pay particular attention to usages such as *I spoke to yourself about it* and *a person cannot help themselves*. Consider what is being expressed and what other options there are. Try to establish whether the usages are new or have always been there. If the latter, why are they not considered 'correct'? Read about the dynamics of language change and acceptability, to predict what might happen next.

159 Find examples of *alot, aswell*, and other non-standard spellings of this kind. Collect data by borrowing essays from a local school or your fellow students. Which word strings are now being perceived as single items and which remain consistently separate? Use basic phrase-structure analysis (such as Burton-Roberts 2010, Thomas 1993) to establish whether there are structural reasons for this. For some background and example data, see Wray (1996).

160 Explore the role of dictionaries as prescribers or describers. By comparing their forewords, their format and what information they include, find out who they are targeted at and what their aims are. Interview native and non-native speakers of English about how and why they use dictionaries, whether they always believe what they find there, and what they do if they can't find the word or meaning they are looking for.

OTHER PROJECT IDEAS

161 Investigate the form and usage of idiomatic and 'rule-breaking' expressions such as *He was sleeping like the proverbial* or *I've just had himself on the phone*. Explore the nature of their form and usage, taking account of the syntax (including any

restrictions they violate) and the pragmatics (shared information, about whom or in what circumstances they would be used, the effect of using them rather than an alternative and so on).

162　Take a selection of jokes from a joke book or website and catalogue them for humour based on pragmatics, ambiguity (phonological, lexical, and structural), and non-linguistic factors such as situation. Give the jokes (intermixed) to groups of participants and get them to rate them for funniness. Do 10-year-olds give consistently different ratings from adults for the different types? What about men and women? Nash (1985), Chiaro (1996), Blake (2007) and Ritchie (2003) provide a good introduction to the pragmatics of humour, and ideas to follow up for projects.

163　Find Monty Python's *Dead Parrot Sketch* on YouTube, for example, or a sketch of similar anarchic complexity, and categorize the lexical, structural, and pragmatic sources of its humour.

164　Explore the origins of idiomatic expressions such as *spitting feathers* or *raining cats and dogs*. Ask informants what they think the expressions mean. We found most people think that *spitting feathers* means very angry but one informant is adamant that it means very thirsty. How might such differences come about?

165　Track changes made to in entries in Wikipedia (http://en.wikipedia.org/wiki/Main_ Page) by watching the pages themselves and also the discussion pages associated with the entries. Use this information to comment on how meaning and accuracy are negotiated, with particular attention to how people cope with multiple beliefs about 'facts'. Consider the extent to which meaning and information are being created or revised rather than simply discovered, and how this process relates to more traditional ways of presenting information. To get yourself started, look at the 'recent changes' list (http://en.wikipedia.org/wiki/Special:Recentchanges) and follow up several topics for a few days, until you see which ones are most active and most interesting.

166　Ask musicians who do not know the Italian language to identify, from a list, common Italian musical terms that they are familiar with and would not need to look up if they occurred in a piece of music. Examples might be *andante, staccato, forte, largo*, and *legato*. Then, for each term, ask your informants to explain the meaning and how they would obey the instruction in a piece of music. Compare the explanations: do all musicians share a common understanding of a term? Is a term differently interpreted according to the instrument? Now look up the terms in a good Italian-language dictionary, to discover what the words literally mean (for instance, *legato* means 'bound together'). If possible, check with a native speaker of Italian whether the terms still have their literal meaning in everyday Italian or whether they are now solely musical terms. Use your results to map out the ways in which the original meaning of the Italian words can shift when used by musicians who do not know the language.

167 Conduct an analysis of the hand signs described in the science-fiction novel *The Foreigners* by James Lovegrove (2001). How different are they to words, and how plausible is Lovegrove's proposal that humans could use them to communicate with aliens? Get some friends to learn the signs (and perhaps invent some more of your own) and then try to communicate messages using only the signs. Write methodically about the problems that arise and how the group attempts to solve them.

You can find lots of information that will inspire ideas for projects by reading Chapters 8–16 of Crystal (2003b).

6

Style in spoken and written texts

In any successful communication, whether we are giving the message or receiving it, we are sensitive not only to the content but also to the way in which the message is encoded. The encoding is dependent on very subtle features of what the speaker wants to achieve. How might you ask someone to open the window for you? A simple request? An indirect request? Or by simply pointing? Each of those ways will be appropriate in some situations and less appropriate in others. As communicators, we learn to be aware of the response that each might provoke from the message receiver. Now compare the way you might write an essay on a linguistic topic with the way you might organize a web page on the same topic. The possibilities of the medium and the expectations of the reader will be different in each case, leading you to make different choices of linguistic and paralinguistic features.

The characteristic structural and stylistic features of texts are well worth exploring and, since language is all around us, there are many types of text to choose from. You might like to consider legal texts or literary texts, or the instructions for assembling or using a gadget. You might take an interest in specialized technical texts (on any topic that interests you) or simplified texts (how has the text been simplified and for what audience?).

In this chapter we suggest projects that focus on the lexical, syntactic, and structural choices in text construction. If you are doing work in **text analysis, discourse analysis,** or **stylistics**, you may find information and ideas here to help you.

The questions that one can ask about a spoken or written text include:

- What makes a text a *text* rather than just a set of sentences?
- How does a spoken text differ from a written text on the same topic?
- How does changing the language used in a text change the message?
- (How) have stylistic conventions changed over the years?
- What makes some texts easier to understand than others? Can the study of style help us to produce texts that are more comprehensible?
- Do different types (genres) of text have discernibly different styles?
- What is the effect on the reader of a text *not* being in the style normally associated with it?

- Can a stylistic analysis reliably determine the authorship of a text when that authorship is in doubt?
- How do poets, advertisers, politicians, and other professional 'wordsmiths' exploit style to create an effect?

The answers to such questions rely on the analyst's examination of patterns in the words and structures, as well as its presentation (spelling, punctuation, font size, use of illustrations, and so on).

Writing is a person's opportunity to have his/her say in a monologue. Although, of course, a writer aims to create a reaction from the reader, a single written text is not really a dialogue, because the reader cannot feed responses directly back to the writer in time to influence what is written next. A spoken monologue is somewhat similar and can be subjected to many of the same questions as those listed above.

However, *interaction* is different. It is the creation of text, in which what one person produces is influenced by what one or more others say. We mostly think of speech in this regard but, in fact, writing can also be interactive. For instance, a series of letters between two correspondents would display some of the same patterns as a conversation, as each writer reacts to the other. The same goes for on-line discussions, which, though not by any means identical to spoken conversations, imitate them in some regards, while also retaining some features only found in writing.

The feature of interaction in spoken and written texts introduces other interesting questions, such as:

- How are the participants working out when it is their turn to contribute?
- How are they signalling that they have finished their turn or have more to say?
- How are they indicating that they understand, agree, or disagree with others' contributions?
- How are participants moving from one topic of conversation to another?
- How are they bringing the interaction to a close?
- To what extent are the different participants picking up topics or lexical or stylistic features from each other and re-using them, and what effect does that create?

As you will no doubt have realized, many of the ideas that we describe in this chapter coincide with topics in other chapters. In relation to language and gender (Chapter 8), you could examine male–female differences in interaction or in the creation of written text. In a study of second-language acquisition (Chapter 4), you could examine how stylistic features in speech or writing are adopted from the first language, so that the second language sounds un-native-like in subtle ways. In an investigation of how children acquire language (Chapter 3), you could examine the process by which the skills of text assembly or of conversational behaviour develop.

Textbooks and major journals

The broad scope of this chapter means that there are a great many books that you can turn to. In the area of discourse analysis, Schiffrin *et al.* (2003) and Gee and Handford (2011) offer an excellent grounding and are sure to inspire project ideas. From the structural perspective, Hillier (2005) analyses a wide range of texts within a Hallidayan framework.

Carter (2004), Have (2007), and Cameron (2001) focus on oral-language use. Crystal (2006) addresses some of the varieties found in electronic use of language. Useful journals for projects on spoken and written style include the following:

JOURNALS

British Journal of Social Psychology

Communication Monographs

Discourse and Society

Discourse Processes

English Text Construction

Journal of Communication

Journal of Politeness Research: Language, Behaviour, Culture

Journal of Pragmatics

Language and Dialogue

Language and Literature

Narrative Inquiry

Research on Language and Social interaction

Text and Talk (previously *Text*)

Written Language and Literacy

Central themes and project ideas

Texts are created for so many different purposes, and in so many different forms, that there are several approaches that one can take to researching them. We have divided the themes according to the *level of analysis*. This enables you to consider the options for how you engage with the construction and function of a text, either alone or as part of a comparison. Text comparison is a very fruitful approach, and it is possible to focus both on how even quite similar texts can differ and how very different texts still have similarities.

But what types of text are there, that you might consider working on? Each text type has characteristics that you can exploit in your investigation. An oral text (that is, spoken language) will have different features from an equivalent written text: consider the difference between someone reading a story out of a book and telling the same story directly in the oral medium. Within the oral medium, a television discussion will differ in certain kinds of ways from a radio discussion: to get a feel for how, try listening to a television discussion without looking at the pictures. In the written medium, linguistic researchers are currently very interested in the way that certain features of spoken language might be 'leaking' into new forms of written text, such as web-logs and text messages (see Chapter 11). For each of these types of text – and there are many more subtle divisions within them – you can ask certain basic questions about the sounds or letters, the words, the grammar, the meaning, and the interpersonal function. Furthermore, you can ask those questions of just one text type, or use the analysis as a means of comparing one text type with another.

Sound patterns within texts

In some texts, the sound patterns created by the writer are clearly the most important feature. Although we associate rhyme, alliteration, assonance, and consonance with poetry, advertisers or politicians also frequently use such devices as a way of making a slogan or soundbite more memorable. Whether you are describing a Shakespearean sonnet or a soap-powder advert, the formal description of the phonetic patterns will use the same approach and terminology. Stress and intonation are also often used to great effect.

Nursery rhymes often follow strong metrical patterns, the heavily stressed rhythms making them easier to memorize. *Twinkle, Twinkle Little Star* is a good example of a nursery rhyme with a particularly strong metrical rhythm. In *Three Blind Mice*, on the other hand, we see reflected the wider potential of the stress-timed pattern of everyday English speech, with different numbers of unstressed syllables packed in between equally spaced stressed ones. **Iambs**, **dactyls**, and other metrical patterns and rhyme schemes are explained in most of the introductory books on literary stylistics (such as Leech 1973) or in the dictionaries of literary terms (such as Baldick 2009). Freeborn (1996) gives some examples of sound patterning in a range of verse and prose texts, including Chaucer's *Canterbury Tales*, *Remember* by Christina Rossetti, and Dylan Thomas's *Under Milk Wood*.

A writer may use onomatopoeia: the choice of words could imitate the noise of walking through crisp leaves in the forest in autumn or the sound of a snake slithering through the grass, for example. These effects can be captured in analysis by using phonetic or phonemic transcription to highlight common sound features that may be obscured by the complex spelling system of English. Indeed, even more general assonance and rhyme in a text benefit from this treatment: the words *all, haunch, lawn, broad, floor, more, pour, sure* appear to have little in common when spelled, yet a phonemic transcription reveals that, in many varieties of English, they all contain the same vowel.

PROJECTS

168 Look at the work of one or more poets (such as Gerard Manley Hopkins or Benjamin Zephaniah) to see what makes their work sound so different from that of other poets.

169 Focus on an advertising campaign that uses puns. For example, Perrier once used a play on the word *eau* (French for 'water') to illustrate occasions when their product could be consumed, including: *Sleau lunch* (with a picture of a snail), *A reau at the regatta* (during the Henley Regatta), and *Eau, I say!* (during Wimbledon, where one commentator was known to exclaim 'Oh, I say!' to a good shot). This last example demonstrates very clearly what is often called intertextuality: our interpretation of any one text may require a knowledge of other texts or situations. A new twist to this intertextuality came from a 'piggyback' advertising campaign (where one advertiser exploits the idea of another) by Nestlé-Rowntree. An advertisement for Polo Mints used the slogan *The mint with the heaule* with a picture of the mints looking like the bubbles in a glass of Perrier. Look for examples of wordplay and piggybacking in advertising: what options are there for different mediums? That is, what can a written advertisement achieve that a spoken one could not, and vice versa?

170   Record some political speeches at election time or at the annual party conferences, or consider party political slogans. Examine specifically the sound patterning that is used and how it reinforces the meaning. Look for ways in which subtle cues in the language help to differentiate the political persuasions of the different parties and/ or how linguistic choices are made in order to appeal to particular sections of the electorate.

Lexical choice within texts

To work in this area, you need to be familiar with the field of semantics. Carter (2012) and Kearns (2011) provide good introductions to areas such as connotation and denotation, and to semantic relationships like synonymy, antonymy, and hyponymy. Crystal (2003b) has a whole section on the lexicon and English vocabulary, including discussions on 'loaded' vocabulary (p. 170) and 'doublespeak' (p. 176).

A lexical analysis of style will ask: Why have these particular words been chosen and not others, and what are the connotations of the chosen words? For example, if *white* is mentioned, is it being used simply to indicate the colour of a physical object, or also to imply a sense of purity? (If the latter, there is a heavy cultural dependency, as white has different symbolism in different parts of the world.)

In newspaper reporting, the lexical choice of the journalist can indicate the ideological standpoint from which he/she is writing. Is a gunman described as a *terrorist*, a *guerrilla*, or a *freedom fighter*? Was a victim *shot by a marksman* or *picked off by a sniper*? In fiction, the author's perspective and opinion of characters are often indicated through the choice of nouns, verbs, and adjectives with positive or negative connotations. Consider this description of Zoltan Kaparthy's dancing, in the musical *My Fair Lady*: *Oozing charm from ev'ry pore, he oiled his way around the floor.* Carter and Nash (1990) focus on how individual characters are presented in Galsworthy's *The Man of Property* by analysing the way a dinner-party conversation is narrated. In an essay at the end of his novel *Nineteen Eighty Four*, George Orwell explains in some detail how lexical choice can be manipulated as a tool of political and personal repression. Freeborn (1996) shows how different newspapers report the same incident in different ways.

In Chapter 8 of Freeborn (1996), you can find a discussion of the notion of 'styleless prose', or that style that the semiologist Roland Barthes described as 'neutral writing'. Freeborn uses parts of Orwell's *Animal Farm*, Seth's *A Suitable Boy*, and Camus's *The Outsider* to explore this from a grammatical and lexical perspective, and concludes that, while the stylistic details can differ greatly from one text to another, there is style in all texts.

PROJECTS

171   Compare two translations of the same original text. By making different choices, the translators can create distinctly different texts. You can do a study of this sort even if you don't understand the original language: it is possible to compare the implications of the lexical and syntactic choices made by two translators of the same original text without any reference to that original, providing you don't want to make any judgement about which version is 'better'. To gain an idea of how two translations might differ, look at Short and Leech (2007), where, in 'Passages and Topics for Further Study', two translations of the first paragraph of Kafka's *The Trial* are juxtaposed.

172   Compare the way that writers achieve different effects from the same word. Choose something that is neutral enough to carry positive or negative connotations, e.g. *family*; *rain*; *compromise*. Add a dimension to your study by taking certain examples from across your texts and asking people with different backgrounds, ages, and attitudes for their views on the use of the words. This will give you insights into how the reader as well as the writer can play a part in constructing meaning.

173   Are the words used in a given text largely of Latin or of Anglo-Saxon origin? Books on the history of the English language (see Chapter 10 for references) will give you some insights into the significance of this distinction, as well as how to spot the difference. Are the words in a text morphologically simple or complex, and what is the effect of this on the reader? Freeborn (1996) considers the effect of lexical choice by looking at different versions of part of the Sermon on the Mount from the Bible, and by looking at two translations of an extract from *The Swiss Family Robinson*. He also compares three versions of the first verses of St John's Gospel from different periods.

174   Find two or more texts on the same subject and see how *few* words they have in common and how they cover the same ideas in different words. For example, compare a poetical and a prose description of a tiger.

175   Find examples of words that have a particular meaning and resonance in advertising. Examples are *crispy*, which is used as a desirable attribute for processed food that is high in fat, and *creamy*, which is intended to give the impression of a luxury product (soup, soap, etc.). Try replacing the words with others that have a similar meaning (e.g. for these examples, *crisp, hard*, etc. and *thick, viscous*, etc.). Work out the boundaries of the words' use – which products are and are not so described – and, by interviewing informants, assess the precise connotations and images that the words create.

176   How do puns work? Collect examples of puns and show how the pun depends on multiple meanings for an individual lexical item. Carter (2004) and Ritchie (2003, Ch. 9) give some examples. Ask informants to rate puns as to how funny they are, and analyse the funniest and unfunniest to see what it is about them that has this effect. Do adults and children have similar views?

Grammatical structure within texts

Specific effects can be achieved by using short sentences with a simple clause and phrase structure on the one hand, and long and complex sentences with many embedded clauses and phrases on the other. A structure may be repeated for effect, while a passive construction may enable the agent to remain unnamed. Useful guidance on basic clause and phrase structure can be found in Freeborn (1995), Bloor and Bloor (2004) and Merrison *et al.* (forthcoming). You can find out how to apply this knowledge to text analysis in

Freeborn (1996), as well as in Fairclough (2001), Carter *et al.* (2007), Bloor and Bloor (2007) and Conboy (2007). You should also read Chapter 5 in this book.

Questions you can ask when approaching text analysis from this angle include:

- Are the sentences of equal length and complexity throughout the text?
- Is the clause structure always neutral (unmarked), or have particular elements sometimes been emphasized by being placed at the beginning of the sentence or deliberately held back until the end?
- Have any structural patterns been created by cohesive devices such as repetition or ellipsis, anaphoric or cataphoric reference?
- Are any of these patterns then deliberately broken to create a particular effect?

Creating and then destroying a structural pattern is a technique employed by many writers to highlight a particular point, as this extract from *Yes, Prime Minister* (Lynn and Jay 1987: 107) illustrates:

> The Times *is read by the people who run the country.*
>
> The Daily Mirror *is read by the people who think they run the country.*
>
> The Guardian *is read by the people who think they ought to run the country.*
>
> The Morning Star *is read by the people who think the country ought to be run by another country.*
>
> The Independent *is read by the people who don't know who runs the country but are sure they are doing it wrong.*
>
> The Daily Mail *is read by the wives of the people who run the country.*
>
> The Financial Times *is read by the people who own the country.*
>
> The Daily Express *is read by the people who think the country ought to be run as it used to be run.*
>
> The Daily Telegraph *is read by the people who still think it is their country.*
>
> And the Sun's *readers don't care who runs the country providing she has big tits.*

PROJECTS

177 Reading schemes for young children or second-language learners are often graded in terms of the structures used in the text. Examine the books in such a scheme. How precise is the grading? What effect does the limiting of available structures have on the flow of the text?

178 There are many simplified versions of classic texts for learners of English as a Foreign Language. How has the original text been modified in terms of structure? Ask some native and non-native speakers of English to compare the two and say which they prefer and why.

179 Compare old and recent versions of the Bible or a church liturgy. What differences are there in the grammar and form – or are the changes all lexical? Have the changes made the text more accessible?

180   Are business letters today written following the same grammatical conventions as, say, in the 1930s? Do the differences extend to personal letters and to public letters (e.g. to newspapers)? You can gain a sense of the differences by trying to rewrite a modern letter in 1930s style, and vice versa.

181   Collect a series of different types of joke that rely on a formulaic structure and examine exactly how the discourse structure remains the same even though the detail differs. You might use *knock knock* jokes, or comic aphorisms such as *One sandwich short of a picnic, One can short of a six-pack,* and *Is the Pope a Catholic? Does a one-legged duck swim round in circles?* Ask members of the older generation to help you collect similar lists that have been popular in the past, such as *Old lecturers never die, they just lose their faculties, Old farmers never die, they just go to seed.* Once you have a type, you can search for further examples on the Internet (e.g. www.ahajokes. com). Focus your analysis on questions such as: What makes a good and bad example of the set and why? How easy is it to create new items for the set? You could explore the second question by asking informants to do exactly that. What rules can you identify as implicitly underlying their choices?

182   As for Project 181, but focus on the extent to which children are able to understand the content and structure of such jokes. Try 8-year-olds and 11-year-olds. Check out Chapter 3 for guidance on developmental issues.

Interpersonal function of texts

Linguists recognize that not everything about a text is contained in its words and structures, because texts are received as well as produced. Thus, it is possible to ask what the effect of a text is (and is intended to be) on its readers or hearers. Why was the text produced in the first place? Sometimes this will be obvious, but quite often, particularly in advertising and in propaganda, the superficial aim of the text disguises a deeper message. For example, an advertisement that appears to be explaining how little servicing a particular car requires is, of course, actually trying to sell the car. A newspaper report of an event and an entry about the same event in a personal diary or a web log will read quite differently because they are written for different audiences, as will an account of that same event provided in a radio or television interview. Cook (2001) gives you some idea of how to approach advertisements as samples of individual texts, as well as indicating some of the more generic features of advertising. For ideas on how to tackle the analysis of propaganda, see Chilton (1985) or Bloor and Bloor (2007).

PROJECTS

183   Choose a specific brand-named product and compare the way in which it is advertised in different places (print, radio, television, the Internet). You will find most variation where there is fierce competition between brands and where the product is not in itself geared to a niche market. A good example is mobile phone advertising. How is the same product described differently for different readers in the different

media? Consider the extent to which the same individual is addressed differently according to the medium – does this somehow imply that he/she is perceived as having different interests or priorities simply by virtue of opening a magazine as opposed to a web page?

184   Compare texts in a single medium, on the same topic, and for the same purpose, but from different countries. You could look at advertisements for the same product (say, the same make of car) or feature items in an internationally marketed magazine such as *Cosmopolitan* or *National Geographic*.

185   In a report in the UK daily newspaper, *The Guardian* (13 August 2005), a paragraph about Omar Bakri says:

> To his enemies, he is the Preacher of Hate, the benefit-scrounging suicide bomber's cheerleader, and a test of Tony Blair's resolve in the battle against terrorism. To his small band of followers, he is a distinguished Islamic scholar, a devoted family man persecuted in the same way as was the prophet Muhammad.

Collect reports and discussions from different sides in some major or local political conflict and compare their use of language in accounts of the same event or issue. Decide which medium to draw on: newspapers, journals, radio, television, and the Internet are all possible. You might want to draw on materials with an international circulation or audience such as *Time* and *New Statesman*, BBC World Service, CNN, and so on. Remember to consider the collusion of readers and listeners/viewers in deliberately choosing to access one source rather than another, because they know or sense what ideology will be reflected. Keep focus in your project – a small quantity of text analysed carefully may gain you more credit than a superficial description of a larger amount.

186   Using the public library archives, compare the coverage of an event (such as an election or a disaster) 30 or 50 years ago with the coverage of a similar event much more recently. Look not only at the reports during the day or two after it, but also the coverage in the longer term. One comparison might be the disaster in 1966 in Aberfan, Wales, and the shootings in Dunblane, Scotland, in 1996, and Columbine High School in the USA in 1999, all of which resulted in the death of many children in their school building. How have styles of reporting changed, and how are the changes best characterized linguistically?

187   Reports of violent events change from day to day as more information emerges. Research how the language used in reporting, say, the shootings by Anders Breivik in Oslo in 2011, changed as more information became public about the identity of the perpetrator.

188   Travel texts can be a fruitful area for linguistic analysis. Compare descriptions of a specific location or hotel as found in a holiday brochure, a guidebook, or a diary, and on a postcard sent home.

189   For a piece of household equipment (such as a hi-fi, microwave, personal computer, smartphone, or iPod), compare the description in the user guide with the one in the sales literature that is trying to persuade you to buy the item and, if appropriate, with the technical description for the engineer or installer.

190   Compare the style in which recipes for the same dish are written in a range of cookery books. Alternatively, choose any other activity that interests you and analyse any texts relevant to it. Aim to identify features that can be changed as an expression of style as compared with those that cannot. Is there any variation in the role given to the reader in terms of responsibility (e.g. instructions to judge quantities or textures, etc.) and, if so, how might this affect the way that the reader perceives the task and his/her role in it?

191   Look at estate agents' descriptions of various houses, considering the stylistic characteristics of detailed descriptions that are intended to persuade the reader to buy the property. Interview some estate agents about how these descriptions are compiled and whether a depressed housing market changes the way in which they are formulated.

192   Compare the reporting of sporting events by different interested parties. For example, you could analyse reports of a football match in the newspapers local to each of the teams, and again on each team's website. Alternatively, follow the accounts of events, including the performance of individual players, over the course of a major tournament (e.g. Wimbledon tennis, Ryder Cup golf, Ashes cricket, World Cup soccer, the Olympics) to see how the reports change over the duration of the competition, particularly as a player or team comes to the fore or fails to meet up to expectations.

Formality and informality

The language used in relation to an event often reflects the level of formality: consider how a top-class hotel might describe a cup of tea and a piece of cake as 'de-luxe afternoon tea', while a local café calls it 'shopper's tea' – both are different from how you might talk about the same thing in your own home. A written text is not necessarily more formal than an oral text where the topic is the same. There can be formal written texts (e.g. legal contracts, degree certificates) and informal ones (e.g. postcards, shopping lists), just as there can be formal spoken texts (e.g. launching a ship, giving a presentation) and informal ones (e.g. chatting over a drink in the pub, telephoning your best mate to pass on some gossip). Some events can only be transacted orally but have a written document to confirm that the event took place (e.g. getting married), whereas other events are only transacted in writing (e.g. writing a cheque). Some texts seem to show some of the characteristics of both oral and written texts, including emails and text language, both of which are still developing their own identity as genres (see Chapter 11).

PROJECTS

193   Compare how language is used orally and in writing to achieve the same interpersonal function. Record someone as they instruct another person on how to pitch a tent or how to make spaghetti bolognese. Then ask the same person to write the instructions for the same activity for the same audience. Analyse how the oral and written text are different from each other.

194   Ask your speaker to give the same set of instructions to, say, a child and to an adult, and see how the language varies, or ask them to give the same instructions to a male and female of the same age to see if the language changes.

195   Compare the initial notes for an essay with an early draft and a final version of the same essay and see how the text changes as it is worked on by the author. What are the main driving forces in changing the text (e.g. the addition of new ideas, changing old ones, additional clarity, imposing more structure)? You might find it easier to work on someone else's essay rather than your own. If you do, you could interview the author in order to gain additional insights about the process.

196   Many people choose to write their own versions of formal ceremonies. Compare the 'official' version of the marriage vows with those written by couples who chose to write their own. A similar task could be carried out comparing funeral rites. What motivates people to write their own version? To what extent do they continue to adopt features of the original, in order to preserve, for instance, dignity and formality, a clear marking of a significant moment, etc.? Are there common elements in rewrites that might indicate the need for updated official versions?

Ideology and power

Language is often used to exercise power over people in subtle ways and you need only think of the use of language in courtrooms, in doctor–patient interviews, in the classroom, and in news reporting (oral and written) to see but a few examples of this use of language. Some of the research into such areas goes under the name of **critical discourse analysis (CDA)**. CDA aims to uncover implicit ideology in apparently innocuous language. You can read about this work in Bloor and Bloor (2007), Caldas-Coulthard and Coulthard (1996), Fairclough (2001, 2010), Kress (1990), Meinhof and Richardson (1994) and Widdowson (2004), among others. A critique of CDA, with practical proposals, based on corpus analysis, to make it a more watertight pursuit, is given by Stubbs (1997). For an account of institutional language, see Thornborrow (2002), and see Hutchby (1996) for an account of power in talk-radio discourse. For a broader range of insights into language at work, see Drew and Heritage (1992).

PROJECTS

197   Stubbs (1995: 383) presents the following distributions from his corpus research:

Table 6.1 Distribution of *little* and *small* with *boy* and *girl*

little girl or girls:	146	little boy or boys:	91
small girl or girls:	8	small boy or boys:	46

He examined the collocations of *little, small, big,* and *large* and concludes that *little* tends to have a connotation of cute and likeable, or else 'it can convey that a speaker's attitude is patronizing or pejorative' (p. 385). In other words, *little* has 'strong cultural connotations' (Stubbs 1997: 113), which give it certain associative attributes and which then, through the collocational patterns, apply these attributes differentially to males and females. Use a corpus (see Chapter 19 for how to do this) to make your own search for the collocations of a word that you suspect may have gender-, race-specific, or other (for example, negative) weightings. You are aiming to see whether the words occurring within, say, a ten-word stretch either side tend to have particular associations that have resonance for our contemporary culture and/or politics. Some you might try are: *handsome, pert, jolly, communist, feminist,* and *clever.*

198 Adopt a CDA approach to examine a range of stylistic devices in different newspapers and link these to their implicit ideologies. Fruitful topics might be reports on:

- the Gaza Strip in pro- and anti-Israeli publications;
- socio-economic issues or the rights of the disabled in charity and more militant publications;
- race issues in an extreme right-wing publication and in newspapers written for and by minority-ethnic groups;
- human rights issues as reported by Amnesty International, broadsheets, and tabloids;
- the portrayal of women in men's and women's popular magazines and in feminist publications.

199 With a focus on environmental or humanitarian issues, explore how language can be used to empower or disempower people. The journal *New Internationalist* often provides a different political perspective from that of the daily newspapers. How is this achieved linguistically? The nuclear-power industry and world poverty are two useful focuses for such a study.

200 Perhaps using historical material, examine the subtleties of propaganda, where the intention is to present a one-sided account as if it was the whole truth. Or analyse the same historical event (e.g. the Gunpowder Plot of 1605) to show how a reinterpretation of the same events is encoded differently. In 2005, when the 400th anniversary of the Gunpowder Plot was being celebrated, Guy Fawkes was described in some articles as a 'suicide bomber', a very modern term applied to a historical event.

201 Use eye-witness accounts of historical events to consider the extent to which people who were present at an event might not agree with how the history books now present it. For an excellent collection of such accounts, see Carey (1997). To what extent do you feel that individual perspectives *should* be taken into account in the study of historical events? (That is, to what extent are they consistent with the purposes of those writing the official histories?)

202 Sit in the observation gallery at your local courtroom and make notes on the language used to express and maintain power relationships. As you go into court, explain to the usher that you will be taking notes (you are not allowed to make recordings in a courtroom in the UK) and why. The usher will then be able to inform other people in court who may wonder what is going on.

203   Observe the way in which power relationships between doctor and patient are portrayed in a range of television programmes (from more than one country if possible). What linguistic devices are used by the scriptwriters to indicate to the viewers who has the power? Which of the portrayals strike you as the most true to life, and what is it about them that makes them seem so?

204   Analyse official correspondence that arrives in the home, for evidence of the power that the writer appears to be claiming over the householder. How does the reader know that it is imperative to respond (as with a final demand for a utilities bill, a fine that must be paid, the compulsory submission of a tax return)? In contrast, how does the reader know when an apparent imperative (e.g. *Call now! Do not throw this away!*) is not actually a true imperative, just a device for advertising? The cues are subtle – can you identify them? Ask other people to act as informants for an experiment in which you manipulate wordings to see where the boundary lies.

Authorship

Stylistic studies have been used to ascertain the authorship of disputed texts. These days, the research is often supported by computer analysis. Such research can help establish whether a newly found sixteenth-century play is by Shakespeare, but it can equally well be used forensically, to compare a ransom note with written material known to be by a given suspect. For general information on how these investigations are carried out, see Crystal (2010, Ch. 12) or Hall *et al.* (2011, Ch. 12). Much more detail about the procedures involved and how the techniques can be applied is given in Farringdon *et al.* (1996). Chaski (2001) and Grant and Baker's (2001) commentary on it are a useful way to understand some of the issues. A more wide-ranging introduction to forensic linguistics can be found in Olsson (2008) and Coulthard and Johnson (2010).

PROJECT

205   Show a selection of short newspaper pieces to informants and ask them to judge whether they were written by men or women. Get them to identify what it is that helped them decide. Does the accuracy or otherwise of their judgements indicate that these apparent pointers are reliable?

Oral texts

In any project that focuses on conversation, you will have to transcribe your data accurately and according to current practice in the field. For guidance on how to do this, see Chapter 17 in this book. You will also need a full grasp of the basic features of conversation: turn-taking, transition relevance points, interruption strategies, topic management, minimal response tokens, and so on.

Scripted versus non-scripted conversation

It is almost always possible to tell, within a few seconds of turning on the radio or TV, whether the conversation you are listening to is scripted or not. It is extremely difficult, in fact, for an actor to sound entirely 'natural' when speaking from a script. There are a number of reasons for this, including:

- the way a script is constructed: many of the features we associate with conversation are simply not found there;
- the purpose of a script: there is an external audience that needs to be given sufficient contextualization to understand what is going on;
- the non-spontaneity of a script: much of what makes spontaneous speech sound the way it does is because it is constructed at the time, while scripted speech is not. This affects the interaction between speakers too. In a script, each actor knows precisely when the next person will speak, whether there will be an interruption, and, if so, who will win the turn, and so on. This is entirely unlike most natural conversation, where these 'battles' have to be fought out at the time.

Some directors make a point of not using written scripts, but plan the 'route' of the conversation with the actors and allow them to *ad lib* until they have settled on a comfortable expression of the ideas.

PROJECTS

206 Compare a scripted conversation from a radio play or a TV soap with a real one on a similar subject and taking place in a similar environment, perhaps from a fly-on-the-wall documentary. Write about the differences in the appearance of your two transcriptions and compare the way in which turns are taken and relinquished and topics are managed, and how those present contribute verbally outside their own turn.

207 Ask some actor friends to learn an extract from a play and to experiment with different ways of performing it so that it sounds as natural as possible. Allow them to try changing the words, improvising, and so on. Record their 'performances' and transcribe them. Ask some independent 'judges' to rate the recordings for naturalness. What characterizes the versions that are judged most natural? How might scriptwriters help the actors to perform more naturally? Include a commentary on the problems that arise in attempting to define and quantify naturalness in conversation.

208 From a film or a television or radio drama, focus on a stretch of conversation that seems particularly naturalistic. Assess what it is that gives it the appearance of naturalness, and identify the ways in which it is still not like real conversation. Are these 'shortfalls' intentional or accidental? In either case, why might they be unavoidable? Good places to look for improvised or semi-improvised dialogue are the films of Mike Leigh and some Woody Allen films. The comedians French and Saunders also sometimes improvise around a previously written script. You could also analyse the television shows *The Office*, *Extras* and *Outnumbered* from this perspective.

Radio and TV interviews

Since interviews tend to have a fairly predictable question-and-answer format, they can be an interesting opportunity to observe other aspects of conversational behaviour, particularly in relation to interruptions on the part of both the interviewee and the interviewer.

PROJECTS

209 Collect three or four conversations with the same political figure or personality, each conducted by a different interviewer. Compare not only the interviewing styles themselves, but also the ways in which the different interviewers draw different conversational behaviour out of the interviewee. Perhaps he/she is more argumentative in one interview than another, or interrupts more, or takes longer turns.

210 Collect a number of interviews (radio or TV) conducted by the same interviewer and compare the style of questioning used with different interviewees. What might be determining the contrasts? For instance, is it the way the interviewees present themselves, or whether or not they are being viewed as responsible for some problem as compared with offering a solution to it? Other issues that you might consider include: Does the interviewer remain neutral through the questioning or does his/her opinion become apparent and, if so, how? Does the interviewer's style change from radio to TV?

211 Drawing on a live radio news and current affairs programme such as the BBC's *Today* on Radio 4 (www.bbc.co.uk/radio4), compare the way in which a chosen presenter copes with interviewing (a) a seasoned interviewee such as a politician; (b) a specific 'expert' who has been thrust into the media as a spokesperson for a current news item; and (c) a member of the public who probably has no experience of public speaking and no expertise to offer, but who has a 'bystander' or 'aggrieved victim' story to tell. How does the interviewer's management of conversational features vary in terms of such matters as aggression, insistence on pursuing a theme, putting words in the interviewee's mouth, and in opening and closing the whole event?

OTHER PROJECT IDEAS

212 Look at the feedback provided in student assignments where the lecturer has chosen to comment on language use. What elements of language use are focused on in the feedback? Is the tutor adopting a prescriptive or descriptive approach? On what grounds might you agree (or not) with the tutor's comments on the student's language use? For detail about language attitudes, including prescriptive influences in teaching, see Edwards (2006).

213 There are several means by which punchlines in jokes can be signalled as such, including text structure, timing, emphasis, and intonation. But what about in comic songs? In a song, the text is constrained by the rhythm and often by rhyme patterns too, timing is dictated by the music, emphasis is difficult to separate from the natural rhythm and may be hard to achieve on a low or high-pitched note, and intonation is heavily constrained by the melody. Collect recordings of comic songs from the twentieth and twenty-first centuries (there are many classic performers to consider, including George Formby, Arthur Askey, Flanders and Swann, Jake Thackeray, and Victoria Wood). Analyse the means by which the punchline is made prominent, if it is. Play selected extracts to informants and ask them to judge how funny they find the line. Do you see a relationship between delivery and the effectiveness of the joke or are other factors in play as well?

7

Sociolinguistics

Sociolinguistics studies the relationship between language and society. Trudgill provides a good summary of some aspects of its coverage:

> Whenever we speak, we cannot avoid giving our listeners clues about our origins and the sort of person we are. Our accent and our speech generally show where we come from, and what sort of background we have. We may even give some indication of certain of our ideas and attitudes, and all of this information can be used by the people we are speaking with to help them formulate an opinion about us.
>
> These two aspects of language behaviour are very important from a social point of view: first, the function of language in establishing social relationships; and, second, the role played by language in conveying information about the speaker. (Trudgill 2000: 2)

Sociolinguistics has been a thriving area within linguistics since the 1960s and there are now numerous sub-areas within it. It would be impossible to summarize them all in a single chapter, but you will gain a feel for the subject here, and you should follow up leads in the books recommended below. In addition, remember the chapters in this book on language and gender, accents and dialects and style, all of which border on and link into this area. Chapters 14, 15 and 16 are also important reading before you embark on a project in sociolinguistics. Themes and questions in sociolinguistics include:

- How and why do accents and dialects develop?
- Is there a link between a speaker's use of regional accents or dialects and his/her social characteristics (e.g. age, gender, social background, and ethnicity)?
- What is the relationship between 'standard' and 'non-standard' accents and dialects?
- How do we decide what is a dialect or accent and what is a language?
- What do people's attitudes towards accents, dialects, and other aspects of language use tell us, and why are some accents, dialects, or languages, and their speakers, perceived in particular ways? How accurate are these perceptions when compared with other types of evidence?
- How does language change across time and geographical areas?
- How and why does language vary from one social context (situation) to another?
- What happens when languages come into contact, or when speakers of a country need to use more than one language on a regular basis (bilingualism or multilingualism)?
- How do pidgins and creoles come into existence? Are they more like dialects or languages?

- Why do speakers sometimes change their accent, dialect, or even the language spoken when in conversation with others, and what sorts of changes do they make?
- How do speakers signal their identity in the language they use, and why do people who live in specific communities sometimes speak in a similar way?
- What is the link between language and disadvantage (e.g. the language of minority groups) or language and power/powerlessness?

Terminology and central concepts

Within sociolinguistics there is a division into **micro** and **macro** research. **Microlinguistic** studies 'typically focus on very specific linguistic items or individual differences' in language use and look for 'wide-ranging linguistic and/or social implications (e.g. the distribution of *singing* and *singin'*)' (Wardhaugh 2010: 16). They often involve the detailed study of interpersonal communication. **Macrolinguistic** studies, on the other hand, 'examine large amounts of language data to draw broad conclusions about group relationships' (Wardhaugh 2010: 16) and relate these to social factors. Aspects of bilingualism, multilingualism, and language planning are issues that often fall under this heading.

The roots of sociolinguistics lie in the work of key figures such as William Labov, often referred to as the 'father of sociolinguistics', who has conducted studies in **modern (urban) dialectology**. Some of the techniques used in sociolinguistics for collecting data (such as questionnaires and interviews) stem from the older field of **traditional dialectology** (**rural dialectology** or **dialect geography**). However, traditional dialectology largely ignored social variation: few young or female informants were used and town-dwellers were excluded, since their dialect was thought to be too new or inconsistent to reflect the older forms of 'pure' dialect that researchers assumed existed. Language change was to some extent the enemy of traditional dialectologists rather than their focus, since it 'muddied the waters' in their search for older forms.

An essential characteristic of language is **variation**. While some approaches within linguistics (such as Chomsky's) expressly do not focus on variation in language, but rather on its structural properties and rules (linked to 'linguistic competence'), *socio*linguistics studies how speakers use language *appropriately*, in terms of what Dell Hymes first called **communicative competence**: 'when to speak, when not, and … what to talk about with whom, when, where, in what manner' (1971: 277). In other words, sociolinguists stress that language varies not only in the sense that words can be combined together to form an infinite number of sentences or longer discourses, but also **systematically**, according to a range of factors such as age, sex, background of speaker, and the situation or social context where the language is used (see below).

Language variation can be approached from a number of angles, including: what the variation consists of, which groups display it, in which situations it occurs, and the approaches that can be taken to its analysis. Language features that vary in precise form from speaker to speaker are known as **linguistic variables**. The detailing and analysing of linguistic variables requires tools such as orthographic and phonetic transcription, and draws on the research techniques of conversation analysis, phonetic, phonological and structural analysis, discourse analysis, and so on. The *causes* of variation are known as

extralinguistic variables and, where there is a relationship between linguistic and extralinguistic variables, this is sometimes referred to as **co-variation**.

We can identify three main types of extralinguistic variable: speaker, group, and situation. The sorts of speaker characteristic that are a backdrop to variation include age, gender, ethnic origin, social background, regional origin, level of education, occupation, and religious persuasion. If variation exists between the language varieties of two or more groups, the sociolinguist needs to identify a pre-existing group membership. He/she might decide there are grounds for saying that these people belong to this group and as a result speak differently. Alternatively, there may be evidence that people belong to a group only by virtue of the fact that they speak differently.

Group variation can shed light on **language change**. Labov tried to demonstrate that, contrary to earlier beliefs, it is possible to see language change in progress, if you know where to look. Variability in language use found within a community of speakers and uncertainty about what constitutes 'correct' or acceptable usage often give clues to what aspects of language may change in the future.

Situational variables are observable where the same person speaks differently in different environments. Studying language from this angle often means thinking about the role or function that language is playing in a situation. This, in turn, means that you can gauge the status and mutual familiarity of speakers and their reasons for needing to communicate, from the style or **register** that they use. Consider, for example, how a politician might speak to his parliamentary colleagues and to prospective voters. The linguistic variation might be seen in the manner of address, including the use of colloquialisms, jargon, and regionalisms, in the selection of topic and examples, and in the level of detail.

Textbooks and major journals

Holmes (2008), Romaine (2000) and Merrison *et al.* (forthcoming, Chs 12 and 13) are introductory textbooks that will set the scene. Coulmas (1998), Eckert and Rickford (2002), Paulston and Tucker (2003), Coupland and Jaworski (2009) and Gumperz and Jacquemet (2006) are readers or edited collections containing classic papers that have shaped the field and/or specially commissioned articles from prominent contemporary researchers. Stockwell (2007) provides many valuable resources that could inspire projects, as might the discussion questions in Coulmas (2005). For methodological guidance, Milroy and Gordon (2003) will be useful.

Check for a sociolinguistic perspective on child language, second-language acquisition, conversation, and so on. For journals relating to those areas, see the relevant chapters in this book. Useful journals for projects in sociolinguistics include the following:

JOURNALS

Applied Linguistics Review

Discourse and Society

English World-Wide: A Journal of Varieties of English

International Journal of the Sociology of Language

Journal of Language and Social Psychology

Journal of Politeness Research: Language, Behaviour, Culture

Journal of Sociolinguistics

Journal of Social Psychology

Language and Communication

Language and Intercultural Communication

Language in Society

Language Variation and Change

Multilingua

Research on Language and Social Interaction

Central themes and project ideas

Quantitative approaches

One of the key features of linguistic variables is that they can often be counted or **quantified**. For example, a group of speakers' pronunciations of /t/ in words like *better* and *bottle* can be scored according to whether they use the 'standard' [t], the 'non-standard' glottal stop [ʔ] or something in between. Scores for different sexes, social backgrounds, or age groups can then be compared to see whether there are consistent patterns of usage by different groups. Features in the speech of the same person in different situations can also be counted and compared. Labov devised a means of eliciting five different **speech styles** in interview situations. He elicited a careful or formal style by asking participants to read 'minimal pairs' (pairs of words that differ by just one key sound – see Chapter 17), and gained increasingly less formal styles from, respectively, read lists of words, read passages, and careful and casual conversation.

The **Labovian paradigm** is the name given to Labov's framework and classification. It provides a methodology for sampling speech styles and is heavily associated with the quantitative studies of accent features that he conducted in the United States, especially in Martha's Vineyard and New York City (Labov 1972). Trudgill's (1972, 1974) work on Norwich speech adopted the same paradigm. Trudgill gathered informants' responses to recordings of particular words, pronounced with accents ranging from RP to broad local ones, and compared these to the tally of features in their own spontaneous language. He was able to demonstrate that women often 'over-reported', claiming that they used pronunciations that were nearer to RP more frequently than they actually did, whereas men often 'under-reported'. Trudgill concluded that the men and women had different notions of 'prestige language'.

When deciding which features to study, check in the published literature for information on the most characteristic features of that accent or dialect. For example, Trudgill (1974) looked at *-ing* in Norwich speech (see above) and Cheshire (1978) looked at forms of *do* (among other things) used by Reading teenagers. A good source for pronunciation features in various accents of British English is Hughes *et al.* (2012), and for non-British English, Trudgill and Hannah (2008) or Melchers and Shaw (2011) (see Chapter 9). Vowel pronunciations (**continuous** variables) are more 'fluid' and can therefore be very difficult to distinguish and score for. Consonants, especially where you are simply listening for their presence or absence (as in /h/ dropping on words like *hammer*), are often easier to handle and score. Reduce extralinguistic variation by using participants who are as similar as possible in all respects except for the one you are interested in.

PROJECTS

214 Select one or more features in a variety that has previously been researched and conduct a replication study to see if the same patterns still hold. If they do not, consider social and other reasons why this might be the case.

215 Undertake a study of the pronunciation and/or dialect features of a group of speakers, eliciting samples of language from them, using methodology similar to that of Labov or another researcher (see Como 2006, for an overview of approaches). This should yield information on how the speakers actually use language. Then, by replicating an aspect of Trudgill's work (see above), investigate the speakers' attitudes to the accent, to ascertain whether these are linked to current changes in the local accent or dialect.

216 Compare two varieties of international English, taking account of the social and historical forces that have brought about the differences. To what extent has the 'new' variety of English taken on systematic new forms that are causing it to diverge from British, American, or other varieties of English? Are these divergences more marked in younger or older speakers? Are they more marked in men or women? For information on features of international English, see Trudgill and Hannah (2008) or Melchers and Shaw (2011). Edwards (2004) and Jenkins (2009) also cover English in the international context.

Social networks

One of the criticisms of Labov's work was that he concentrated too heavily on collecting data from rather superficially defined 'social class' groupings. The concepts of 'social groups', 'speech communities', and, moreover, 'social networks', were borrowed from the social sciences by sociolinguists such as Gumperz (e.g. 1982). Gumperz's aim was to find ways of showing how language use was linked with membership and allegiance to certain clearly defined social *groups* (such as adolescent peer groups, unusually tight-knit communities, and so on), rather than 'classes'. Speakers often, consciously or unconsciously, use language to convey their social identity, so members of a group may sound alike in their speech. Sounding alike also helps groups to seem distinctive when compared with others. The concept of social networks is explained very simply in Coates (2004, Ch. 5). More detail is given in Wardhaugh (2010), and especially Milroy (1987; Milroy and Milroy 1978), whose study of Belfast pronunciation was based on the social-network framework. Where large-scale studies, such as Labov's New York City work, lose the profiles of individuals in the group scores, this approach allows a much closer examination of the individual and is far more ethnographic in nature.

PROJECTS

217 Labov (1972), Cheshire (1978, 1982), and Milroy (1987) all observed how language can be used, even at a subconscious level, as a 'badge' of belonging. Focusing on a group in your own life (or of someone close to you), collect data that can enable you to judge whether commitment to the group affects individual members' language. You may be able to judge how central a member someone is by the strength or frequency with which the group's speech forms are used (e.g. catch phrases, special vocabulary, or grammatical structures). Many types of groups may be appropriate for this kind of study, but groups that share an ideology or specialist knowledge, or who have a strong motivation for seeming 'different', should be particularly fruitful. Possibilities include sports and hobby clubs, and religious, political, and environmental action groups.

218 Make a study of a family that is well known to you. Examine specific language features used by different members of the family and compare them. To what extent can differences be attributed to different group membership? Are there any *similarities* that might relate to the family being a group in its own right?

Qualitative approaches

Qualitative approaches, by definition, involve description and analysis rather than, for example, the counting of features. They often have much in common with linguistic work on discourse and pragmatics (see Chapters 5 and 6). The emphasis is on exploring the types of strategy that particular speakers use in specific contexts with particular people. For example, how does a hospital consultant or GP (a 'high-status participant'), inform a patient that he/she must take more exercise or stop smoking? Is it achieved by negotiation (e.g. *Could you try to take some exercise? Do you think your smoking is affecting your health?*) or more directly (e.g. *You need to stop smoking and lose weight now.*)?

This kind of research often involves longer-term observation, very detailed and close perusal of the data, and relatively small numbers of participants. Findings can therefore only be said to hold true for that particular group until comparative work can be undertaken with other groups. Some researchers feel that purely qualitative approaches lack the rigour of research supported by frequency figures. They feel that, without such figures, no generalizations about trends in language usage can be made. Others, however, feel that the process of eliciting data suitable for counting and comparisons may prevent truly 'natural' and spontaneous language from being produced (the 'observer's paradox' – see Chapter 1).

It is possible to combine elements of all the approaches. Cheshire, in her social-network research with teenagers in Reading (Cheshire 1982/2009), not only examined the frequency of certain types of language structure (such as *you was* as opposed to *you were*) but also explored how these forms were used by individuals on particular occasions. Cheshire was able to show a connection between one speaker's use of vernacular forms and his/her central position in one of the teenage gangs.

PROJECTS

219 Document the key daily routines in the lives of recent immigrants to your country or region. What part does language (in general, or one language in particular) play in these routines? Are special registers (or styles) of language used for particular activities (such as religious worship, speaking to elders)?

220 Focusing on **diglossia** (the use by a whole community of different languages or distinct language varieties in different situations), make a study as described in Project 219, but looking at the way in which your participants switch between languages during their day according to where they are and what they are doing.

221 Investigate the phenomena of **code-switching** (where bilingual speakers switch between their two languages on the basis of topic and/or addressee) and **code-mixing** (where they mix languages within a single conversation or even a single sentence). What appears to determine when they use each language? For further information, see Appel and Muysken (1987/2005), Romaine (1995), or Li Wei (2006b).

222 Make a study of how a language or a language variety under threat from a dominant surrounding language or variety interfaces with that dominant language or variety. For example, if you know Welsh, use data from Welsh TV and radio programmes to examine borrowing from English. What kinds of words are borrowed from the dominant language and why do you think this happens? Your study could incorporate both quantitative and qualitative techniques.

223 Study the linguistic behaviour of individuals who operate together in more than one domain with different power relationships. For instance, you might look at the interaction between a shopkeeper who is also a non-stipendiary church leader and one or more individuals who are both customers and parishioners. Alternatively, you could study how a schoolteacher interacts on parents' evening with a parent who is also his/her heating engineer or pharmacist. You will need to observe interactions in both contexts to establish how variation in the power dimension is expressed. For information on language and power, see Thomas and Wareing (2003), Fairclough (2001, 2010), Simpson and Mayr (2010) and Mooney *et al.* (2011). Specifically in an institutional setting, see Thornborrow (2002).

OTHER PROJECT IDEAS

224 Focusing your project on language change, collect samples of written and/or spoken English, and look for aspects of usage about which people seem unsure (what might be termed 'inconsistent usage'). Obvious examples are constructions such as *would of, could of* instead of the standard *would have, could have*, and the linking of words in writing, as in the case of *aswell, alot* (see also Project 157). How frequently do the constructions appear in your sample? Who uses them? Are they more common in written as opposed to spoken language? Why might they be occurring, and is there any reason to believe that they indicate language change? Your study could incorporate both quantitative and qualitative techniques.

225 Embed some examples of non-standard usage in sentences or paragraphs and present the texts to a range of 'judges' selected carefully with respect to such characteristics as age, gender, background, or regional origins. Ask if the language samples are acceptable to them and, if not, where the problems are and how they would resolve them. How similar are people's attitudes and identifications of what is problematic? Decide in advance whether you want your data to be quantitative, qualitative, or both, and use the appropriate techniques (see Chapters 14 and 15). For examples of similar types of study, see Freeborn *et al.* (1993, Ch. 1).

226 Over a period of at least several months, examine the linguistic behaviour of a recently arrived non-native speaker in an English-speaking area. What patterns emerge regarding the situations where English is used? Does your informant cope with the distinction between colloquial and formal language?

227 Undertake a primarily qualitative study of the language used with elderly people. To what extent does it resemble the 'carer talk' used with children (see Chapter 3) or 'foreigner talk'? Does the selection of this 'register' seem necessary for successful communication in the situations where it is used? You might ascertain this by finding out whether *all* people speaking to an elderly person appear to see the need for features of this register to make themselves understood and whether elderly people seem to understand less well when the features are not used. What does your study tell you about how elderly people are viewed by society? For fuller discussion of language and the elderly, see Coupland *et al.* (1991) and Nussbaum and Coupland (2004).

228 Make a study of language and power by observing the forms of address or politeness strategies used in one of the following situations: a university tutorial setting; transactions at a bar, shop, or some other form of agency. What range of linguistic structures or strategies is used? Are there any patterns regarding which types of people are most polite? Determining factors might be: age, apparent social status or occupation, gender, and so on. If you have the means of recording and analysing them, extend your study to include intonational features or paralinguistic features such as gesture or facial expression. Your study could incorporate both quantitative and qualitative techniques.

229 Explore the ways in which dress affects the way people speak to someone. Visit several times a range of shops selling a particular product (e.g. jewellery, cars, bikes, furniture, antiques) but, each time you go, wear different styles of clothing (smart and elegant, casual, scruffy). Keep notes on key features in the language used in addressing you: are you given a title such as 'sir' or 'madam'? How direct are enquiries? How solicitous and complimentary are staff towards you when you take interest in a particular product? Spread your visits out over a month or so, so that there is less likelihood of being recognized by the sales assistants. You might want to persuade a friend to 'act' as the customer so that you can observe closely what happens and then make notes later.

230 Investigate the attitudes of some carefully selected participants towards language varieties by surveying their reactions to particular accents. This could involve using the 'matched guise technique' (see Chapter 14).

231   We know that many people have a 'telephone voice'. People often adapt their pronunciation to fit particular situations and/or to blend in with other speakers. The latter, in particular, is **convergence** – part of what linguists call **accommodation**. The opposite of this is called **divergence** – when someone changes their accent or dialect (or even their language choice) on a specific occasion in order to distance themselves from the people they are among. Collect samples of someone's language from several situations in which contrasting varieties of English are used by the other speakers involved. Observe the extent to which your informant converges or diverges from the language of the others present. One way to do this would be to ask someone to record their telephone conversations for a week, using their home answering machine. (Allow your informant to delete any conversations that they consider too personal or private in nature.) Avoid revealing until afterwards the true focus of your interest in the data, as knowing what you are looking for may affect the way your informant speaks. Look for things like style-shifting between the informant's initial phone-answering style and his/her subsequent accent and dialect use, as he/ she accommodates to the language variety used by the caller. For more information on accommodation, see Bell (2006).

232   The language used to talk about taboo topics can be very interesting. How are death notices or obituaries written and how do they differ from each other? Are they written in all cultures and, if so, are they written in the same way?

233   What euphemistic terms are there for discussing taboo topics? In what social contexts are the euphemisms used as opposed to the direct terms? To what extent are the euphemisms metaphors and what is the source of the metaphor?

234   There has been a lot of work done on linguistic politeness but what about linguistic rudeness? (See, for instance Bousfield (2008), Bousfield and Locher (2008).) You might like to explore the language use of fictional characters such as Basil Fawlty (from the BBC sitcom *Fawlty Towers*) and compare it with everyday rudeness. Anne Robinson often appears rude to contestants in *The Weakest Link* on BBC TV. What is it about her use of language that makes her appear rude?

235   In discussions of religion, how do believers and non-believers signal position through language? Bring together socially some people who do not know each other and engineer a discussion of some religious or spiritual issue (e.g. reincarnation; religious foundation schooling; whether empty churches should be sold off as houses, etc.). Record the conversation and identify how individuals use language to position themselves and check where others stand.

236   Over the course of a week or two, attend the meetings of a number of organizations that you are not a member of, such as hockey club training, a church service, an environmental action group meeting, an evening class, or discussion group. What language is used that is unfamiliar to you as an outsider and do the members make assumptions about your own use of that language? How does their use of language with you minimize or maximize your identity as an outsider?

8

Language and gender

Gender is just one of many variables that linguists consider when they examine the conscious and unconscious choices that we make in relation to our linguistic behaviour. We have singled it out for its own chapter because it is a particularly fruitful topic for researchers and a good focus for a project. Among the questions addressed by research into language and gender are:

- In what ways do males and females use language differently (e.g. grammar, pronunciation, vocabulary choice, amount of talk, topics selected for talk, strategies selected in conversation, use of taboo words, politeness, accuracy in written language)?
- Are the patterns equally observable in all societies?
- Do males and females speak differently in single-sex groups and mixed groups?
- What are people's attitudes towards male and female language, how do they relate to the genuine observable differences found through research, and are they changing?
- How are males and females portrayed as communicators in literature, commercials, comedy, and so on?
- What happens to individuals whose language does not fit the popular stereotype of how a man or a woman should behave?
- What is the role of gender differences in linguistic change?
- What is linguistic sexism, where does it exist, and why?
- Can political correctness change people's attitudes and behaviour regarding language and sexism?
- How do children learn to speak and write appropriately for their gender?
- How does the linguistic signalling of sexual orientation relate to gender stereotypes?

Terminology

In the context of language and gender research, gender is not just a synonym for sex: '*Sex* refers to a biological distinction, while *gender* is the term to describe socially constructed categories based on sex' (Coates 2004: 4). That is, 'Generally speaking, gender-linked patterns of language-use arise not because men and women are naturally different, but because of the way that difference is made significant in the organization of social life and social relations' (Cameron 2006: 733).

Textbooks and major journals

Introductions to language and gender include Litosseliti (2006), Coates (2004), and Talbot (2010). Eckert and McConnell-Ginet (2003) develops ideas beyond the introductory level. Holmes and Meyerhoff (2005) and Coates and Pichler (2011) are readers containing many useful key papers. Coates's (2003) account of male talk balances an earlier focus on women talk, including in her own previous book (Coates 1996). Curzan (2009) takes a historical perspective. Sunderland (2006) examines the features of discourse about gender. Cameron and Kulick (2003) include consideration of gay language, and Leap and Boellstorff (2003) focus on gay language worldwide. For project ideas, try Goddard and Mean (2008) or Sunderland (2006).

Because of the broad scope of the area, there are many journals where papers on language and gender issues might appear. Gender is often the focus of a special issue, as with *Journal of Pragmatics* volume 38, issue 1 (2006), on gender and humour. Useful journals for projects on language and gender include the following:

JOURNALS

Applied Linguistics

Communications (European Journal of Communication Research)

Gender and Language

Journal of Language and Social Psychology

Journal of Pragmatics

Journal of Sociolinguistics

Language and Communication

Language and Education

Language in Society

Merrill-Palmer Quarterly

Psychology of Women Quarterly

Women's Studies International Forum

Central themes and project ideas

Due to the popularity of projects in language and gender, certain topics have been 'done to death'. Look for a focus that can add something new, no matter how small, to the field. Discussion with a tutor should help with this.

The gender variable in linguistic research

In spite of their training, many linguists in the past were not curious about gender differences in language, sometimes because they allowed themselves to be influenced by popular opinions on female language (see *Attitudes towards male and female language* below). Coates (2004) gives a good overview of some of the main themes, particularly in Chapters 2 and 3. Chambers and Trudgill (1998) give coverage on the methods of traditional and urban dialectology.

The first studies of gender differences in language were formal studies. Formal studies place emphasis on quantitative techniques, relatively small units of language (sounds, words), large groups of participants about whom comparatively little is known, and relatively small samples of speech collected from a fairly restricted range of situations, using structured questions in an interview format. Formal studies are now less popular than studies focusing on interaction between speakers of one or both genders.

PROJECTS

237 Look in detail at some of the material from a major linguistic survey, such as the *Survey of English Dialects* (Ortan *et al.* 1962–71), and examine the extent to which the questionnaires reflected issues of interest or relevance to women. Many university libraries have copies of the full survey and related publications.

238 Contact researchers who have worked on published surveys that have taken gender as a variable. Try to establish where their motivation for studying gender comes from and how they view early work in the field. Study their results in order to gauge the extent to which the gender variable has been a fruitful focus for our understanding of language more generally.

239 Survey recent books and journal articles to find out what the most popular issues in language and gender research currently are. You could combine this with a survey of the questions and approaches followed in these studies. Write a critical comparative evaluation of the issues and how they are researched, aimed at establishing the extent to which gender, as just one variable, has gained disproportionate attention or simply what was needed to redress a previous imbalance.

Attitudes towards male and female language

Gender-based attitudinal research involves looking not so much at real language use as at society's perceptions, attitudes, and stereotypes of it: sometimes termed 'folk-linguistic beliefs'. If attitudes and stereotypes are not based on truth, how and why have they arisen? Do they exert any influence on how males and females acquire or use language?

Use Coates (2004, Chs 2 and 3) as a starting point for information on gender-related language attitudes in Western society. Niedzielski and Preston (2003) cover language and gender from the folk-linguistics perspective.

PROJECTS

240 Using Coates (2004, Chs 2 and 3) as a reference resource, survey key writings of prominent authors, commentators, and early linguists, to investigate the kinds of opinions that were held concerning male and female language. Supplement this with general reading from books about language written in the nineteenth and early twentieth centuries. Identify one or two specific linguistic features from these sources and carry out your own survey of current attitudes towards them.

241 If you have contacts with native speakers of other languages, especially if they are from markedly contrasting cultures, probe their perceptions of male and female language, at the same time asking about wider beliefs in their culture. This may involve using some kind of structured interview technique or questionnaire (see Chapter 14 in this book).

242 What do children think of adult male and female speech, and at what age are their perceptions strongest? Again, Coates (2004) can provide some orientation. Source studies include Edelsky (1976).

243 On the basis of what the research literature identifies as strongly and mildly indicative features of male and female written language, assemble some short tests and give them to male and female informants. Can they tell which are which? Ask them to write commentaries on their decisions so that you can see what they are homing in on.

244 How is male and female speech portrayed in novels, cartoons, or TV and radio drama? Investigating these issues can be an oblique way of asking questions about society's attitudes. One source reference for cartoons is Kramer (1974). Smith (1985) has summary coverage of relevant issues.

245 Replicate or adapt Trudgill's (1972) study of male and female speech. He found that women tended to think they used standard forms more than their real language data showed they did, whereas men did the opposite. The roles of males and females in society have changed since then – will that lead to different results? For similar ideas, but with a different slant, see Projects 218 and 251.

Gender differences in accent and dialect

Several key studies, such as Labov (1966) and Trudgill (1974), have identified certain groups of women as the driving force behind pronunciation change within their communities, and have provided insights into the different models of prestige that males and females adopt, as well as helping to shape a picture of how and why accents change. Cheshire (1978) studied non-standard verb forms used by three adolescent peer groups (two male, one female) in Reading, by 'hanging out' with the groups and becoming accepted by them. Cheshire saw how the girls and boys became socialized into their adult roles and linguistic patterns. This type of approach, because it takes the emphasis away from gender differences and places it on gender 'behaviour', legitimizes studies that look at only one of the sexes. See also 'Gay language' below, where research into the dialect *Polari* is mentioned.

PROJECTS

246 Conduct a study of your local dialect, paying attention to the gender dimension. Replicate or adapt the methodology of one of the key studies, and write about the particular problems encountered in making the adaptation and/or in collecting representative data from both sexes.

247 Much of what we know about male and female dialect patterns stems from work done more than 30 years ago. Social conditions have changed markedly since then. Conduct your own survey of male and female language and compare your findings with those of an older study in the same locality. You will need to gather information on any changes in lifestyle, employment, population (immigration and emigration, for example), that might have led to changes in the roles of males and females with a corresponding change in their language.

Differences in conversation and style of language use

Studies following this theme tend to focus on differences in **communicative competence**, i.e. broad features of language use, including the issue of *appropriate* language use (Coates 2004: 85ff.). One central question is whether males and females have different models of communicative competence, such that there are identifiably male and female 'styles'.

One of the pioneer studies in this area was Lakoff (1975). She proposed a set of so-called **women's language** features. Although Lakoff's list was based largely on her intuitions and informal observations of friends rather than on systematically gathered evidence, it was for many years a starting point for other studies that set out to find empirical evidence for or against the existence of these features. One informative 'spin-off' study is published as Chapter 7 in Coates and Cameron (1989). Other key sources include Kramarae (1981), Maltz and Borker (1982/1998), and Thorne and Henley (1975).

Lakoff's work has encouraged and inspired research in several areas. One is gender patterns in conversational styles and strategies, including turn-taking, topic selection and control, minimal responses (also known as backchannel behaviour or sympathetic circularity), interruption and overlapping speech, and the initiation and ending of conversation. Studies have tended to find that women are far less domineering in conversation and tend to favour co-operative or supportive participation. Coates (2004) provides an excellent starting point on these issues. Coates (1996) gives a more detailed account of women's talk, while Johnson and Meinhof (1996) and Coates (2003) examine men's talk.

Politeness also reveals gender patterns. Although 'politeness' clearly involves more than saying 'please', 'may I', and so on, writers differ in what they put under this heading. Holmes (1995) considers 'hedges' and 'tag questions', apologies, and compliments as politeness features, whereas Coates (2004), for example, sometimes classifies them differently. Findings on these features have usually suggested that women use more politeness strategies than men. As regards **talkativeness**, Western society often stereotypes women as the more talkative gender. However, research has frequently indicated that this is not the case. Summaries of key studies on these issues can be found in Coates (2004: Ch. 6) and Spender (1998). Coates and Cameron (1989: Ch. 8) and Johnson and Meinhof (1996) cover 'gossip' from female and male perspectives respectively, and Talbot (2003) examines it as a gender stereotype. See also Coates (2011). **Swearing** and **taboo language** is another of Lakoff's themes where folk-linguistic beliefs seem to be undermined by research findings. Both genders seem to swear more in single-sex company than in mixed, but there is only limited evidence to support the view that men swear more than females overall (see Coates 2004: Ch. 6).

PROJECTS

248 Are there gender differences in forms of address? Brouwer *et al.* (1979) investigated politeness and forms of address used by males and females at the ticket office of Amsterdam Central Station. Both ticket sellers and customers were studied. Find an environment where you could collect data from a large number of transactional exchanges (do you know anyone who owns a shop or works in a bar and can give you permission to observe or record exchanges?). You might find yourself looking at a relatively small range of speech features and variations, but your work would have a clear focus and the features would be easy to count. Remember to consider the ethics of recording in specific environments (are you likely to capture material which you shouldn't record without the speaker's consent?) and problems with background noise (see Chapter 12).

249 Observe a mixed group of friends, and examine the frequency of swearing, the 'strength' of the terms used (this could be evaluated by a questionnaire to the participants after recording), and the word classes that swearwords typically occupy (such as noun, verb, or adjective). Are there male–female differences in any of these criteria? McEnery (2006) is a good source of information.

250 Is it true that female students swear a lot, relative to male students? Do a gender-controlled survey of what your informants consider to be swearing. When might they use swearwords and of what strength? Ask them to characterize their own swearing behaviour and that of other people in your survey (assuming they know each other). Are there male–female differences in the way that people admit to swearing, and characterize swearing in others? Remember that neither a person's own evaluation nor that of others actually tells you how much a person really swears – to find that out, you would need to observe their discourse.

251 To examine single- and mixed-sex conversational strategies, try the following procedure. Ask a small group of mutual friends, half of them male and the other female, to your house for a meal. Ask the females to arrive earlier than the males (or vice versa) and record their conversation. When the other gender group arrives, record some mixed-sex conversation and, at some point, arrange for the first group to leave the room. You can then record the second group talking. This methodology has the advantage of using the same informants for each gender in both the single- and mixed-sex interactions, and gives you data sets from the same time and context. Remember the ethical issues involved in recording people's speech – you will have to tell them afterwards what you have done, and give them the option of withdrawing from the study. To help them agree to stay in it, reassure them that you will replace names in your transcripts, and remove anything that might be hurtful or embarrassing (e.g. what was said about someone when they were out of the room).

Gay language

Studies of gay and lesbian language are increasingly common. See Coates (2004: Ch. 12) for an overview, and Livia and Hall (1997) and Baker (2005) for studies. At the interface of gender and dialect studies, Baker (2002) tells the story of Polari, a secret language among male homosexuals in the twentieth century.

PROJECTS

252 Do your own study of Polari, using Baker's (2002) book and his web resources at www.ling.lancs.ac.uk/staff/paulb/polari/home.htm. Assemble examples of sentences containing words from Polari and ask informants to explain their meaning. Look for patterns regarding the words that are generally known and those that are not. Do gay informants know more Polari words than non-gay informants do?

253 Adapt Project 251 to focus on gay discourse.

Explanations of difference

There have been various explanations of gender differences in language, starting with claims (since refuted) about the mental or cognitive inferiority of women. Subsequent explanations were less judgemental but suggested that biologically programmed tendencies or properties might account for the differences (see Coates 2004: Ch. 3). However, researchers generally agree that most differences (those relating to language acquisition are one possible exception) are culturally determined (Cameron 2006: 733).

Accounts in the 1960s and 1970s focused on women's status in society. Trudgill (1972) suggested that women's greater tendency to use prestige forms was the result of the profile of their lives: they were less likely to be able to signal their status via their occupation, so they signalled it through the way they spoke. Lakoff (1975) suggested that women's social inequality made them unassertive, and her work has become associated with so-called 'dominance' explanations. Some women reacted to this viewpoint by trying to eliminate the 'female' characteristics from their language style and by striving to be more assertive, which often meant copying male speech strategies. O'Barr and Atkins (1980/2011) used data from courtrooms to suggest that Lakoff's features related not to gender but to status, and propose that they be renamed **powerless language**. However, subsequent research has challenged this (see Coates 2004: Ch. 6).

In the 1980s, there was some re-evaluation of the features of **women's language**. Coates, for example, has stressed the co-operative (rather than weak or unassertive) nature of female style (see Cameron 2012; Coates 1996; Coates 2004: Ch. 6; Coates and Cameron 1989). This links with accounts of how children are pushed towards different interactional styles by socialization in predominantly single-sex groups (see Maltz and Borker 1982/2011). In making sense of all these explanations, one very useful framework to be aware of is Tajfel's theory of inter-group relations and social change (e.g. Tajfel and Turner 1986; Tajfel 2010).

PROJECTS

254 Investigate the language of an informant who has an atypical male lifestyle (for example, acting as prime child-carer). Does he display any of the characteristics of the typically female co-operative style? If so, is the style 'female' at all, or just the product of a social role, and is he displaying female language because of his role or does he find the role more comfortable than most men because of his 'female side'?

> **255** Examine the discourse of a female informant who has reached a powerful position in a male-dominated work environment. Collect data from situations in which she is heavily outnumbered by male colleagues of equal or higher status, and also from professional interactions with women only. Do your results suggest that she is 'in disguise' when she interacts with men? Or is it the power dimension rather than a gender one that is operating?

Language and sexism

Sexist language can be found in adverts, film dialogue, posters, comedy, many types of written document and conversation. Some sexism is inherent in language, such as the generic *he* in English. Graddol and Swann (1989: 110) point out that English 'has no direct feminine equivalent of *virility*' to reflect female sexual potency. Some research investigates how derogatory or potentially patronizing terms are applied to women. One antidote to sexism in language has been political correctness, in which deliberate linguistic choices are made, to raise awareness of entrenched biases.

PROJECTS

256 Investigate the origins of forms of address used to males and females. Ask informants for their perceptions of the connotations of different forms and compare their replies with what you have discovered about the forms' histories. Map out trajectories over time for how individual forms may have changed their meaning. Read about language change to establish what the role of political correctness has been, or may yet be, on the use of the forms.

257 Investigate the assumptions made about gender for people in certain jobs. Examples would be a nurse, cleaner, mechanic, hairdresser, brain surgeon, judge, and so on. Does the vocabulary of English offer the possibility of non-sexist job descriptions?

258 Ask two groups of different ages to provide specific types of terms for men and women (for example, relating to sexual promiscuity or untidy personal appearance). Does your data bear out the claim that there are more derogatory terms for women and that they are considered 'stronger'? If there are differences between the two age groups, what is the significance of these?

259 If you have a working knowledge of another language, focus on one of the above issues from the perspective of speakers of that language and compare the results with patterns identified in English that you have found in textbooks.

Gender-differentiated language in first-language acquisition

Much of the research into the acquisition of structures has focused on the rate of development of grammar, phonology, or lexis. Early work either assumed or suggested that girls acquire language faster and better than boys, perhaps because of earlier maturation. However, later research has questioned whether girls' acquisition patterns are markedly superior at all. For a summary of views, see Coates (2004: Ch. 9) and Wells (1986b). Research on

communicative competence concerns how girls and boys learn what it means to speak and write appropriately for their gender in a given society. Edelsky (1976) investigated how children perceived stereotypes of male and female language and how these perceptions might influence them (see Coates 2004; Swann 1992). There is some evidence that girls become aware far earlier than boys of the need to 'style-shift' towards standard pronunciation in formal contexts (Romaine 1984, Ch. 4).

Other studies have focused on how parents speak to children of each gender and the way they encourage girls and boys to speak to others. One question has been whether parents provide a good model of the language they require from their children (e.g. does the father constantly tell his son not to interrupt his sister and then interrupt her himself?). Wells's (1986b: 124) study on when and with which gender parents will initiate conversations found a focus on 'helping/non-play' activities with girls and on 'playing with an adult' contexts with boys. Recent studies on **socialization** have suggested that girls and boys are socialized in single-sex peer groups and that this is a key means by which they learn how to talk like boys and girls. Coates (2004, Ch. 9) reviews studies suggesting that adult female 'co-operative discourse' can already be seen in the ways in which girls' peer groups are structured and in the activities they engage in.

PROJECTS

260   Conduct a case study of a pair of mixed-sex twins. By studying brother and sister, you eliminate extralinguistic variables, such as differences in social background and family structure. If, in spite of both participants belonging to the same family, there are differences in their stages of language development (see Chapter 3), accent, and dialect, or conversational style, is it reasonable to attribute these to the gender differences? What else might have caused them (e.g. parental models, friends, other models from TV)?

261   Compare male and female children of the same age, background, and educational level describing a picture or retelling a story they have previously watched on video. Do the girls exhibit the sorts of style features found in adult female language? Is the boys' language different in specific ways and, if so, how would you evaluate the differences?

Language, gender, and education

Are gender differences in children's oral and written language the result of boys and girls being treated differently by teachers? Conversely, do teachers treat boys and girls differently because the children use language differently in the first place? Related issues are: whether teachers exercise as much equality as they intend to or as they believe they do; strategies that boys use to get more conversational turns than girls in classroom settings; and the implications, for their educational achievement, of girls' tendency to be more quiet and passive than boys in the classroom (see Coates 2004; Swann 1992). White (1986) explored the ways in which some girls' literacy skills, combined with more modest career expectations, were leading them into low-status secretarial jobs rather than other professions, and the extent to which girls' literacy skills led them away from science-based topics at school, college, or university (see Swann 1992). Many changes have taken place in educational curricula since then, with an upgrading of the value of 'female' oracy skills like co-operative discourse features. This fact makes the education domain an excellent choice for research on language and gender.

PROJECTS

262 Study the types of reading material (such as fiction or non-fiction, and sub-genres within these) used by a mixed group of children. How far can you identify patterns of preference, according to gender, for particular types of material? Can these be linked in any way to styles of language (such as descriptive, imaginative, or factual)? What might the implications of your findings be?

263 Investigate how a group of girls and boys feel about the writing tasks they are asked to do at school. Which tasks do they enjoy most and why? Collect samples of their writing and analyse the styles, or the presentation, punctuation, spelling, use of non-standard grammar, and so on. Do any trends emerge?

264 Since computers became a normal part of the work and home environment, the traditional 'secretarial' career for women has changed its identity. Interview older women in typical office support jobs (your university or college is one place to look, but you could also approach private businesses), about the role that text writing, note-taking, and transcription play nowadays, in comparison with when they began their career. To what extent is there any indication that the jobs that women do in these posts today are best suited to women?

9

Accents and dialects of English

Accents and dialects are the focus of interest for various groups of linguists. The main two groups are sociolinguists studying how people use pronunciation, vocabulary, and grammar to express and retain social identity, and phoneticians and phonologists, who study the sound systems of accents. Although this chapter focuses on varieties of English, most of the methods would be the same if you were collecting information about another language. The sorts of questions that you might ask in research into accents and dialects include:

- Where are the geographical borders between different pronunciations of the same word?
- Where are the geographical borders between different words or expressions for the same entity, action, and so on?
- Are such borders consistent across a large set of words or expressions, or must they be differently drawn for each?
- How are past settlements of communities reflected in the pronunciation, vocabulary, and grammar of a local variety?
- How are social and cultural differences in society expressed through language?
- What level of variation can be observed in an individual's pronunciation, vocabulary, and/or grammar in different social situations?
- What differences are there between the pronunciation and vocabulary of men and women using the same regional variety?
- In what ways do TV and film actors exaggerate, under-represent, or successfully reproduce a given regional accent?
- How do the grammatical forms of a given dialect differ from Standard English, or from another variety, and why?
- How mutually comprehensible are dialects and accents from different places?
- To what extent is dialect used, and should it be used, in schools?
- What subtle differences in pronunciation and vocabulary mark out subgroups within a single local community?

Research on accent and dialect often requires a baseline for comparison. It is entirely feasible to compare any variety with any another. However, you may well find it easier to compare the variety that interests you to the national 'standard', or another variety that is frequently described in books. A good place to start is Trudgill and Hannah (2008).

Describing pronunciation will require phonetic script. Phonemic transcription will probably not be sufficient to capture the detail you need and, in any case, it builds in assumptions about the phonological system that may not apply to the variety under investigation. See Chapter 17 for guidance on transcription.

If you are short of actual data to analyse, there are several ways to obtain some. You could enquire at your local library about recordings, either made for the sake of the language itself or for some other purpose such as an oral-history project. Alternatively, find out about sound archives in national libraries or in museums of local culture and life. However, check first whether you will be able to make a copy to take away, as this isn't always permissible. Local radio programmes and national radio phone-ins are another good source of data. Television news bulletins where onlookers to an incident are interviewed can provide usable, though short, soundbites. Excellent data for studying non-native accents can be gathered from television and radio current-affairs programmes, where politicians, sportspeople, and so on are interviewed. See also the section below on 'Obtaining data'.

Terminology

The terms **accent** and **dialect** are often used rather imprecisely, even interchangeably. According to the glossary in the *Encyclopaedia of Language and Linguistics* (Brown 2006), a dialect is 'a variety of language associated with a particular regional and/or social background, marked by features of grammar, vocabulary, and (for some linguists) accent' (vol. 14: 35), while an accent relates to 'features of pronunciation associated with a speaker's regional or social background' (vol. 14: 2). In other words, dialect is a broader concept than accent, covering also words and grammar. Linguists avoid the suggestion that some people have an accent and dialect while others do not: '*all* of us speak with an accent, and *all* of us speak a dialect' (Trudgill 1999: 2).

Textbooks, reference sources, and major journals

Crystal (2003b, Chs 20 and 21) gives a brief, well-illustrated account of regional and social variation. Bauer (2002) offers insight into why regional and international varieties exist. Elmes (2005) is an accessible introduction to regional variation in English. Hughes, Trudgill, and Watt (2012) offer specific descriptions of regional varieties of British English and this book comes with a CD-ROM. Collins and Mees (2008) also has an extensive audio collection of accents of English. Foulkes and Docherty (1999) describe urban British varieties and Gordon *et al.* (2004) and Hay *et al.* (2008) do the same for New Zealand English. Trudgill and Hannah (2008) and Melchers and Shaw (2011) cover international varieties of English, with audio recordings available. Jenkins (2009) is a useful resource book on world Englishes. For a considerably more in-depth look at varieties of English from the point of view of phonology, morphology, and syntax, there is the two-volume edited collection (including CD-ROM) by Kortmann and Schneider (2005). The older three volumes of J.C. Wells (1982a, b, c) also remain a classic resource. A detailed survey of Scots can be found in Corbett *et al.* (2003) and one of Irish English is found in Hickey (2004). For detailed research on specific accents and issues arising, see Waniek-Klimczak (2008, 2010).

There are specialist publications for specialist jobs: dictionaries and books on place names and surnames, dialect dictionaries, and dictionaries of slang, jargon, and euphemism. A very handy book for British varieties is Upton and Widdowson (2006), which provides maps from the *Linguistic Atlas of England* (see below), showing the distributions of sounds and vocabulary in different regions. An excellent resource regarding how ordinary people perceive their varieties is the two-volume *Handbook of Perceptual Dialectology* (Preston 1999 and Long and Preston 2003).

For examples of how data can be collected, look at the publications spawned by the major national surveys, including the *Survey of English Dialects* (Orton *et al.* 1962–71), *The Linguistic Atlas of England* (Orton *et al.* 1978), *The Linguistic Atlas of Scotland* (Mather and Speitel 1975), *A Word Geography of the Eastern United States* (Kurath 1949), and *The Atlas of North American English* (Labov *et al.* 2006). Samples of the data in these are given in Crystal (2003b, Ch. 20). Information on other languages is given in Veith (2006).

Sources such as the above will help you identify lists of words and forms that you can use as stimuli. For information on particular varieties, use local libraries and bookshops, which will often have books or pamphlets not easy to come by outside that area (for example, the Yorkshire Dialect Society publications). Bear in mind, however, that not all of these will be taking a strictly 'linguistic' approach. Classic sociolinguistically focused accounts of specific varieties include the work by Labov on New York and Martha's Vineyard (Labov 1972) and Black Vernacular English (Labov 1969), Trudgill (1972, 1974) on male–female differences in Norwich, Cheshire (1978, 1982/2009) on Reading, and Milroy (1987) on East and West Belfast. Much of this work is reviewed in Chapter 7 in this book. Ideas for interesting topics can be found in Görlach's (1991b, 1995, 1998 and 2002) collections.

Useful journals for projects on accents and dialects include the following:

JOURNALS

American Speech

Dialectologia et Geolinguistica

English and Germanic Studies

English Studies

English World-Wide: A Journal of Varieties of English

Folklore

International Journal of the Sociology of Language

Journal of English as a Lingua Franca

Journal of English Linguistics

Journal of the International Phonetic Association

Journal of the Lakeland Dialect Society

Journal of the Lancashire Dialect Society

Language and Speech

Linguistics

Orbis: Bulletin International de Documentation Linguistique

Scottish Language

Social and Cultural Geography

Transactions of the Yorkshire Dialect Society

Word

World Englishes

Which accent/dialect to choose

One important question to consider is whether you are going to study a variety of accent or dialect that you use yourself. The advantage of studying your own variety is that you are yourself a source of data. This means that if a form or a pronunciation is missing, you know what it is and can confidently add it to the list. Working with a variety that is not your own can make it difficult to identify the pattern underlying a set of features, because it is hard to judge what another example would do. This problem can be eased by using published work on the same or a similar variety to get some ideas. Other advantages are that you can plan with more confidence how to elicit the forms you need and that, when interviewing informants, you are not putting them off by using a different pronunciation or vocabulary.

However, there are some serious disadvantages too. You may not have an identical variety to that of your informant, and you may unwittingly remove some of the more subtle layers of data by influencing the informant into your way of speech. Studying a variety requires some perspective and it is very hard to get this when it is very familiar to you. It may be difficult for you to tell which words are part of the standard variety, a 'national slang', or specific to your own variety. We can tend to be quite blind to aspects of our own speech, so you may miss some detail. You can reduce the risk of this by getting a friend who does not use that variety to listen to your data and check your assumptions. A variety you know very well, but which is not your only variety, may provide a compromise, offering the advantages of both scenarios above.

It is accents and dialects that bring us to the realization that there is no single version of English that can be considered *the* reference point. The concept of **World Englishes** (see, for instance, Jenkins 2009, Kachru *et al.* 2009, Kirkpatrick 2010, Melchers and Shaw 2011) focuses on the fact that English 'belongs' to many different people around the world, all bringing to it certain distinctive characteristics. Within the worldwide community of native speakers we find the use of national and regional varieties. There are also many millions of speakers of other languages who have learned English, whether in their early years as the language of education, or later, for use in business or leisure pursuits. In some countries English is one of the official languages, so there is a recognized national variety taught by local teachers, as with India, parts of Africa, and parts of Malaysia. Elsewhere, such as in France, Spain, and Poland, English is a foreign language. In addition, there are speakers whose native language is not English but who live in an English-speaking environment, like Punjabis in Britain, Greeks in Canada, Hispanics in the USA, and so on. There are, in short, many opportunities for studying the accents and dialects of English, wherever you live. If you are interested in researching varieties of a language other than English, start off by finding out about the range of places and circumstances in which the language is spoken around the world, in order to keep your horizons broad.

Obtaining data

It is much easier than it used to be to obtain good-quality audio data, since many recordings are now available on the Internet. Digitally broadcast radio, such as the BBC, offers its material on line and for MP3 download: see www.bbc.co.uk/radio. For accent analysis, even very short extracts can be sufficient. The International Corpus of English (ICE) website www.ucl.ac.uk/english-usage/ice/ provides links to ICE team sites around the world, on many of which sound files have been made available. Although only a few seconds long, they could be a useful resource for a single or comparative study. The BBC voices website has a large collection of audio recordings of local UK accents, www.bbc.co.uk/voices/wil/. For longer texts in international and regional accents, try the Audio Archive, http://alt-usage-english.org/audio_archive.shtml#spoken. The extensive set of international readings of a single passage, available in the Speech Accent Archive at http://accent.gmu.edu/browse_language.php could provide the basis for your own comparative study, using the same text. Since phonetic transcriptions and key observations about the accents are also given here, you will be able to relate your own transcriptions to those in the Archive. The Australian slang site, http://www.aussie-slang.com/ may also be useful. An excellent collection of audio collections of UK accents and dialects has been issued by the British Library (2010), and Meier's (2009) practical guidance for actors includes phonetic transcriptions and audio recordings of many different varieties.

What to look for in an accent

If you are interested in pronunciation, structure your study by listening out for specific sounds and transcribing them in some detail. A list of English phonemes, based on British Received Pronunciation (RP), is provided in Chapter 17. Use this to write down your own examples phonetically, next to the appropriate phoneme. Try to find several examples of each phoneme, in case it is pronounced in different ways in different environments in that variety. As your chosen variety may have a different set of phonemes from those of RP, do not be surprised if some categories collapse together and others divide: that is something that you can write about in your study. Kreidler's (2004, Ch. 4) representation of English variety types, as determined by their phonemic inventories, may help you. Hughes, Trudgill, and Watt (2012) also provide a wordlist suitable for eliciting all the phonemes of RP.

What to look for in a dialect

In order to analyse a dialect, you need an understanding of basic grammatical categories, both so that you can accurately describe what you find and so that you know what sorts of phenomena to look for. You may find it helpful to write a 'translation' of your material in Standard English alongside the original, so that the differences become clear. You must categorize your data according to word classes, and really get to grips with morphology (word forms and endings) and grammar, as well as vocabulary. The relationship between grammar and vocabulary, on the one hand, and pronunciation, on the other, is not always clear-cut. Some words which seem to just be 'lazy' pronunciations of the standard form are actually very different, with a separate history. For example, *'em* in *sort 'em out* appears to be a shortened form of *them*, but it is not (Brook 1978: 105). If you have enough data, you should be able to construct tables of pronoun and verb forms. Use the lists of standard forms in Table 9.1 to help draw up a corresponding set of dialect forms.

Table 9.1 Standard forms

Parts of speech	Form
Subject	I, you, he, she, it, we, they, who, which
Object	me, you, him, her, it, us, them, who(m), which
Possessive	my, your, his, her, its, our, their, whose
	mine, yours, his, hers, its, ours, theirs

Pronouns and possessives

Some languages and, indeed, some varieties of English may have additional forms that you need to check for, including: a difference between singular and plural *you* forms, a difference in politeness and/or intimacy in *you* forms, a difference between plural forms referring to two and to more than two, a difference between *we* forms which include and exclude the addressee, and separate *they* forms for male and female. For further details on pronouns, see Trudgill (1999: 87–101). Remember to note carefully the pronunciation of all pronoun forms, along with the context in which they have occurred.

Verbs

Besides variations in the meaning or inventory of verbs from place to place, the key things to look for are the different tense forms (present, past, past participle), especially those of the common irregular verbs such as *to be* and *to go*. If you find an unusual form of a verb, check the rest of its forms. Dialect forms are likely to differ from the standard by having a different strong past tense form, or else a weak (*-ed*) form instead of a strong one, or vice versa. Different varieties can also sometimes use the verb tenses differently. For example, a British southerner would say: *The burglar broke into the house and he ransacked the place*, while further north you might hear: *The burglar has broken into the house and he's ransacked the place*, using the present perfect rather than the simple past. There may also be contrasts in the use of conditionals and subjunctives: where a speaker of standard British English says *If I had seen him I would have chased him*, an American might say *If I would have seen him I would have chased him*.

Nouns

You should find the richest pickings of regional vocabulary here, particularly, of course, where a word is needed locally for something that does not exist elsewhere. (For illustrations of regional variation in nouns, see Crystal 2003b, Ch. 20.) Some terms require local or topical knowledge to explain: according to the *Dictionary of South African English* (1996), Township vernacular contained (at that time) the words *Mary Decker* (a fast police vehicle) and *Zola Budd* (a slow one), named after an American and a South African who were rival athletes in the 1980s. As this example indicates, an interesting question can be how long certain words will remain in a variety after the local conditions that created the opportunity no longer exist. In addition, look out for non-standard plural forms of familiar words.

Negative forms

Languages have many ways of forming negatives but, even within English grammar, there is regional variation. Some people say *Don't you?* and others say *Do you not?* Some varieties use the **double negative**, e.g. *I ain't seen nothing.* Trudgill (1999) is a very useful source of insight into this.

Tags

Tag questions are a hallmark of English. Compare: *It's raining, is it?*, *It's raining, isn't it?*, and *It's not raining, is it?*. Different varieties use tags in different ways. In South Wales you might hear: *So you've moved into your flat, is it?* Other varieties replace the standard tag forms with a general *yes* (*yeah*) and *no*: *So it's raining, yeah?* or with *innit*. Consider what your variety does: it might make the basis of an interesting study.

Adverbs

Differences between varieties in their use of adverbs can be quite striking when heard for the first time. The following example illustrates how an analysis might progress. In Yorkshire (and some other places), it has been common for a long time to hear *He was well happy* and *They were well tired* for *He was very happy* and *They were very tired*. What is the underlying pattern? One might hypothesize that Yorkshire English simply uses *well* wherever Standard English would use *very*, but this is refuted by the fact that Yorkshire English does not say *You're the well person I was looking for*. To understand how Yorkshire English works, it is necessary to examine the way that Standard English itself distributes *very* and *well* (e.g. *She had been well taught*; **She had been very taught*; *The tyres were well worn*; *The tyres were very worn* – the asterisk indicates that the sentence is ungrammatical). If it is the case that *very* is used with adjectives and *well* with verb forms, then where does *He was well pleased* fit in? It turns out that there is a subtle relationship between adjectives and past participle forms in Standard English and, returning to the Yorkshire variety, this leads to the following question: does the difference between the two varieties lie in the meanings of *very* and *well* themselves, or in the underlying categories of the words they are modifying?

Possible angles and project ideas

You can, of course, just focus your work directly on the variety. However, it is often useful to get an 'angle'. This gives you something to aim at and provides a motivation for exploring some aspects more than others. Most importantly, it can help you avoid simply ending up with a list of forms you have found, without anything very much to say about them.

Comparing the speech of three generations

This is a study of how a variety is changing at the moment. Providing you can get access to compatible recordings of three individuals from the same regional and social background, and at least a generation apart, you can potentially uncover interesting differences that may characterize change within their variety across time. However, remember that other variables may explain the differences that you are attributing to age. For example, it has been suggested that males tend to display more pronounced regional characteristics than females (see Trudgill 1972, and the discussion in Aitchison 2001: 71–3). Avoid this variable by studying only one gender. Alternatively, perhaps the informants have had different amounts and types of contact with outsiders (such as travel or work experiences). Perhaps they watch different quantities of TV or different programmes, and/or are differently influenced by them. Remember here that it is clearly not reasonable to say that the youth are exposed to youth culture through TV and yet to deny that older generations are also exposed to external cultures. You need to take a sensible sociolinguistic approach to the whole question of identity (see Chapter 7).

PROJECTS

265 If you have family members who have lived for several generations in the same area, compare the language of a grandparent, parent, and sibling or cousin. Bear in mind the following advantages and disadvantages of this sort of study. There is a good chance of getting good-quality data without very much effort and the research is fairly well controlled, provided the only major difference between the informants is age (not place of birth or residence, social class, extent of travel, gender, level of education, and so on). However, while you bring an insight and intuition to a description of your own family's variety, it can also be quite difficult to detach yourself from it and see it for what it is (see earlier discussion). Furthermore, the chances are there that there is little, if any, published material about the variety used in your town or village. This is not disastrous, but it can leave you out on a limb, particularly with those observations that you find hard to interpret. For guidance on sociolinguistic factors that may be relevant to this, see Project 218.

266 Rather than studying your own or a friend's family, find recordings of three generations of a famous family (the British Royal Family is one obvious choice), and compare their accents.

267 Or, using videos of classic films and TV programmes, study the accents of members from three generations of one of the great acting families such as the Redgraves. Of course, you must restrict yourself to material in which the actors are not adopting an accent different from their natural one.

Comparing the accents of different non-native speakers

Second-language-acquisition research proposes that a person's accent when speaking another language is largely determined by the phonology of his/her native language (see Chapter 4). This being so, predictions can, in theory, be made on the basis of a given language, about the likely characteristics that will become evident when speaking an L2.

PROJECT

268 Select a non-native accent of English from the list in the Speech Accent Archive at accent.gmu.edu/browse_language.php. Find out about the phonological features of the native language of the speakers and use this information to explain the key characteristics of the accent that the informants have in their English.

Explaining why a variety has come about

This is a study of the accent or dialect of a place, incorporating its history. Clearly, you are going to have to rely on reading for a considerable chunk of your work. This is fine, providing that the language of the place you choose has been fairly extensively studied before. Do check first that that is so. Unless you are looking at a variety with a high profile like Geordie (Newcastle) or Scouse (Liverpool), you may have considerable difficulty in finding more than the odd page in a few books about the history of the place, let alone its language. Writing about the history of settlement in a place is not the same as writing a linguistic history and, if you are not careful, you will end up with a political or social history of the area that you cannot easily relate to the modern variety of English except to say that the dialect 'probably reflects the history of settlement in the area'.

PROJECTS

269   Focus a study on one of the historical centres of immigration, such as inner London, Liverpool, New York, Melbourne, or an industrial city that drew many rural populations to it in a short space of time. The later the settlement, the better documented it is likely to be. There may be useful local records about the origins of settlers in the USA, Canada, and Australia, if your study is focused there. To identify linguistic signs of the settlement in an urban accent, compare it with the less-influenced surrounding variety. Can you spot specific features that might reflect the variety (or foreign language) that was spoken by the immigrant population?

270   Find a locality that has a specific story of recent unusual settlement. For example, Corby in Northamptonshire (in the southern Midlands of England) received a sizable settlement of Scots workers when a steel plant was relocated there. Collect data from the original settlers (if any survive), their descendants, and individuals (or their descendants) who were part of the receiving community. Compare the varieties used for signs of a retained social identity and/or linguistic integration.

The political dimension of a variety

This approach takes a sociolinguistic or historical perspective, focusing on the status of a variety within a community. Read Chapter 7 in this book for background on the social aspects of accent and dialect use. For ideas on the specific social impact of certain dialects, look at Burke and Porter (1994), where the papers include a study of the significance of dialect at the beginnings of the trade union movement, Quaker language, an account of the research done by a seventeenth-century dialectologist, and how language is affected by political conquest.

PROJECTS

271   Gather data on attitudes to non-Standard English in the education system. This is a large and lively issue, so use newspaper archives to assemble recent views and reactions to reports and events. You could make recordings in a school in an area

where the variety is particularly strong, to see how 'standard' the English is in different contexts, such as formal teaching, discussion and group work, sports or gym, recreational time, staff meetings, and in the staffroom at breaks.

272   Write a carefully considered account of the differences there might be in the accents and dialects of a country if some political event or policy or the status quo had been different: for example, if York had been the capital of England in the Middle Ages, if Edinburgh, rather than London, had developed as the centre of British culture, or if Australia had been settled largely by Scots rather than English emigrants. In every case, you will need to assess the long-term effects of the political domination of a variety. Some study of the way that standard and non-standard varieties of English came about will help to give you insight (for references, see Chapter 10).

Accent and dialect in literature

This is a study of an accent or dialect as depicted by a certain author, and it offers an interesting slant on accent and dialect work because authors are not dialectologists and their purpose is not linguistic. When examining accents in literature, take a linguist's eye to what is, in effect, a literary device. You may well find that the author permits him-/herself certain liberties in 'spelling' words 'phonetically' (for example, keeping silent letters in a word to help indicate the meaning, as in *y knaa* for 'you know', where the 'k' is actually silent). Use phonemic script to clarify your understanding of what is depicted in 'spelled' forms. You can read more about this topic in Beal (2006).

PROJECTS

273   Do an analysis of, say, the London accent of one or more of Dickens's characters, the West Country accent or dialect in Hardy's novels, or the speech of the yokels in Shakespeare. Evaluate its accuracy against published descriptions. Assess the extent to which the differences are simply a function of the time lapse between the literary description and the more recent linguistic account. Alternatively, draw on a linguistic description that is contemporaneous with the work of literature, to remove this variable.

274   Compare an author's depiction of an accent or dialect (as above) with your own data from the same area.

275   Compare an actor's rendering of a local accent with the real thing (try to use an actor who is not from that area). A notorious example is Dick van Dyke's attempt at a Cockney accent in the film *Mary Poppins*. At the other extreme, Meryl Streep is one actor who has tackled many accents with success. What tends to make an actor's rendition more or less convincing? Does a bad attempt tend to exaggerate, under-represent, misplace, or incorrectly define features? Search the Internet for examples, e.g. http://unrealitymag.com/index.php/2009/01/29/eight-american-actors-with-great-foreign-accents/, http://fandomania.com/5-actors-that-should-have-been-forced-to-use-their-natural-accents/.

> **276** Find a book with lots of colourful characters in it, including some from different places if possible, and audio record an extrovert friend reading extracts aloud, with different voices for each character. Transcribe the examples of each character's speech and identify the markers that the reader has used to make the voice sound distinctive. You could also see how the presentation of that voice changes over time, if the reader has provided several examples of the same character. What has been used to indicate an unpleasant personality, female speech (if your reader is male) or male speech (if female), various regional accents, sadness, annoyance, and so on?

Update study

This is a comparison of a published description of a variety with data of your own and it has the makings of an excellent project. Instead of simply making observations that, while valid in their own right, may not fit easily into a wider pre-established context, you can anchor everything that *you* find into something that has been found, or not found, before. It is best if you can replicate as many aspects of the original work as possible – ask the same questions in a similar way, use a similar questionnaire, record in a similar environment with people of the same age, gender, and background as the original, etc. Beware of becoming too simplistic and narrow when you have a good single source for comparing your data. Read other descriptions of the variety and see in what ways your chosen study differs from others of the time: if there wasn't full agreement at the time about what this variety was like in its finest detail, it will not be surprising if your findings are different too!

PROJECTS

> **277** Find a study from, say, 40 years ago. The Survey of English Dialects, carried out between 1948 and 1961, is one place to look. Replicate the procedures of the original study as closely as you can. Concentrate your discussion on whether any differences in your findings are a function of the 40-year gap or not. You should, in this case, consider some of the other factors that might make a difference, such as the procedures used, how comparable the informants were, the precise geographical area they came from, and how the population of an area may have altered in nature.
>
> **278** Using the maps in Upton and Widdowson (2006) or a similar publication (see earlier in this chapter), identify, for your geographical area of interest, a boundary between two pronunciations, dialect words, morphological forms, or structures. For example, the map for terms meaning 'silly' shows the boundaries for the use of *silly, daft, barmy, gormless, fond, addle-headed, cakey,* and *soft.* Conduct your own survey in the area around your chosen boundary, to see whether it is still in the same place as it was when the survey was carried out.

Comparison of two varieties

In one sense, any study of a single variety entails this anyway, because there will be implicit or explicit comparisons with Standard English. However, there is no intrinsic reason why

Standard English (British or otherwise) should represent the point of comparison. If you choose to compare two non-standard varieties, the rationale for your choice should be made obvious: a historical or geographical link or else one relating to cultural or educational influence.

PROJECTS

279 Compare a Scots variety with Geordie or with Northern Irish (in both cases there are historical links that make them sensible to compare).

280 Find out the national and regional origins of settlers in a particular area of a former colony of Britain (e.g. Canada, Australia, New Zealand, or the USA) and compare the varieties used today in the two places. For example, are there similarities between London Cockney and the variety used in an Australian settlement originally founded for or by Londoners?

281 Compare the varieties used in two adjacent towns or villages where there is known to be variation.

282 Compare the English of, say, two French informants, one of whom loves British culture and one of whom identifies with American culture.

283 Research the level of similarity between the names for common edible fish in two distant parts of the English-speaking world. For instance, is a *cod* on the fish counter in Australia the same as a *cod* in the UK? Is it even the same thing from fish shop to fish shop? How about *hake* or *mullet*? You may need to contact fish marketing boards and/or interview fishmongers or fishermen. Consider the means by which names might travel with immigrants and the reasons why some names retain their original reference while others do not.

284 Download the 'Stella' passage from one of the examples in the Speech Accent Archive at http://accent.gmu.edu/browse_language.php and record your own informants reading it. Transcribe the readings phonetically, and compare them to each other, and/or to appropriate examples from the Archive.

Things to think about

- To explain why a variety is as it is and put it into context, read up on the history of English. Features of regional varieties often shed light on the historical development of the standard language and/or retain features that used to exist in Standard English. In their turn, historical developments can often help explain regional differences.
- On the whole, you will get stronger accent and dialect features if: (a) you can understand your informants when they use their variety – if you have to keep asking them what they meant, then they are likely to modify towards the standard to help you; and (b) the informant speaks about particular subjects such as family or home life. Children talking about playground games and elderly people talking about their childhood may also be fruitful.

- Beware of a tendency for informants to make value judgements about the language variety that they speak and perhaps to understate what they know and/or use.
- Be aware that an informant may tell you that they use a form that they don't actually use. This is clearly problematic if you are trying to get an accurate picture of the variety as it is today, especially if you are comparing different ages of speaker. But it can be turned to your advantage in a couple of ways. If you focus on identifying the features of the variety *in general*, it may not matter that your informant's perception of it is rather old-fashioned. Simply mention this somewhere in your study, as a feature of the way people can sometimes identify with defunct forms. Alternatively, if you have enough data, you could compare *what* your informants say with *how* they say it, looking for examples in their speech of the things they have described. Thus, you can take the interesting angle, for all or part of your study, of how speakers may have limited ability to recognize the form of their own language.

10

History of English

There are innumerable questions to be asked about a language at every point of its history, about every aspect of its form and function, and about the relationship between the language forms at different times. Whatever may be asked about one language can be asked about every other, though languages vary considerably in the amount of research already done on them and, indeed, in the amount of primary documentation that is available for researching them. For convenience, most of the ideas put forward below will make reference to English. This is undoubtedly one of the best-documented and most-researched languages, as well as being one that is unusually rich in its mixture of vocabulary. It also has a striking **diachronic** ('across-time') profile, largely because of its political and economic history. In many cases the suggestions made for English can be transferred to the study of other languages, but it will be important to establish that the information you need, be it historical documents or commentaries upon them, is available.

There are two basic ways of finding out what a language used to be like. Where possible, evidence comes directly from written records. However, writing is not only a recent phenomenon in man's cultural development: it is also highly selective, and much of the information that would most interest the linguist is therefore simply not available that way. Where there are no written records, it is possible, to some extent, to reconstruct features of a language using either other linguistic information from that time or information that we have about one or more languages from a subsequent period that have descended from it. In this way, it has been possible for scholars to reconstruct aspects of the vocabulary and grammar of the prehistoric language Proto-Indo-European, using information from its many descendants today. The same method could be used, however, to reconstruct the dialect of the 'criminal' class in London in the eighteenth and nineteenth centuries by using the modern London dialects and the variety of Australian English that developed in the penal colonies.

Because we cannot time-travel, care must be taken, when working on the history of a language, to ask only questions that it is possible to answer from where we are today. This immediately excludes, for example, questions such as how much aspiration Shakespeare's wife used on a word-initial /t/ or whether the English nobility at the time of the Norman Conquest spoke French as fluently as they wrote it. Unless these specific things happen to have been written about at the time, there is obviously no way of finding them out.

It may seem, then, that the only questions we can ask are the ones that are, by definition, already answered. But this is far from being the case. Nor is it true that we cannot know anything about the spoken, as opposed to the written, language. Linguistic information documented at the time, combined with the many superb surveys and investigations done since, can provide you with both the materials and the theoretical background for exploring a wide range of questions.

Textbooks, reference sources, and major journals

We can mention here only a few of the many excellent books that your university or college library is likely to hold. Studies of the history of language do not go out of date as quickly as those in other areas, and you may find books that are 30 or more years old that still can offer you useful information. Your local public library is also likely to hold some books on the history of English.

For readable overviews of how language changes, try Aitchison (2001), Crystal (2010: Ch. 54), and Trask (2007). Trask (1994) has many practical exercises that might inspire projects, as does Culpeper (2005). Graddol *et al.*'s (2006) thematic approach to the historical origins of diversity in English may inspire project ideas. For a first overview of the history of English, go to Crystal (2003b) or Bryson (2009). Fuller accounts of the history of English include Algeo (2010), Barber *et al.* (2009), Baugh and Cable (2002), Burchfield (2002), Gramley (2011), McCrum *et al.* (2003), McIntyre (2008) and van Gelderen (2006). Williams (1986) takes a particularly imaginative approach to the social history of English that may give you ideas for projects. It includes excellent chronologies of political and linguistic events. More scholarly descriptions can be found in the edited collections by Hogg and Denison (2008), and Mugglestone (2008), and in Strang's (1970) classic account, which works backwards through time. Singh (2005) brings in literary and sociolinguistic perspectives and, like other recent studies, includes material on English outside Britain and America. Watts and Trudgill (2001) provide histories of an impressive collection of non-standard varieties. For data, use Freeborn (2006), for which there are MP3 audio examples of the texts at http://www.palgrave.com/language/freeborn/, and where there are also plentiful activities that may prompt new project ideas. For information about Early Modern English (*c*.1400–1650) specifically, try Barber (1997) and Görlach (1991a). There is an excellent electronic resource, Early English Books Online (EEBO) that will enable you to view scanned images of thousands of books published between 1473 and 1700. Check whether your university/college library subscribes and if not, ask the librarian to help you find out the location of the closest library that does. If you want to check out the origins of words, go to the complete *Oxford English Dictionary*, Onions (1966), or the very readable Partridge (2008). For the origin of proper names, use Room (1999) and, for the origin of slang words, Partridge (2002) or Dalzell and Victor (2006), and Green (2005).

When it comes to journals, it must be said that much of the research on historical linguistics is highly technical and takes for granted a firm understanding of linguistic theory. However, you may get some ideas from flicking through journals such as these:

JOURNALS

Diachronica

English Language and Linguistics

English Studies

Folia Linguistica Historica

Journal of English Language

Journal of Historical Linguistics

Language

Language and Communication

Language Variation and Change

Studies in Philology

Transactions of the Philological Society

Central themes and project ideas

Researching words and names

Many people find the history of English words very interesting. The ordinary vocabulary of English is particularly rich and derives from a great many different sources. However, a project on words must be very carefully managed. It is excessively tedious to look up word after word in dictionaries, particularly as you really need to check each one in more than one place. Furthermore, it isn't always very obvious what to do with a set of word definitions – just putting them down in a list, even organized under *words from French, words from Arabic,* and so on, will not convince your assessor that you have done much thinking! It is, therefore, important for your sanity and that of your assessor to provide yourself with a solid theme that allows you to *interpret* your data.

Names can be particularly interesting to research (for inspiration, try Redmonds 2007). Much less is genuinely known about the history of surnames than you will be led to believe by any given book on the subject. Look a name up in one book and you may feel confident of knowing its origin. But look the same name up again elsewhere and it will probably seem less certain that any of them have got it right! So, be very sceptical about what you read. Look for interesting questions to ask. For example, while it is true that many surnames derive from place names or geographical features, occupations, physical characteristics, or personal names, some apparently straightforward cases are more obscure. At first glance, 'Pope', 'Monk', and 'King' might seem to have derived from occupations, with the surname passed from father to son in the normal way, but a moment's thought indicates that this is fairly unlikely. For an excellent overview of personal names, see Hanks (2006).

Place names (see, for instance, Cameron 1996) can be easier to research than surnames, because while people move from place to place, taking their name with them, places tend to stay put, so you can trace at least the spellings of a place name as far back as there are maps or local records. Again, different books may give different meanings to the same name. The best single source for place-name meanings is the 69 volumes of the English Place Name Society, such as *The Place-Names of Dorset* (Mills 1987) and *The Place-Names of Rutland* (Cox 1994). To avoid just ending up with a list, find a way of *using* place-name research to address a slightly different question to 'what is the origin of these place names?'

PROJECTS

285 Choose a small number of surnames, look them up in every book you can find, and make a critical comparison of what the different sources say. Then try to account for the variation and discuss the significance of it.

286 Choose two very different areas of the country and, using the telephone directory, find out what the most popular local surnames are. Use this as a way of discussing possible differences in the communities today and in the past. For example, London has been a target for waves of immigrants: French Huguenots, Eastern European Jews, Indians, and so on, whereas a rural area may have had a very settled local community for many generations.

287 Draw up a list of specific queries to investigate, such as: why *are* there so many people with the surnames 'Pope', 'Monk' and 'King'? Why is the name 'Smith' spelled in so many different ways? What surnames *don't* exist that could, and why (e.g. Mrs Computer-programmer; Mr Obese; Ms Tea-drinker; Mrs Pylon, and so on)?

288 Take a wider, more comparative, approach, asking why surnames arose in the first place and how different communities (local and worldwide) have dealt differently with the same problem that surnames were intended to solve. Ask whether they are appropriate and/or sufficient in our modern world and, if they are not, how naming practices could be reformed.

289 Track the changes in the spelling of surnames within particular families over many centuries: what sorts of more general linguistic and social change do these changes reflect? Focus on families whose history is well documented.

290 Research the reasons why immigrants have changed their surname on arrival in their new adoptive country. Your study might include work on nineteenth-century immigrants to America registering on Ellis Island, Jewish immigrants to Britain before and after the Second World War, and into the state of Israel from 1948, and subsequent waves of settlers from Vietnam, Somalia, Afghanistan, and Iraq into different countries. Remember to consider the widest possible range of reasons, such as: transcription errors, deliberate alterations to hide identity or origin, direct translation, making the name easier to spell, attempts to transfer from one cultural naming tradition to another, and so on.

291 According to a report in *The Observer* in October 2004, people in Mongolia did not have surnames until modern practicalities made it necessary: being listed in the phone book and the introduction of identity cards. Research the issues that have arisen in Mongolia as a result (one was that most of the population chose the same surname) and use books on the social history of English to compare these modern issues to the pressures that led to the introduction of surnames in Britain many centuries ago.

292 Focusing on a local area of interest to you, find out how the place names have changed their spelling (and pronunciation, if you can manage it) over the years and why. Who would have determined how the name was spelled and what would the status of any given spelling have been?

293 Are there patterns to the place names in an area that indicate the history of settlements of different peoples? Yorkshire is particularly good for this. Look for indications of who lived on the hills and who lived in the valleys. You don't need to live in the area to do this sort of work: get a good map and read up about it. You may find Cameron (1965) a useful model. He looks at how place names in the five boroughs of Derby, Nottingham, Lincoln, Leicester, and Stamford reflect Viking settlement patterns.

294 What do street names tell us about the history of an area? Consider how the basic vocabulary for thoroughfares must have changed its meaning over the years: what was the difference between a *road*, a *street,* and a *lane* 300 years ago? What do they mean today? Focus on a suburb and use modern and old maps to trace its development as a residential area. Extend your study to look at new towns and/or street names in new estates. Find out who decides what to call them, and look for patterns in the choices from place to place.

295 Look at a particular recurrent word or syllable in place names. What pattern is there to its occurrence within an area and across a region or beyond? Among the useful sources are Zachrisson (1909) on Anglo-Norman influences, Ekwall (1923, 1925, 1928) on place names with *-ing* and on river names, and Sandred (1963) on *-stead*.

296 Make a critical analysis of pub names. Rather than simply recounting the history of a few interesting ones, interview publicans and brewers to find out their preferences and policy on keeping or replacing long-standing names and choosing new names (do they like to make a new pub *sound* traditional, or might they call one *The Website* or *The Heliport*?). Do they feel that the name of a pub has an influence on its image, so that different names would be used for different clientele? By examining the names that pubs have been given in past centuries, attempt to ascertain whether the influences then (such as market forces) were the same as they are now.

297 Compare local street maps for two different towns in the English-speaking world, one that has been settled only in the past couple of centuries (e.g. in New Zealand or Australia) and one that dates back to very ancient times (e.g. in England). Look for indications of the same natural processes of naming in the streets and local areas, which should still be fairly transparent in the new settlement, but will only be revealed by dictionary research for the more ancient settlement, because of historical changes to the name. For instance, look for roads named after the people who lived there (in many places they still will do – why not email the local librarian or a school or college and ask?). Also look for places that have evidently been named after the town or village from which the settlers came – all of the ex-British colonies are full of such names (small towns called London, Halifax, Brentwood, and so on) but can you track down equivalents that indicate Viking or Saxon naming? Using overviews of how place-naming traditionally happened, draw up a comparison: have some naming practices fallen out of use and/or others been introduced? Use the Internet to make contact with people who may be able to tell you about the origins of local names. Before making your final selection of places to study, sample several to be sure you have interesting ones. Steer away from cities that were obviously designed all at one time, because the naming of streets and local areas may have been a corporate decision (for which see Project 298).

298 When a new housing estate or town is built, who decides on what the street names will be and how are the decisions reached? Interview local town planners about this and see if you can find records of the choices that were considered and the processes undertaken in deciding. Compare these processes with the natural development of place names, choosing, where possible, either geographically adjacent places that contrast the two extremes or paired examples where one street has an ancient name and another has, by quite different modern processes, ended up with the same name.

299 Choose a theme and look up the words that relate to it. This could be equestrianism, things you eat for breakfast, words for modern machinery and gadgets (many of which are much older than the things they describe), plant names, names for zoo animals, or words relating to warfare (see Partridge 1948). Then *use* what you find out to account for the ways in which words come about in languages, and how technological advances, or changes in a culture or society, will require new words. Read up on language change so that you can back up your claims. Useful reading, especially for ideas and serendipity, includes Groom (1934), Ayers (1986), and Barfield (2002). A wide-ranging source well worth using is Serjeantson (1935). To look up specific words, use Onions (1966) and Partridge (2008). The latter usefully indicates the links between rather unlikely words, such as *turban* and *tulip*, *asterisk* and *disaster*, *shrub* and *sorbet*, *wench* and *lapwing*, and so on.

Pronunciation and spelling

English has a fascinating history as far as pronunciation is concerned and our modern spelling system bears witness to much of it. Almost all the introductory books will give you an overview both of the sound changes and the spelling system and there are specialized works by Bradley (1916), Brook (1957), Barber (1997), Burchfield (2002), Kökeritz (1953), Zachrisson (1913), Vallins (1965), and many more. For spelling, Baugh and Cable (2002) is useful and includes, on pages 422–8, examples of contemporary writings to illustrate the spelling changes that English has undergone. A dedicated history of English spelling is provided by Upward and Davidson (2011). For a recent study of the nature of English spelling, see Mitton (1996). A practical account of the reconstruction of pronunciation for performances of Shakespeare can be found in Crystal (2005) and reconstructions done over 100 years ago are available in Viëtor (1909/2007).

PROJECTS

300 English is renowned for having many different spellings of the same pronunciation. Find out which spellings are the most 'characteristic' by reading out made-up words to participants. Tell them to write down the non-words in whatever spelling will enable them to read them back to you correctly. (Do *not* use linguistics students for this, as they will probably use phonetic script!) Do the participants all tend to spell a sound in the same way when being impressionistic? (For example, is /u:/ always written *oo*, or are *ue* and *ough* also used? Does it depend on what consonant precedes?) Are the preferred spellings of each sound today the most long-standing ones (e.g. has *oo* represented the sound /uː/ for longer than the other spellings?). Vallins (1965: 46–9) gives lists of the different spellings for each sound, but you will find other lists quite easily, or you can construct your own.

301   Take a piece of verse (by Shakespeare, for example) and identify which rhymes still work and which don't. What about puns? What pronunciation changes are reflected by them? Argue in a balanced way for and against performing works of literature in their original pronunciation. What wider implications are there for the performing arts?

302   Borrow from your local library some CD recordings of vocal music written in the 1500s, in which the English is performed using historically informed pronunciation. Play selected items to some informants and ask them to write down as many of the words as they can recognize. Then play the pieces again, but this time let them read the texts in advance – does that help their recognition? Finally, interview them about their views of whether the pronunciation enhances the performance or not, and why.

303   What have been the motivations of the spelling reformers in England (and France, perhaps) during the past few centuries? For some ideas to get you started, look up the *inkhorns*, the *Académie* and *George Bernard Shaw*.

304   What would we lose by modernizing our spelling system to match modern pronunciation? Why has no such reform been achieved before now? When did spelling start diverging from pronunciation and why, and what was people's reaction?

305   Examine books issued in facsimile by Scolar Press, or electronically on Early English Books Online, for contemporary views of issues in the history of English. For example, read the introductory note to Mulcaster's *The First Part of the Elementary* (1582/1970) for an idea of his attitudes towards spelling, and then describe the alphabet that he presents. Alternatively, use John Hart's *An Orthographie* (1569/1969), one of the most linguistically informed and accurate descriptions of English pronunciation of its time, incorporating his own phonetic spelling system. Which issues of that time still apply today and why? What role do you think such writers played in the way that English has turned out?

306   Write a critical evaluation of a nineteenth-century or early twentieth-century essay on the 'decay' of language, such as Bridges (1913). Use the modern descriptive linguistic approach to put the other side of the arguments.

307   Interview actors and musicians about the validity of performing works from the sixteenth century and earlier in original pronunciation. For insight into the issues, see Wray (1992a and b, 1995, 1999).

308   Using Mitton (1996) as a basis, evaluate the influence on English spelling that computers and also texting have had since he wrote that book. Collect data from friends, and interview teachers, lecturers, journalists, and/or publishers about what changes they are aware of.

History of English dialects

Be careful what you choose here, because some dialects are better documented than others. Read Skeat (1911) to gain a clear idea of how the four major dialects of Old English fit together, and work forward from there. Try to avoid giving just a straightforward chronicle of developments.

PROJECTS

309 Investigate why it was that the variety of English spoken in the East Midlands became the standard English. By careful reading about Northumbrian and about the nature of standardization, speculate about what English would be like now if Northumbrian had continued to be the high-prestige variety that it was in Bede's day.

310 Draw on a range of reading to ask to what extent a topography of the British Isles can account for the development of Standard English.

The profile of a feature of English across time

Aspects of English grammar, meaning, and style have all changed across time, and there are plenty of documents that provide evidence of this. Use what you know about syntactic, semantic, or discourse theory to inform your analysis.

PROJECT

311 Focus on a feature such as the passive, the subjunctive, the negative, or how speech is quoted, and compare its occurrence in a couple of sample texts for each of, say, three periods between Chaucer and the late eighteenth century – or even up to modern times. You can keep the variability down by choosing a text that has been rewritten many times, such as a Bible passage. Examples of such passages can be found in many textbooks, including Fisher and Bornstein (1984), Burnley (2000), and Freeborn (2006).

Sociopolitical trends and influences on English

One much-described aspect of the history of our language is the way in which the Norman Conquest affected, among other things, the vocabulary of English. There has also been some interesting work done on the later 'social' history of English, including the way in which dialects were used to support the trade union movement (Joyce 1994). See Burke and Porter (1987, 1994) for ideas, and Leith (1997) for a more general but socially oriented view of the history of English.

PROJECTS

312 Using the chronologies in Williams (1986), write an account of what linguistic life would have been like in Norman England for, say, three or four individuals from different social classes. What language would they have used when, and with whom? How does this relate to the changes in the vocabulary of English between 1066 and 1400?

313   Draw up a list of the proverbs mentioned in Obelkevich (1987). Interview a small group of elderly people and ask them which ones they know, what they mean, and in what circumstances (for example, in conversation with whom) they might use them. Do the same with a group of young adults or children. Comment on the following possibilities: the use of proverbs is dying out; proverbs vary from generation to generation; you only really learn (or learn to use) proverbs later on in your life.

314   Make a study of euphemisms and when they are used. Read the introductory pages of dictionaries of euphemisms for an impression of their range. Make a list of euphemisms for the same thing (e.g. words for having sex, for excrement, or for parts of the body) and interview a group of informants about when they would use each one. Which do they consider shocking, which 'cute', and which old-fashioned? What words do they consider to be non-euphemistic (i.e. the direct term) for each concept? Look these words up to establish whether they, too, are, or have been, euphemisms. Consider the 'shelf life' of euphemisms and when they need replacing. For an outline of the scope of taboo words, including their use as swearwords, see Crystal (2003b: 172–4).

English as a world language

Read Crystal (2003b, Ch. 7 or 2003a) to gain a clear impression of the current status of English as a world language, and Phillipson (2003) for an in-depth consideration of the role of English in Europe. Kirkpatrick's (2010) collection brings in a number of historical perspectives on world Englishes (see also Melchers and Shaw, 2011). Issues arising from the worldwide dominance of English Language Teaching are explored in Block and Cameron (2002).

There are many interesting questions that we can ask, including how English came to be such a widespread and influential language, what mark it has left on other languages, and what mark they have left on it.

PROJECTS

315   Assuming an unaltered basic political history for Europe and America, how would foreign policy and/or social structures have had to be different for the English language *not* to have become so important? You can get ideas by looking at other nations that have had plenty of political, but less linguistic, influence. This sort of project is based on speculation and, for it to be successful as a piece of research, you *must* draw upon a range of established theories to support the points you make. You will need to research the processes by which English became so important, and draw on sociolinguistic research to demonstrate how social and political influences filter through to the individuals in a speech community, leading them to decisions about their own needs and priorities.

316   Make a comparison between English today and Arabic in the Middle East, or Latin during the Roman occupation of Europe.

317 Interview a range of different types of people, both native and non-native speakers of English about the future of English in the world. How likely do they think it is that English will become even more dominant in the political and commercial spheres? Does it matter if it does? What about the domestic use of English around the world, where at present other languages are used in the home? How do your informants' views compare with those expressed in the recent literature?

The influence of literacy on language

By researching the history of basic literacy education in Britain over the past thousand years, and linking that to who had influence over whom as far as language was concerned, one can develop a picture of the effect that being able to read and write has on the development of a language. Remember to consider the people at both edges of literacy: those who maybe had to write letters from time to time but who had almost no schooling and those who were highly educated not only in English but also in French, Greek, and Latin. There is plenty of information about the latter in introductory books like Baugh and Cable (2002) and Crystal (2003b).

PROJECT

318 Find out who was teaching the basic literacy skills to the less privileged in a period of history of your choosing. How good were *their* skills? Link this debate into literacy practice in the modern world, both locally and internationally, but remember to consider to what extent the demands of our society today require different levels of literacy and education from those of the past.

OTHER PROJECT IDEAS

319 If you, or someone you know, has already researched their family history, select a handful of members of the family and construct a linguistic profile for them. For instance, you might write a short paragraph in which each of them introduces themselves, their family and their occupation. Think about how to represent their vocabulary, grammar and pronunciation, given when and where they were born. Even if you can only track back to the early twentieth century, you will be able to find recordings that can help pinpoint features they might have had in their language. Then, use the assembled profiles to comment on how language might have changed subtly and less subtly within that family. Perhaps each member might have an opinion about how another family member talks!

320 Compare an eye-witness account of a historical event (Carey 1997 is an excellent source) with a similar one today in a blog. Which of the differences are due to linguistic change and which to changes in culture (e.g. attitudes to what has been witnessed) or technology (e.g. the mode and speed of writing)?

Things to think about

- It is possible to download from Early English Books Online (see earlier), or the Internet, lengthy texts that may not be easily available any other way, by doing a search on a name such as *Paston* (a family whose letters through the fifteenth century have been much studied), or the name of an event or monarch.
- Studies of pronunciation require a working knowledge of phonetic script; phonemic script will not be sufficient for anything other than the most general kinds of observations. For the difference between these two transcription systems, see Chapter 17.
- The more research you do into the history of a language, the more you will realize how much of what is presented as *fact* is actually an *interpretation* of what is often rather ambiguous and confusing original data. Don't be content with reading just one account; expect another one to be different, and take note of where the disagreements occur. The art of writing a good project is to use the disagreement as a pivot for developing your own views (see Chapter 22).

11

Computer-mediated communication

One of the most significant changes in human communication in recent years has been the explosion of new opportunities to gather and exchange information instantly using electronic devices, including texting and apps, Internet searches, social-networking sites, GPS navigation, blogging, Twitter, and so on. The speed of these developments is startling. The Internet did not become widely available until the mid-1990s. It took less than seven years (2004–2011) for Facebook to accrue 600 million active users (Carlson 2011). Twitter was created in March 2006 and five years later was 'estimated to have 200 million users, generating 65 million tweets a day and handling over 800,000 search queries per day' (Wikipedia: Twitter). Even Google has only been available since 1999. Yet these, and other electronic amenities, are so much part of our lives that we find ourselves asking how anyone managed before they existed.

Computer-mediated communication (CMC) is a broad term that can cover not only language but also images such as photos and video, as well as music. Crystal (2011) explores in some detail how what he terms 'Internet language' differs from more traditional forms of speech and writing. But not everyone agrees that there really is a specific 'language of the Internet' distinct from the language in other media, and some point much more to the linguistic differences *within* CMC than those between CMC and other media (e.g. Androutsopoulos 2006a).

Many aspects of linguistic research into CMC are still in their infancy, so doing a project in this area could mean you are breaking new ground. Some topics we can explore in this domain are paralleled by ones already addressed in relation to spoken and written language, but some are only meaningful in relation to these new media. The kinds of questions that researchers might be interested in include:

- What is really different about CMC? Does it mark a fundamental change in how we communicate or is it just another way of packaging what we have always done?
- Are the characteristics of electronic communication, including abbreviated spellings in texts and the different uses of communication, likely to alter the 'standard' form of languages permanently?
- Does the fast-pace exchange of short packages of information permanently alter our capacity to concentrate on long passages of text?

- To what extent do new technologies make us reassess our beliefs about how language works?
- Is digital text – the language of blogs, Twitter, simultaneous messaging, and so on – a form of writing, a form of speech, or something different again?
- Are the patterns of difference that we see in spoken conversation between, say, males and females, older and younger people, or people from different places, also observable in (different types of) electronic communication?
- What are the characteristics, pros and cons of being able to present different identities in CMC?

Terminology

The terminology associated with CMC is often, as with 'CMC' itself, in abbreviated form, which makes it difficult to work out if you don't already know it. In fact, this observation becomes a potential focus of research in its own right. Terms such as SMS (short messaging service), SNS (social networking site), URL (uniform resource locator), GPS (global positioning system), MP3 (Moving Picture [Experts Group Audio Layer] III)) and PC (personal computer) are used by millions of people who may not actually know what the letters stand for. On the other hand, more people probably do know that 'www' stands for World Wide Web. Some abbreviations were popular for a while, but have now gone out of use again, such as PDA (personal digital assistant), the name for the devices superseded by the smartphone. Besides the terminology describing the technology itself, there are thousands of terms for ways of communicating, e.g. *tweet*, *blog*, and plenty for expressing oneself on line, e.g. *lol* (laugh out loud, or, for some older users, lots of love). While printed dictionaries struggle to keep up, it should rarely be difficult to find out what a term means, since one can use the Internet to look it up. However, not everyone necessarily *does* look terms up, and that provides opportunities for us to observe language development and change at work.

Textbooks and major journals

Good introductory books on CMC include Barnes (2002), Baron (2008), Crystal (2006, 2011) and Thurlow *et al.* (2004). Myers (2010) is entirely dedicated to the discourse of blogs and wikis, and Boardman (2005) explores the language of websites. There are also some excellent collections of research papers that might give you ideas and information for your own project. They include Danet and Herring (2007), Hunsinger *et al.* (2010), Thurlow and Mroczek (2011). There are also overviews in certain papers (e.g. Herring 2004) and in encyclopaedias. Since this research area is so fast-moving, look out for new publications that capture the latest technological developments. You can find them by checking publishers' websites, or by going to the Amazon page for a recent book on the topic and following links to other similar titles, or to the titles that other people also examined.

There are a number of journals specifically dedicated to CMC, and it is also a popular topic for special issues in journals focused on discourse, sociolinguistics, etc. (e.g. *Journal of Sociolinguistics* 2006; *International Journal of Multicultural Societies* 2004; *Journal of Computer-Mediated Communication* 2003). More generally, since the Internet is often simply the source of data for a linguistic study, it's a good idea to check the journals linked to the approach or topic, rather than just the medium. For instance, studies of computer-mediated approaches to language learning might be reported in language-learning journals, and examinations of how people express their identity on line might be found in sociolinguistics journals. Journals more specifically dedicated to CMC include:

JOURNALS

Computer Assisted Language Learning

Computers in Human Behavior

Electronic Journal of Communication

Human Communication Research

Human IT (a Swedish journal, but most of the articles are in English)

Interacting with Computers

International Journal of Web-Based Communities

Journal of Computer-Mediated Communication

Journal of Sociolinguistics

Language Awareness

Language Learning and Technology

Language@internet

Media, Culture and Society

New Media and Society

New Review of Hypermedia and Multimedia

Research on Language and Social Interaction

The Information Society

Central themes and project ideas

Research into CMC is very broad, because it entails the interface between a medium and all the relevant aspects of linguistics, and beyond. For this reason, remember that other chapters of this book also contain some project ideas relevant to CMC. Here, we can broadly divide the CMC themes into two types – first, those relating to the language used, and, second, those concerning processes of communication.

Impoverished language

There has been considerable debate about whether certain sorts of practices, some forced on CMC users by the limitations of the technology, are likely to have a lasting impact on the standards of the language. These practices include short-spellings in texting and the restrictions of overall message length in Twitter and SMS (140 characters). Research has shown that in fact many of these practices predate the modern technologies, and are not as widely used as often claimed (e.g. Crystal 2011: 4ff). This indicates that popular opinion is only partly driven by the hard evidence, and suggests that in some regards CMC may be taking the rap for anxieties arising elsewhere. See Thurlow (2006) and Jones and Schieffelin (2009) for studies of popular perceptions of the language of CMC.

PROJECTS

321   Keep a log of your own behaviour when typing messages on your phone, in email or on web-based sites. What decisions are you taking about punctuation, spelling, abbreviations, and so on, and why? Do you have just one, or more than one way of expressing certain meanings? If you do, what are the patterns behind how you use them? Ask a couple of friends to do the same thing, so you can make comparisons – or sit at their shoulder while they type, and ask them questions.

322   Wood *et al.* (2011) report research suggesting that the use of abbreviations in texting correlates with *better* not worse spelling in school students. Interview some teachers to get their view on whether that is true, and if so, why.

323   Collect some typical examples of statements or conversations on a social networking site such as Facebook and ask their authors to edit a copy so they are more 'standard' in spelling and punctuation. Examine the sorts of changes that are made, and use the information to gauge the extent to which authors have control of more than one variety of language, or have 'lost' or failed to develop knowledge of what were previously considered 'correct' forms. For each major difference, consider what the feature does in the language and whether there are any potential consequences for permanently losing the 'correct' form. For instance, would it matter if we started spelling the first person singular pronoun *I* with a lower case letter? Why?

Changes in vocabulary

New processes and products require new words, and everything of importance in our new technological world needs a name. How do these words get chosen, and by whom? How straightforward is it for others to pick them up, particularly if they are not formally defined, just used? Do they always end up meaning exactly the same as originally intended? Given the historical patterns by which vocabulary has entered language (see Chapter 10), it is interesting to consider the processes occurring now. For instance, in the past, many new words were coined for English by assembling morphemes from Greek and Latin, but nowadays few of the people who invent new objects, ideas or software applications have studied Latin and Greek, so they must seek inspiration elsewhere. Some words are amalgamations of existing words, e.g. *blog* (web log), or are acronyms, e.g. *grep* (globally search for the regular expression and print). Some are inspired by ideas in books or movies, e.g. *iPod*, from the film *2001: A Space Odyssey* (Wikipedia: *iPod*). The name *Google* was a misspelling of another word, *googol* (Koller 2004). *Twitter* and *tweet* were existing words adopted for a new purpose (Sarno 2009).

Historically, many words have been borrowed *into* English from other languages, reflecting the origin of the item in question (see Chapter 10). But in the CMC domain, English is exporting rather than importing words, and many languages have adopted them. For instance, on the site http://www.languageguide.org/im/computer/jp/ you can hold the mouse over a set of objects relevant to computing and read the Japanese terms used. They include: *koNpyuutaa* (computer), *kiiboodo* (keyboard), *supeesu baa* (space bar), *furopiidisuku doraibu* (floppy disk drive), *rappu toppu* (laptop), *puriNta* (printer) and *keeburu* (cable).

PROJECTS

324 Crystal (2011: 115) writes: 'a large number of software terms are picked up in the *scrape*.' Elsewhere, he refers to *grepping*. How do we learn the meanings of new terms? Identify some words that reflect new developments in CMC, and find out what people think they mean. If they don't know, see how they go about guessing. Compare their responses to a technical description (e.g. for *scraping*, see Wikipedia: Web scraping) or the opinions expressed in the Urban Dictionary http://www.urbandictionary.com/. Compare your findings for different words to see if different types of word lead to different strategies, or if different individuals take different approaches.

325 List some texting/Internet abbreviations, e.g. *lol, brb* (for a lengthy list, see http://en.wiktionary.org/wiki/Appendix:Internet_slang), and ask people of different generations what they mean. Where they don't know the meaning, ask them to guess, and include some bogus ones, to ensure you get some guesses from everyone. Look at the patterns of their guesses. What are the thought processes that are determining them – e.g. what sort of information are they assuming these abbreviations carry? Do your findings enable you to predict any of the characteristics (meaning, form, function) of future abbreviations?

326 How do people use emoticons, and what do they mean, exactly? It would be quite easy for them to be differently understood by different users. For example, Crystal (2011: 23) describes the meaning of ☺ as 'sympathy, delight, amusement' – but does everyone use that symbol for *all* of those meanings? Also, find out how aware users are of the risk that a reader of their message might interpret an emoticon in a different way than intended, or might not understand it at all. How does that influence how emoticons are used? See Crystal (2006, Ch. 2 and 2011: 24) for some additional ideas and pointers regarding emoticons.

Linguistic variation

Are the classic linguistic differences between sub-groups of speakers or writers, whether on the basis of gender, age, ethnicity, sexual orientation, replicated in CMC? Herring's work (e.g. Herring 2003) suggests that there are consistent male–female differences in how language is used on line, but, in the context of blogs written by teenagers, Huffaker and Calvert (2005) found little gender difference.

PROJECT

327 Waseleski (2006) examined text from two discussion lists to test the hypothesis that since women had been found to use exclamation marks more than men in other mediums, the same would be true in CMC. It was, but she discovered that they were not using them to express surprise, but friendliness. Read Waseleski's paper and design a replication of it, using different texts. Keep in mind the possibility that practices might have changed since she ran her study, and that writers are not all the same. Either try to find texts by authors comparable to hers, or deliberately choose a different type of author group (e.g. by using a gardening or sports discussion list).

Discourse structure

Leaving aside the matter of falling standards (see earlier section), there are some rather interesting questions that can be asked in relation to how text is organized in CMC. **Multi-party talk** online, instant messaging, the interspersing of replies within emails, and the use of **hypertext** all end up presenting information in a different order from that in which it was originally produced. But is this as new as it seems? Student essays often get feedback on the body of the text, so that the original essay and the comments interact – to create meanings that neither creates on its own.

PROJECT

328 When replies are interspersed into previous electronic messages, or when several people engage in an online chat, it could be argued that, to understand the way the text operates you need to be there, observing it as it develops. Is that true? Capture some complex interactions, in which the threads of the discourse are interwoven in a complex way, and ask people who were not part of that conversation to talk you through the conversation. Observe how they jump backwards and forwards, and how they home in on particular topics or people to help them work out what is going on. You might focus on how references to time, person and place are handled, since these are typically sensitive to a current context and previous mentions.

Semantics and pragmatics

The meaning we take from texts is not divorced from our awareness of where we find that text. For instance, if we are looking for information on a health topic, we will interpret what we read on a web-page differently, according to whether the page is from an official health service site, a commercial drugs company, or an informal set of postings on a discussion board. But sometimes it may not be clear what the origin or authority of a site is, leaving us to look for clues in the language or presentation.

PROJECTS

329 Select some web-pages and either print them out or show them on screen to some informants. Ask them to grade the likely reliability of the information there, and ask them how they are judging. Compare the grades and the reasons of your different participants. Choose websites of different kinds, looking for evidence that some or all of the following might contribute to the judgement: presentation (typeface, colour, design, business, professionalism), content (general plausibility, types of claim, evidence for them, one-sidedness, role of personal opinion), external validation (reference to recognized authorities such as published studies), evidence of age (dates, broken hyperlinks), etc. You may find Boardman (2005) a useful resource for this project.

330 Compose a list of the functions that interaction can have (e.g. sharing information, congratulating, gossiping, warning, commiserating, sacking someone, notifying competition winners). Next, list the different ways in which messages can be conveyed (e.g. face to face, phone, voicemail message, letter, email, etc.). For each type of function, ask informants to rank the different mediums for their acceptability and appropriateness. Give them space to comment, so that if they say 'it depends', they can explain. What patterns are there? For instance, is it more acceptable to convey good news than bad news via CMC? If so, why? Does the anticipated response of the receiver make a difference?

331 Some people say that CMC makes it too easy to act in a hurry and regret at leisure, particularly in relation to politeness. Interview some people about their experiences of being and not being polite in CMC, and the reasons – how much is due to the fact that it was CMC? Also ask them for their experiences on the receiving end of impolite or unkind CMC from others. Think carefully about what sorts of informants to use in this study – it might make a difference.

332 Track some on-line discussions over a period of time: how do topics develop? If they stick to the point, how is that achieved? If there is drift, how does it happen? Are there any patterns to the drift (e.g. Does it first get jokey, then chatty and general? Is there always a drift away from facts into personal experiences?)? What might explain the patterns you observe?

Language production

The processes and pressures associated with language production are different in different media. The language used in CMC is considered by some to be a blend of speech and writing. What impact might it have on us as language users if the production processes of speaking and writing are operating simultaneously?

PROJECTS

333 How fast can your friends type compared with how fast they can speak? What differences does this make to the quantity and nature of the information they offer in a web-chat compared with a face-to-face chat? You can investigate their typing in real-time chatting, and you can also get them to do a basic typing speed test on line, e.g. http://speedtest.10-fast-fingers.com/, though bear in mind that tests can make people emphasize speed over accuracy and content.

334   When you type on your computer, do you make typing errors? If so, which do you leave and which fix? Download software that can track your keystrokes, e.g. http://www.actualkeylogger.com/ and examine what you do in detail. Note: be sure to restrict access to only yourself, since it will be picking up your pin numbers and passwords. Useful reading on this topic can be found in Sullivan and Lindgren (2006).

Interpersonal communication

CMC research often distinguishes between **asynchronous** and **synchronous** communication. These terms have a technical meaning, relating to how the data is sent, which in turn is determined by whether the sender and receiver are both present at the same time (synchronous) or whether they are not, or at least don't have to be (asynchronous). For instance, Skype communication is synchronous – you can't Skype someone unless they are there to interact with you. Email and Facebook wall posts are asynchronous – when you open your email or go onto Facebook, you are checking for updates that may have been sent or added while you were off-line.

It's important not to confuse the technical meanings with the kind of experience you have in interaction. For instance, when someone emails you, you might be on-line, receive the message immediately and respond within seconds – the experience is pretty synchronous, but technically this is still an asynchronous exchange because the way the message is sent uses software that accommodates your *not* being there to reply. The reason for pointing out this distinction is that the experiential aspect will often be uppermost in your mind (you may not even know how the data is transmitted), so it would be easy to become confused by the technical uses of the terms.

There are many foci of interest regarding how people interact in CMC. For instance, Cherny (1999) undertook a two-year study of the linguistic behaviour of members of an on-line community, tracking how they achieved the things they wanted despite the limitations of this kind of interaction.

PROJECTS

335   Study how your relationships with your friends are shaped by the different ways in which you communicate (e.g. face to face, talking on the phone, Facebook, texting, etc.). List some facts that you know about some of your friends (e.g. what they did last weekend, whether they like a particular band, what they thought of the party you went to last night, whether they regularly watch a particular TV programme) and work out how you came to know those facts. Is there a pattern to which sorts of information are shared using which kind of medium? If so, why, and could it easily be

very different? For instance, how are the most personal details shared? What about the one-off facts (place of birth, number of siblings)? How do you get to know the very latest information?

336 How does CMC technology impact on our face-to-face interaction? Undertake a survey, to discover what people do and don't like in the behaviour of others in relation to new media. For instance, is it acceptable when spending time with a friend, to take and make phone calls, receive and send texts, go online on a smartphone, etc.? Should people be allowed to make phone calls in restaurants, planes and trains? Is there a good match between what people would like, and what they feel actually happens? How does their own behaviour fit into the picture?

337 Thurlow (2006: 691) quotes the following from a Hewlett Packard press release: 'In a series of tests carried out by Dr Glenn Wilson, Reader in Personality at the Institute of Psychiatry, University of London, an average worker's functioning IQ falls ten points when distracted by ringing telephones and incoming emails.' Survey some people who work in an environment where this sort of interruption might be common (e.g. administrators and academics in a university or college). Ask them if they believe they are less able to work effectively with distractions from phones and emails, what their personal strategy is for managing such distractions, and what sort of changes to policy, practice or software they think should be made to help alleviate the problem. Also ask them how easy they find it to switch their phone off or deliberately not to connect to the Internet, and under what circumstances they might do so. Do they agree with the claim that 'technology rules us, rather than us ruling it'?

338 Compare and contrast some netiquette guides. What do they tell us about (a) normal expectations of communication, and (b) the particular risks of the differences between Internet communication and those normal expectations?

339 In universities and colleges, staff and students can take very different positions regarding the centrality of email as a mode of communication. Interview students, academic staff and administrators in your university or college about how well communication between staff and students works, what they think could work better, what they think causes problems, and what ideas they have for solutions. This sort of study could conclude with some practical proposals for your college or department.

Identity and anonymity

How we present ourselves in electronic media has become a source of some interest for two main reasons. One is that CMC gives us opportunities to take some control over how others perceive us – from the decisions we make about what personal information and which photos to put on a Facebook page, to completely new fantasy identities in virtual worlds like **Second Life**. Since language plays a major role in how we convey our identity, there are plenty of opportunities to explore how a person's linguistic choices vary in different CMC contexts.

The other reason for interest in the matter of identity is that people can deliberately mislead others through their choice of identity, so as to behave irresponsibly or commit a crime. For instance, in 2011, there was considerable international media interest in a blog written by a gay woman in Syria, who was involved in anti-government protests and feared for her safety. Later, an American man living in Scotland admitted to having written the blog, but justified his actions as a means of drawing attention to the political situation in Syria: 'While the narrative voice may have been fictional, the facts on this blog are true and not misleading as to the situation on the ground' (http://www.bbc.co.uk/news/world-middle-east-13744980). There are interesting issues to research around the way that this man was able to sustain this alternative identity linguistically, and his claim that it is socially and ethically acceptable to do so, if the motivation is a 'good' one.

It is very difficult to track criminals down if they are easily, and legally, able to disguise their identity. Linguistic research can be used to help demonstrate that criminal activity is taking place. For instance, Crystal (2011, Ch. 7) describes a project that demonstrated differences between a paedophile's interaction with an under-age victim on an instant messaging site and the language of bona fide users.

Governments struggle with the conflict between the rights of individuals to privacy and the many ways in which CMC can be misused for criminal or antisocial activity. Since 2007, the South Korean government has required everyone using the Internet to register under their own name, cross-referenced to their national identity number (Weigand 2011). The US government proposes to strengthen the security of individuals' identities in CMC by creating an 'Identity Ecosystem' (Schmidt 2011) that can cross-check user credentials (e.g. prevent a child accessing an adults-only site) while preventing companies from collecting personal information about its customers, reducing the risk of information falling into the wrong hands and removing the problems associated with individuals needing to remember many passwords and/or using the same password for too many things (see http://www.nist.gov/nstic/identity-ecosystem.html). National initiatives that impose new systems are typically viewed with suspicion by those fearing excessive surveillance. There are some interesting discussions to be had about how to navigate the path between the freedom and the protection of the individual.

PROJECTS

340 Not everything we write or say is deliberately calculated to create or mould our identity. But even if we are not conscious of it, our decisions about self-disclosure do impact on how we are perceived. Examine the discourse on some typical discussion sites and grade the information offered by contributors for its relevance to the discussion. What purposes might self-revelatory information that is irrelevant or semi-relevant have within the discourse? What would be the impact of omitting it?

341 Interview some regular users of CMC about the range of identities they have used. In particular, ask them how close they have got to deliberately presenting themselves as 'somebody else' and why. For instance, have they ever posed as someone older or younger, so they could ask a 'dumb' question? Have they written an endorsement of a friend's restaurant, pretending to be a real customer? Use the information you collect to consider how the knowledge, assumptions and fears that we carry with us into the CMC context can lead us to want, or need, a different identity in specific circumstances. How do these pressures differ from those we might carry into other contexts, such as letter writing, making a phone call, etc., and why?

342 Collect some email phishing spam (e.g. letters inviting you to send your banking details to a stranger; requests to enter your password or pin). Analyse what it is that marks them out as inauthentic. In order to understand what is really *new* about being 'street-wise' in CMC, interview an older friend or relative about the kinds of scams they can remember during their life (in phone calls, letters, people calling at the door, approaches on the street). Does CMC put us at greater risk of criminal behaviour now than in the past, once we take into account the level of awareness that Internet users (should) have?

343 Using the examples on the US Government's 'identity-ecosystem' webpage (http://www.nist.gov/nstic/identity-ecosystem.html), develop a detailed evaluation of what would be entailed in introducing this system in your country. Consider the advantages and disadvantages of having such a system, the potential risks, the practicalities, and likely response to the system of different types of user (including any who might be inadvertently excluded from full use of the Internet), the ways that criminals might try to undermine it, and how the new procedures should be explained and justified to users.

Technology and information

The technology of CMC creates the environment within which we communicate, offering new opportunities but also imposing limitations. One of the bonuses is the easy access of information, including the linking of one resource to another. Another is the capacity to collaborate in the creation of new knowledge (see Myers 2010 for more on these topics). However, **accessibility** has another important aspect. While people with disabilities can hugely benefit from the new technologies, they can also be disadvantaged if too little thought is put into what they need.

There are some 'holy grails' of IT development that are still to be achieved, including fully effective automatic conversion of speech to writing and writing to speech, and the automatic translation of texts between languages. Google Translate (http://translate.google.com) offers one opportunity for the latter but is currently far from perfect. For instance, compare passage 1 below, from a UK newspaper website (21 May 2011) with passage 2, which was created by translating the original from English into Welsh, the Welsh into Hindi, the Hindi into Basque and the Basque back into English.

(1) The pod of pilot whales, about 20 of which had severe head injuries, was spotted late Thursday night as the mammals attempted to beach themselves on the rocky shore of a remote Scottish island. Dozens of healthy whales had also followed them into the shallow water raising fears that up to 100 of the animals could strand themselves.

(2) These pilots had serious head injuries about 20 pods of whales, mammals, was seen late Thursday night in a remote Scottish island to try to beach themselves on the rocky

coast. Dozens of whales and surface water, have a healthy fear of large animals in the 100 helix, they can be.

Of course, we would not expect to regain the precise original even using expert human translators – but we might hope for an end-product that made reasonable sense. The differences between the translations, which can be tracked in more detail by translating each interim version back to English as well, can tell us a great deal about how language works, and so provide us, unintentionally, with a new approach to linguistic analysis.

PROJECTS

344 There are still people alive who, though born in the industrialised world, recall a time when motor cars and aeroplanes were an uncommon sight. For them, the home computer, the Internet and the mobile phone were all unheard of until they were well into retirement. This makes our current era a fascinating one for observing how different generations engage with technology. Interview some silver surfers (aged over 70 if possible), some 40-somethings and some teenagers, and find out how differently they use CMC. Which differences are simply a reflection of their lives (e.g. teenagers don't need to check car-hire websites or find out about pensions) and which might be caused by other factors? What do your findings predict about how current teenagers will use CMC when they are in the 40s and, how the 40-somethings will use it in their 70s?

345 What do people do with their old mail messages and why? Find some people who are good at deleting, and some others who keep or archive most messages. Find out what the consequences are of these practices. What differences do you perceive in their attitude towards the messages and the senders? You might add another dimension to this study by asking people how their electronic practices compare with what they do with hard-copy materials such as receipts, guarantees, certificates, postcards and letters.

346 Look at a range of web-pages on a single topic of your choice and compare how the language and presentation on the websites differ from that in written documents on the same topic. In your view, are websites simply a new forum for providing the same information held in books and magazines? Does the evidence suggest that the linguistic nature of web material will gradually become more like that in books and magazines or less like it?

347 What *can't* you do or find on the Internet? Ask as many people as you can to jot down – maybe over a couple of weeks – what information they just can't track down, or what information it takes them a really long time to locate. Why do these gaps exist?

348 'The Internet is too cluttered with old information. When you're looking for a restaurant and you find places listed that you know have closed down, it means you know you can't trust anything else on the list. It's particularly annoying when a new site has obviously just copied old information across without checking it.' Interview some Internet users for their views on how up to date the Internet is. Does the amount of clutter vary across topics or types of information? How do they think outdated information should be dealt with? What danger is there that the Internet will become unusable because obsolete sites overwhelm the useful material?

349 There are now several technologies for changing written language into spoken language, including the Text-to-Speech feature on Kindle. Analyse the output of one of these products, testing its ability to pronounce difficult words, join words together in phrases, disambiguate meanings and apply convincing intonation.

350 Dragon Naturally Speaking and other speech-recognition software can turn a user's speech into print. But how successfully? Test such a product to find out where its strengths and weaknesses lie. For instance, what is the limit of its capacity correctly to recognize words in different accents, or in fast speech? Are there any specific patterns of errors that reveal inherent weaknesses?

351 Experiment with translating and retranslating some texts using Google Translate (http://translate.google), to explore the parameters and limitations of its ability. How well does it manage with single words, and if they are not translated back identically, can you figure out what has happened? For instance, do semantically complex words become simplified (e.g. *incessant* → *fixed*), or less frequent words get replaced with more frequent ones (e.g. *spectacles* → *glasses*)? What happens when you introduce simple and more complex grammatical patterns? What solutions would you recommend to the software designers?

352 Do software or hardware features determine your language choices? For example, do you rely on automatic spelling corrections, and thus confidently use words that you are not sure how to spell? Do you make certain typing errors over and over again, because of the layout of the keyboard? In instant messaging, is the text you write influenced by the way the software operates? Does the fact that smiley emoticons end with a bracket prevent you putting comments with an emoticon into brackets? Do people who write a lot of tweets believe that it has made them think in shorter bursts in other contexts? Consider whether these sorts of constraints could permanently influence the way you or others compose language.

353 How can CMC support people with disabilities and what aspects of their needs are not really taken into account yet? Search on the Internet for guidelines on how to make a website accessible, and then evaluate some sites against those criteria. Tools available to help you include the Wave accessibility tool http://wave.webaim.org/, and the W3C web accessibility initiative http://www.w3.org/WAI/eval/. The webaim site also has simulations that can help you experience what it is like to have a particular disability, http://webaim.org/simulations/. A useful paper to consult might be Kennedy *et al.* (2011).

Multilingualism and minority languages

How do people who regularly use more than one dialect or language in their speech and/or writing use them in CMC? Some research into this question is reported in collections of papers by Hawischer and Selfe (2000), Danet and Herring (2003, 2007), Wright (2004),

Cunliffe and Herring (2005) and Androutsopoulos (2006b). Each situation is different, so there is plenty of scope for an original project on this topic.

PROJECTS

354 If you are multilingual, explore your own practices in language choice, including how you open a new conversation with someone else you know also knows your languages, how you decide which language to use on a forum, and what prompts you to change language. Perhaps you have a rudimentary command of another language – explore your comfort zone by accessing sites in that language or contacting a speaker of it, and observing how you feel about using the language.

355 There are a number of social networking sites that aim to help learners practise a foreign language, e.g. http://www.italki.com/. Join such a site and undertake an evaluation of the reliability of the information that learners can access. For instance, how easy would it be to pose as a native speaker of a language you didn't know very well? How accurate is the feedback from native speakers?

OTHER PROJECT IDEAS

356 In the old days, a student who wanted to pass off someone else's work as their own would have to find a suitable text in the library or get it from a friend, and copy it out by hand – quite a time-consuming task. Now it is possible to find a much wider range of texts very quickly, cut and paste the electronic text and create a new essay in minutes. Universities and colleges try to detect this sort of activity by using plagiarism software, but it's clear that many students still succeed in beating the system. How do they do it? Interview some students (guarantee to keep their identity confidential, of course) about how they manage to avoid getting caught when they embed other people's text in their essays. What weaknesses in the software or the assessment system are they aware of and how are they exploiting them? How much skill and work does it take to plagiarize really well?

357 If you play Internet games, spend some time examining the language used by players. Which features of that language are determined by the activity, and which by the fact that the game is played on-line?

358 Increasingly we do our shopping on-line, and there can be huge competition for customers, but not always. What are the key common features of the websites of highly successful Internet retailers? Can you see a difference between companies that easily command the majority market (e.g. Amazon, iTunes) and companies that are in fairly equal competition with others (e.g. electronics, clothes and insurance retailers)?

359 A lot is said about how the older generation does and doesn't engage with CMC, and we know a little about why they don't. But what do they understand about what these different technologies do? Interview some people over 70 years old who are not users of CMC. Ask them what they believe the advantages and disadvantages are of the Internet, mobile phones, texting, blogs, Twitter, etc., and as part of that, ask them what they think people use them for. Are they in fact aware of all the things these media offer? For instance, it would be interesting to see whether they see the Internet as primarily a way of staying in touch with family or of shopping. They may not even know that you can receive news-feeds or stream films and music, blog, or play Internet games.

You can find some additional project ideas in Crystal (2011: Ch. 9). See also Project 308.

Things to think about

A number of practical challenges associated with researching Internet communication are identified by Crystal (2011). They include:

- If you want to examine private emails, how will you get people to let you use them? Even if they were sent to you, who would you say owns them?
- If you are analysing material from Twitter, be sure to save it at the time, because it may not be available again later.
- With text from the Internet, it may not be practical to use it unedited. See Crystal (2011: Ch. 3) for some consideration of why, and what to do.
- While information on the Internet can be viewed as being in the public domain, you may have problems if you want to dig deeper, such as asking a company why it chose its logo, how it decides on its webpage design, or how many people access its site. Such questions can be viewed as commercially sensitive.

Part II

TECHNIQUES FOR COLLECTING DATA

12

Audio- and video-recorded data

Many kinds of researcher use audio- or video-recording in order to avoid having to make frantic notes at the time and missing important information. But, in linguistics, the speech itself is often the subject of analysis, and so it is especially important to have a good-quality recording.

Places to get data

Provided you take note of possible problems with background noise and interruptions (see below), you can record in many places: the home, a pub, a train, a café, a school, a retirement home, a student room, a club or meeting, a consultation room, and so on. You can also get material from the radio, TV, and archives, and from the Internet, subject to copyright.

Audio or video?

In most circumstances, audio data is sufficient, but it is certainly worth considering using video equipment. With modern digital technology, either audio or video should provide you with excellent sound quality, provided you have a good microphone but, if you have several informants, especially children, it may be difficult to tell their voices apart if there is no visual corroboration.

Naturalistic data

Researchers need to be aware of how the act of recording might make the data less naturalistic. However, the inhibitions associated with informants knowing that they are being recorded are usually fairly short-lived. Therefore, although you may be inclined to conceal your microphone or camera, do not assume that this is the only way of getting the data you need. Most people will soon forget about the recording as they become involved in the activities.

Ethics and legality

There are important ethical considerations when it comes to recording people. Either ask their permission first or, if you feel that your data will be less 'genuine' if they know you are recording, ask them afterwards. You should be prepared to let them hear what you have recorded and you must give them the option of asking for part, or all, of it to be erased (see Chapter 16).

Recording from the radio or television and downloading from the Internet do not entail such ethical problems, because the material is in the public domain. However, some broadcast and Internet material is copyright and, if you intend to use it in a publication or other public presentation, you should ask the permission of the copyright owner. Increasingly, digital-radio broadcasts are offered for download from official websites (e.g. the BBC, www.bbc.co.uk) and there copyright is unlikely to be an issue for researchers.

Quality

Golden rule number one in collecting recorded data is to remember that you will have to listen to it over and over again till you're sick of it. You will need to listen for detail, so it must be well recorded, otherwise background noise will increasingly become a problem. When you are deciding where to record, think about the noise implications. Pubs, trains, cafés, schools, and retirement homes can offer wonderful opportunities for natural conversation or interviews, but they can also be excessively noisy, so do a trial recording before you commit yourself to collecting the data there.

How much data do you need?

The amount of data you need depends on two key things. One is what questions you are asking of your data, and how thick and fast the answers will come. If you want to know how the word *the* is pronounced in continuous speech, you won't need more than a few minutes' worth, because *the* is such a common word. But, if you are interested in how topics are linked together in debates, you will need enough material for sufficient topic changes to occur. As you collect the data, listen to it to gauge how many examples you have accumulated so far.

The second thing that determines how much data to collect is the detail of your analysis. A narrow phonetic transcription of speech will take a great deal of time, and it may be sufficient to analyse no more than a set of short stretches of a few seconds each. A detailed conversation transcription will also take a lot of time to complete and four to five minutes in total may well be plenty. You should be discerning about what you choose to transcribe – not just everything you recorded!

- The first five minutes of a conversation might not be the most interesting part. Go for interesting features such as story-telling or argument.
- If you are studying accent, you will want to find at least a few examples of each phoneme. Some of the sounds may be quite rare and it will be frustrating if you find you have too little data to provide everything you need. So record more, in order that you have more to select your examples from.

- For dialect studies you may need a longer recording, because certain forms and structures may not appear in a five-minute stretch.
- If you need specific forms or examples to occur, don't leave it to chance. Design interview questions or a task that is likely to elicit them.
- If you plan to record on more than one occasion, transcribe or do a preliminary analysis of the data you already have before you get the next lot, as this may help you to see what you still need.

Practicalities

- Record digitally if you can, because the quality will be better and there is software that will help you with transcription.
- Use a good machine, and make sure you know how it operates.
- Make sure all your recordings are labelled immediately, with a unique code that you will still be able to interpret later, or you could spend a long time looking for extracts, or might even delete something by mistake.
- Back up your data as soon as you can – for example, both on the hard drive of your PC or laptop and on a memory stick.
- If storing data on disks (e.g. CDs, DVDs), use new ones on which you can rewrite and add new data.
- If your machine has limited capacity (e.g. digital memory), buy a second memory card, and if it runs on batteries, have enough spare ones to change the entire set at once. Or, especially if it has its own rechargeable battery, consider having a second machine set up and ready to record, to switch on as soon as you can see that the other is about to stop. The overlap will help with continuity later and it avoids interruptions, which remind interviewees that they are being recorded, just when they had forgotten.
- If making a recording using your mobile phone, check that the quality is going to be good enough for your purposes, and that you can transfer and store the recording appropriately.
- Experiment with using an external microphone, especially if you need a very good quality recording. It will also give you more scope for where you locate it, while still being able to operate the recorder controls.
- If using video, consider whether you want to hand-hold the camera (more flexible but quite intrusive) or put it on a tripod (leaving you free, but risking the action falling outside the frame).
- If you decide to conceal a camera or audio recorder, plan carefully how you will achieve this. If there is any danger of it being discovered midway through the recording, or if you will have trouble secretly retrieving it afterwards, you might be better off making it visible in the first place.
- Where possible, get informants to identify themselves on the recording, so that you have a reference to link their voice and their name later. When a new speaker contributes, make a note of their name and the time elapsed.
- You may want to plan to collect data from more subjects than you need, in case anything goes wrong with the recording.

- Make an edited copy of your original data, containing just the extracts you are focusing on; this reduces the endless fast-forwarding and reversing. With digital data, insert bookmarks at the important locations.
- With video data, ask at your institution if there are studio facilities for editing your material.

What to submit

When you submit your project, you may need to provide a copy of your audio/video data for the assessors.

- It does *not* need to be a complete recording of everything. Create a short, edited version that contains just the parts that you report on. Provide a menu list of what you have supplied and where it can be found.
- Check what data format your assessors prefer (e.g. some may want MP3 files in a folder, others a DVD). Data saved to CDs and DVDs may not be playable on all machines, so check what format to save to. You may want to hand in a memory stick with adequate (but not excessive) memory capacity. If you want it back, make sure you say so, and provide a mailing address.
- Listen to the start of the recording, the end, and any transitions between tracks, to make sure you have presented what you intended.
- Label CDs, DVDs and memory sticks with your name (or student ID number if your institution operates anonymous marking), module number, and the contents. Label files in a way that will make sense to other people.
- Keep a copy of all data and of the project write-up itself, in case it gets mislaid.

Things to think about

- How well do you know your informants? It can save a lot of time if you already know them, and many friends and family members will be pleased to help you with your research. On the other hand, a small child who knows you well may mess around, whereas one who knows you less well might be more co-operative.
- If recording in a public place, remember that not everyone will necessarily take kindly to being on your recording!
- Particularly if there is a high risk of extraneous noise, or interruption, request a quiet room if possible.
- Plan carefully whom you will record, how long for, and what the agenda will be. If you are interviewing, write a plan of your questions (see Chapter 14).
- TV and radio programmes provide good-quality sound. But remember that the sound from a TV doesn't come out of the screen where the mouths are, but from a speaker, often round the side or back. If possible, download the programme from the Internet.
- Scripted speech may not be appropriate to your study, so if you are recording from the radio or TV, look through the schedules to find the most appropriate material to record.
- If you want accent features or natural conversation from TV or radio, target 'passer-by' interviews on news broadcasts, programmes that use interviews with children, and 'fly-on-the-wall' documentaries.

13

Experiments

Language is a complicated phenomenon and sometimes its occurrence in natural settings does not enable you to see what is going on. Certain kinds of research questions are best answered by creating an artificial situation, where you compare what happens when one specific detail ('variable') is changed, while everything else remains constant. If you find a contrast in what happens in the two conditions, you can reasonably claim that it must be due to that variable.

However, no single individual can be guaranteed to produce behaviour that is consistent or representative of the population as a whole. Therefore, experiments are normally conducted on groups of similar participants, rather than on single individuals, in the hope that the pooled results will be representative of the wider population.

Conducting experiments can be very rewarding, but it can be a nightmare if the procedures are not carefully planned and executed at every stage. Think twice before embarking on experimental research unless you have a good supervisor who is experienced in it himself or herself.

It is vital to design your experiment round a clearly thought-through research question and with your focus firmly on what you will do with the results and what all the different possible outcomes will mean. The skill in running experiments lies in making sure that everything except the variable being investigated remains as similar as possible. For instance, two groups of participants should be compatible and treated the same way. If you compared women with men on some language-based task and the women performed better, but it turned out that the women were all university graduates in their twenties, while the men were all in their sixties and had left school at 14, it would not be possible to determine which variable (gender, age, or education) accounted for the difference in performance.

What does experimentation involve?

Participants

Normally, you will want to use ordinary people, representative of the general population or some subset of it. However, gathering a sample of practical size that genuinely represents the whole population is virtually impossible so, if it is easiest to only use, say, female undergraduates, do so. In your write-up, just acknowledge the limitations of your participant pool in representing only one subgroup of society.

Since you are likely to need to run statistical tests on your results, you need a statistically viable number of participants. As a general rule, the problems arise when you have too few participants, because just one odd result can skew the outcome for the whole group – the more participants you have, the more that result will be watered down. However, different group sizes can attract different statistical tests. See Chapter 20 for more information.

Conceptual structure

It's absolutely essential to have a clear-cut, well-planned experiment from the outset. Keep it simple and don't be tempted to complicate it while you're running it. It will become complicated of its own accord once you take some basic procedures into account! You should be able to explain in one sentence what you intend to find out and, in another one, how you intend to do it.

How do you keep it simple? By generating your design on the basis of a claim in the research literature, and *only* testing that claim. For example, if you read that women tend to use a wider vocabulary of colour terms than men, you might design an experiment to test this claim, by getting comparable groups of men and women to name unlabelled colours on a paint chart, and counting how many different names they come up with.

The **theory** that women use a wider vocabulary of colour terms forms the basis for a specific **hypothesis** about the outcome of your experiment: *Experimental hypothesis: women will produce more different names for colours.* You can then also identify the **null hypothesis**, which states what will happen if the theory you are relying on is incorrect: *Null hypothesis: women and men will not produce a significantly different number of names for colours.*

At this point in your planning, you will need to think through all the possible outcomes of your experiment. List them and consider what they will mean. This is a good way to check that your experiment will work, and it will greatly speed things up later. In our example, there are three possible outcomes:

1 The women produce significantly more names, supporting the experimental hypothesis and confirming the theory it is based on. 'Significant' is a technical term (see Chapter 20).
2 There is no significant difference between the number of names produced by men and women, supporting the null hypothesis, though there is more than one reason why one might get this result: there really is no difference between men and women; there is a difference, but not a large enough one to show up as statistically significant; there is a difference, but the experiment did not manage to capture it.
3 The men produce more names than women. This would be something of a surprise! Since your experimental hypothesis was not based on a hunch but on apparently reliable claims in published sources, you can ask whether, perhaps, the claims were wrong. By examining the evidence that led to the original claim, you may find an explanation for your finding (e.g. the difference had only ever been observed in natural conversation, not in controlled experiments, so could be a matter of choice rather than vocabulary knowledge).

Procedure

An experimental task should be carefully chosen to be appropriate to the abilities of the participants. Plan meticulously and run through the steps in a rehearsal and/or pilot study (see Chapter 1). Locate a suitable environment: this must be available when you need it and be within your control. If you use a language lab, make sure you can operate the machinery; if you use a quiet room, make sure the porter, caretaker, or secretary will not come and turn you out midway. If you use your own room, negotiate with your flatmates and unplug/turn off phones. If you are testing participants in sequence, think ahead about the problems of an appointment system – what if someone is late or doesn't show up? If they're early, will they interrupt proceedings and/or overhear something they shouldn't? Perhaps you need an assistant to keep participants out of the room till the appropriate time, help present stimuli, or take notes.

Equipment

You may need equipment for the presentation of stimuli and/or for the collection of data (e.g. recording equipment, a computer, flashcards, a timer). Some procedures used in the published research rely on complex equipment. Computers can display words or pictures for timed periods and can accurately record reactions to them. Fairly simple programs can achieve this. Be practical about what you can achieve and, if necessary, use the old pre-technology methods of, say, flashcards and (if it will give sufficient accuracy) a stopwatch. As always, take advice on what is expected of you and how best to achieve your objectives.

Designing an experiment

If possible, base your experimental design on one that has been run before. You can try to match it exactly (replication) or alter one dimension. Published experimental reports vary in how much information they give you about exactly what was done and what stimuli were used, so you may only be able to approximate to previous work. If so, aim to identify what was central to the experimental design.

Experimental comparisons can be made in different ways and may require different statistical treatments (see Chapter 20). The major comparisons are as follows.

Two identical groups ...

The assumption is that the two groups would perform in the same way given the same conditions and input, so that, if you vary the conditions or input, that is why their performance varies. Assigning people to groups can be done randomly if the numbers are large enough. Alternatively, share the genders and ages equally between the groups. Do the same for any other factor that you feel could be relevant (such as ethnic origin, past experience, educational background, or handedness). Don't go mad, though: hair colour and favourite ice-cream flavour are unlikely to have a bearing on most experiments.

... Doing different things

Here, the experiment is based on the assumption that Group A would perform like Group B if it was given Group B's task and vice versa. The reason for not giving both groups both tasks (which is certainly permissible in the right circumstances) is that doing one task spoils you for doing the other. Example: memorizing household items on a tray, compared with memorizing the names of those objects on a list (see Project 2).

. . . Doing the same thing in different conditions

There are several variations on this, including the following:

- Both groups perform the same task, but Group A is prepared one way, Group B another: do different things happen? (Look at Project 27.)
- Group A undergoes a process (such as training), Group B doesn't: do different things happen? Here, B is acting as 'control' group, against which the effect of a process can be measured: in medical trials, one group receives the new drug and another receives a dummy (placebo) drug, to see whether any recovery is due to the drug itself or due to the patient's reaction to being treated (as in Project 3).
- Both groups complete the same task, but the conditions under which they complete it are different (see Project 1).

Two groups that are different in some specific way doing the same thing

Here, you want to keep the stimuli, training, and procedures the same and just compare the effect of being a Group A person as opposed to a Group B person. You need to be able to explain why you think the two groups might perform differently: are you assuming that their brains are wired up differently; that different lifetime experiences will influence their behaviour; that one group will have more confidence than the other? Examples: a comparison of children of different ages; a comparison of males with females; a comparison of native speakers with non-native speakers.

One group doing two different tasks, or one task in two different conditions

This is appropriate where doing the first task (or in the first condition) will not invalidate the results of the second. It is best to take precautions, however, against possible order and practice effects (see below). For example: participants recite familiar nursery rhymes (or days of the week) and a poem they've only just memorized while bouncing a table-tennis ball on a bat: is their physical accuracy different when they have to think more about what to say next?

Using published results as your control

If you are replicating a published experiment, you can compare your results with those in the original, instead of building a comparison into your own experiment. However, this really does require you to have matched your stimuli, participants, and conditions very closely with those of the work you are replicating.

More than two groups?

You can compare more than two groups or conditions, but this complicates the results because each group and condition needs to be compared with each other one. Keep to two if you can: to find an age difference, you can compare 18–24-year-olds with 50–55-year-olds: you don't need the ages in between. Don't split groups after the event: if you didn't plan to compare males and females, then don't try to do so after you have the results.

Things to think about

- Will you tell your participants what you're looking for before they do the experiment? What effect would it have? If you don't tell them, are they likely to try to guess (thereby adjusting their behaviour in uncontrollable ways)?
- Will your participants be intimidated by the experimental set-up (see Chapter 16)? How can you alleviate this without compromising the rigour of the experiment?
- Are your stimuli unambiguous? For example, young children may have difficulty interpreting line drawings. Do the stimuli reflect any cultural and social stereotypes that may be inappropriate for some of your participants?
- What exactly are you testing? How will you know if you have found an effect? Does your experiment really measure what you intended? How will you score or assess the data?
- Where are you going to get enough participants and will they be homogeneous enough?
- How will participants, parents, teachers, and so on feel about the 'testing' dimension? Can you explain clearly your plans and how the data will be used?
- Where can you run it? Do you intend to bring the participants to one unfamiliar place, so that none of them have the advantage of feeling at home? Can you avoid external interruptions?
- Will you have to run the experiment lots of times (on individuals or small groups)? If so, how will you ensure that all the conditions are identical each time?
- Do you need special skills or techniques for presenting the stimuli (for example, with child participants, in operating puppets convincingly)?
- Look after your data: summarize your data into clear tables and remember to label them fully. Refer to the content of the tables explicitly, pointing out the important information. Do calculations carefully and check them. Make sure that totals tally.

Order effect

If one group is doing more than one task, or in more than one condition, or with a series of stimuli, how are you to be sure that any differences you find are not simply to do with the order in which the tasks or stimuli were presented? The most straightforward way to cancel out order effects is to split the group in two and present the tasks or conditions in one order to one group and the other order to the other. Then add the results together. If participants always scored better on, say, the first task or condition, then the differences will cancel out, because half the participants will have done one task or condition first and half the other.

Floor and ceiling effects

If you make a task too difficult, then everyone will score zero and you'll have nothing to compare! This is called a 'floor' effect. If the task is too easy, everyone will score the maximum and the same problem will occur. This is called a 'ceiling' effect. Your task should be pitched so that everyone performs well inside the range of possible performances (so that, say, if the score potential is 0–20, then the lowest score is about 3 and the highest about 17). Don't expect to know intuitively how to achieve this: that's what a pilot study is for (see Chapter 1).

Practice and fatigue effects

If you were to draw a graph of an individual's performance in a task, you wouldn't be surprised to find that they performed better as they got more accustomed to the task (the 'practice' effect) and worse as they got tired and/or bored (the 'fatigue' effect). Provided that everyone's scores went up and down symmetrically for practice and fatigue and that everyone became accustomed and got tired at the same rate, you could find a way of making allowances for this. But people aren't like that. However, there are ways of reducing the potential of these two effects to skew the results:

- Give everyone some practice sessions, so that they don't use the experiment itself to build up to speed.
- Design the experiment so that the activities don't go on too long. Obviously, you can't pre-empt at what stage people will become tired, but you can use a pilot study to ensure that you don't seriously overstep the mark.
- If some important types of stimuli are positioned at the beginning of the test and there is a general tendency for the scores to be lower than on later ones, you will not be able to tell whether this is due to the nature of the stimuli or the practice effect. Counter this by dividing the different types of stimuli randomly across the test and having different random orders for two randomly split groups. The idea is that a practice or fatigue effect will show on the first or last stimuli irrespective of what those stimuli are, while a genuine stimulus-specific effect should show up on those specific stimuli irrespective of when they are presented. Do not aim to run statistical comparisons on the two groups who get the stimuli in different orders. The results should be pooled, to minimize the effect of those orders.

Emergencies

It can be very distressing if, after all your hard work, your experiment 'goes wrong', whether that simply means that you can't support your hypothesis or that the procedure is actually unworkable, though the latter can be avoided in most cases by running a pilot study. Unforeseen circumstances such as a fire in the building or a breakdown of the equipment are just bad luck. However, many apparent 'disasters' are salvageable:

- If the results are inconclusive, that is a result in itself – maybe the claim from the literature upon which you built your hypothesis is not correct or the phenomenon is not measurable in the way you thought. Try to find some possible reasons why you got what you did, especially identifying whether there was any problem with the experimental design. This is how real research actually works: you use each experiment as a way of understanding the bigger picture and working out what to do next time.
- If the procedure has gone completely awry, you may have time (or be able to negotiate time) to rerun the experiment, in which case you can treat the original as a(nother) pilot. Alternatively, you may be able to salvage some of the results and report just those.
- If there really is nothing to show for it, obviously you need to negotiate with your tutor, but do so in the confidence that anyone who has run experiments has experienced bad luck or bad judgement and so you should get a sympathetic hearing. Offer to write up the experimental design critically and discuss what the various possible results would have meant. Add a section on ways in which problems of the kind you experienced could be avoided in the future.

- Occasionally, an experiment turns out to have been a poor way of finding out the thing it was designed for, but incidentally to have ended up measuring something else. So consider whether it is possible to find other patterns in it: you may find that you have another experiment embedded within the one you actually ran. Obviously, however, be careful with this strategy and take advice, because most investigations are only suitable for answering the question they were designed to answer.

Advantages of experimental research

- The history of science in the Western world clearly demonstrates how important experimental investigation is seen to be. Indeed, there are many who find it hard to conceive of valid research that is not experimental.
- A well-planned experiment gives you results that can be processed easily, to provide clear evidence for or against a pre-specified hypothesis.
- There are (in theory) no loose ends or awkward corners, and results are easy to relate to each other and to other experiments done in the same way.
- A clearly described experiment can be improved upon in future work or replicated by others.
- Experimental data is much more focused than, say, a recording of spontaneous speech or informal interview/activity data, so it is easier to make sense of, to process and to evaluate.

Disadvantages of experimental research

- Experiments pare the situation down to its bare minimum. Some situations can be treated in this way, but others can't. There is a danger that in the process of controlling the experimental design you lose the very essence of what you are trying to examine.
- It is easy to measure the behaviour of people operating in experimental conditions but how could you compare it to their behaviour in non-experimental conditions? (You couldn't do it by experiment, so what would be your basis for comparison?)
- Experiments usually end up being harder than they look, and it is easy to bite off more than you can chew.
- The more participants you have, the less likely you are to know a lot about them; there may be hidden variables contributing to your pattern of results. Experiments on people are always subject to much more 'unexplained' variation than those on white rats or vials of potassium permanganate, and they are liable to give ambiguous results. There is a good chance that, when you have made your calculations, there will be no statistically significant differences at all. However, this does not mean that your experiment has been a failure. You can write it up with every bit as much confidence as you would if you had made a major new discovery.
- Some people (children, for example) do not make good experimental participants. They may have too short an attention span, feel uneasy about being tested, or be inhibited with a researcher.
- You may only discover when you analyse the results that a participant has not really understood what he/she is supposed to do.
- Avoiding design faults, such as potential ambiguities in the stimuli or instructions, can be difficult.

For guidance on writing up your experimental work, see Chapter 1.

14

Questionnaires, interviews, and focus groups

If you want to find something out about people's knowledge or beliefs, one very obvious way is to ask them. There is a range of techniques for doing so, from formal tick-box questionnaires sent by email, to open face-to-face discussions. Although you are quite likely to choose only to use questionnaires *or* interviews, rather than both, we discuss them together in one chapter, because they share a lot of features.

For present purposes, when we refer to the 'questionnaire' we mean a document that is filled out in writing (or electronically) by the informant. An 'interview' entails the researcher presenting the questions to the informant orally and recording the responses either in written notes or on an audio recording for later transcription and analysis. Thus, we include under 'interview' what is sometimes referred to as the 'spoken questionnaire'. Mixed formats are also possible, however. You could administer the questions in writing and ask the respondents to record spoken responses on audio or video. Conversely, you could administer questions orally (say, to a group of respondents) and ask them to write their responses down. A 'focus group' involves interviewing a group of people together about a particular topic, in order not only to discover their individual views but also to observe how the group's interaction develops those views towards patterns of consensus and/or disagreement. You can find useful guidance on all three of these techniques in Bryman (2012), Dörnyei (2007) and Sealey (2010). For guidance on using questionnaires in second-language research, see Dörnyei (2002) and Dörnyei and Taguchi (2009).

Focus groups, interviews, and questionnaires can help you find out about people's linguistic and social behaviour, attitudes, beliefs, and perceptions. They can also be used to elicit comments on a recording, text, or picture.

Deciding if you need a questionnaire, interview, or focus group

What exactly is it that you want to know? Is asking your informants the best way to find it out? If you want to know how good people are at something, then asking them to tell you how good they are may not be as effective as testing them. But, if you want to know what they think or believe about something, or what they do in situations that you cannot observe, asking them may be the obvious approach. Whether a questionnaire or an individual or group interview will work best may depend on the potential impact for *your* investigation of the key advantages and disadvantages of each approach (see later). It is worth considering all your options at first, until you are certain you have what is best for your needs. As a general guide, remember that certain consequences arise from each method. Questionnaires administered without your being present are capable of providing a large quantity of data that you cannot easily control the detail of, while interviews tend to give you detailed information from a few people. Focus groups enable you to 'interview' more people, but you will not end up with a totally clear impression of each individual's views – the strength of the focus group lies in the construction of a group view. Which approach is most appropriate for answering your research questions?

Common uses of interviews, focus groups, and questionnaires

These are as follows:

- Traditional dialectology, to help produce linguistic maps and atlases
- Urban dialectology, to elicit information on how speakers' accents and dialects change between informal and formal situations, vary according to sex, age, and social background, and change over time
- Sociolinguistic work on attitudes towards language, including such matters as non-standard accents and dialects, slang, new vocabulary or pronunciations, female vs male speech features, dying or minority languages, and multilingualism.
- Second- or foreign-language teaching and learning, including motivation, learning style, aspirations, and needs analysis
- Language surveys, investigating, for example, which languages are spoken in a specific area, when these languages are used, and proficiency levels in the different generations of speakers
- Ethnographic ('whole-culture') research (see Chapter 7), to gather a wide range of information about aspects of specific cultures and societies, including linguistic data
- Data-gathering about perceptions and memories of a linguistic experience, such as asking jury members about their reaction to technical explanations provided in the course of a trial.
- Focus groups are particularly useful when investigating topical issues, on which people may not yet have formulated a clear individual opinion, so that discussion with others helps them think through aspects of the issues for the first time.

Logistics

Participants

Any participants can be used, provided they are able to understand the questions and can provide responses (that is, that they can write and/or speak intelligibly in at least one language or dialect shared with the researcher). See Saville-Troike (2003: 99–103) for considerations relating to the selection of subjects, including child respondents.

The number of participants you use often depends on entirely practical matters. Focus groups need a critical mass to work well (between six and ten participants seems to be effective), and you will normally need more than one group in order to establish the range of views that can emerge. Although questionnaires work with any number of respondents, their true usefulness is with large numbers of them. A large sample will be more representative and can lend greater weight to your claims. Interviews cannot be administered to as many people, and care needs to be taken that the few whom you select for interview are truly representative of the population you are interested in.

Indeed, for all three approaches, the participants have to be selected carefully to ensure that as reliable and representative a sample as possible has been obtained. You may work either with a 'random' sample, where 'everyone in the population to be sampled has an equal chance of being selected' (Wardhaugh 2009: 158) or with a 'judgement' sample, where you select your participants according to your preferred criteria, or else a range of representative criteria such as social class, age, gender, or education.

If you use a judgement sample, you need to consider two major things: compatibility and representativeness. To ensure compatibility, you need, where feasible, to obtain at least minimal reliable background information on your respondents. To compare responses from a group, there need to be some baseline features in common, so that it is clear why a comparison is valid. For example, if you were comparing attitudes to mother-tongue teaching in a Polish immigrant community and a Somali immigrant community, it would make sense to ensure that all your interviewees had children, that all used the mother tongue to a similar extent at home, and perhaps, even, that all of them were of the same sex, as differences in any of these variables could otherwise confound your results.

Representativeness is not always easy to achieve. Saville-Troike comments that 'often the people who make themselves most readily available to an outsider are those who are marginal to the community, and may thus convey inaccurate or incomplete information' (2003: 102). She also notes that such 'marginal' group members may 'interfere with the acceptance of the researcher by other members of the group' (ibid.).

Personal information, confidentiality, and anonymity

In seeking personal information, a balance needs to be found between getting what you need and being intrusive, or costing people time and extra work. With child subjects, be aware that they may not even know their own name and address, and that school records may not be up to date. If you promise anonymity or confidentiality to subjects, you must keep your word (see Chapter 16).

Limitations of self-report

The 'self-report' element of an interview or questionnaire means that you gain a direct window onto the informants' own views and beliefs. However, there are some limitations:

- Respondents cannot always tell you what they actually do, only what they *believe* they do – self-reporting is not necessarily very accurate because we often don't know ourselves very well. This limitation is difficult to overcome but it is important to report your findings appropriately: rather than saying 'All the teachers prioritized content over accuracy', say 'All the teachers said that they prioritized content over accuracy', for you only know the latter, not the former.
- The information you get will heavily depend on the way that the questions are formulated and what choices, if any, you offer as possible responses. Thus, care must be taken not to

unintentionally influence the findings by building assumptions into the formulation of the questions, or omitting potentially important details.

Ways of getting information

The best way to get information is not always the most obvious. Your aim is to help the informant give you the information you need, and you must think about whether the questions you have formulated will do that successfully. There is a lot to be said for the **direct** (or **explicit**) **approach**, where you are straight and truthful about your interests. It minimizes the risk of being misunderstood and can help your informants to trust you and your questions. However, there can be disadvantages too. Saville-Troike (2003: 102) notes that respondents will sometimes try to provide the answer that they think will please you (courtesy bias) or, conversely, may deliberately try to mislead you (sucker bias). In addition, if your topic includes stigmatized or distasteful issues, they may feel negatively about participating if you tell them directly what you are aiming to research. Direct questioning takes quite a lot of preparation. Investigating a dialect, you would need to go armed with wordlists to elicit pronunciation, and objects, pictures, and/or carefully worded probing questions to elicit vocabulary.

In an **indirect (inexplicit) approach**, the questions you ask are a distracter, and provide the information you want indirectly. For instance, if you wanted to gather data on an elderly person's pronunciation, you might get better data by asking them about their childhood than by asking them about pronunciation itself. You might find out more about a teenager's use of swearwords by asking about emotive issues than by quizzing him/her about the words. Thus, for some kinds of investigation, an indirect approach will make the informants' responses more reliable: there is less motivation to hide or distort anything. On the other hand, your informants may well develop their own opinion about what you are really looking for and perhaps, in trying to be helpful, go off at an irrelevant tangent.

The form of a question matters too. An **open question** offers the respondent a chance to talk or write at length, and that is often just what you want. The classic open question begins with *Why*, or *Can you tell me about* … In an interview, open questions are the gateway to following up interesting issues. In a questionnaire, they provide you with qualitative detail. On the other hand, they can lead to digressions, leaving you with irrelevant material. Open questions are particularly effective in focus groups, where the intention is to generate discussion.

A **closed question** requires only a short answer, with no direct opportunity to expand. Examples include: *What other languages do you speak?* and *Do you like the sound of this voice?* One advantage of closed questions is that they allow you to gather a great many pieces of precise information. However, they have drawbacks too. One is that they can appear rather patronizing. Informants do not want to feel that they are being treated like idiots and you run the risk of receiving flippant unhelpful answers. Another disadvantage is that closed questions may tend to prejudge the issues and possible responses. Open questions might reveal things you did not know were even there to ask about.

The reason why closed questions nevertheless remain a popular and valued means of gathering data is because they provide answers that are easier to process and score for. Closed questions make possible a range of formats for tallying and comparing responses, and often lead to quantitative analyses. Two of the most familiar types of closed question are **true/false questions**, and **yes/no questions**. However, these are rarely useful in linguistic research because, on their own, they give so little information. Fortunately, several other, more useful, closed-question designs also exist.

A **semantic differential** scale provides respondents with pair of adjectives with opposite meanings, at either end of a scale. Respondents indicate the approximate position on the continuum between the two that best represents their attitude to, or impression of, a stimulus (see Figure 14.1). It is a means of eliciting subjective reactions to words, speakers' voices on tape, and so on. In order to avoid the respondent construing one end of the scale to be 'worth more' than the other, it is a good idea not to use numbers for the points on the scale, though they can, of course, be added later by the researcher in order to make the data processing easier. One objection to using the semantic differential scale is that it relies on respondents having the same understanding of the adjectives you use. So avoid using adjectives for which this problem might be particularly acute – those, for instance, that are likely to be interpreted on the basis of personal experience, such as *motherly, educated,* or *stressed.* For examples in second-language research, see Larsen-Freeman and Long (1991: 35–6).

Your impressions of voice A on the recording:								
friendly	—	—	—	—	—	—	—	unfriendly
unintelligent	—	—	—	—	—	—	—	intelligent
inactive	—	—	—	—	—	—	—	active
reliable	—	—	—	—	—	—	—	unreliable

Figure 14.1 Semantic differential scale

Another scale that elicits informants' subjective responses is the **Likert scale**, also known as the **attitude scale**. A statement expressing an attitude is presented and the respondents indicate how strongly they agree or disagree with it (see Figure 14.2).

It is important to preserve endangered languages						
1	2	3	4	5	6	7
Strongly disagree			Neither agree nor disagree			Strongly agree

Figure 14.2 Likert scale

One disadvantage of using the semantic differential and Likert scales is that you force people to choose from a range of responses, of which, perhaps, none might really fit their ideas. You may find that interview respondents sometimes offer an explanation along with, or instead of, a straight response, and questionnaire respondents alter the categories by hand or do not indicate any response on the scale. In both cases, you will then have problems when you come to analyse the data, which you will have expected to be clear-cut and complete. Another problem can arise if all the scales are oriented in the same direction. In written presentation, the positive adjective (semantic differential) or the 'strongly agree' category (Likert scale) might always be to the right, say. Some researchers like to swap the direction between questions, to ensure that respondents have to read each one carefully. However, if you do reverse the scale, and respondents do not notice, they may mark the wrong location on the scale, giving a different answer from the one they intended. Since you may have no way of knowing if this is the case or not, you could have some data that you suspect, but cannot prove, is invalid.

A different kind of limitation with Likert scales arises if you want to apply statistical tests to check significance (see Chapter 20). Although you can derive frequency scores for each category choice on the scale, it is often desirable to have values that are more like 'scores'. One solution is to use a program like ImageJ (http://rsbweb.nih.gov/ij/features.html), which measures the exact location of a mark on a line. Your participants indicate how far along a continuous line from, say, 'strongly disagree' to 'strongly agree' their view falls. You scan in the hard copy and, using the cursor, pinpoint the start of the line, the participant's mark, and the end of the line. The program calculates the response as a percentage of the total line. (Keep all the scales facing one direction, see above.) Since these are 'quantitative data' (see Chapter 20), it is possible to calculate averages and standard deviations and do parametric statistical tests. However, it is worth considering whether researchers can be certain that participants truly are equally able to place a mark *anywhere* on the scale, as such tests assume, or whether their choices are biased towards certain positions.

Another way to elicit closed-question judgements from respondents is using a **ranking scheme**. This approach will be familiar to you if you have ever entered a product-promotion competition where you had to put a set of desirable features into their order of importance. In the linguistic domain, Dorian (1981) asked English/Gaelic speakers to order a set of 13 reasons for being a Gaelic speaker into their order of importance (see Dorian 1981: 166; Romaine 1995: 313–14). For general information, see Fasold (1984: 152).

A technique most people are familiar with, though it is by no means the easiest to design well, is **multiple choice**. The respondent is presented with a question (or an incomplete statement, or stem), and must select the appropriate answer (or completion) from a list of several possible alternatives (see Figure 14.3). Whereas in a multiple-choice test of knowledge each question has one correct answer and a set of three or four distracters, in an exploration of attitude or motivation, all the answers might equally be valid, with the choice indicating a range of potential views. Multiple-choice questions benefit from a written format, because it is difficult to keep several choices in your memory at once if you only hear them spoken.

| I have known her _____ three years now |
| (a) whilst   (b) for   (c) since   (d) besides   (e) at |

Figure 14.3 Multiple choice

The **matched guise technique** is a specific technique that is often used in association with a questionnaire investigation of language attitudes. Though the precise format may vary, the basic technique usually involves respondents being played recordings of voices and then being asked to evaluate them, using semantic differential scales (see above), on a range of criteria including intelligence, friendliness, co-operativeness, reliability, honesty, and so on. The technique can reveal which languages or linguistic varieties (accents, dialects) the respondents unconsciously associate with the most positive and most negative personality attributes. On the basis of such tests, several large companies have located their telephone sales or services departments in regions where the local accent is associated with high ratings for intelligence, friendliness, and trustworthiness. The recordings typically involve a single person speaking first in one dialect, accent, or language and then in another (that is, in two 'guises'), giving the same information. The respondents must not realize that both recordings were made by the same person. See Fasold (1984: 149–58) for more information. Hughes *et al.* (2012) and Wardhaugh (1993) also provide summary examples.

Things to think about

- There are many potential pitfalls with interview and questionnaire studies and a potentially high price to pay if the main study encounters practical problems. So it is very important to run a pilot study (see Chapter 1).
- How will you make your respondents trust you and want to help you with your research? Do they really understand who you are and why you are asking them questions?
- Do not make too many assumptions about your respondents, especially if they are much older or younger than you are, differently educated from you, or from a different country. Will they know what a questionnaire is? Might their previous experience of interviews have led them to perceive them as threatening or intrusive? Will they understand your speech? Can they read sufficiently well to cope with written questions?

Having considered some of the general approaches and issues relevant to asking people questions, we now consider separately the details of the three main techniques, the questionnaire, the interview, and the focus group.

Questionnaires

Questionnaires can be used to collect both qualitative and quantitative data, and are suitable for a range of research questions, including ones that require several types of information. At their most tightly controlled, questionnaires allow data to be collected in the same, replicable way from a large number of informants. This makes a comparison of the results easier and the conclusions clearer.

For some research, the questionnaire can act as the sole source of data. For other research, it is best used in association with other methods of data elicitation (e.g. interview, test, observation) to gain the full picture. Because of this, questionnaires often do not operate as a substitute for transcription and analysis, but rather complement them.

Advantages

- Useful for surveying a lot of people in many different locations.
- The identical format means you can easily find corresponding answers across your cohort of informants.

Disadvantages

- If an interesting issue is mentioned, about which you would have liked to ask more, you will not know until afterwards.
- If you send the questionnaire to people (by post or electronically), you may have a low response rate (perhaps only 20 to 30 per cent). Low response is not only disappointing, but may skew the sample, since taking the trouble to reply may reflect a personality trait that also colours the answers. Those who do not respond might have given different answers.

- Unless you are there when the questionnaire is completed, you will never be certain whether: the right person filled it out and without help; it was done in one sitting; the questions were answered in sequence order; all the respondents took roughly the same amount of time over it, and completed it in comparable circumstances.
- If you have had to rely on someone else to distribute or administer the questionnaire (e.g. in another country), there are inevitable risks. No one will understand the aims as clearly or be as committed to obtaining good data as you are. If you have left it to someone else to identify 'suitable subjects', you have lost control of that aspect.

Formulating your questions

The aim of designing an effective questionnaire is to make it as easy as possible for your informants to provide you with good-quality reliable information. Think through the stages carefully and try things out before committing yourself. With limited space, every question must be there for a good reason. Aim not to collect any information that you have not already planned a specific use for. The test is: point to a question on your questionnaire and ask yourself 'Why do I need this information?' If you can't think of a good reason, consider dropping the question.

Questions must be **simple and unambiguous**. Be careful not to combine several questions into one big one, because you may not get a complete answer or know what exactly the answer refers to. For instance, a question like 'If you have visited a Spanish-speaking country, where did you go, or if you have not, where would you like to go, and why?' is far too complex. Also avoid **loaded questions**, where an underlying assumption is built in. For instance, in 'Why do people think that the Birmingham accent is unpleasant?', you do not allow for the possibility that people *do not* think that the accent is unpleasant. Similarly, don't use **leading questions**, where the wording suggests the 'right' answer, e.g. 'If someone has a strong regional accent and dialect, don't you expect them to be from a lower social class?'

Begin the questionnaire with some easy questions, so that the respondents feel they are getting on well. If there are several harder or more time-consuming ones, space them out, or, alternatively, preface them with a statement such as: 'The following three questions require slightly more detailed answers.' This indicates to the respondent the nature of the new task and how much of it there is.

If you provide a choice of answers, make sure that you cover all the possibilities. Try to imagine a range of different people trying to find an answer to match their precise circumstances. Alternatively, include 'other' and a space for a comment.

Include one or two cross-referencing questions, in which you ask, in different words, for the same information as in a previous question. This gives you a check on the reliability of the responses. It is often possible to 'turn the question round' so that a positive response in one version corresponds to a negative one in the other. Be particularly careful, however, that, in doing this, you do not alter the emphasis. For the answers to be comparable, you must have asked for exactly the same information.

Presentation

The single most common response to questionnaires is to throw them in the bin, whether that is immediately they arrive, when completing them gets too difficult, or six months after the deadline, when they turn up in a pile of 'things to do some time'. How can you minimize the risk of non-return?

- Provide a covering letter or other form of explanation of who you are, what you are doing, and why, and why the respondents' help will be so valuable to you. Also explain your intentions regarding confidentiality or anonymity (see earlier, and Chapter 16).
- If your informants are geographically dispersed, think about whether you will post them a hard copy, or whether you could perhaps email one. The latter is quicker and cheaper, and although people ignore or forget electronic documents as much as they do paper ones, at least they don't have to buy a stamp and find a postbox.
- Postal questionnaires are cheaper than telephone interviews but the costs are not negligible, especially if you need to pay for the photocopying and both directions of the postal charges.
- If your informants are all in one place but too far away for you to go to, how about asking someone else to administer the questionnaire for you, at a set time and place, such as at a meeting or in a class? There are potential disadvantages (see above) but it might be the best solution all the same.
- If you can be present, would it be better to ask people to complete the questionnaire while you wait than to let them take it away with them? (It may depend on how long the completion will take and how detailed you want the answers to be.)
- Electronic questionnaires give you data that are already transcribed for quick searching and analysis.
- Even more analysis-friendly might be a web-based questionnaire, where the responses are automatically catalogued in the format you need, and stored in an archive – if you cannot set this up yourself, see if anyone in your university's computing service can. The basic SurveyMonkey package (http://try.surveymonkey.com/) enables you to ask up to ten questions of up to 100 respondents free of charge, and you may find your institution pays an annual subscription that can provide access to the other packages on offer with this, or another similar, provider.

You can learn a great deal about the design of questionnaires by considering your own response to the ones that you have had to complete in the past. For example, have you ever:

- not felt that any of the answers on offer actually reflected your view?
- not really understood what the question was getting at?
- not wanted to answer a particular question because it was too personal, painful, or difficult?
- not really cared whether you gave accurate or truthful answers, because the whole thing seemed rather silly, or ill thought-out?
- been reluctant to give certain details because the questioner wanted your name and address and you were worried about where the information would end up?

These common reactions, and many others, can seriously compromise the success of a questionnaire survey. Do a careful pilot study (see Chapter 1) to ensure that you have not made it in any way difficult for your respondents to provide accurate and honest information.

- Make sure that the instructions make the task look easy. If there are different routes through the questionnaire, mark them clearly and ensure they look logical (e.g. If you answered 'No', please move to question 13).

- Give it a clear and roomy presentation, including adequate space for answers, but …
- … don't let the questionnaire get too long.

Here are some key points to consider:

- How clear are your instructions and the questions themselves? If something turns out not to be clear, will circumstances make it possible for you to clarify it to everyone, or just to the person who queries it? Is there any risk that different understandings of a question will make your results difficult to interpret? How can clarifications be provided that do not suggest particular answers?
- Even one question that respondents consider to be too difficult or too intrusive could jeopardize the number of returns you get, if the questionnaires are completed out of your sight.
- Have you experimented with different formats for different questions? You might want to combine various of the closed-question formats described above, with requests for more open-ended answers.
- If you are using closed questions, give opportunities for 'comments', if you think they might help you interpret the responses you get. However, only do this if you plan to write about your data in a qualitative way: if you only need to count up how many of each response you have got, then you won't want to engage with discussion based on voluntary comments.
- At the bottom of each page (paper or electronic), give an instruction to go to the next page. It may seem obvious, but it is not worth risking even one respondent missing a whole page or more of questions by not realizing they were there.
- What will happen if pages get separated on your paper questionnaire? See if you can think of a way to make sure you will be able to reunite loose pages with the right document.
- At the end of the questionnaire, invite and leave a space for final comments, thank the respondents for their trouble, and provide clear instructions about who it is to be returned to, how, and by when.
- Have your respondents ever seen a questionnaire before? They are relatively unfamiliar in some communities, and respondents may not be sure how to deal with them. Children may never have filled one in before.
- Some people may be suspicious of what looks like an official form.
- People with low levels of literacy, or whose native language is not that in which the questionnaire is written, may find the whole exercise intimidating.
- People can suffer from 'questionnaire fatigue', if they have been confronted with too many other questionnaires before yours. This may make them less willing to take part or they may tend to give irresponsible answers.

Interviews

Interviews are stressful to administer and must be carefully planned. You will need a list of questions that you know will work – if you modify your questions too much during the course of a set of interviews, then you may find that the answers from the earlier ones and the later ones cannot be pooled or compared. You need to find a balance between simply barking out questions in a preordained order, and letting the interviewee take over and tell you things you don't want to know.

Open questions (see earlier) are highly desirable in order to get detail and depth, but they can create difficulties if the informant digresses in one question into the territory of a later question. You need to be able to quickly assess the risks and benefits of curtailing an account now and returning to it later, versus letting the interviewee continue, and perhaps losing the logical flow you had planned for your questions later on. Because they don't fully understand the 'routine' of questionnaires, children are particularly prone to digress and to think it strange if information that has already been given is asked for again.

One solution is to plan out a series of potential pathways through your list of questions, according to how the interview is developing. Doing this can also enable you to include questions that become relevant only if a particular previous question has been answered in the affirmative, say, or others if it has been answered in the negative. While it is impossible to anticipate every possible answer, the more you are ready for, the less likely you are to be disorientated by what a respondent says.

Conversely, you can deliberately plan to control the order in which topics are covered, so that you gradually develop a particular line of thought in your respondent. It is even possible to pose the same question twice, once near the start of the interview and again near the end, and quite naturally elicit different answers, because of what has happened in between. This sort of sequential control is much easier to achieve in an interview than in a written questionnaire, where the respondent might look ahead, or go back and alter an earlier answer. However, carrying it off requires a lot of confidence.

Be aware of your own personality. How well do you think you will succeed in getting the kind of rapport with your subjects that you need for your particular study? Doing a pilot study can make this easier to judge and will give you practice in approaching the task in a way that works for you.

Similarly, consider whether your respondents might be influenced in their responses by who you are, or what (they perceive that) you represent. If your racial, social, or gender identity might influence what they say, is there anything that you can do about it? Perhaps someone else could do the interviewing? In all events, remember to mention any such concerns in your write-up, and to comment on what effect they might have had. Respondents might also be affected by the very fact of sitting face to face with someone, particularly if the information being provided is sensitive or embarrassing. Remember that your primary aim is to get answers to your research questions. If your respondents would be more comfortable with the anonymity of a questionnaire that does not bear their name, then this might better meet your research needs in the end.

General procedures

Where possible, you should expect to audio- or video-record interviews. Although this means that you must allow time for transcribing the key points later, it is well worth it. You can concentrate all of your attention on the interviewee(s), rather than continually having to break eye contact by looking away while you write things down. You can also avoid having to make snap judgements about what to note down and what to omit. A third advantage is that you are not a victim of your own handwriting, which may be less than legible during hurried note-taking.

You can interview people individually or in a group. Group interviewing enables you to collect data from a lot of people very quickly and individuals can spark off ideas in each other. On the other hand, you may find that one person influences others by inhibiting them from saying what they really think or by leading the group into apparent agreement. People may speak at the same time, so it is hard to hear all the different points being made and might possibly be difficult later on to tell who is who on the tape. One type of group interview is the focus group, which we consider separately below.

Interviewing makes possible the collection of certain types of information that would be less easily gathered by questionnaire or in a focus group. In **data elicitation**, you deliberately set up situations, or ask specific questions, that will give you the data you want. This gives you a considerable level of control. For obvious reasons, an interview is particularly suitable for collecting oral data, and is often used for dialect studies.

Questions can be asked either directly (e.g. 'What is your word for this?', 'Do you like the local accent here?'), or by tightly controlling the conversation so that relevant information naturally emerges. Although direct questioning about language or attitudes towards it is a well-tested technique (as in, for example, the Survey of English Dialects – see Chapter 9), it does have its disadvantages. While it is straightforward to ask someone directly about their memories of the war or what their school years were like, asking them questions about language does not always produce useful results, as speakers do not always know much about how their variety works and/or may be self-conscious about it.

In conversation, the different forms of a verb can be explored by asking questions like: 'So, did you do that often?' and 'What did you do exactly?' This might provide replies like: 'Oh, we were always X-ing' and 'We only X-ed when it was a games lesson.' For more guidance on investigating accents and dialects, see Chapter 9.

Asking for intuitions is rather different from general questioning or eliciting linguistic forms, because you are trying to get a 'view round the back' of the process that has led your informants, or would lead them, to their linguistic responses. As we do not by any means always know what we are doing when we speak or write, this technique has a limited scope but is quite useful within that. It requires the subject to have self-knowledge and the vocabulary to talk about language (metalanguage). Unlike other types of data collection, it is important that you conduct the interviews yourself, rather than delegating the job to someone else. Questions can be concurrent with a task (such as 'Tell me how you're working that out' or 'Why did you choose that one?'), retrospective (such as 'Look at the video/listen to the recording and tell me what you were thinking as you wrote/said that'; 'Why do you think you said it that way?') or even more direct, such as asking a simultaneous interpreter 'Do you think that you plan a whole sentence before you start speaking? Why?'

Subjects' accounts of their own opinions and intuitions, possibly alongside the results of a task they were completing, will appear initially chaotic and may add up to several hours of material. When recording, try out the position of the microphone in advance, as people tend to speak quietly when they are talking about their thought processes.

There are several advantages to intuition data. There is a real sense in which you can get inside the mind of the subject. Whereas in experiments you are trying to interpret the mind of the subject solely from observing his/her behaviour, here you can actually get the subject to help you. Also, subjects know that they are being recorded, so there's no need for clandestine activity. The fact of their knowing is unlikely to compromise the results, unless they are inhibited from being totally honest, for some reason (e.g. if you get them doing word association for sex vocabulary). Disadvantages, however, include the following.

- Data based on people's intuition is scientifically imprecise and will never give you more than a rather cloudy view of what is 'really' going on. Not everyone sees intuition studies as valid. It can be argued that intuition is like an iceberg: nine-tenths hidden, so the little bit you can get at is not representative of the whole.
- There is no way of controlling how much information of a particular type people either have access to or choose to give, nor whether it is accurate or not (they could even lie).
- Respondents who are not used to talking about language may lack the knowledge and analytic tools to give you anything but brief and vague answers.
- Finally, the intuition itself is filtered through the interpretation and expression of both the informant and the researcher. This is not insignificant: to what extent are we able to verbalize our intuitions at all? And how compatible are the experiences of two people (interviewer and interviewee) or their vocabulary for talking about internal processes?

As with most types of research, what you get out depends on what you put in. In this case, what you put in must be designed to access information that the informant may not even know they had, and also to provide you with something that you can make sense of.

If you have a long set of comments from different informants, you need to find some way of presenting them thematically, to tell more of a story than you'll get from just listing them.

Gathering general data for later analysis

In this approach, you are conducting a general interview simply in order to gather a body of language data. You might do this if you wanted to avoid the participants knowing what you were looking for (because if they did, they might behave differently). Alternatively, you could simply want to use this 'personal' method to obtain data from particular individuals (such as elderly neighbours), as an alternative to, say, taping speech from the radio.

By definition, you will be letting the conversation go where it will, even if you prompt with questions. Certain types of topic may elicit good accent and dialect material, such as reminiscences; others may increase the likelihood of language that is not influenced by the presence of the interviewer, as in the case, say, of emotive issues, such as recalling a bereavement or an emergency situation. You can usually increase the chances of getting speech that is relaxed and that contains informal features (such as strong dialect or accent) if the speakers talk about things they are familiar and comfortable with, and/or things associated with their childhood. If you want to avoid them knowing you are interested in their language, enlist them to help you draw their family tree, or say that you are studying changing fashions in forenames, the history of games played in the street and playground, childhood pranks and punishments, or changes in occupations and work patterns. Alternatively, you could ask about the history of the local area. If possible, have some old photographs and read up on the area beforehand.

With children, you may need props in order to elicit the data. Practise in advance with any pictures, toys, games, flashcards, and so on, and have a trial run with participants like the ones you will use in the data collection. Check with parents or teachers that the activities you have chosen are appropriate for the age of the informants.

A word of warning: the general questioning technique might seem like a good way to collect data before you have developed a clear idea of what you want to study, but it is not.

You could well end up with a lengthy set of data and not know what to do with it. In other words, make a positive decision to gather data in this way, for reasons related to the specific analysis you have planned.

Focus groups

Focus groups have been used for years in commercial settings, to find out how consumers react to products, and they are increasingly used to canvass the political views of 'ordinary people'. They can also be very productive for linguistic research of many kinds but, before you decide to use them, be sure that they are the best way to meet your needs. The word 'focus' is there for a reason and they are most successful where the topic under discussion is very clearly focused. The focus comes from some shared topic, often a video that everyone has just watched, or an experience they have jointly been through. This focus enables the researcher to be confident that everyone is talking about the same thing, since there is no opportunity, as there is in an individual interview, to probe about each person's specific experiences or understanding of key concepts under discussion.

Effective focus groups tend not to be heavy on formal questioning, as you might find in a group interview, but rather facilitate guided discussion. Part of your interest needs to be the way that being in a group affects how the individuals respond – that is, how individuals develop or defend their views in the light of what others say. If, conversely, the group dynamic will be a complication for you, as you try to find out what each individual would have told you on their own, then you should be conducting individual interviews.

The role of the 'interviewer' minimizes in an effective focus group, and becomes closer to that of a 'facilitator', who sets the ball rolling and then tries to stay out of the way as much as possible. Doing this effectively is a skill that may require some practice. A major advantage of the reduced role of the interviewer is that it is left to the participants to determine which of the issues is foregrounded and which others are backgrounded. Even though you will expect to intervene at certain points to introduce new topics, you will find that each group discusses different things, and indeed not necessarily the things you had expected or hoped – something you need to anticipate and be prepared for. The more that different groups go off in different directions, the more you may be tempted to conclude that it is something *about* that group's characteristics (jointly or individually) that determined its focus. However, that may not be so: conversations in groups reach crossroads at regular intervals, and going down one path rather than another can be somewhat arbitrary – the same group on another day might have done something different. So you need to develop a sense of how much it is reasonable to read into the specific outcomes that you got.

Organization

Organizing focus group meetings takes time and thought. Where should you meet? Where will people go if they arrive early or late? Can they park? Do you need to pay their travel expenses? Should you provide them with refreshments? What will you do if some people don't turn up? If someone arrives late, when you have already started the meeting, should you let them in even though they have not received the same briefing? But the biggest question of all is: Whom should you invite? This depends, once more, on what you are trying to achieve. A useful test is to write, at the planning stage, the following extract from your write-up: 'This particular profile of participants was selected because ...' and then try to fill in the rest of the sentence with an eye to how it will fit in with your research account. Suitable completions might be 'they were all within an age range that made them likely to have done X/studied Y/confronted Z' or 'they had all identified themselves in a survey as having an interest in X/experience of Y', and so on. Try to avoid putting yourself in a position where you would have to say 'they were the only people I could find in the Student Union bar'.

Since you will expect to have several groups, you can decide whether you are interested in how *similar* the discussions from similarly constituted groups will be, or how *differently* things develop in groups of different types. In the first case, you may be able to assemble a full list of participants and assign them randomly to groups. However, you may have to be pragmatic in accepting that people's availability on certain days or at certain times will play a role in who ends up with whom. In the second case, you will need information in advance about each person that will allow you to allocate them to the appropriate group. 'Appropriate' groups are determined on the basis of what you are trying to find out. For instance, if you were interested in the question 'Should minority languages be used in nursery schools?', you might choose to have contrasting groups: minority-language-speaking mothers of nursery-age children; teenagers whose parents speak minority languages and who did and did not attend nursery schools that used the language; nursery-school teachers from ethnically mixed and unmixed areas; and so on. In this way, you would hope to demonstrate that the issues are complex, and differently perceived by different parties – something that might not emerge so clearly if you had random groupings.

Reporting

What you can report from a focus group will be different in kind from what you can report from questionnaires and interviews, since you will not necessarily have a clear sense of anyone's full view, nor, if the group has worked well, that any individual has only one unchanging view.

For fairly obvious reasons, it is a particularly good idea to video-record focus groups and, if possible, with more than one camera, so that you can capture everyone visually. Without that visual record, you may struggle to work out who is saying what. For more guidance on recording, see Chapter 12. When it comes to transcription, you may be faced with a great deal of complex conversational data. Don't assume that you must transcribe everything before you start. Wait until you know what you need, and transcribe just that. Remember also that orthographic (conversation) transcription (see Chapter 18) is a device for representing speech so that it can be analysed structurally. If you are interested in the *content* of the conversations and not how the conversations are conducted, then you may in fact not need to transcribe them using the full orthographic conventions at all. Once again, the rule is: ask yourself what you are trying to achieve and then consider the best way to achieve it. With focus groups, in particular, don't make unnecessary work for yourself, for your data will be rich enough to occupy you with relevant analyses.

For more information on focus groups, see Bryman (2012), Krueger and Casey (2000), Litosseliti (2003) and Sealey (2010).

15

Observation and case studies

The terms 'observation study' and 'case study' are not mutually exclusive: you may be doing both. Observation studies involve the collection of data without manipulating it. The researcher simply observes ongoing activities without making any attempt to control or determine them. In a case study, some or all of the data may result from observation but it is also possible to collect data in other ways. In this chapter, we first of all consider observation studies and then case studies.

Observation studies

Normally, you would study ordinary people or people with some recognized disability, about which generalizations can be made. You can use any number of participants. Remember, however, that you may need quite a lot of background information on each participant and that each will produce quite a large quantity of unsorted data, so small numbers are advisable. Data from participants who are expected to share patterns of behaviour can be pooled. Participants with contrasting characteristics can be compared. They can be of any age, gender, or background but, if you are pooling results, the fewer variables there are of this kind, the more compatible the participants will be. You may gather your data in various ways, including audio- or video-recordings when you are present or absent, recording from the radio or TV, or re-using data previously collected for some other purpose (but in this case you may not have access to all the background material that you need).

Observation data is qualitative in the first instance, consisting of recordings, transcriptions, and notes relating to your participants' behaviour and language (spoken and/or written). You may subsequently derive quantitative data from it (such as the number of words in each utterance).

Advantages

While many types of research can only measure *elicited* behaviour because specific tasks are presented in a controlled environment, observation enables you to examine non-elicited behaviour as and when it occurs (e.g. slips of the tongue, paralinguistic behaviour, interactional behaviour, and pathological phenomena). This allows a much more 'holistic' view of how language is being used in context. For this reason, it is a technique much favoured by ethnographers (see Chapter 7). It is also more flexible than, say, a controlled experiment, where any extraneous or unplanned event could potentially invalidate the results. Another advantage is that observation studies are relatively easy to administer. Indeed, by using pre-recorded or broadcast material, you can avoid many of the practical difficulties of data collection. Observation can be used at the planning stages of other types of project in order to get ideas or to determine the feasibility of the main procedure and can supplement information gathered by other methods.

Disadvantages

Making secret recordings is generally considered unethical, yet sometimes the participants' awareness of an observer or of recording equipment can affect how they behave (the observer effect or the observer's paradox). Another disadvantage is that some observable phenomena (such as slips of the tongue) are not densely packed in data, so you may need a great deal of material to get even a small set of interesting observations. However, you do not need to transcribe or analyse anything that is irrelevant to your study. Also, it can be difficult to predict what sort of material you will get: topics may shift, the things you were looking for may not occur, and observation studies are difficult to replicate on another occasion because there are so many uncontrolled variables. Finally, it may not be easy to produce well-focused conclusions because the data is so unstructured and multifaceted. It may be hard to decide which parts of the data to submit to the assessor as part of the project, as the points of interest may be spread over a large quantity of material.

Things to think about

- Be very sure of precisely what you are looking for. While you may not be able to envisage what specific *examples* of a phenomenon you will gather, you should know before you start what phenomenon you are investigating. In other words, don't just switch on an audio recorder and hope that something of interest will materialize! Try to ensure that you are looking for something that is likely to occur reasonably often.
- To remain within ethical guidelines, you should normally aim to get consent in advance of your observation and/or recording. If you do collect the data secretly, you will need the participants' permission after the event. With child participants, you will always need the consent of parents and schools.
- Different types of phenomena will come from different sources. For example, if you wanted to look at spontaneous slips of the tongue, there would obviously be no point in recording a play from the radio. Nor would you be likely to find many in an interview between an experienced journalist or presenter and a politician. Slips of the tongue tend to occur when the speaker is tired, nervous, flustered, or drunk, so you would need to consider how best to record someone in that state. Asking your participant to read out loud some very complicated unfamiliar text would be one way to increase the likelihood of observing speech errors.
- Be aware of what role you, as the observer, might be playing in the dynamics of the situation you are observing (see Chapter 1). You might put participants at their ease by being a full participant in the procedures. You would be counted by them as one of the group and you would join in with what they were doing on an equal basis. However, it is important, as a 'participant observer', not to try to direct or manipulate, nor to test or interview.

- Alternatively, you may decide not to be present at all during the recording, and leave a recording device on while you are out of the room.
- To help summarize your results, devise a checklist for features based on other studies and use this as a framework. For each feature, systematically record whether the participant(s) used it or not. At the end of each section, you can then produce a table or list, bringing out any patterns. If you have a transcript available, remember to note line numbers for occurrences for features, so that these can be stated in the project.
- Consider carefully how to draw conclusions from your results. Focus on finding patterns in the data that relate to your original research questions. Are there any differences between individuals for the features you were interested in? If you have not found the differences you expected, explain why this might be. Scrutinize your sampling, data collection, and analysis procedures for possible causes. Perhaps previous studies on which your expectations were based were flawed and your results have helped to demonstrate this.

Case studies

A case study is usually most appropriate where a given individual has some behaviour worth observing, but where the circumstances are so individual or rare that there would be no benefit in combining the results of observations of that person with those of others. A case study would also be appropriate if the phenomenon being observed is so complex that a variety of different kinds of data is needed in order to gain a full picture, with the interest lying in how that particular individual manages the different processes. Case studies are particularly suitable for longitudinal research (where you observe the individual change over time and the focus is on comparisons of the individual's performance on a sequence of occasions). They are a vehicle for both qualitative and quantitative research.

Data can be collected using the techniques of observation, interview, and/or testing, and will often be supported by additional information, both linguistic and non-linguistic, from parents, carers, and official records. Whether you are dealing with language plus a special circumstance or creating a 'profile' of a normal individual's development or progress in one or more aspects of language, you will also need to accumulate background knowledge of what the range of normal development is, so that you have a baseline against which to interpret the patterns you observe.

You will normally need the consent of the participant and anyone else involved (doctor, speech therapist, teacher, family) and you must be able to demonstrate strict confidentiality. You may have to travel to your participant on several occasions and fit in with others' schedules. Remember to take into account the cost in time and money and to consider how you will transport any equipment you need. If you are administering tests, you can design your own or ask the therapist, doctor, or teacher for access to some of those that are standard as diagnostics.

Advantages

You can study someone you already know, in his/her own home or some other environment familiar to him/her; this increases the likelihood of observing representative behaviour. Often there are good opportunities for observing the language of carers and/or teachers as well. The data is valid in its own right, irrespective of how representative of a population the individual is. If you are conducting a longitudinal study, this gives a more genuine picture than can be gained by comparing individuals at each of the different stages (a cross-sectional study). As you become more familiar with the case, you can develop your investigation in new directions.

Disadvantages

Relying totally on data from one person can be risky. The participant's personality, disabilities (or limitations), prejudices, and anxieties may be difficult to deal with. If you are collecting data over a period of time, the participant might move away or the circumstances change so that your visits are no longer welcome. If your ideas about the study change as you proceed, your early data may be less useful than you hoped or you may be stuck with a test design or observation procedure that is not appropriate to what you later want to find out. Working over an extended period it can be difficult to remain objective. Also, a child participant may take things less seriously as the level of familiarity increases. Other disadvantages of case studies include: the time they can consume, not only for you but also for the participant and his/her carers, teachers, and so on; the small sample size, which means that few generalizations can be made; and the fact that relevant data can be elusive.

How to set up a case study

Accessing a participant can take time, so it's better to know someone already. If you do not, work through a professional such as a teacher or speech therapist. If you are approaching a patient you don't know, take advice about how to do this or get yourself introduced by someone they know. Do what you can to make it clear to the patient and his/her family that you are *not* an expert and that you are there only because they are kindly doing you a favour. If negotiating with a parent about access to their child, explain your intentions in as much detail as possible. Don't insist on the parent being excluded from the room if they would rather stay. Keep the parent on your side by asking for advice and insights.

A foreign- or second-language learner can be contacted through a school or college, or through an agency providing language support. However, you could also set up your own arrangement with a friend who fancies studying a new language; but remember you will be relying on them to see it through, so make sure they are serious about it and are in a position to continue the study for as long as you need.

Before you begin collecting data, do some initial observation to identify likely areas of interest (you can't look at everything). This will help you to design any tests you need to elicit particular phenomena.

Remember that you are dealing with real people (participant and carers) who may be in a delicate state and/or sensitive about their language performance or their role in supporting and teaching the participant. So be scrupulous in your preparation and sensitive and professional in your approach. Ensure that the participant *really* does not mind being observed or tested and *really* understands what's involved. Think carefully about what you expect the participant to do and how you will cope if they don't, can't, or won't. Part of this entails finding out as much as you can about how to do your research *before* you get there: read journals, ask the professionals, and be guided by them.

Dealing with the results

Avoid accumulating hours of recorded material or other observations without any clear idea of what you will do with it all. Try to transcribe and analyse the data as you go along: it reduces the amount to be done in the final stages and it gives you a chance to see if any of your data-collection methods need refinement. By knowing what you are looking for, you can transcribe just the material that is relevant, saving a lot of time. If you have several types of data to analyse (spoken, written, tests, observed, elicited, and so on), keep a careful eye on staying within your project word limit.

It is not sufficient simply to list (even in summarized form) what you have seen; you need to pull out patterns and relate them to models and/or theories. It is fine to home in on one or two interesting aspects and leave the rest aside – don't feel you have to describe everything in equal detail and depth. However, it is important to indicate when you *have* left some things aside, so that your assessor doesn't think you have failed to see them.

16

Ethical considerations in research projects

For obvious reasons, there have always been strict rules about trying out new drugs on people in medical research but, in recent years, attention has also been paid to the rights and welfare of those who are used in other types of research, including language studies and linguistics.

Ethics policies and guidelines

Most universities and colleges have their own ethics policies and you should check with your supervisor whether there are any procedures you have to follow in order to have your research plan approved. Ethics policies generally focus on ensuring that data is handled sensitively, that there is no unnecessary deception or distress caused during the data collection, and that participants have sufficient information to make an informed decision about their participation.

The key points most relevant to linguistic research are:

- The welfare of the participant is paramount.
- All research procedures should be within the law and in line with the recommendations of the appropriate community, academic, or professional bodies.
- All participants (and guardians and/or carers) should be told the purpose and nature of the research project with information on potential benefits being put into the context of any potential risks.
- All explanations of the project should be in a form that the participants can understand. This means that you need to:
  - think carefully about the participant's language ability or level of understanding,
  - be sensitive about the demands that your research is putting on any informants with special needs,
  - ask for the consent of an appropriate adult (usually parent or guardian) in the case of a child and the consent of the school if you are carrying out your research in the classroom.

- Informed consent should be obtained in writing from all participants.
- Participants must know that they have the right to withdraw from the project at any stage without any obligation to explain their decision.

- Confidentiality or anonymity should be assured for all participants in any reports of the project and, if this is not possible, participants should be told so, as part of the consent procedures.

The difference between confidentiality and anonymity

With anonymous data, even *you* do not know who has provided what. For instance, you might issue a survey questionnaire that does not require respondents to give their name, only information about, say, their age and gender. Generally, there is no way for you to trace back a specific response to an individual. Where data is confidential, you *do* know who is who, but you undertake not to let anyone else know. For example, you might interview or observe people and, in your transcription and write-up, give them a different name and (if necessary) alter certain personal details that do not have a bearing on your analysis.

Anonymity precludes you from using any sort of code number that can lead you back to an identity for each respondent. If you feel you will need to know, for example, who has and who has not returned the questionnaire, or if you may need to do follow-up interviews, then do not offer anonymity, but rather confidentiality. You might favour anonymity when, for example, you are investigating delicate issues, such as names for intimate parts of the body or knowledge and use of swearwords. It is often assumed that respondents will be more candid when anonymous. However, they can also be less responsible, and you may be left unsure about the validity of their answers.

Is your data really anonymous?

Handwriting and linguistic style can be distinctive. If you believe that you will recognize certain responses and it might matter to the respondent (e.g. the information is sensitive or embarrassing), consider designing your data-collection tool to gather multiple-choice responses rather than lengthy written ones. If you cannot do this, you could suggest to your respondents that they write in capital letters (to make writing less identifiable), or in note form (to minimize the opportunities for language errors). Alternatively, they could respond electronically, if you can arrange for the files to be deposited in a central database that does not store their identity (ask your computer-services support team for advice).

Is your data really confidential?

You must remove *all* clues to identity before submitting your work. This includes the labels on your files and disks, and the identification data on any sample transcriptions or analyses in your appendix. It also means *not* thanking the participants by name in your acknowledgments section! If you are submitting audio or video data, then clearly there is a potential problem with confidentiality, since someone might recognize participants even if they don't know their names. You should make clear to the participants that the data you are collecting will be seen by your assessors. You could take the precaution of a statement in your write-up such as:

> The material provided in this project has been collected on the understanding that confidentiality will be observed in relation to identities of and details about individual participants. The author respectfully requests that those reading this project maintain this confidentiality code. Thank you.

For further guidelines on ethical considerations in linguistic research, see http://www.baal. org.uk/dox/goodpractice_full.pdf. A useful chapter on ethics in social science research is given in Bryman (2012).

Data Protection Laws

Many of the ethical issues that researchers need to bear in mind are legislated for. In the UK, this is done through the Data Protection Act (1998), the Freedom of Information Act (2000) and the Human Rights Act (1998). The Office of Public Sector Information (www. opsi.gov.uk) website allows you to read the legislation online. Most countries have some equivalent laws and you should be able to find out about these via your local or university library. The following information about the situation in the UK should provide pointers as to the issues that you need to consider.

The purpose of the **UK Data Protection Act 1998** (http://www.legislation.gov.uk/ ukpga/1998/29/contents) is to protect the rights of people about whom personal/sensitive information is stored on computer. This is achieved by two basic means. Anyone who stores data on individuals must *only store what they actually need*, and must *register as a data user*, saying what the information will be used for. The law does not give an individual the right to control what is done with information stored about them, but it is possible to request a copy of what details are being held and/or distributed. This right was established in the UK in the **Freedom of Information Act 2000** (http://www.legislation.gov.uk/ukpga/2000/36/ contents). The Human Rights Act (1998, effective from 2000 in UK, http://www.legislation. gov.uk/ukpga/1998/42/contents) was incorporated into UK law to 'give further effect to rights and freedoms guaranteed under the European Convention on Human Rights'.

The problems that the Acts are designed to address are mainly as follows:

- gathering data for one purpose and then using it for another, without the permission of the individual involved;
- storing information that is incorrect.

How does Data Protection legislation affect academic research?

Data Protection legislation is not designed with academic researchers in mind, but it can affect them. For example, under the UK's Data Protection Act (DPA), if you were doing some case studies and you kept computer files that had personal information in them, then you might need to register. The easiest and most sensible procedure would therefore be to keep any personal information about your research participants on paper. Note that in the UK, if you put the information onto computer solely as part of the word-processing of your work, that is, just for presentational purposes, it is *not* subject to notification. There are some special provisions in the UK's DPA for data that is for 'research, history and statistics'. These permit data to be kept indefinitely (not normally allowed) and also allow researchers to use data for research that was not collected for that purpose. Data can be held for research purposes, provided that it is not used for anything else and the identity of individuals cannot be worked out from the write-up.

Note

The information provided in this chapter is for guidance only. If you are unsure if you are in breach of ethical or legal requirements, you should check with an authoritative source.

Part III

TOOLS FOR DATA ANALYSIS

17

Transcribing speech phonetically and phonemically

In most situations, slight differences in the pronunciation of a sound by different people, or by the same person on different occasions or in different linguistic contexts, can be overlooked. It is enough to recognize what the words were, or that a given sound was a kind of 't' or a kind of 's'. But, where pronunciation is the focus of your work, you need finer distinctions. The sorts of studies where this may apply include:

- accents
- first-language acquisition
- second-language acquisition
- language impairment
- speech errors
- conversation
- language and gender.

The difference between phonetic and phonemic transcription

If you are focusing on pronunciation, it will soon become clear to you that you need a means of transcribing sounds in some detail. Specifically, you need to be able to demonstrate on paper the often subtle differences between two sounds that do not contribute to any change in the identity of the words but which are, nevertheless, salient within the study you are doing. This is done using *phonetic* script, and transcriptions are enclosed in *square brackets*. On the other hand, in order to write about the *relationships* between two pronunciations, you will also need a transcription system that allows you to consider a sound in general terms, independently of its detailed realization on a particular occasion. For this, you need to use *phonemic* script, enclosing transcriptions in *slanted brackets*. This may seem like a mere difference of degree, but it is not.

Phonetic transcription

Phonetic transcription can be likened to an infinite palette of paints. It is possible, in theory, to depict in phonetic script differences as subtle as the most finely attuned ear can hear. To achieve this, there is a large inventory of symbols, including a set of **diacritics**, which act as pointers to exact articulatory positions or ways of making a sound. Thus, to give just two examples, the diacritic [₊] written beneath a symbol indicates *tongue further forward* and [ː] written to the right-hand side of a symbol means *of greater duration*. A full set of symbols, including the diacritics, can be found on the IPA chart on page xii.

Because the detail that can go into a phonetic transcription is potentially infinite, a phonetician needs to make a decision about what to include and what to leave out. In practice, the relatively untrained ear simply does not hear much of the detail, and so the rule of thumb for most students is *if you can hear it, write it down*. However, as detailed transcription is time-consuming, avoid transcribing material or detail that you know you will not need. A detailed phonetic transcription is termed *narrow* and a less detailed one *broad*. A broad transcription may only use a few more symbols than a phonemic transcription, but it is *not* one, for all the reasons outlined in this chapter.

Phonemic transcription

Phonemic transcription is like having an infinite palette of colours organized into sets called *green*, *blue*, *red*, and so on, with any given shade belonging to one of those sets. Each language – indeed, each variety of each language – has a small set of **phonemes** (such as /t/, /m/) and each actual utterance of a sound can be categorized as being an **allophone** (**phonetic realization**) of one of the phonemes (see below). Most (but not all) allophones have a phonetic identity that is predictable from the surrounding environment. The kind of /p/ that you get at the beginning of a word like *patch* in English is, characteristically, an aspirated one [pʰ] and the kind of /d/ that you get at the end of a word like *reward* is normally a devoiced one [d̥]. Linguists have worked out the distributions of the different phonetic realizations of the different phonemes by studying how English works. Each language is different. This implies that you cannot transcribe a language, or a language variety, phonemically until you know what phonemic category to put every sound that you hear into. If you do not – and often part of your analysis will be establishing the phonemic categories – you must use phonetic script.

In summary, phonetic script *describes* what you are hearing; phonemic script *interprets* it. Beware of using phonemic script as an easy option: there are hidden implications within it, which, if not accounted for, could seriously compromise the validity of your analysis.

A few notes on phonemes

Phonemes are *notional* sounds: they are *categories* of sound. You can't hear a phoneme, only example phonetic realizations of one. Compare the category 'red': it is not a colour in its own right. Rather, to illustrate 'red', you need to find examples of it. In the same way, the phoneme label /t/ is just a cover term for the complete set of its possible phonetic realizations, i.e. for what you could actually *hear*. So you will be writing that a speaker's realization of the phoneme /. . ./ is [. . .]. This enables you to compare different speakers (or different speech events in one speaker) while being sure that you are comparing like with like.

Two sounds may be superficially rather similar, but belong to different phonemes. We demonstrate these phoneme categories by identifying words that are identical except for the choice of that phoneme. These are called **minimal pairs.** For example, in English, /ɛ/ and /ɪ/ must be phonemes because there are minimal pairs such as *led* and *lid*, in which the difference in the sound of the vowel is the only thing that keeps the words separate. So part of the definition of the phoneme is that, if you swap one phoneme with another, you can make another word. Contrast this with some sound characteristics that are *not* phonemic for English. Suppose, on one occasion, a person said *sitting* as [sɪtɪŋ] and on another said it as [s:ɪtɪŋ] (i.e. with a longer, hissy /s/). This would not stop it being a pronunciation of the word *sitting*, because in English the sounds [s] and [s:] do not contrast in a way that could create a new word. They are therefore not separate phonemes of English, but just different examples (allophones) of the phoneme /s/. However, we can imagine a language in which this contrast *was* phonemic, because there was a minimal pair /sɑɪt/ (meaning, say, *blossom*) and /s:ɑɪt/ (meaning, say, *big toe*). In this language, you would have to be very careful how hissy you made your 's', otherwise you could end up saying that the big toes in the garden smell very beautiful this year. Native speakers of Japanese and Korean sometimes struggle to differentiate the English phonemes /l/ and /r/, because in their languages this phonemic distinction does not exist, and [l] and [ɹ] are just allophones of the same phoneme.

Categorizing the sounds we hear into phonemic classes allows us to retain a view of the phonological structure of a language, even when the pronunciation is rather odd. If we aren't sure what we heard, we use our knowledge of the language at all levels to make sense of the message, so that we can work out which phonemic category the rogue sound must belong to. Thus, if a foreign learner of English said *I sailed on a* [ʃiːp], we could tell from the context that he meant *ship* and not *sheep* and conclude that, for him, either [iː] was an allophone of the phoneme /ɪ/, rather than of /iː/, as it would be for native speakers, or else he had not, so far, succeeded in creating two phonemes, /ɪ/ and /iː/, at all (perhaps because his native language did not have that contrast).

You can read more about phonemes in Roach (2009, Chs 5 and 13), Collins and Mees (2008), Davenport and Hannahs (2010, Ch. 8), or virtually any other introduction to phonetics and phonology.

Phonetic and phonemic symbols in word-processing

There are a number of specialist fonts that you can download for phonetics, including the ones used by the Summer Institute of Linguistics (SIL) http://scripts.sil.org/cms/scripts/page.php?item_id=DoulosSILfont. However, it is increasingly possible to use symbols from your word-processing program, so do check the options there. The choice may be greater for some base fonts than others, so if necessary write your entire document in Times Roman to maximize what you can do. If you search for fonts on the Internet, remember only to download from a reliable site and ensure you have your antivirus software switched on. Bear in mind that if you are submitting your work electronically, your supervisor or assessor may not be able to read or print the symbols correctly, if they don't have the same font on their own computer. It is best to send a test document to check this. Alternatively, save the file as a pdf – but check that the symbols are correct there, as some pdf writers won't reproduce symbols they don't recognize. Ask your supervisor or a technician for help if necessary.

Hints on writing about pronunciation

When you are writing about a real piece of data (or about how a real piece of data would sound if only you had a recording of it), use square brackets and give as much phonetic detail as you can hear, or as much as you need to make your point. When you want to say that the sound in square brackets is an example of, say, a 't' or an 's', use slanted brackets for the latter (/t/, /s/), because you are referring to the categories, that is, the phonemes.

When you explore the pronunciation of an individual speaker, use a phoneme checklist such as the one given below, or the one in Hughes *et al.* (2012) to help you find examples of each phoneme. Next to the phoneme symbols on the list, transcribe your examples with square brackets (because they are real sounds that you have heard) and put in as much information as you can. You are then in a position to compare the pronunciation you have heard with other possible pronunciations of that phoneme.

Despite what most of the books imply, there is *not* simply one inventory of phonemes for English. In other words, it is not simply the case that different varieties of English have different pronunciations for a given phoneme. In some varieties, the actual set of phonemes is slightly different. So, look out for examples of a phoneme on the checklist dividing in two parts, or of two phonemes on the checklist collapsing together. The best example of collapse for British English is the phonemes /ʌ/ and /ʊ/. Both phonemes exist in most parts of the south of Britain, giving minimal pairs such as *could* /kʊd/ and *cud* /kʌd/, and *put* /pʊt/, and *putt* /pʌt/. But, in many parts of the north of Britain, these words all contain the same vowel: /kʊd/, /kʊd/, /pʊt/ and /pʊt/. A second example derives from the fact that some varieties of English are **rhotic** (i.e. pronounce the *r* in *car* and *card*) whilst others are non-rhotic. Non-rhotic varieties may not differentiate between words like *law* and *lore*, *spa* and *spar*, which, provided the vowels do not differ, will form minimal pairs in a rhotic variety. Kreidler (2004, Ch. 4) provides a useful set of phoneme inventories for English, into one of which most, if not all, national and international varieties should fall.

You can find some examples of the phoneme inventories for different varieties of British English in Hughes *et al.* (2012). A good impression of the way in which phonemic and phonetic transcriptions will differ for the same data can be found in Brown (1990, Ch. 4). For a very practical approach, written to help learners improve their pronunciation of English, try Hewings (2007), which comes with audio CDs and CD-ROM. Note that textbooks on pronunciation have to reflect a particular variety. Thus, it is a good idea to use a book written in your own country or in the country that uses your target pronunciation. Collins and Mees (2008) offer, with a justification, an alternative to using British Received Pronunciation (RP) as the reference point, preferring Non-Regional Pronunciation (NRP) instead. The notes in the Checklist of Phonemes below give some indication of why this might be worth considering in your own practice.

Checklist of phonemes

Symbol	Example based on British RP	Notes
/iː/	b*ea*t	
/ɪ/	b*i*t	
/ɛ/	b*e*t	
/a/	b*a*t	Also often written /æ/; /a/ is arguably the better choice because the phonetic realization in modern RP is closer to [a] than [æ], which tends to sound old-fashioned
/ɑː/	b*a*rd*	
/ɒ/	b*o*dy	
/ɔː/	b*o*rd, b*oa*rd*	
/ʊ/	w*oo*d	These two phonemes collapse into one in some parts of Britain. That is, *wood* and *mud* rhyme, whether they both have [ʊ], [u], [ə] or (even) [ʌ]
/ʌ/	m*u*d	
/ɜː/	w*o*rd*	
/ə/	winn*er**	
/eɪ/	b*ai*t	Also often written /ɛɪ/, /ei/ or /ɛi/
/əʊ/	b*oa*t	
/aɪ/	b*i*te	Also often written /ɑɪ/, /ai/ or /ɑi/
/aʊ/	br*ow*n	Also often written /ɑʊ/, /au/ or /ɑu/
/ɔɪ/	b*oy*	Also often written /ɒɪ/, /ɔi/ or /ɒi/
/ɪə/	b*ee*r*	One increasingly common phonetic realization of this in RP is [ɪː]
/ɛə/	b*a*re*	One increasingly common phonetic realization of this in RP is [ɛː]
/ʊə/	p*oo*r*	This is a good example of how the phonemic inventory has got out of date. In RP today (except among older and particularly 'posh' speakers) there is no separate phoneme /ʊə/, because it has collapsed with /ɔː/. However, many regional varieties do retain this phoneme. You can check by asking informants to say the words *poor, pore, pour, paw* and *pause*.
/aə/	f*i*re*	Also written as /aiə/, and pronounced in a variety of ways, including, by some British southerners, /aː/
/p/	ro*p*e	
/b/	ro*b*e	
/t/	wro*t*e	

/d/	ro*d*e
/k/	spo*k*e
/g/	ro*g*ue
/tʃ/	broo*ch*
/dʒ/	hu*ge*
/f/	loa*f*
/v/	dro*v*e
/θ/	brea*th*
/ð/	brea*the*
/s/	gro*ss*
/z/	grow*s*
/ʃ/	fa*sh*ion
/ʒ/	vi*s*ion
/h/	*h*eart
/m/	roa*m*
/n/	loa*n*

/ŋ/   wro*ng*   Watch out for varieties in which the *ng* in spelling is pronounced /ŋg/. In these cases there is no phoneme /ŋ/ at all, because [ŋ] only ever occurs before /g/ and /k/ and never on its own, making it an allophone of /n/.

/l/	ro*ll*
/r/	*r*oll
/j/	*y*ear
/w/	*w*ear

*In *non-rhotic* varieties like RP, an *r* occurring between a vowel and a consonant, or at the end of a word, is not pronounced and therefore should not appear in the transcription. It is important not to be influenced by the *r* in the spelling of words, and to *listen* in order to decide whether or not there is an /r/ present. In *rhotic* varieties you will be able to hear the *r* in these positions and should transcribe it.

18

Transcribing speech orthographically

Fundamental points to bear in mind whenever you are planning to transcribe a stretch of speech include:

- For any analysis to be valid, the transcription of the data must be accurate. This is a time-consuming activity, as you may have to listen to the same stretch of sound many times, especially where several people are speaking at the same time. Therefore, don't be over-ambitious about the quantity of data you transcribe. Only transcribe what you need, and do not put in detail that is not relevant, such as phonetic details of the speaker's accent, unless you have a reason for doing so.
- For audio material, see if you can borrow a transcribing machine, which offers the facility to slow the speech down, so that the duration of the pauses can be measured more accurately. For digital data, software is available so that you can listen to data on your computer, with click-on options for starting, stopping, repeating, and slowing down the data.
- Never transcribe from the original. If an accident can happen, it probably will. Always make a copy and then lock the original away somewhere safe. Work from the copy. Some pessimists work from a copy of a copy.

How to organize the presentation of a transcription

Vertical alignment

The biggest challenge with this kind of transcription is in aligning different material vertically. In order to avoid problems with tabs and spaces, which look ugly and often don't transfer from machine to machine, create a table for your example, using different rows for each line and columns to match up the vertical alignment. Set the column dividers where they need to be for that particular example. Finally, select the option that makes some or all of the table's lines invisible. In example (1a) the lines are still visible. In (1b) you can see the effect of removing the lines (other than between the transcription and comment). You can dispense with the headings line once your reader can see what you are doing.

(1a)

Line	Speaker			Comment
17	L:	could you br-	[bring that with you	
19	F:		[I can bring this along yeah	*laughs*

(1b)

Line	Speaker			Comment
17	L:	could you br-	[bring that with you	
19	F:		[I can bring this along yeah	*laughs*

If you prefer not to use tables, you can use a non-proportional font such as Courier. In a non-proportional font, each of the letters takes up the same amount of space, so it is much easier to align your material. Compare the phrases in Table 18.1. On the left, the fact that some letters are wider than others means that the two phrases take different amounts of space, even though they contain the same number of letters. But on the right, all the letters are the same width, so words and phrases can be easily aligned.

Table 18.1 Proportional and non-proportional fonts

Proportional: Goudy Old Style font	Non-proportional: Courier New font
Illicit illusions	Illicit illusions
Ambulatory aspect	Ambulatory aspect

The key

Always provide a key to your symbols. This is because (a) not everyone uses the same conventions; (b) there are choices regarding how to transcribe some features; and (c) the assessor wants to be reassured that you know what you're doing. Quite deliberately, we are providing only one convention for each feature here. Be particularly careful to include in the key any symbols that might be mistaken for punctuation symbols (they usually mark intonation – see later). Otherwise, you might get penalized for apparently not knowing that punctuation itself is not used!

What to include

- Number every line. This makes it possible for you to refer to specific lines and for the reader to find your examples easily and check the wider context if required. Try to ensure that the numbers are not so far into the left margin that they are obscured by the binding or file grip. There is a convention for highlighting a particular line (see example 38) in a transcription.
- Many researchers like to use a column on the right-hand side of the transcription for comments, so that they don't need to be incorporated into the main transcription (see examples 1a and 1b above, and various other examples below).

Long turns

A short turn in the conversation on a single line does not lead to any difficulties for the transcriber. But suppose a speaker talks for a long time. If no one interrupts, you can simply run the speech on like normal text. But if someone says something during that speaker's turn, there will be an intervening line for the second speaker. To show that there is no break in the first speaker's utterance, use the latching symbol =.

(2) 81   W: tha- was [it? (.)] yeah we ha- we had eighteen of=

82   R: [yeah]

83   W: =them here a- all at once

Transcription conventions

The information below is organized in terms of what usually happens in conversation, and addresses the procedures of orthographic transcription from the inexperienced user's point of view. The conventions are based on those of Gail Jefferson, as described in Psathas (1995: 70–8) and Jefferson (1989: 193–6). Bloomer *et al.* (2005) or Merrison *et al.* (forthcoming) provide a similar list linked to examples from some well-known data.

Turn taking

As in a play script, name the speaker in the left-hand margin. Use a short form, such as an initial, to save space, giving a key at the beginning or end (each speaker should have a different initial or short form). If you wish to protect the identity of the speakers, use letters such as A, B, and C. A line of transcription should have one, and only one, letter or name in the margin. If the same speaker has several lines of speech, it is sufficient to label only the first. If several people speak at once, each should have a separate line. The only exception to this would be if two or more people deliberately co-ordinated an utterance in unison (like singing 'Happy Birthday'); in this case, it is acceptable (but not obligatory) to list them on one line:

(3) 19   J: C-come on then

20   R: Yeah (.) ri-

21   J: (sung) Happy birth =

22   J,R,K,S: (sung) =day to you: happy birthday to you . . .

If two people start at the same time, give them separate lines, beginning with a double opening square bracket:

(4) 12   W: [[Take it if y-

13   E: [[I mean (.) no I

Where one person begins when someone else is already speaking, use a single opening square bracket before the new speaker's words, aligned vertically with another at the appropriate point in the established speaker's line (example 5). If two people interrupt in close succession, do the same again with a third line (example 6).

(5) 57   R: so we didn't have to   [wait long
     58   T: [no we didn't

(6)   34   S: would you   [li-(.) like o-orange or ap[ple
      35   M: [we've got
      36   E: [yes please

Where one person finishes while the other continues speaking, use a closing square bracket in both lines:

(7)   9   T: till it cam- (0.5) we   [weren't all that] all that s-sure
      10   G: [but did you]

If someone starts speaking immediately another has finished, this is called **latching**. Use an *equals* sign at the end of the first component and the beginning of the second (example 8). If two people latch at the same time, mark them both (example 9). Latching can also be marked within the turn of a single speaker, if one idea immediately follows another (example 10).

(8)   132 A: before Sunday if you can=

      133 K: =I'm really busy at the weekend

(9)   19   R: so why didn't you after all that=

      20   F: =[[yeah

      21   G: =[[I was going to

(10) 172 E: after y-you turned him down=why did you anyway

Silence and non-verbal communication in conversation
Pauses

A pause too short to measure is indicated by a dot in brackets: (.). Pauses of measurable length are indicated in seconds and tenths of seconds. Give the duration numerically in brackets, e.g. eight-tenths of a second (0.8); one-and-two-tenths seconds: (1.2). Where the silence is in the middle of the speaker's turn, simply put the brackets on the same line as the speaker's words. If the silence comes between one speaker's turn and the next, give the brackets their own line. If there is a very long pause, this can be marked as ((pause)) but it is perhaps more consistent simply to time the pause and insert the time length in brackets.

In-breaths and out-breaths

Most of the time you don't need to indicate breathing, because it is a background activity. But an audible breath, in or out, should be marked. An in-breath might indicate that someone is trying to get into the conversation, for example, or an out-breath might be interpreted as a sigh. Breath is indicated by one or more '*h*'s, as follows:

• breathing out: followed by a dash

(11) 13   K: He was (0.6) hhh- no I s'pose not

- breathing in: preceded by a dot.

> (12)   51   O: Erm (0.4) .hhhh try the other (1.1) way roun-

- breath sounds associated with sobbing, laughing, being out of breath: in brackets.

> (13)   12   E: Then (hhh) he said wha(h)t ti(h)me d'you ca(hh)ll this (hhh)

Head movements

To indicate that someone nods (without saying anything), simply write *nods* in double brackets (14a) or in your comments column (14b). The same goes for other gestures, such as pointing, smiling, or head-shaking.

> (14a)   27   S: Who told you=don't tell me=Karen
>   28   E: Mmm ((nods))
>   29   S: ((smiles)) Okay

> (14b)   27   S: Who told you=don't tell me=Karen
>   28   E: Mmm   *nodding*
>   29   S: Okay   *smiling*

Dealing with unusual pronunciations

How to show that a word has been started but not finished

Use a hyphen at the point where the word ends (example 15). Note that because of English spelling it will not always be clear what the sound was that was uttered. If it matters, use phonetic script (see below). This notation works for slips of the tongue too (example 16).

> (15)   08   P: hurt him an- and hit his head on the ste- on the top of the
>   09   steering wheel

> (16)   42   F: there'll be pi- mist patches and some drizzle in the east

How to show an unusual pronunciation of a word

Because orthographic transcription was invented by sociologists, not linguists, it lacks some of the features that linguists are accustomed to employing for the close transcription of speech. Although phonetic script would be by far the best way to depict any pronunciation that could not be adequately indicated by conventional spelling, it is not often used. There are several ways of coping with the need to show a pronunciation more exactly. You can use conventional spelling and indicate, in double brackets or in the comments column, the relevant feature (example 17). Alternatively, use conventional spelling to approximate the pronunciation (example 18).

> (17)   05   D: he's a real bastard ((northern pronunciation))

> (18)   98   R: you need to move in really slooooly

Alternatively, skirt the issue in the main transcription and use phonetic transcription in the comments column and when discussing the item in the analysis (example 19). Remember to indicate in your key what an entry in square brackets in the comments column means.

(19)   16   P: an. then (.) y. you just got to go | [gɔɹə]

How to show a word that has been stretched out

Use a colon immediately after the lengthened sound. The more colons you use, the longer the sound:

(20)   12   S: we- well it was (.) eno: : : : : rmous

Coughs and sneezes

Write *cough* or *sneeze* in double brackets (21a) or use a comments column (21b).

(21a) 36   T: oh God ((cough)) tha- ((cough)) Go- could I h-have

       37   ((cough)) that wa- wa((cough))ter

(21b) 36   T: oh God ((hhh)) tha- ((hhh)) Go- could I h-have |
                                                                           coughing
       37   ((hhh)) that wa- wa((hhh))ter |

Transcribing unclear utterances

Sometimes a speaker mumbles. Sometimes there are several people talking at once and one or more of them is virtually drowned out by the rest. Listen to it again. Listen to it yet again. Sit back and try to hear it as if for the first time. Imagine you are there: what is the speaker *likely* to say? Play it to someone else and see if they can decipher it. Do whatever you can to minimize the quantity of indecipherable speech. If it really is impossible to understand, indicate that the utterance is there by putting empty single brackets for the appropriate duration (example 22). Alternatively, put 'indecipherable' in double brackets (example 23) or in your comments column if you have one. It is also quite common to use an asterisk for each indecipherable syllable (example 24). (In these examples, speaker W's turn is long enough to run onto a second line – (see example (2) earlier).

(22)   3   W: so he's (0.2) he's about to   [run off the guy c-come=

       4   T: [oh God (   )]

       5   W: = comes o]ver and

(23)   3   W: so he's (0.2) he's about to   [run off the guy c-come=

       4   T: [oh God (indecipherable)]

       5   W: = comes o]ver and

(24)   3   W: so he's (0.2) he's about to   [run off the guy c-come=

       4   T: [oh God (* * *)]

       5   W: = comes o]ver and

It may be that you know what was said but not who said it. In this case, put empty single brackets in the margin:

(25) 7 R: for a few minutes till=

  8 ( ): =huh you'll be luc-

If you are able to have a guess about what has been said, put your guess inside single brackets – this indicates that you have some doubt about it:

(26) 407 R: taken [it over again

  408 E: [(likely to be)

If you can hear the sounds but cannot work out what the words are, the convention is to make an orthographic representation of them inside single brackets. It is not standard to use phonetic script (but see example 19):

(27) 75 D: (mekka bunit cor)

Marking pitch, emphasis, volume, and speed

How to show standard intonation patterns

The intonation of speech is not represented in orthographic transcription with anything like the accuracy that a phonologist would expect. If you want to give greater detail, do a separate transcription of the relevant extract, using one of the standard systems of intonation transcription for phonology (see, for example, Kreidler 2004, Ch. 10 or Roach 2009, Chs 15–19). As indicated above, punctuation symbols are used for transcribing some of the specific intonation patterns of English. Although each represents the sort of pattern that we associate with it when it is punctuating written text, the application of the symbols is much more rigid, and they must be reserved for their defined purpose, as follows:

- a **falling tone** is marked with a full stop (period). To indicate a particularly noticeable fall, put a downward arrow immediately before it begins:

  (28) 3 R: There was ↓ nothing there.

- a **fall–rise** pattern, as when listing, or continuing at the end of a clause, is marked with a comma:

  (29) 9 K: I had (.) um (0.7) a ball, (.) a cricket bat, an (.) tha. (0.4)

  10   um a ball and a cricket bat

- a **rise** is marked with a question mark (but beware of using the symbol as punctuation by mistake – not all questions rise at the end, and not all rises are questions!). For a particularly noticeable rise, use an upward arrow immediately before it begins:

  (30) 21 F: Well would you ↑ like to be left behind?

- **animated tone** is indicated by an exclamation mark:

  (31) 732 B: You've got (.) to be joking!

For changes in pitch not associated with these familiar intonation patterns, see below.

Pitch features

Pitch movement is closely tied up with intrinsic (word, phrase) and emphatic stress. In addition, it often requires the stretching of the syllable so that there is time to achieve the effect. Because of this interrelationship, it is possible to mark pitch features by underlining parts of the stretched syllable. Basically, the underlined item is higher in pitch than what surrounds it, as illustrated below.

- a **drop in pitch** in a stretched syllable is marked by underlining the vowel immediately before the colon that indicates the stretch. To indicate a prolonged drop, extend the line backwards, i.e. towards the beginning of the word.

    (32)   65   G: It wasn't pounds it was do: llars

             66   R: What d'you mean do: : llars.

- a **rise in pitch** is indicated by underlining the colon following the vowel. A lengthened version is achieved by extending the underlining forward, towards the end of the word:

    (33)   74   L: a sto : : : rage container?

- a **rise and fall** can be shown by underlining the point of the highest pitch, implying that what comes before and afterwards is lower:

    (34)   08   T: ((sarcastically)) Oh yeah it was rea: : : : : : : : lly good

- a **fall and rise** cannot be shown using these tools, so use an arrow to indicate the fall (see example 28).

Emphasis

Underline the relevant words and combine this, as appropriate, with indicators of how the emphasis has been achieved, e.g. a falling tone (see example 28) or a change in volume (see below). If it is associated with a marked change in pitch, you cannot show emphasis independently of that, because underlining is intrinsic to it already. In all events, you can add comments in a right-hand column to describe what is happening.

How to show a change of volume

Use capital letters to show loudness, and a degree sign (superscript circle) either side of a quiet passage. Indicate whispering by writing *whispered* in double brackets or in the comments column:

    (35)   4   H: Mummy look there's FIVE!

             5   R: °don- (.) make so much [noise°

             6   H: [((whispered)) Mum[my there's=

             7   R: [°yes I know°

             8   H: = ↓five!

How to show a change of speed

A faster passage is enclosed in inverted angle brackets, or, to put it another way, in 'arrow heads' with their points inwards (example 36). There is not normally any need for specific symbols to indicate a slower speed of delivery. If someone speaks slowly, they must either be extending the words (in which case, use colons to show the 'stretch') or leaving gaps between the words (shown by the symbols for pauses).

> (36)   18   K: yes (0.5) if you like (0.1) cooking = > if you do like cooking it's <
>
>   (0.3) well it's no problem then

External events

The purpose of the transcription is to record everything that is part of the conversation. This means that an extraneous noise (a fire engine going past or the telephone ringing) does not need transcribing if it is ignored by the participants. But anything that provokes a reaction (e.g. a slight hesitation or a comment) should be transcribed. If in doubt, put it in. Notate it with a description in double brackets, e.g. ((telephone rings)) or a comment in the right-hand column. You should follow this up with a later entry ((telephone stops ringing)) unless it is clear from the context that this is the case. There is a special convention for notating applause, using upper- and lower-case Xs for loud and soft respectively, as in example 37 (Atkinson and Heritage 1984: xv):

> (37)   14   Audience: xxXXXXXXXXXXXXXXxxx

Presenting the transcription

To draw the reader's attention to something

Put a horizontal arrow in the margin, to the left of the speaker's name/initial (example 38). Alternatively, use a large dot. Only mark things that are central to your discussion, and remember to refer to them in your account.

> (38)   11   E: Leave that will you?
>
> →   12   K: Wh- ↓ what!

To show that you have omitted something

You are more likely to need to do this when you are quoting from your transcription in the discussion than when doing the transcription itself because, by omitting things, you are expressing an opinion about the relative importance of different parts of the whole. Show that you have missed out bits of a speaker's turn by using a horizontal sequence of dots:

> (39)   43   L: and I said . . . don't just don't try it

Use a vertical line of dots to indicate that turns have been missed out. Give the line numbers to make it clear what quantity of material is missing.

> (40)   123   F: so he go- .hhh goes um what's that! and she
>
>   .
>
>   .

.

.

131   F: so an he goes what's that an she says (0.3) it's your

132   birthday pre(hh)sent

When all else fails

To show something for which you have not found, or cannot use, the conventional symbol, invent your own symbol that is not going to be confused with anything else, and indicate clearly in the key what it stands for.

Presenting the audio data itself

To assess your work properly, the marker will need to listen to a sample of the original material, to satisfy him-/herself that it has been adequately transcribed. Doing this for everyone in the class is a time-consuming affair and you can help the assessor to look favourably upon you by making the job as easy as possible. For guidance on how, see Chapter 12.

For further transcription conventions, see Atkinson and Heritage (1984: ix–xvii), who cover gaze-direction, for example. You can also model your work on research papers themselves, many of which contain a key at the end (for example, Jefferson 1989: 193–6). For guidance on the transcription of spoken data for computer analysis, see Leech *et al.* (1995).

19

Using computers to study texts

The study of language has been hugely influenced by advances in computer technology. Previously, the only way to discover patterns of words in texts was to read the texts and find the examples by eye. Now, it is possible to conduct electronic searches that are sophisticated, reliable, fast, and much more extensive than would be possible by other means. Computers have not only provided linguists with new ways of answering old questions, but also helped identify new questions and new ways of thinking about what language is and how it works.

What is a corpus?

A corpus (the plural is **corpora**) is a set of texts in computer-readable form. Many of the first large corpora worldwide were constructed as part of dictionary projects funded by publishers. A corpus may consist of written texts, transcriptions of spoken material, or both. Corpora are assembled for various reasons, and these reasons will determine both what is included and how the text is **tagged**. Tagging is the process by which the material in the corpus is marked (or coded) to make it searchable. Linguists often like to use corpora that have been tagged for word class (so that it is possible to search for all the examples of, say, *record* as a noun, without also accessing the examples of *record* as a verb). **Lemmatized** tagging makes it possible to find the different forms of the same root, such as *swim*, *swimming*, *swam*, *swum*, without searching for them all separately. Other useful tags might enable one to find examples from speech only, or from different genres of text; to identify recent rather than less recent material; or to select examples from only one gender or age of speaker/writer. Tagging for semantic and discourse features is also occasionally found. For more detail about tags, see 'Making sense of corpus annotation' below.

Why is a corpus useful?

Often, to make a meaningful comment about some aspect of the language in your own data set, it is necessary to refer to a wider tendency in the language. Imagine, for instance, that in a study of the English of a non-native speaker, you find the phrase *a sympathetic friend*, meaning *a good friend*. You want to propose that this expression is not nativelike, but you would like to back up your claim more robustly than just by stating that it seems non-nativelike to you. One solution would be to look up the phrase in, say, the British National Corpus, and see how often it occurred relative to other expressions with the same meaning, such as *a good friend, a kind friend*. You might go further too, and access a corpus of English by non-native speakers with the same first language as your informant, to see if the expression is prevalent there. To take another example, opinion seems to be divided about the current balance of use of the forms *–er* and *–est* (as in *bigger, biggest*) and the forms *more _* and *most _* (see the exercise in Chapter 22). A corpus search on selected examples could provide you with evidence for your own contribution to the debate (for example, in projects 172 and 173).

How do corpus searches operate?

The corpus is just the raw material. Even if it is tagged, it is still just a set of data. In order to discover what it contains, search tools are needed. All of the main corpora come with certain tools for doing searches, but different tools look for different things. Both because of the tagging and because of the search tools, different corpora may be needed for answering different questions. Some search tools can be applied to a corpus that you have assembled yourself. The main sorts of searches that the tools make possible are:

- **Word frequency:** If you are interested in knowing which words occur most frequently in the text(s), you will be using a text-analysis program that tells the computer to count up the occurrences of each word form and list them in descending or ascending order of frequency, or alphabetically, say. Figure 19.1 shows the first 25 words in an alphabetical word-list and in a list of the most frequently occurring words for Thomas Hardy's novel *Far from the Madding Crowd*, produced by means of the WordSmith Tools program (see 'Text analysis tools' below).

- **Co-occurrences of words:** You might want to know what sorts of words tend to occur in the immediate environment of a given word. This requires a concordancing program. You choose your key word and the program searches for all the occurrences of it and displays and/or prints them with your preferred amount of context (for example, one line or one sentence). Different orderings are also possible. Figure 19.2 shows a concordance of the word *red* from Hardy's *Far from the Madding Crowd*, again produced using WordSmith Tools. The concordance has been sorted according to the alphabetical order of the word to the right of the search word. The actual appearance of this concordance on the screen would be slightly different: the search word (*red*) would be picked out in one colour and the word to the right in a different colour. Further investigation of the occurrences of this word, using a larger context, reveals interesting connections with the characters in the novel. For guidance on understanding concordances, see Sinclair (2003).

- **Distributions of words:** It may be of interest to you to discover how certain words or sets of words are distributed through the various parts of a text. Figure 19.3 shows the distribution of the name of the character *Troy* in *Far from the Madding Crowd* (again produced by WordSmith Tools). The horizontal bar represents the book, and each vertical line is an occurrence of the word. We can see from this that there are only two mentions

WORD	FREQ.		WORD	FREQ.	
1. A	3710	(2.91%)	1. THE	7650	(5.73%)
2. A'MOST	1		2. AND	4152	(3.11%)
3. A'S	1		3. A	3845	(2.88%)
4. A'TERNOON	1		4. OF	3744	(2.81%)
5. AARON	1		5. TO	3575	(2.68%)
6. ABANDON	1		6. IN	2336	(1.75%)
7. ABANDONED	1		7. WAS	1958	(1.47%)
8. ABANDONMENT	2		8. I	1630	(1.22%)
9. ABASEMENT	1		9. IT	1511	(1.13%)
10. ABASHED	4		10. THAT	1480	(1.11%)
11. ABATED	1		11. HER	1461	(1.09%)
12. ABBEY	1		12. HE	1361	(1.02%)
13. ABEDNEGO	1		13. YOU	1361	(1.02%)
14. ABEL	1		14. SHE	1226	(0.92%)
15. ABIDE	2		15. AS	1180	(0.88%)
16. ABIDING	2		16. HAD	1142	(0.86%)
17. ABEL	29	(0.02%)	17. HIS	1137	(0.85%)
18. ABNORMAL	7		18. SAID	980	(0.73%)
19. ABOARD	1		19. FOR	979	(0.73%)
20. ABOAT	1		20. WITH	969	(0.73%)
21. ABODE	1		21. AT	937	(0.70%)
22. ABOUNDING	1		22. NOT	828	(0.62%)
23. ABOUT	252	(0.20%)	23. BE	796	(0.60%)
24. ABOVE	40	(0.03%)	24. IS	741	(0.56%)
25. ABRADED	2		25. ON	734	(0.55%)

Figure 19.1 Alphabetical and frequency-ordered word lists in *Far from the Madding Crowd*

of this character's name in the first third or so of the book. Information of this kind could be useful if you were exploring the stylistics of narrative in one or more pieces of fictional or non-fictional writing.

- **Collocations:** Corpus research has revealed to linguists the truth of J.R. Firth's observation that 'you shall know a word by the company it keeps' (Firth 1968: 179), i.e. that the meaning of a word is somewhat determined by the words that it occurs with. Many unexpected patterns have been revealed through collocation research. Stubbs (1995) for instance found that *little* occurred only two-thirds as often with *boy(s)* as with *girl(s)*. Furthermore, when it collocated with *man*, there were likely to be other, pejorative words associated with the pairing, such as *ridiculous*. Both findings suggest that *little* has connotations that extend beyond its basic description of size. Figure 19.4 takes the words that occur in the immediate environment of *red* in *Far from the Madding Crowd* (i.e. one, two, three, four, or five words to the left or right of it) and shows how often each one is found in each position.

1. y Ball out of breath, his mouth	red	and open, like the bell of a
2. t visible burnt rayless, like a	red	and flameless fire shining ov
3. ms. In the midst of these shone	red	and distinct the figure of se
4. panting like a robin, her face	red	and moist from her exertions
5. his eyes, which where vermilion-	red	and bleared by gazing into it
6. and clinging to her hair, were	red	and yellow leaves which had c
7. spring waggon, picked out with	red,	and containing boughs and fl
8. re marked with great splotches	red	as arterial blood, others wer
9. tight warm hide of rich Indian	red,	as absolutely uniform from e
10. silent awhile. He regarded the	red	berries between them over and
11. nted holly bush, now laden with	red	berries. Seeing his advance t
12. usual into the furnace with his	red,	bleared eyes. From the bedro
13. heba was unusually excited, her	red	cheeks and lips contrasting i
14. art of the circle, covered with	red	cloth, and floored with a pie
15. a sergeant, and good looking a	red	coat with blue facings? miss
16. ne upon the bright gown and his	red	coat my! how handsome they lo
17. I, his face turning to an angry	red.	Coggan twirled his eye, edge
18. th a single pane, through which	red,	comfortable rays now stretch
19. the snow, till it shone in the	red	eastern light with the polish
20. t, and to see how strangely the	red	feather of her hat shone in t
21. ed and hornless blue flocks and	red	flocks, buff flocks and brown
22. lly, some of the natural, rusty	red	having returned to his face.
23. ssment. She became more or less	red	in the cheek, the blood waver
24. The man was Sergeant Troy. His	red	jacket was loosely thrown on,
25., save the foremost, who wore a	red	jacket, and advanced with his
26. bled ropes of black hair over a	red	jacket. Oak knew her instantl
27. ness of aged men, and the rusty-	red	leaves of the beeches were hu
28. he close compression of her two	red	lips, with which she had acco
29. e keenly pointed corners of her	red	mouth when, with parted lips,
30. he saw a dim spot of artificial	red	moving round the shoulder of
31. few minutes she noticed the fat	red	nape of Coggan's neck among t
32. do we'll have another. A large	red	seal was duly affixed. Bathsh
33. astening itself, till the large	red	seal became as a blot of bloo
34. preceding day, at the insistent	red	seal: me, he said aloud. the
35. ily, if not quite, an enlarging	red	spot rising in each cheek. Ca
36. The sun went down almost blood-	red	that night, and a livid cloud
37. eturned Liddy promptly: rose is	red,	the violet blue, Carnation's
38. d Betegueux shone with a fiery	red.	To persons standing alone on
39. d. A young cavalry soldier in a	red	uniform, with the three chevr
40. g waggon with the blue body and	red	wheels, and wash it very clea
41. heat, as if they were knots of	red	worms, and above shone imagin
42. ntly. I, said Boldwood, growing	red.	You needn't stay here a minu

Figure 19.2 An example of a concordance

MADCROW2.TXT
304 hits in   133,456 words   2.3 per 1,000 words

Figure 19.3 Distribution of *Troy* in *Far the Madding Crowd*

1.	RED	42	0 0 0 0 0	-	0 0 0 0 0
2.	THE	24	3 3 1 4 3	-	1 1 4 4 0
3.	AND	22	1 1 1 1 2	-	7 5 1 2 1
4.	OF	15	2 2 3 2 1	-	0 3 0 0 2
5.	A	14	2 1 0 2 5	-	0 0 0 2 2
6.	WITH	14	1 0 2 1 3	-	0 3 2 2 0
7.	HIS	9	1 0 0 1 3	-	0 0 2 1 1
8.	HER	8	0 0 1 2 2	-	0 0 1 2 0
9.	WERE	6	1 0 1 1 1	-	0 0 0 0 2
10.	SHONE	5	0 1 1 0 1	-	0 0 0 1 1
11.	TO	5	1 1 1 0 0	-	1 0 1 0 0
12.	BLUE	4	0 0 2 0 0	-	0 0 2 0 0
13.	IN	4	0 0 0 2 0	-	1 0 1 0 0
14.	WAS	4	0 2 0 0 0	-	0 2 0 0 0
15.	WHICH	4	0 0 1 0 1	-	0 0 1 1 0
16.	AS	3	0 0 0 0 0	-	2 0 1 0 0
17.	BLOOD	3	0 0 0 0 1	-	0 0 1 0 1
18.	EYES	3	0 1 0 0 0	-	0 1 0 0 1
19.	FACE	3	1 0 0 0 1	-	0 0 0 0 1
20.	FLOCKS	3	0 0 0 1 0	-	1 0 1 0 0
21.	FROM	3	0 0 0 0 0	-	0 0 2 1 0
22.	JACKET	3	0 0 0 0 0	-	3 0 0 0 0
23.	LIKE	3	1 0 0 1 0	-	0 0 1 0 0
24.	LIPS	3	0 0 0 0 0	-	1 0 1 0 1
25.	OUT	3	1 0 0 1 0	-	0 0 0 0 1
26.	OVER	3	0 0 0 1 0	-	0 0 0 1 1
27.	SEAL	3	0 0 0 0 0	-	3 0 0 0 0
28.	SHE	3	1 1 0 0 0	-	0 0 0 1 0

Figure 19.4 Collocations

How do you find a corpus?

Although some corpora can be accessed free via the Internet, others are only available for purchase or subscription. Therefore, the first thing to check is whether your university or college library has, or subscribes to, any corpus products. For any resources within your university there is likely to be a manual or set of introductory guidelines. If there is a staff member or postgraduate student in your department who uses corpora, you might do well to ask for some help with getting started.

For a general listing of available English-language corpora, try http://nora.hd.uib.no/text.htm or http://torvald.aksis.uib.no/corpora/sites.html. There are now many corpora for languages other than English: see http://www.uow.edu.au/~dlee/corpora2.htm. The main corpora for English that you might want to target are:

- The **Bank of English**, containing several hundred million words of written and spoken English, collected at the University of Birmingham and used for the well-known COBUILD series of dictionaries and grammars. Access to more than 50 million words of this corpus is available in Wordbanks Online http://www.collinslanguage.com/word-banks/, via subscription (but often with a free trial-period of one month).

- The **British National Corpus** www.natcorp.ox.ac.uk/ (100 million words), involving Oxford University Press, Longman, Chambers, the British Library, and the Universities of Oxford and Lancaster. The material is from a wide range of styles of written (90 per cent) and spoken (10 per cent) British English, and each word is grammatically tagged. The corpus is accessed using the search tool SARA, though other tools can also be used. The full BNC (100 million words) can be accessed on-line (see http://bnc-web.info/) or by purchasing the World Edition CD-ROM. There is also a cheaper CD-ROM called BNC Baby, which includes one-million-word subcorpora for each of four text types (academic, fiction, newspaper and conversation), a two-million-word 50-50 written/spoken representative sample of the full BNC, the one-million-word Brown corpus of American written English from 1961, and search software. An alternative and effective way of using the BNC is via the free-access facility provided by Mark Davies at Brigham Young University, http://corpus.byu.edu/. For further information about resources, see the BNC site http://www.natcorp.ox.ac.uk/Wkshops/Materials/specialising.xml?ID=online

- Now dwarfing the Bank of English and BNC are the **Corpus of Contemporary American English (COCA)** with 425 million words, the **Corpus of Historical American English (COHA)** with 400 million words from 1810 to 2009, the **Oxford English Corpus** with 2 billion words, and the **Google Book corpus** with 155 billion words. COCA, COHA and the Google corpus can be explored via http://corpus.byu.edu and access to the Oxford English Corpus can be granted to researchers through an application (see http://oxforddictionaries.com/page/oecresearch)

- The **International Corpus of English (ICE)** consists of one million words of spoken and written English (500 texts of about 2000 words each) from each of a growing set of countries where English is a first or second language. Each corpus is tagged in the same way, to make comparisons possible. The British and New Zealand corpora must be purchased but those from East Africa, the Philippines, India, and Singapore are available free on CD-ROM or for download. For the latest list of available corpora see: www.ucl.ac.uk/english-usage/ice/avail.htm

- The **International Corpus of Learners' English** (http://ice-corpora.net/ice/) contains over two million words of written English produced by learners of English as a foreign language with different native-language backgrounds. All the material is from essays written by advanced students and is tagged to make cross-comparisons possible. Although the corpora themselves are not available without special access rights, a number of the partners (listed at http://www.uclouvain.be/en-317605.html) do provide results of analyses, such as the top 100 words and their concordances in the Brazilian English component (BRICLE): http://www2.lael.pucsp.br/corpora/bricle/index.htm.

- The **World Wide Web** is for many researchers the ultimate corpus, with many billions of indexable words. Such a huge resource makes possible searches for rather rare examples (those where a mere 100 million words of text might provide only one or two instances). However, there are some disadvantages too: variation in the reliability of the language – some examples will be non-standard and non-native, and you cannot easily identify which; repetition of material – as any Google search for a wordstring reveals, the same text is sometimes reported many times as separate hits; changeability – the web is changing all the time, and so any figures you get will probably not be replicable even a day later, nor specific examples necessarily retrievable. Having said that, with a resource so huge, minor differences ought not to impact much on your findings. To search the web as a corpus, either use your preferred search engine (e.g. Google, Yahoo!, Bing) or the Webcorp tool described below.

- **Literary works:** If your interest lies in the use of words by one or more literary authors and your searches do not need to be sophisticated, you can access thousands of complete literary works available for download on the Internet, such as from the Gutenberg Project, www.gutenberg.org/.

What are the main text analysis tools?

- **WordSmith Tools** is a reasonably user-friendly software package for text analysis. It is available from http://www.lexically.net/wordsmith/, but there is a good chance that your university already has a copy. Examples from WordSmith have been used in this chapter.
- **Corpus.byu.edu** is a powerful search tool that accesses a number of very large English language corpora including the British National Corpus. It is free to use, and there is a useful three-minute guided tour on the home page, http://corpus.byu.edu/
- **Webcorp** is a search tool for linguists who want to use the World Wide Web as a corpus. It operates in a slightly different way from a normal search engine, having been designed specifically to access linguistic data. Webcorp is free to use, and details can be found at www.webcorp.org.uk/guide/.
- **Dante,** http://www.webdante.com/the_dtd.html, is a lexical database of English based on the analysis of 1.7 billion words. It can be searched for single words and word strings, and for groups of words performing the same function (e.g. adverbs of degree).

Making sense of corpus annotation

As noted above, the most useful corpora to linguists have been tagged in various ways. In SGML (Standard Generalized Markup Language) and XML (Extensible Markup Language), a tag is enclosed in angled brackets < >. Programmers can put any information that they wish in these brackets and know that it will be identified as a marker, as specified in their program. Thus, words in a play might be tagged for Act, Scene, and line numbers, while in a general linguistic corpus that is tagged for word class, each word will be labelled with <noun>, <verb>, etc. (or codes meaning the same thing). An example, from the Lancaster Oslo Bergen corpus (LOB) of written English is given in Figure 19.5. In Figure 19.5, the tag **NN** indicates a singular count noun, **BEZ** the third person singular of BE, **AT** the indefinite article, **JJ** an adjective, and so on. Texts can even be tagged with information on the syntactic structure of the phrases and sentences (that is, they can be **parsed**). The abbreviations used for tags and the theoretical rationales for which tag to use where will normally be provided along with the corpus itself, so look there for a list of glosses of the terms.

Hospitality_**NN** is_**BEZ** an_**AT** excellent_**JJ** virtueNN,_, but_**CC** not_**XNOT** when_**WRB** the_**ATI** guests_**NNS** have_**HV** to_**TO** sleep_**VB** in_**IN** rows_**NNS** in_**IN** the_**STI** cellar_**NN**!_!

Figure 19.5 Part of a corpus with word-class tagging

Using corpora effectively in your work

- Why reinvent the wheel? Some very useful analyses have already been done and are available on the web for you to draw on. For instance, Adam Kilgariff has listed the frequencies with which all the words in the British National Corpus occur: http://www.kilgarriff.co.uk/bnc-readme.html, or you can visit http://ucrel.lancs.ac.uk/bnc-freq. There are separate listings for lemmatized and unlemmatized forms (see above). Remember, of course, that if you use information that someone else has produced, it becomes a *resource* for your own work, not a replacement for it. You need to acknowledge it like any other published source, and use it to help you answer your own, different questions.

- As with any research, it is a very good idea to think through in advance what you can use any information from a corpus for. It can become rather easy to spend hours at the computer looking up more and more examples, only to find that you have a long list, and nothing much to say about it. Try to formulate a research question that will lead you to a conclusion. For instance, you might ask, as Stubbs (1995) did: *Are the meanings of 'small' and 'little' differently weighted for negativity, when used to refer to 'man', 'boy', 'woman', and 'girl'?* A question like this always gives you an answer, whether it is 'yes' or 'no', and if it is 'yes' (as it was for Stubbs) you can explore exactly what the distributions are by drawing out examples from the corpus. In contrast, a research question like *Is 'horse' a more frequent word than 'cow'?* is only worth asking if you have a good reason: if you find out that it is, what will that enable you to conclude? In short, corpora are simply resources – they will furnish you with good answers, but only if you ask good questions. Since there are still many good questions that cannot be answered using corpora yet, take note of the kind of work that has already been done, as a guide to what you may be able to do yourself.

Compiling your own corpus: potential problems

It is possible to create your own corpus but in the context of a project this is probably not advisable because you need so much text and it takes so much time to assemble and make suitable for use. (We mean here 'corpus' in the technical sense used in this chapter. In a less technical sense, any dataset might be referred to as a 'corpus', but it would not have the features we are referring to here.) Here are some key observations:

- To create a corpus, you need to convert very large amounts of material to computer-readable form. This can be done using a scanner, but the results are by no means 100 per cent accurate and need careful proofreading.
- It is illegal to put copyright material (that is, almost all published works) into a computer corpus without permission.

- Spoken data, if that is what you want in your corpus, must first be collected and transcribed before it can go onto the computer. The permission of the speakers will also be needed.
- It is difficult to ensure that your corpus is truly representative of the type(s) of language you want to study.

Because of these difficulties, you should consider using an existing corpus, as long as it will provide the data you require in the format you need.

Limitations of corpora

Large general corpora may be presented as representative of the language in use. But remember that:

- Most corpora only give a snapshot of the language at a particular time.
- They are reliant on what is electronically available and not restricted by copyright, with the result that certain genres of writing, particularly journalism, tend to be over-represented.
- Spoken data needs to be transcribed, which is complicated, expensive, and time-consuming, so considerably less spoken data is available than written.
- Searching any corpus is constrained by what the tool can look for, and by how the text has been tagged. In both cases, there may be major theoretical models and/or practical aims underpinning the decisions that have been made.

Further reading

For general overviews on the nature of corpora and of corpus linguistics, see Tognini-Bonelli and Sinclair (2006) and Hunston (2006). Useful introductions to English corpus linguistics are Meyer (2002), Anderson and Corbett (2009), Lindquist (2009) and Cheng (2011). An excellent collection of overview essays by corpus specialists is given in O'Keeffe and McCarthy (2010), and in the four volumes of Biber and Reppen (2011). Sinclair (2003) is a guide to reading concordances. For ideas about what corpora can contribute to linguistic research, look at Stubbs (2001), Hoey (2005), Teubert and Cermakova (2007) and McEnery and Hardie (2011). For practical guidance on using corpora for projects, see McEnery, Xiao, and Tono (2006), and Baker (2010) if your interests lie in sociolinguistics, including language varieties. For more technical guidance on the analysis of corpus data, see Gries (2009).

20

Statistics and your project

Do you need graphs and calculations in your project?

If your project provides you with results in the form of numbers, there is a good chance that presenting them in graphs and/or analysing them using statistical tests will enhance your work. But how far should you go? How sophisticated is such work expected to be?

It is unreasonable for your assessors to expect you to use any analytical techniques for which you have not been given input/training unless they are part of the compulsory curriculum of a (high-)school education or part of a preparatory curriculum you have followed at university.

As a general rule, it might well be expected that everyone will have previously learned how to draw simple bar charts and pie charts and how to calculate percentages and averages. So it would be quite fair for your university assessors to expect you to use those skills in your project.

However, anything more complicated than that, such as determining whether one figure is *significantly* larger than another (see 'The point of statistical analyses' below) requires specific training that you will not be assumed to have had elsewhere. If your university department expects you to use statistical analyses in your project, they will have made provision for you to learn how to do so. If no such provision has been made, stick to graphs, percentages, and averages. But if you did attend classes on how to do statistical analyses, then even if you didn't enjoy or understand it all, it is likely that you will lose marks for not using such analyses if they are appropriate.

The good news is that your lecturers will understand that not everyone finds this aspect of analysis easy and, as part of the requirement that you will do such analysis, they will expect to offer you support. Find out what support is available, and do everything you can to make yourself helpable (see 'How to avoid common problems' below), because even a wizard statistician cannot turn chaotic figures into a reliable finding. Getting help with this sort of thing, whether from a dedicated statistics expert, your supervisor, another student, or a friend or relation, will not normally be viewed as cheating, unless it has been made clear to you that you are being specifically assessed on this aspect of the work (as would be the case in a statistics module, of course). If in doubt, ask. For the sake of honesty and courtesy, if you have had a lot of help, you should acknowledge this, either in an acknowledgments section at the front of your project or in a footnote at the point when you present the relevant material.

Of course, if you have studied mathematics at a high level, you may have command of certain techniques and confidence about learning new ones: if so, go for it (but do still read the books carefully and take advice, just to ensure you are on the right lines).

In this chapter, we aim to help those who are rather intimidated by the idea of statistical presentations and analyses. We hope to bridge the gap between where many students feel they are and the level at which most of the books (and courses) start. The first golden rule for the mathematically insecure is: *don't panic*. This is easily said, of course, and harder to achieve, but panicking will definitely not help. Divide your work into small clear tasks that you will easily manage and that you will know you have completed. Avoid multi-tasking (e.g. trying to count three different things at once). Keep a record of what you have done and what it is for.

First we shall look at how to present your findings using *descriptive* statistics: graphs, percentages, averages, and so on. Like your assessors, we are assuming that you have done this kind of thing before, though maybe not for a while. If this is not the case, then you need to find a good textbook to take you through the principles or get a friend to show you what to do. Then we move to considering why statistical analyses are worth the effort and how they work. Finally, we identify some useful textbooks and offer some basic information for the 'mathematically insecure'.

Descriptive statistics and basic calculations

Types of data

Numbers have to be handled carefully and with common sense. You need to have a clear sense of what you are counting and, indeed, when you are not really counting at all. For instance, imagine you asked people what they thought would most enhance the effectiveness of warning instructions on pharmaceutical products: (1) non-technical vocabulary; (2) short sentences; or (3) pictures. Although these three categories have been given numbers for convenience, they are just labels.

In the textbooks, you will find reference to three or four types of data: **quantitative data** (subdivided into **ratio data** and **interval data**), **ordinal data,** and **nominal data**. Below, we simply indicate what sorts of data fall into each category, and then provide illustrations for comparison. If you want to know why, or have data that you cannot relate to our examples, then look up the terms in a good introductory textbook, such as Hinton (2004: 21–3), Coolican (2006), or Coolican (2009, Ch 11).

The two easiest types to contrast are **quantitative data** and **nominal data**, so we'll begin there. The question to ask is: what am I counting? If the answer is 'actual scores achieved on a test' or 'actual time taken to do something', or 'actual number of words in each utterance in a spoken text', or 'actual number of interruptions in each line of a conversation', etc., then your data is quantitative. At every point when you are scoring, you are saying 'does this score a point or doesn't it?' You are *not* saying 'I have a point to award, so do I add it to this set or that set?' If you are doing that, you are dealing with nominal data.

Nominal data entails categorizing: you might have a list of languages spoken by different non-native speakers of English in a class, and want to categorize the class members according to which language is their mother tongue. Or you might have a list of ways of learning languages, so that you can ask people which they prefer. Or you might have a list of different words in a text and want to know how often each one occurs. 'Nominal' relates to 'naming', and for as long as your categories are named, you should not have any difficulty recognizing nominal data. However, be careful if you number your categories for convenience. Just because Arabic is referred to as '1' and Punjabi as '2', they have not stopped being nominal data. Ask yourself: 'Have I, or could I have, named the categories with which I am operating?'

Nominal categories are used to gather frequency information by distributing a fixed number of people or pieces of information into the categories. That means that your figures (the frequencies) will always add up to the number of pieces of information you had. For instance, if you categorize a class of 30 children according to their mother tongues, you might have 3 native speakers of Arabic, 7 of Punjabi, 4 of Greek, 12 of English, and 1 each of Japanese, Chinese, Spanish, and Italian.

Next, we consider **ordinal data**. Ordinal scores superficially look like quantitative data, but are not the same, because the intervals between the different possible scores cannot be precise. Consider the marking system used in your university, where, perhaps, you are awarded marks out of 100, with a pass mark of, say, 40. Gaining a mark of 65 does not entail any real counting: it is an impression based upon how well you have met the criteria for the work. There is no guarantee that someone with 62 and someone with 68 have performed exactly equal amounts worse and better than you. The issue is even more extreme if you try to imagine what would justify the ten-mark difference between 80 and 90 or between 15 and 25. Because the scores are impressionistic and unequally spaced, we cannot perform the same calculations as we could if they were genuinely out of 100 (as they might be in a test with 100 questions, where each correct answer got one mark). However, we can still use the fact that all the scores are placed in a particular order: if you get 65, it definitely does mean that you did better than the person with 62, who did better than the person with 58.

Another example might be data derived from asking people to rate voices on a scale of 1 to 5 for friendliness in a set of recordings. We could certainly say with confidence that a voice with an average rating of 4.2 had been considered more friendly than a voice with an average of 2.1, but it would not make sense to say that the first voice was considered twice as friendly as the second: ratings are just not that exact.

There are particular calculations that use the order of the scores without placing too much importance on the score itself. They focus on the relative *order* of the participants or categories on a scale of performance, popularity, or whatever. This process of **ranking** is the only option for ordinal data, but it is also possible to convert quantitative data into ordinal data. Doing so can be very useful if you want to compare two aspects of performance, one of which is ordinal and the other quantitative, because it lets you bypass the need directly to relate the worth of, say, 15 out of 20 in a spelling test, with a score of 3.82 on a progressive reading scale.

When you rank, you lose some information. If Bob comes top with 17/20, Carol comes second with 12/20 and Phil comes third with 11/20, you cannot capture the fact that the difference between Bob's and Carol's scores was greater than the difference between Carol's and Phil's scores.

Here are some examples of fictional studies that produce the different types of data.

Quantitative data

The figures in Table 20.1 are quantitative (ratio) data. The researcher has given 16 participants a memory test, for which the highest possible score is 20. Deciding what score each participant should get has been a question of looking at how he/she responded to each of the 20 items and asking 'Does this response get a point or not?' Getting 12 points makes a person twice as good as someone who got 6 points. The researcher has, in fact, used two groups of eight participants: the first eight were prepared for the memory test in one way and the second eight in a different way. Therefore it will be possible to calculate the average (mean) score for each group (see 'Reporting your data' below) and use that to work out whether the two groups performed significantly differently from each other.

Table 20.1 Scores on a memory test (out of 20)

Participant ID number	1	2	3	4	5	6	7	8	9	10	11	12	13	14	15	16
Score	7	11	12	9	3	8	18	12	15	10	10	11	6	7	13	17

Nominal data

Table 20.2 Country that Chinese learners of English would most like to visit (number of votes)

	USA	South Africa	Canada	Ireland	UK	New Zealand	Australia	Singapore
Popularity as destination for visit	178	9	53	17	92	71	143	2

To generate Table 20.2, the researcher asked Chinese learners of English 'Which English-speaking country would you most like to visit?' Each participant got one 'vote' and it is allocated to a particular category (country). If you add up all the scores, it will equal the number of votes cast (i.e. the number of people in the survey). Such data might be used to explore the effectiveness of the marketing of each country to potential Chinese visitors or to evaluate the influence on Chinese learners' aspirations of the destinations featured in the textbooks they use or of the English native speakers that they meet in China. Alternatively, it could be converted into ordinal data (see later).

Ordinal data

Line A of Table 20.3 has taken the same information as in Table 20.2, and converted it into ranks. The ranking tells us that the USA was preferred over Australia as a destination, but we have lost the information about how much more popular it was. On the other hand, by changing to ranks, we are in a position to make a comparison with the quite different 'scores' in Line B. These are also ranks, but they have been derived not from nominal data but from quantitative data (sub-type ratio): the actual number of kilometres distance between Beijing and the capital of each country. By converting the kilometre figures to ranks, we have, again, lost the information about how *much* further away one country is than another. But we have gained something useful too. Using the two sets of ranks, we can find out whether the desire to visit a place is determined by how far away it is. We could not do that with the raw scores, unless we believe that, say, each additional 1000 km of distance justifies an extra vote!

Projects in Linguistics and Language Studies

Table 20.3 Rank orders of countries according to: (A) where Chinese learners of English would most like to visit; (B) distance from Beijing to each country's capital

	USA	South Africa	Canada	Ireland	UK	New Zealand	Australia	Singapore
(A) Rank of popularity as destination for visit (1 = most popular)	1	7	5	6	3	4	2	8
(B) Rank of distance from China (1 = closest)	7	8	5	3	2	6	4	1

Making types of data work for you

You need not feel that you are 'victim' to the kind of data that your study produces. You have two kinds of control over what kind of data you deal with. First, you can decide to design your study to produce the sort of data you are comfortable with. You can even model your entire investigation around the data table that you want to end up with. Then you will know you can handle what you get. The second kind of control is in how you choose to formulate your data and what questions you ask of it. While you will not be able to convert nominal or ordinal data into quantitative data, you may well be able to do the reverse, and that may free you up to make choices about the presentation and analysis of your material.

Reporting your data: averages, percentages, and graphs

What you can do with your data depends on what kind of data it is, so don't try to do everything! If you produce a figure or graph that looks like nonsense, it might well be so. Before you calculate anything or prepare any kind of graph, identify a specific question that you want to know the answer to. Usually, that question will help you work out what sort of treatment to give to your data. Here are some examples, using the tables from the previous section.

Table 20.1 reported quantitative data: the scores out of 20 that 16 people got in a memory test. Participants 1–8 (Group A) had been trained in one way, and participants 9–16 (Group B) in another. A sensible question to ask would be: *Did the training method affect the scores?* That is, *Did Group A do better than Group B?* Looking at the distribution of scores, it's clear that some did and some didn't. You need to find out what each group did *on average*, by calculating the mean. We explain in the notes at the end of this chapter how to calculate the *mean*. The means for the two groups from Table 1 are: Group A = 10.00, Group B = 9.875.

Do you think that this indicates that the training made a difference? The figures are very close. You could put them onto a graph and see if that helps you judge. You can create a graph from a table in many word-processing programs, so look in the Help guidance of the program to find out how to do it.

The graph in Figure 20.1 shows how careful you have to be with automatically generated graphs. The difference looks enormous and you might easily choose to conclude that the training for Group A was much more effective. But the scale of the graph indicates that only the difference between 9.8 and 10 is shown – yet individual participants could only score whole numbers on the test, so the range of actual scores would fall outside the range of that graph! We can see a truer picture if we force the graph to show us the entire scale (Figure 20.2). Now the difference looks tiny. You may think 'Well, how am I going to know what to say? Was there a real difference or not?' This is where statistical analyses would come in – see 'Using statistical analyses' below.

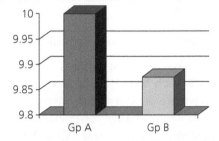

Figure 20.1 Mean scores on a memory test: the ranks for 'Visit' and 'Distance'

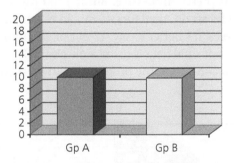

Figure 20.2 Mean scores on a memory test (rescaled): the ranks for 'Visit' and 'Distance'

Nominal data, as in Table 20.2, invites a different question such as: 'What was the relative popularity of different destinations?' This information can be shown on a bar chart (see Figure 20.3). Since you are dealing with the relative distribution of a set number of bits of information (in this case, the share of votes out of a total of 565), you can also state the results as percentages.

A percentage is the number of instances *per hundred*. The calculation, therefore, amounts to saying: if there are in total 565 votes (as there are in Table 20.2), and 53 of them were for Canada, how many would there have been for Canada if there had been 100 votes? We show you how to calculate a percentage in the notes at the end of this chapter. The answer is just over 9 per cent. To calculate a percentage, you have to know what a score is *out of*. If you cannot provide that *out of* figure easily, then a percentage may not be appropriate. For instance, you cannot provide percentages of reaction times like 817 milliseconds: what are they *out of*?

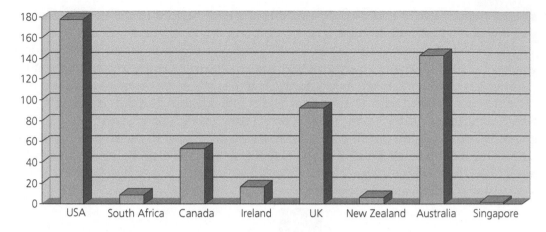

Figure 20.3 Distribution of preferences for visit to English-speaking country (bar chart)

It is also a good idea not to give percentage values for very small figures. If 7 out of 10 schoolchildren prefer reading French to writing it, does this really mean that if you had asked 100, exactly 70 would have preferred reading? Surely not, because if just one of your 7 had chosen something else, that would change your percentage by 10 – that's ten people out of the hundred. As a result, percentages based on less than 100 in total are not very accurate. If you say that 33.3 per cent of the parrots in your study were capable of reciting an entire nursery rhyme, this sounds pretty impressive. But if you only studied three parrots, that's only one individual! Don't be afraid, therefore, to talk in real figures rather than percentages when you have small samples: it's better to say '17 out of 25' than to use a percentage.

Another way to display nominal data is using a pie chart (Figure 20.4), which divides up the whole 'pie' into slices according to the proportions in your data.

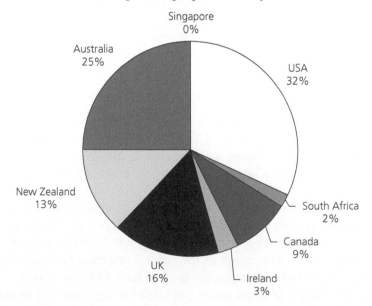

Figure 20.4 Distribution of preference for visit to English-speaking country for 'Visit' and 'Distance'

With **ordinal** data, you are asking different questions again, and so a different kind of presentation is likely to help. In Table 20.3 we had two sets of ranks and a good question would be 'Are English-speaking countries that are further from China more attractive as destinations?' How might we use a graph to answer the question? The clearest presentation will result if one of your categories shows a nice rising line. You can then see whether the other ranking follows the same trajectory or not. Thus, you might re-order the information in Table 20.3 so that the 'Visit' ranks are in order – do this by moving the entire columns around, so that the 'Distance' rank and the name of the country also move (see Table 20.4). A line graph can then be generated (Figure 20.5). This shows that, in fact, there is not much of an obvious relationship between the popularity of destinations among Chinese learners of English and the distance of the place from Beijing.

Table 20.4 Re-ordered information from Table 20.3

	USA	Australia	UK	New Zealand	Canada	Ireland	South Africa	Singapore
Visit	1	2	3	4	5	6	7	8
Distance	7	4	2	6	5	3	8	1

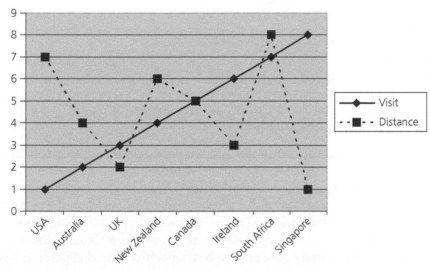

Figure 20.5 Comparison of the ranks for 'Visit' and 'Distance'

Using statistical analyses

Why go any further than graphs and averages?

As we have already indicated, your decision about whether to go any further will depend on what is expected of you and what you are comfortable with. As should have become clear by now, even if you had planned to stick to just noting percentages and drawing graphs, you may find that you are dissatisfied with the limitations of doing so. The tell-tale sign is when you find yourself asking: 'Yes, but what does all of this mean actually happened?'

or 'What is the answer to my original question?' or 'Is that difference big enough to take seriously?'

Statistical analyses assess the degree of confidence we can have that our small set of results is representative of what we would get from a larger **population** of the same type. ('Population' is a technical term, meaning *the entire set of people (or things) from which the sample in the research has been taken*.) In other words, statistical analyses check whether a hypothesis is valid when it proposes a certain relationship between two or more sets of data. And they investigate, in an open-ended way, relationships between different variables. A **variable** is any property whose value may vary (such as gender, age, test score, or reaction time).

The point of statistical analyses

The fundamental point of doing a statistical analysis of your data is to find whether the results you got are worth taking seriously. In statistical analyses for the social sciences, a probability value of 0.05, that is 5 per cent, is generally viewed as sufficient to be termed *significant*. The lower the probability value below that 0.05, the *more* significant it is and, if you can attain a probability value of 0.01 or lower (that is 1 per cent), then it is often called *highly significant*. If you read a published research report that contains statistical tests, you will see statements like the following:

$\chi^2 = 35.95$, df = 2, $p < 0.01$

t = 2.65, df = 7, $p < 0.05$ (one-tailed, related)

The statement of probability is the part that begins $p <$. This means: 'the probability is less than…' Thus, $p < 0.01$ means 'the probability is less than 0.01, or 1 per cent', and $p < 0.05$ means 'the probability is less than 0.05, or 5 per cent'. But what does *that* mean?

What is a statement of probability?

Imagine you toss a normal coin ten times and count how many times it turns up 'heads' and how many times 'tails'. Because the coin is balanced, there is no reason why one side should 'win'. However, experience tells us that there is no guarantee that you will get an exactly equal number of heads and tails. Yes, you might get five heads and five tails, but you might get six and four, or even seven and three – chance can do that, because the coin can't remember what happened last time and so, every time you throw the coin, there is an equal chance of either outcome, irrespective of what has happened up to that point. It's even possible that you could throw the coin ten times and get heads every single time. Having said that, provided the coin *is* balanced, we would consider a score of 10–0 to be very unusual.

Now let's think of a different coin: one that you *believe* (but do not know) to be weighted so that it comes up heads more often than tails. You throw this coin ten times and you get 10–0. What does this mean? It might mean that the coin is indeed weighted. On the other hand, maybe the coin is not weighted and it just happened that you got the unusual outcome of 10–0, which, as we have seen above, can happen just by chance. The obvious thing to do next would be to throw the coin some more and see what happened. If the coin is balanced, you are likely to get a score closer to 5–5 this time, and that will help you interpret your first finding as the result of chance. But if you get another 10–0 or a 9–1, then you may feel more confident that the original 10–0 was down to the coin being weighted. The more you throw the coin, the more of a picture you will develop. But suppose that you only had that one set of ten throws to work from, because the coin is now lost. You are looking at the original 10–0 score and you don't know what it means. You can't throw the coin any more, so how can you find out what the likelihood is that it was weighted?

Mathematically, this can be worked out. The assumption is made that the coin was *not* weighted, that is, that it was equally likely to fall down on either side. It is possible to calculate, using simple principles of probability, how many times in, say, 100 lots of ten throws, a score of 10–0 was likely to come up: not many! In contrast, scores of 5–5, 6–4, and 4–6 would be predicted to occur very often. On the basis of such a calculation, you could state that, were the coin to be balanced, the chances of your getting the outcome 10–0 were very small, though not, of course, impossible. In fact, they are *very, very* small: the probability of 10–0 for a balanced coin is 1 in every 1024 sets of ten throws, or 0.0009, less than one-tenth of 1 per cent.

This is the important bit: if the probability of something happening is one in 1024, it means that, assuming the coin is *not* weighted, then you will only get that outcome once in every 1024 times you try the experiment. The other 1023 times you do the experiment you won't get such an extreme result. It follows that since you have a suspicion that the coin *is* weighted, and you predicted that the weighting would indeed lead to more heads than tails, there's a very high chance that the reason you got 10–0 is because it is weighted. It would be very bad luck indeed to be testing the belief that a coin was weighted to favour heads, and to get a 10 heads to 0 tails result when in fact it wasn't weighted at all!

What should be clear from this is that *part* of what gives you confidence in interpreting your outcome is the mathematics. But the other part is that you had made a prediction in advance (a hypothesis) about what the outcome would be, and you did indeed get that outcome. Thus, the hypothesis is a crucial part of your design and should be firmly based on existing theory and findings from research, not just on a hunch (see Chapters 1 and 13).

Let's get away from coins and think about a language-related example. Imagine you are interested in whether words are easier to remember if you see them written down than if you hear them spoken. What do you predict? On the basis of what you have read, you have come to the conclusion that both visual and auditory information helps with memory. But you have also discovered that when people see a word written down, they are likely to silently 'speak' it, giving them both visual and auditory input – a double chance to remember it. On the other hand, when people hear a word, they do not normally imagine it written down. As a result, you are predicting that visual input will be more effective. Your results show that the scores from the visual input group were, indeed, higher, and now you have done a statistical test on the figures. The analysis reveals the probability of getting those results if there was *no* advantage of visual input over auditory input. The probability comes out as less than 0.05, and is therefore termed *significant*. What this means is that if there was no advantage to visual input, you could still get this result, but only 5 times in every 100 times that you ran the experiment. The other 95 times, you would get a result that showed less difference between visual and auditory. Because of this, it is, as it says, *significant* that you had predicted this particular outcome on the basis of your belief that visual and auditory input were not equally effective. If visual and auditory input *were* equally effective, then running this experiment once and getting the outcome you did would be pretty bad luck, and so it is a reasonable guess that, in fact, you were right all along, and there is indeed an advantage to memory of getting visual input rather than auditory.

How do you arrive at a statement of probability?

It should now be obvious that for many people (though not all, for there are limitations to judging probabilities in this way), the statement of probability is the Holy Grail. Probability levels are the result of statistical calculations, not all of which are as straightforward as the coin-throwing example, because people and the things they do tend to be more unpredictable than balanced coins are. We cannot explain the principles of all the different available tests here. Rather, we point you in the direction of the tests likely to be most appropriate for the main kinds of data generated by research into language. You need to find the test in a good statistics textbook (we recommend some later on in this chapter), and check that it does indeed meet your needs.

The principles of five common statistical tests

- To see if two sets of real scores (quantitative data) are as different as your hypothesis predicts, use a *t-test*. The scores may be from the same group (*related t-test*) or from two different groups (*unrelated t-test*).
- To see if more than two sets of scores (quantitative data) are as different as your hypothesis predicts, you need *analysis of variance* (ANOVA). However, it's a good idea not to use ANOVA until you have got the hang of what the *t-test* does, so try to avoid having more than two sets to compare.
- To see if the increasing values in one set of scores (quantitative data) are matched by an *increase* in a second set (*positive correlation*) (e.g. a low reading score is associated with a low spelling score, a high reading score with a high spelling score); or to see if the increasing values in one set of scores are matched by a *decrease* in a second set (*negative correlation*) (e.g. the more often a word occurs in a text, the fewer letters it tends to have), use a *Pearson's product-moment correlation coefficient test*.
- To see whether the distribution of frequencies (nominal data) is likely to be due to chance, use a *chi-squared* (χ^2) test.
- To see whether two ranks are as different as you predicted, use a *Mann Whitney U test* (for two different groups) or a *Wilcoxon signed ranks test* (for the same group doing different things). (Real quantitative data can be converted to ranks for this test, if a *t-test* cannot be used)
- To see whether two ranks are as *similar* you predicted (positive correlation) or move in opposite directions (negative correlation), use a *Spearman's rho correlation test*. (Quantitative data can be converted to ranks for this test, if a *Pearson's test* cannot be used.)

Remember, if you plan ahead, you can decide *first* what kind of test you can cope with, and then design your research to provide suitable data.

How to avoid common problems with statistical tests

1 Keep your design *very* simple: compare two groups, or one group doing two different things. Don't add in complications.
2 Tests that are termed *parametric* (e.g. *t-test, ANOVA, Pearson's*) must meet strict criteria for the calculations to be valid. For *all* tests, your results will be more reliable if you minimize unintentional variation:

- In groups of participants or informants, keep the balance of gender, age, educational level, etc. the same if you know it might have an effect. However, if you have no reason to believe that a variable will affect the outcome (e.g. there is no evidence that gender is likely to make a difference in the data you are examining), then just say so and stop worrying.
- If using texts as input for comparison, avoid differences in the length or frequency of words (unless, of course, that is what you are trying to test).
- In test conditions, avoid gathering otherwise comparable sets of data in very different circumstances, such as in noisy and quiet environments, early and late in the day, etc.

3 In addition, check *before* you finalize your design how many participants you need in each group to make your chosen statistical test valid. If your sample is larger than the recommended maximum or smaller than the minimum, you may need to use a different test, or convert the figures first. Get advice.

4 Read an account of the statistical analysis you are using. And then read it again, until you can see where your figures will fit in, and what your results ought to look like. If you can't make it make sense, you may have the wrong test. Get help.

5 Take care if using computer software, such as SPSS, that will do the statistical analyses for you. It can be difficult to work out what to put in and, if you get that wrong, you will get rubbish out. *First* work out what test you need. *Then* read instructions on how to do that test using the software. If possible, check your first couple of calculations of such tests by also doing them by hand. If the results don't come out the same, then something has gone amiss.

Textbooks

Statistics is an enormous subject and can get very complicated. Textbooks vary tremendously. Some are for advanced mathematicians (leave these alone), others for researchers and students who have a substantial background in statistical work, and others for people who need leading gently by the hand. Most linguists fall into the last category! It is worth using a book written *for* linguists if possible, or at least one that deals with a similar topic area such as psychology or social sciences, because the examples will be relevant, will make sense to you, and may give you ideas for your own research.

Woods *et al.* (1986) and Hatch and Lazaraton (1991), though old, remain key resources for linguistics students, with Rasinger (2008) a more recent addition. Coolican (2009) is a friendly and practical book for psychology students, which covers the main statistical tests within the context of explaining how to design studies and collect data. The examples are interesting and well illustrated. Coolican's other book (2006) begins at an even more introductory level. Another introductory book aimed at psychology students is Greene and D'Oliveira (2005). Hinton (2004) is written for social science students and is similarly helpful and clear but does not include the study-design aspect. The most logical guide for getting started with SPSS is Colman and Pulford (2008) but it does not explain the statistical tests themselves. Books that bridge the gap include Brace *et al.* (2009), Field (2009), Hinton *et al.* (2004) and Pallant (2010). If you need to engage with Analysis of Variance (ANOVA), Reitveld and Van Hout (2005) have dedicated a whole book to it, aimed at linguists, and it is also covered by Greene and D'Oliveira (2005).

Many linguists are adopting the statistical package R (http://www.r-project.org/) as a way of generating information and graphs. Gries (2009) is a useful introduction to R. To understand how quantitative and qualitative methods can be combined, Dörnyei (2007) is a valuable resource.

Help for the mathematically insecure

Brackets

A sum in brackets should be done first: the brackets indicate that everything inside belongs together. Thus:

$(3 + 2) \times 4 = 5 \times 4 = 20$, whereas $3 + (2 \times 4) = 3 + 8 = 11$

Relationship between adjacent symbols

If you see a figure *next to* a symbol or something in brackets, you need to multiply the two together, e.g.:

4a is the same as: $4 \times a$

$G (5 - 3)$ is the same as: G times the result when you take three from five, i.e. $G \times 2$

Something on top of something else

One figure or symbol, or an array of them, on top of a line, with something underneath, indicates a division sum. First, work out any calculations that are entirely above or below the line. Then divide the bottom value into the top one. Thus:

$\dfrac{5}{10}$ is the same as: 5 divided by 10 = 0.5, i.e. ½

$$\frac{2(6-1)}{20} = \frac{2 \times 5}{20} = \frac{10}{20} = 0.5, \text{ i.e. } ½$$

Squaring something

When you *square* something, you multiply it by itself. We write this instruction with a superscript 2, so 12 squared is written 12^2 (and comes out as 144). To square something on your calculator, enter the figure, press the multiplication key (x) and then the equals key (=). By the way, squaring something gets rid of minus signs (that's one reason why it is used so much). So, $12^2 = 144$ and so does -12^2.

Square root

When you find the *square root* of something, you do the opposite to squaring it – you find out which number you would have to multiply by itself to get the figure you have. So, the square root of 16 is 4, because $4 \times 4 = 16$. The square root of 100 is 10 because $10 \times 10 = 100$. Square roots are hard to guess, so you do need your calculator. To work out a square root, enter your figure and press the square root key ($\sqrt{\ }$).

Which order?

If you see two division sums that have to be added together, do the divisions first, then add the results:

$$\frac{5}{10} + \frac{7}{9} = 0.5 + 0.78 = 1.28$$

See also the section on 'Brackets'.

How many decimal places?

The majority of calculations will give you figures to many decimal places (i.e. numbers after the decimal point). It is customary to use two or three in most calculations. To operate to two decimal places: look at the *third* figure after the decimal point. If it is 5 or higher, then round *up*, that is, add 1 to the figure to its left. If it is less than 5, round *down* – that is, don't change the figure to the left:

0.7777777777 will round up to 0.78

0.7272727272 will round up to 0.73

0.2727272727 will round down to 0.27

Sometimes you may notice that the third figure is *nearly* 5. Should it, itself, be rounded up? Suppose you wanted to round up 0.314999999 to two decimal places. Should it round up to 0.32 or down to 0.31? Answer: the original figure is *less* than 0.315, so don't round up. Think of it like money: if you owed someone £2.49, how would you feel if they said 'Let's call it £3'?

Calculating a percentage

You start with two figures, one a proportion of the other. For instance, you have counted up how many syllables there are in the words of a text. The text is 4131 words long and 716 of the words have more than one syllable. The percentage calculation tells you how many per hundred words of text. Divide the larger figure into the smaller one, thus 716 divided by 4131, and multiply the answer by 100 (move the decimal point two places to the left). Thus: 716/4131 = 0.1733 or 17.33, per cent. If you convert figures to percentages, you can more easily compare them. Another text might have 893 words with more than one syllable, but the text was longer, at 5148 words, so is the proportion the same or not? The percentage works out at 17.35 per cent – virtually identical, but that would be hard to see without the percentage calculations.

Calculating the mean

The mean is the 'average', and is sometimes written as $\bar{x}$. Add up the scores and divide the total by the number of scores, e.g.:

The mean of: 10, 13, 6, 11, and 5 is:

$$\frac{(10+13+6+11+5)}{5} = 45/5 = 9$$

Key to the most common algebraic symbols used in basic statistics

Table 20.5 The most commonly used algebraic symbols

Symbol	Explanation
x	Any single value or score
y	Another single value or score
N	The number of results or participants
Σ	'Sum of', so Σx means 'add together all the values of x'
x^2	x squared, i.e. multiplied by itself. Example: if $x = 3$, then $x^2 = 9$
$\bar{x}$	The mean (average)
$\dfrac{\Sigma x}{N} = \bar{x}$	The sum of all values, divided by the number of values, producing the mean
$\sqrt{x}$	Square root of x, i.e. the number which, multiplied by itself, gives x. Example: if $x = 64$, then $\sqrt{x} = 8$ (use a calculator with a square root button)
$\dfrac{x}{y}$ or x/y	Divide x by y, i.e. the same as x/y. Example: $\dfrac{3}{4} = ¾ = 0.75$
f	Frequency: how often something occurs
df	Degrees of freedom: a figure used to help you find the 'critical value' you need in your test, to establish the probability level. It reflects the number of columns and rows in your data table, and instructions are given with the relevant test
χ and χ^2	Chi: represents a value used in the Chi-squared (χ^2) test
E	Expected frequency in the Chi-squared test
O	Observed frequency in the Chi-squared test
p	Probability (of getting a result by chance)
ρ	Rho: the Spearman's correlation coefficient
σ	Standard deviation (of a population): a measure of how much variation there is between scores
s or sd	Standard deviation (of a sample)
< >	Smaller than, bigger than, e.g. $x < 12$ means *the value of x is less than 12*
≤ ≥	Smaller than or equal to, bigger than or equal to
t, z, U, W, etc	Letters may relate to the value of the *test statistic* for a specific test, e.g. *t* is used for the test statistic in the *t-test*. You will find the relevant letter to use when you read about the test in a good statistics book.

The symbols used in mathematical expressions can be very intimidating. The secret is to treat symbols as your friends: they tell you unambiguously and succinctly what to do to get a valid answer to your calculations. The point of using symbols is that one statement will cope with lots of different individual calculations. To convert a string of symbols into a calculation, you simply work out what number each symbol stands for in your case, and replace the symbols with the numbers (see Table 20.5). The intimidating thing about them is that they look so strange, but, remember, it's just a code.

Part IV

PRESENTING YOUR WORK

21

How to reference

It is crucial to your work that you reference your sources correctly. This chapter aims to answer your questions about why and how to reference.

What is the purpose of referencing?

Referencing has two purposes. First, you must give credit where it is due for the ideas you have used. You do not want to be accused of plagiarism, that is, of passing someone else's ideas off as your own (see Chapter 22), which is a kind of academic theft or cheating.

Second, referencing enables the reader to trace an idea or piece of information right back to its source. The conventions of referencing are such that it should always be possible to do this. The writer is leaving a 'trail', and this trail must be clear all the way back, because:

- One of the major ways in which all researchers come across important new information is by reading about it in another source. Without full references, it would be impossible to track the information down.
- When your project is marked, your assessors are looking to see that you understand the material you are writing about. If you make reference to, or quote, some work that they do not know (which is not uncommon), or if you back up an apparently wacky idea with a quote or reference, it will be necessary for them to check it. Unless you give the full details, including the page number, it may be impossible – and certainly very time-consuming – for them to find it. As pointed out in Chapter 1, the golden rule of project writing is to not annoy your assessor, and incomplete referencing is a sure-fire way to make yourself extremely unpopular.

General tips

- Whatever your precise choice of referencing conventions, be consistent.
- If you do alphabetical auto-sorting using your word-processing program, check carefully for date order in each author's works, and the order of second authors.
- Alphabetical order is not always obvious. You should position names beginning 'Mc' as if they were spelled 'Mac'. List German names with an umlaut over a vowel as if the vowel was followed by an 'e'.
- The ordering of authors' names on a paper or book is significant in signalling the importance of each person's contribution, so, to be a correct reference, it must have the names in the order that the authors of that paper or book have designated. Even for

the same title, the sequence of author names can vary from one edition to another (e.g. Bloomer *et al.* 2005 becomes Merrison *et al.* forthcoming).

• In your text, refer to the authors, unless you expressly mean the publication. Thus: 'Pearson and De Villiers (2006) [the people] argue...', not 'Pearson and De Villiers (2006) [the work] argues...'

What does a basic reference look like?

Examples (1) and (2) below are from a book by Wardhaugh (1993: 109).

(1) The 'tip of the tongue' phenomenon (see Brown and McNeill, 1966) is an instance of this last kind of failure to bring an item immediately and completely out of long-term memory.

By referring to Brown and McNeill's paper, Wardhaugh is giving you, the reader, information about where to look for further details. The short reference given in the text (example 1) is backed up by a full reference in the alphabetical list of references at the back of Wardhaugh's book (example 2). This provides you with all you need to locate the original work, and to read for yourself what they did. In this book, as in most of the other books and papers that you will read, referencing according to these conventions is the norm:

(2) Brown, R., and McNeill, D. 1966. The 'tip of the tongue' phenomenon. *Journal of Verbal Learning and Verbal Behavior* 5, 325–37.

There is more detail later in this chapter about how to format references like this.

What is the difference between a 'references' list and a 'bibliography'?

These terms do tend to get used interchangeably in some contexts, but there is a difference between them. Your 'reference list' gives details of the books and articles that have been mentioned in your text. It should contain all of them, and should not contain anything you have read or looked at but not mentioned in the text. A 'bibliography' is a list of books and articles put together for some other purpose, usually to help researchers and/or as recommended reading for study. According to this rule, the list of sources at the end of your project should be headed 'References'.

Basics of referencing

What happens if I haven't seen the original work, just a reference to it or a quote from it somewhere else?

If you have not had access to the original source of an idea or quote, you will have to adopt the convention of citing or giving a secondary quote:

(3) Noam Chomsky believes that 'The language each person acquires is a rich and complex construction hopelessly undermined by the fragmentary evidence available [to the child]' (Chomsky 1975, quoted in Pinker 1994: 23).

You must include in your reference list the source that you used (in the above case, the work by Pinker). Practice varies regarding whether you should also list the original source (in example 3, the work by Chomsky). It is courteous to the reader to do so – it will prevent the need to find Pinker's book in order to track down the details. However, many lecturers dislike seeing secondary sources (works you refer to without having seen) listed in the reference list, because it makes it hard to tell what you have in fact read. Ask each lecturer for whom you write which practice you are to follow. Alternatively, include the secondary sources in your reference list, but indicate (with an asterisk, for instance) that you have not seen them. This practice is not something that you will see in published materials, and it is just a way of covering yourself when your assessors have different views. Remember, of course, to state what the asterisk (or other mark) signifies.

It is a good idea to keep second-hand quoting and citing to a minimum, by finding the original source wherever possible, and drawing from that instead. The only works that you should be quoting or citing second-hand are those that your library does not have, and which you have not had an opportunity to get sight of in any other way.

What is the difference between 'cited in' and 'quoted in'?

Many students muddle these two terms, probably because they have not really understood their respective meanings. When you *quote* something, you give the words as they appear in the original. Indicate this by putting inverted commas around the quote if it is less than two lines long, or by indenting the quote, with a line space above and below, if it is longer (for an example of this, see the first page of Chapter 7 in this book).

When you *cite* something, you mention it. There is no quotation involved. If you want to mention a source that you have found in another work, then you say 'cited in'. For example, if you read in Wardhaugh (1993) about Brown and McNeill's (1966) experiment (see example 1 above), then you might write:

(4) The 'tip of the tongue' phenomenon can be investigated experimentally, as Brown and MacNeill (1966, cited in Wardhaugh 1993: 109) have demonstrated.

How do I make sure I have managed to list all and only the sources I have mentioned?

One of your jobs as a writer is to ensure that your reference list is complete and accurate. In order to make sure that you have not omitted a reference, make a print-out of the list and then work through the text, ticking off on the print-out every reference as you come across it. If you find a reference in the text that ought to be on the list and isn't, then add it. If at the end of the process, there is any reference on the list that has not been ticked, then there is no mention of it in the text and it should be removed.

To speed things up, use the search facility in your word-processing program. Type in the first few letters of a name from the reference list and search for it. If the first occurrence that the search comes up with is in the reference list itself, then there is no mention in the text and the entry should be deleted. This procedure cannot be used to find out if a reference in the text is missing from the reference list. Alternatively, if you are using the Harvard referencing system (see below), every reference in your text should include round brackets, so if you search for an opening bracket, you should find every reference in the text.

Alternatively, use software such as *Endnote*, which automatically generates your reference list from the works you cite in your text. See next section.

What is the best way to keep track of what references I need to put in the list?

There are various methods, three of which are given below.

Method 1

Construct the reference list as you go. The advantage of this approach is that you have one less job to do at the end. There are a couple of disadvantages, though. First, as your work goes through different stages, you are likely to edit out passages containing references. It is not always easy to remember whether there are other mentions of those works in your project, and so you might not be sure whether or not to delete them from the reference list. Second, you may find that it breaks your flow to keep moving to the reference list when you are in the middle of writing. Alternatively, as you write, highlight each reference (on screen, or with highlighter pen, according to your medium). Then they will be easy to find later.

Method 2

When you have finished writing, do a very careful read, identifying all the references at that stage and building up the list. The advantage of this is that, if you are careful enough, you will end up with a list of all and only the references mentioned. The disadvantage is that you have to be quite disciplined to comb the text for only references. It is tempting to combine this job with a final read-through or a proofread for typing errors, and this division of your attention is quite likely to make you less efficient on all of the tasks.

Method 3

Use software such as *Endnote* to manage your references (see http://www.endnote.com/ for details). *Endnote* is expensive to buy, but your university or college may have a licence, so you can use it on networked computers and/or buy a reduced price copy for your own use at home. There are several advantages to this sort of software. It helps with your referencing because every time you mention a work in your essay or dissertation, it is automatically added to your reference list at the end. You can choose the format it appears in, and add page numbers to the reference in the text, and so on. Furthermore, because you have entered the details of the work into the database, you know you can always find a record of each thing you read. You can add notes on the content, and information about the library call/classification number for a book, or details of where you are storing it (e.g. the number you have given it in your electronic or hard copy store of papers). Another advantage is that if you add key words you can generate lists of just those items with that key word. This is useful if you are reading around many different areas or subareas, as you will in the course of your undergraduate degree or in a Masters or PhD.

Whichever method you use, remember one golden rule: every time you use a book or article, keep a note of the complete details that you will need for referencing purposes. Don't assume that it will be as easy to get the details later. For a start, without the reference details, how will you know where to look? Also, you cannot rely on a library catalogue to give you all the information you need for a reference list: very often no place of publication is given, and no titles, author details, or page numbers will be given for the papers in edited collections. If you assume that you can go back to the library and check the original source later, remember that someone else may have borrowed the book by then.

Is there only one way of referencing correctly?

No. There are two major systems, the Harvard and the Humane, and within each you may spot minor variations. So far in this chapter, and indeed in this book as a whole, we have adopted the Harvard system.

What is the basic difference between the Harvard and the Humane systems?

The distinction between Harvard and the Humane has traditionally been associated with the major division between the sciences (including the social sciences) and the arts, though the Harvard system now tends to be used in both. As linguistics spans the sciences and the arts, both systems can be found in older publications, but it is rare to find Humane referencing in recent books and journals. If you are studying a subject like English literature as well as linguistics, you may well find that you are required to use both systems. Accept this gracefully, and be careful to use whichever is required in each piece of work. Take particular care not to mix them, otherwise you will be using neither!

As to format, the Harvard system refers to works by their author(s) and date in the text, with full references at the end, alphabetically by author surname. The Humane system uses footnote numbers in the text, and gives the references, in numerical order (that is, in the order of their occurrence) at the foot of each page or at the end. In what follows, the guidelines relate to the Harvard system. A summary of how to reference in the Humane system is provided at the end of the chapter.

Details of the Harvard system conventions

How do I refer to a book?

In the text, give the author's name followed by date of publication (example 5). Where appropriate, give page numbers too (example 6).

(5) Asp and de Villiers (2010)

(6) Asp and de Villiers (2010: 35–43)

In the reference list, give the author's name, initial(s), date in brackets (although note that, in some versions of this system, the date is not in brackets, and it is followed by a colon; in others, there are neither brackets nor a colon), and title in italics, followed by a full stop, place of publication followed by a colon, publisher, and full stop:

(7) Asp, E.D. and De Villiers, J. (2010) *When language breaks down: analysing discourse in clinical contexts*. Cambridge: Cambridge University Press.

As you build up your list of references, apply strict alphabetical order by author surname.

What if the book is an edited collection of papers by other people?

In the text, use the same conventions as for a book (examples 5 and 6). In the reference list, add '(ed.)' for one editor or '(eds)' for two, after the author name(s) and initial(s), but before the date:

(8) Barfield, A. and Gyllstad, H. (eds) (2009) *Researching collocations in another language*. Basingstoke: Palgrave Macmillan.

However, consider whether it is really the edited collection itself that you should be referencing. If you are referring to material *within* that collection, refer to the specific chapter, using the name of its author. Thus, to draw on the paper by Groom that is included within the collection by Barfield and Gyllstad, refer to Groom (2009), not Barfield and Gyllstad (2009), and reference the work as outlined below under 'How is a paper in an edited book notated?'

How is a paper in an edited book notated?

In the text, give the author of the paper and the date of the edited book. Do not mention the editor(s) of the book here:

> (9) Smith (1996)

In the reference list, give the author with the initial(s), date, title of paper (not in italics; in some versions of this system the title of a paper is put in inverted commas), followed by a full stop. Then write 'In', followed by the book details, as described above. Finally, give the page numbers of the paper, preceded by a comma (or, in some versions, a colon, or a comma and 'p.' or 'pp.') and followed by a full stop:

> (10a) Smith, P.K. (1996) Language and the evolution of mind-reading. In Carruthers, P. and Smith, P.K. (eds) (1996) *Theories of theory of mind*. Cambridge: Cambridge University Press, 344–54.

Note that, if you are listing several items from the same collection, one option is to shorten the individual references (example 10b) by cross-referring to a single reference for the collection (example 10c). Doing this is only worthwhile if you have at least two items from the same collection, otherwise it increases the word count and space taken rather than decreasing it. Also, it is imperative that you *do* provide the entry for the collection (example 10c), since entries like example 10b are *not permissible* without it.

> (10b) Smith, P.K. (1996) Language and the evolution of mind-reading. In Carruthers, P. and Smith, P.K. (eds.), (1996) 344–54.

> (10c) Carruthers, P. and Smith, P.K. (eds.) (1996) *Theories of theory of mind*. Cambridge: Cambridge University Press, 344–54.

What are the conventions for a paper in a journal?

In the text, proceed as above (example 9). In the reference list, give the author(s) with initials, date, title of paper (not in italics; in some versions of this system the title is put in inverted commas), full stop. Then give the title of the journal, in italics, volume number, part number in brackets if appropriate, and pages, preceded by a comma (or, in some versions, by a colon, or a comma and 'p.' or 'pp.') and followed by a full stop:

> (11) Culpeper, J. (2010) Conventionalised impoliteness formulae. *Journal of Pragmatics* 42 (12), 3232–45.

Note that it is *not* necessary to name the publisher of a journal.

Are there any special conventions for referencing more than one work by the same person?

Practice varies. It is common simply to see the name repeated on line after line in the references list where there are a lot of references to one person's work. That is the practice adopted in this book. However, another option is to replace the name by a long dash after its first occurrence:

(12) Trudgill, P. (1974) *The social differentiation of English in Norwich*. Cambridge: Cambridge University Press.

— (1978) *Sociolinguistic patterns in British English*. London: Arnold.

— (1983) *On dialect*. Oxford: Blackwell.

If you choose to adopt this convention, it is a good idea to wait until the last minute before replacing the repeated names by dashes. This is to avoid accidentally inserting another author's work (here, it might be, say, something by Turnbull) under the first entry, so that the later entries are attributed to the wrong person.

What should I do if I have referred to more than one work by the same person, published in the same year?

Since it would be confusing to have two or more works all referred to as, say, Crystal (2003), the convention is to label them 2003a, 2003b, 2003c, and so on. You should use these letters both in the main text and in the reference list, and ensure that you always use the same letter for the same one. Look at the References in this book for the two works by Crystal that were published in 2003, to see how this operates. Note that the use of letters is local to the piece of writing in question. If you find such a letter in someone else's references, do not simply adopt the letter as if it were a permanent part of the reference – it is not and, if you are only referring to that one work, you don't need it. You should never have in your reference list a date with a letter after it unless there is at least one other work by that author with that date, also with a (different) letter after it. Note also that there is nothing intrinsic in the publication that is referred to as 'a' that means it had to be 'a'. Someone else might list it as the 'b' publication.

What if there is more than one author with the same surname?

In the references, list the authors in alphabetical order of their forenames or initials. In the text, because authors are referred to by surname only, there is the potential for confusion if both authors have published in the same year. If this occurs in your work, add the initial in the text reference, for example J. Smith (2011), so that the reader knows which Smith (2011) reference you mean. In this book we only narrowly missed having this problem with the names Brown, Cameron, Carroll, Clark, Cook, Edwards, Lakoff, Smith, Thomas, and White.

When an author has co-authored with others, which order do the works go in on the reference list?

To illustrate how to do this, we'll use some made-up authors, so that we can imagine various permutations (example 13). We'll call the first author Penelope Wilkinson. First, put all the single-authored work by that person into year order; then sort the co-authored works alphabetically by the second author's name, and list them in that order. Works by the same two authors are in date order:

(13) Wilkinson, P. (2006) . . .

Wilkinson, P. (2009) . . .

Wilkinson, P. (2011) . . .

Wilkinson, P. and Armitage, S. (2007) . . .

>　Wilkinson, P. and Cooper, M. (2002) . . .
>
>　Wilkinson, P. and Cooper, M. (2006) . . .

If a two-author team has also written with a third person, put the three-author work at the end of the list of works by the first two authors, even if it is of an earlier date than some of them. If there is more than one work by the same three-author team, put them in date order:

>　(14) Wilkinson, P. and Armitage, S. (2007) . . .
>
>　　Wilkinson, P. and Cooper, M. (2002) . . .
>
>　　Wilkinson, P. and Cooper, M. (2006) . . .
>
>　　Wilkinson, P., Cooper, M. and Bryant. Q. (2000) . . .
>
>　　Wilkinson, P., Cooper, M. and Bryant, Q. (2003) . . .
>
>　　Wilkinson, P., Cooper, M. and Caradine, K. (2002) . . .
>
>　　Wilkinson, P., Cooper, M., Collins, R. and Bryant, Q. (2009) . . .
>
>　　Wilkinson, P. and Davies, K. (2006) . . .

In other words, clear up all the works by the author on his/her own before doing the two-author works. Clear up everything by each two-author team, including works with extra authors, before moving onto the next two-author team. Remember that the order in which the authors' names appear on a book or paper is extremely important and you must not change it. So, in the penultimate line of example 14, Bryant is listed after Collins, and it is Collins's name that determines the position of the reference, below the publication with Caradine.

If there are lots of authors, do they all have to be mentioned each time?

In the text, on the first occurrence of the reference, give all the names and, after that, use '*et al.*', which means 'and others' (so don't use it to replace just one co-author!):

>　(15)　Barber, Beal and Shaw (2009) . . . Barber *et al.* (2009) ...

In the reference list, give all the authors with their initials, linking them with a comma until the last two, which are linked with 'and':

>　(16)　Barber C., Beal, J. and Shaw, P. (2009) *The English language: a historical introduction* (2nd edition). Cambridge: Cambridge University Press.

What if an author has published more than one work with several other authors in the same year?

If Smith, say, has published two papers with Jones, Brown, and White, both in 2011, then you can refer to them as Smith *et al.* (2011a) and Smith *et al.* (2011b) (see above). If Smith has published with different co-authors in the same year (or with the same co-authors, but listed in a different order), it is more awkward. They will be differentiated in the reference list but, if you refer to them in the text just as 'Smith *et al.* (2011)', the reader will not know which work is being referred to. Yet it would be odd to refer to them as (a) and (b) since the authorship lists are not identical. One solution is to opt out of using '*et al.*' for these particular works and list all the authors each time you mention them. This is the best option if there are only three authors. For more than three authors, see how far down the list of authors the differences lie. You may be able to refer to 'Smith, Jones *et al.* (2011)', 'Smith, Brown, *et al.* (2011), and so on. You can only do this if at least two names remain captured by *'et al.'*.

How do I handle family names with more than one part?

Names like Robert de Beaugrande and Wilhelm von Humboldt can be difficult: should they be listed alphabetically under the second or the third part of the name? Where three names are given, such as Alonso Zamora Vicente, Susan Ervin Tripp or Suzette Haden Elgin, does the middle one count as the first part of the family name, or as part of the given name? Don't give yourself a hard time over this: individuals with such names will have their own preferences, but other forces are at play too, including the practices of individual publishers. Here are some handy hints for what to do:

• Go back to the source of your information. If you have read the name in a book or article, find it in the reference list and follow the practice there. If you have something by the author him-/herself, there may well be citations of his/her other works in reference list, so check there.
• Aim for consistency in your own reference list. So if you choose to list De Beaugrande under 'D', do the same for De Saussure, and list Von Humboldt under 'V'. If you list De Beaugrande as 'Beaugrande, R. de' then it will be 'Saussure, F. de' and 'Humboldt, W. von'.

Some names from other countries can be difficult to list too. In China, it is customary for the family name to precede the given name in everyday usage, and this can mean that in a reference, the given name is inadvertently listed as a surname. Additional complications arise because many Chinese scholars adopt Western practices when presenting their name, and because it is not always easy even for a Chinese person to tell which name is the family name and which the given name. In order to list the name correctly, check the author's own publications to see how reference is made to his/her previous works. You can also search for the author's web pages for the same purposes. For instance, in this book, we list works by Li Wei under L, not W, because that is what he does himself.

Where do I find the information I need?

In a book, the publication details are usually in the first few pages at the front. Be careful to copy the authors' names and the book or paper title correctly. The date of publication will normally be on the same left-hand page as the ISBN number and the British Library or Library of Congress (or other national library) cataloguing data. It is not usually difficult to spot the publisher (but beware of giving the printer or typesetter by mistake). However, it is sometimes difficult to work out the place of publication. If there is an address for the publisher, give the town and, if American, the state as well. If there are several addresses, give the top one, or the one associated with editorial as opposed to marketing concerns. Some large publishing houses publish simultaneously in two countries (such as the UK and the USA): if you can't tell which country the book was probably commissioned in, give both places.

In a journal, the name of the journal and the volume number and part should be printed somewhere on the article as a header or footer. If they are not, and you have the whole journal in your hand or on your screen, look in the front, or on the back cover. If you have only a photocopy, you obviously needed to write down the details when you made the copy. If you didn't, you have a problem, so remember to do that in future! To find details you forgot to write down, use a web search-engine such as Google, to see if anyone has listed it on a website. Alternatively, see what electronic search facilities your library has.

How do I reference a work with no apparent author?

This situation can arise when you cite an official report, a newspaper article, or a large work such as a dictionary or encyclopaedia. For an official report (example 17) or newspaper (example 18), treat the commissioner or publisher of the report as the author. For a dictionary, give the name (example 19). Do the same for an encyclopaedia, unless the author's name is given at the foot of the article, in which case, treat it like a paper in an edited volume (example 20):

(17) Department for Education and Science (1975) *A language for life* (The Bullock Report). London: Department for Education and Science.

(18) *Times* (2005) Google must win 'keyword' battle. *The Times*. 22 October, p.66.

(19) *Oxford English Dictionary*. (2nd edition). Oxford: Oxford University Press.

(20) Cameron, D. (2006) Gender. In Brown, E.K. (ed.) *Encyclopaedia of language and linguistics*. Oxford: Elsevier, vol. 4: 733–9.

If a book has more than one edition, or has been reprinted or revised, which date do I use?

Inside a book all sorts of information is given and only some of it is relevant to academic referencing needs. The basic rule is to give the earliest date for the text in its current form. When a new edition of a book is produced, material is added and the page numbers end up different, so it is important that you indicate which edition you have used, and give the correct date for that edition. Indicate an edition by putting '(nth edition)' after the title, where n stands for the edition number (e.g. 3rd, 4th). However, when a book is reprinted, comes out in paperback or is made available for Kindle, the material is not altered, so you should not make any reference to reprint or paperback dates, or Kindle editions. Sometimes there is a date given for a reprint with revisions. In this case, give the reprint date, and in the reference, put '(revised edition)' after the title.

What if the date of publication is different from the copyright date?

Use the publication date, unless there is evidence to the contrary in the reference lists of others. If there is a large discrepancy it will probably be because the work has been re-issued, in which case the 'copyright' date coincides with the original date of publication. In the case of key papers that end up in a 'reader', it can be useful to indicate the original publication date as well (see the section 'Which date?' below).

If I am referring repeatedly to the same work, do I have to keep mentioning it?

It certainly is possible to overdo referencing of the same work. If you are drawing heavily on one source for a while, it is acceptable to write something like: 'In the following discussion, much has been drawn from the work of Brown (2011).' However, have a think about why you are so dependent on one work. Could it indicate that you have not read sufficiently widely? See Chapter 22 for guidance on how to work effectively with multiple sources.

If you refer more than once to the same work with no other reference in between, it is also possible to use the abbreviations *op. cit.* (short for *opere citato* – 'in the work cited') or *ibid.* (short for *ibidem* – 'in the same place'), to indicate that the referencing information is exactly the same as last time, including the page number, if any (example 21). If the page number is different, indicate this (example 22):

(21) According to Brown (2005: 10) … In addition, …. (*ibid.*)

(22) According to Brown (2005: 10) … In addition, …. (*ibid.*: 17)

However, these abbreviations are used much less frequently than they used to be. If you do use them, only introduce them in the final draft, as they *must* refer to the immediately preceding reference. As text often gets moved around, added or removed in the rewrites, you could end up with an *ibid.* or *op. cit.* referring back to the wrong work if you put it in too soon.

What are the conventions for punctuation in reference lists?

These do vary considerably; however, as long as you are consistent, it doesn't matter too much which conventions you use, unless you are preparing something for publication, when you should check with the notes for authors that are issued by the publisher. Certain conventions, however, are fairly standard. We recommend the practice adopted for referencing throughout this book (giving you plenty of examples to refer to):

- Names: Place a comma after the surname, a space and then the initial(s). Follow each initial by a full stop; after each name in a list of authors, add a comma, except the penultimate (which is linked to the final one with 'and').
- Date: Put the date of publication in brackets.
- Titles: Use 'sentence case' (only the first initial and proper nouns are capitalized); put book and journal titles in italics, but not the titles of papers within a book or journal. Put a full stop at the end of the title.
- Publication: Put the place of publication first, followed by a colon, then the publisher's name, followed by a full stop.
- Pages: introduce the page numbers by a colon.
- Other: Use a full stop after abbreviations such as 'ed.' (for editor). 'Editors' is contracted to 'eds' and 'edition' to 'edn' and neither of these has a full stop.

As the reference list is organized alphabetically, do not use bullet points or numbers to indicate each entry.

What should I do if I can't print italics or I am writing by hand?

Wherever italics would occur (in reference lists and also in the main text), it is acceptable to use underlining.

Is it possible to put into the reference list a work that has not yet been published?

Yes. If you have had sight of a paper or book that is currently being printed but hasn't yet appeared, write *forthcoming* or *in press* where you would otherwise write the date and, if it is a paper and the page numbers are not available, omit them. It is also possible to refer to a work that is at an earlier stage. Do this in the same way as above, but replacing *forthcoming* or *in press* with *in preparation*. Beware of using these labels when you have found the reference in another source. A work that was forthcoming, in press, or in preparation in 2009 is probably published by now, so you need to try and find its publication date (and check that it actually got published at all).

If, in the text, I refer to more than one work at once, what order do I list them in?

There are two permissible orders: alphabetical (example 23) and chronological (example 24). Whichever you choose, be consistent. If you are mentioning several works by the same author, you will save words by using alphabetical order:

(23) … (Brown 1998, 2004; Smith 1999, 2001; White 2000)

(24) … (Brown 1998; Smith 1999; White 2000; Smith 2001; Brown 2004).

Suppose I asked an expert about something face to face or by email – how do I acknowledge the source of my information?

You can write 'Brown (personal communication)' or 'John Brown (personal communication)', depending on whether the reader will know from the context who Brown is – often you check a fact with a researcher whose work you are already engaging with. You should not list anything like this in the reference list at the back. Information from your lecturers, family, or friends will not usually make the grade of a 'personal communication' citation.

How do I reference information from my lecture notes?

Ask your lecturer if it is okay to reference your lecture notes. Usually it is not recommended. If at all possible, go and find the information in a published source and refer to that instead.

Which date?

Sometimes a work has more than one publication date, because it is a re-issue or a modern edition (prepared by someone else) of a classic work, or a reprint (sometimes edited) in a 'reader'. By referring to the original and the later date, you signal to the reader that you have used the more recent one, and that any page numbers will be from that, not the original. Examples in the reference list of this book include Maltz and Borker (1982/2011) and Carroll (1865/1971).

How do I reference something I found on the Internet?

Internet referencing conventions are not fully standardized yet, and you may see various practices. However, keep in mind the golden rules of *all* referencing:

1 Give due credit to the author.
2 Make it possible for your reader to track the work down.

These two principles, between them, lead to the following recommended good practice for referencing a web source. Use the following:

- the author's name or that of the organization that the author represents;
- the title of the piece;
- the address;
- the date on which you last accessed it.

If you cannot tell who wrote or authorized the page, look for a link to a home page, or remove sections of the address from the right, to see if you can find one. Since not all material from the Internet is trustworthy, be suspicious about pages that you cannot associate with a named person or organization with credentials. (See also Chapter 1 for advice on how to avoid ending up with untrustworthy material.)

- *Don't* just provide the web address as the reference. This is the equivalent of referencing a book by saying which shelf it is on in the library. (However, if it is indeed the address rather than the information on the page that you are referring to, then it is acceptable to give the web-page address in the main text, as we do, for instance, in Chapter 19, when we are advising you where to go to. In your project, such a reference is likely to be the exception rather than the rule, so think twice before taking this course of action.)
- Make sure you give the *full and correct web address* for the material, so that the reader can go straight there. For each web address that you give, try entering the address yourself and see whether it does get you to the right place.

By way of illustration of the above observations, it is *not* good practice to write:

> (25) There is no single agreed definition of formulaic language (http://www.cardiff. ac.uk/encap/research/networks/flarn/whatis/index.html).

Instead, you should find out who wrote the material and name that person (example 26a) and/or his/her affiliation (example 26b) and give the Internet reference in the reference list at the end (examples 27a, 27b):

> (26a) There is no single agreed definition of formulaic language (Wray 2011).

> (26b) There is no single agreed definition of formulaic language (Formulaic Language Research Network, Cardiff University, 2011).

> (27a) Wray, A. 2011. What is formulaic language?

> (http://www.cardiff.ac.uk/encap/research/networks/flarn/whatis/index.html). [Last accessed 7th August 2011]

> (27b) Formulaic Language Research Network, Cardiff University. 2011. What is formulaic language? (http://www.cardiff.ac.uk/encap/research/networks/flarn/ whatis/index.html). [Last accessed 7th August 2011]

Details of the Humane system conventions

In the Humane referencing system, a superscript number in the text points the reader to a footnote or endnote containing the reference information. Thus, in the text, place a superscript number adjacent to the word that precedes the reference you wish to make:

(28) Messages in language fall into three situation types: states, events, and actions.[18]
      These situation types are . . .

In the footnote or endnote, adopt the following procedures.

For a book

Give the initial(s), author(s), title in italics, place of publication, publisher, and date together in brackets, and page(s) relevant to the point you are making, if any (example 29):

(29) [18] D. Graddol and J. Swann, *Gender Voices* (Oxford, Blackwell, 1989), p. 77.

If you have to refer to it again, you use a shortened form, with just the surnames, a shortened title if it isn't short enough already, and the page (example 30):

(30) [20] Graddol and Swann, *Gender Voices*, p. 54.

For an edited book

Proceed as above (examples 29 and 30), but add 'ed.,' after the author name(s).

For a paper in an edited volume

Give the initial(s), author(s), title in inverted commas, 'in', editor's name, comma, '(ed.)', title of book in italics, place of publication, publisher, and date together in brackets, and page(s) relevant to the point you are making, if any (not the page range for the entire paper) (example 31). Use a short reference for later mentions (example 32). There are no rules for what the title gets shortened to, provided a reader will be entirely sure which work you are referring to.

(31) [41] G.R. Guy, 'Language and Social Class', in F.J. Newmark (ed.) *Linguistics: The Cambridge Survey IV – Language: The Socio-cultural Context* (Cambridge, Cambridge University Press, 1988), pp. 60–1.

(32) [45] Guy, 'Social Class', p. 63.

For a paper in a journal

Give the initial(s), author(s), title in inverted commas, journal name in italics, volume number, date in brackets, and page(s) relevant to the point you are making, if any (not the page range for the entire paper) (example 33). Use a short reference for later mentions (example 34):

(33) [3] N. Alm, J.L. Arnott and A.F. Newell, 'Discourse Analysis and Pragmatics in the Design of a Conversation Prosthesis', *Journal of Medical Engineering and Technology*, 13/2 (1989), p. 12.

(34) [12] Alm *et al.*, 'Prosthesis', p. 11.

The use of punctuation

This varies somewhat between users of the Humane system. The Hodder guidelines, from which the above information has been taken, require the capitalization of every initial letter in titles, full stops at the end of the entire reference, and commas in the places illustrated in the examples above.

Plagiarism and how to avoid it

What is plagiarism?

Plagiarism is the *theft* of other people's words and ideas. Plagiarism happens when you claim (or *appear* to claim) that an idea, or the expression of it, is your own when in fact it is someone else's. Plagiarism falls into two types: deliberate and accidental.

Deliberate plagiarism

Deliberate plagiarism includes getting someone else to write your essay for you and then saying it's yours or copying chunks of text out of a book or from the Internet, with the deliberate intention of deceiving the reader into thinking they are in your own words. Why would people engage in deliberate plagiarism? Perhaps out of laziness and a disregard for the requirements and expectations of university study. Perhaps when it seems pointless to restate less expertly what someone else has said well. Perhaps because the copied material is in better English. Or perhaps because of the mistaken belief that everyone else is doing it and getting away with it. It would be as well to treat this claim with the same scepticism as you would the claim that 'everyone' is shoplifting or that 'everyone' is using hard drugs. It is not everyone, nor does the fact that some people are doing it make it right or safe. And it's your choice. Leaving aside the very serious penalties for plagiarism – failing your module, losing the credits, perhaps even being expelled from your course – think back to your aspirations when you came to university. Did they include cheating your way to a qualification you are supposed to gain through study and skills development? Will you respect yourself if you know you never really earned your degree? Will you be able to cope in your career if you have ducked out of learning key skills by cheating?

Accidental plagiarism

Accidental plagiarism is, as the term implies, unintentional. However, since it looks identical to deliberate plagiarism, many institutions penalize it equally heavily. It comes about through oversight and/or lack of skill in manipulating information. You need to be alert for the dangers of accidental plagiarism and have the techniques for ensuring that you avoid it (see below). The problem is that we all rely heavily on other people's ideas! How else can we learn? And, unless we have a photographic memory, how are we to be sure that an idea that occurs to us really is our own and not something that we read somewhere? The dangers of accidental plagiarism can seem to loom like hidden icebergs in the sea – you know they are there, but you can't really see if you are going to hit one.

Here are some examples of how accidental plagiarism can happen:

- You make notes from a book or other source, copying out useful passages. Later, you cannot remember what is copied and what is not and you simply take passages from your notes and use them in the essay.
- You find material in a book or other source that covers exactly the area you are dealing with. You are aware that you mustn't copy it out, so you deftly rephrase little bits, replacing 'small' with 'little', 'major differences' by 'main differences' and swapping over the order of two halves of a sentence. *You* think that this is now legitimate but your assessors do not.
- You use entirely your own words but you don't acknowledge the source of your information.
- You draw from notes you made or were given in some previous course of study (school notes, for example), without realizing that these were copied or adapted from some other source.

Will you get found out?

University lecturers are intelligent people! They have read a lot of essays and they know their subject. If you have plagiarized material in your essay, it may not be all that evident to *you*, but it probably will be to them. With the possibility of electronic searches, it is very quick to check whether something is plagiarized, and there are a number of dedicated software programs available too, such as Turnitin (http://turnitin.com/static/index.php), through which institutions now often require coursework to be checked. So, yes, there is a good chance that, if you have plagiarized, you will be found out.

How to avoid accidental plagiarism: some strategies

There are four key skills that will enable you to avoid plagiarizing by mistake: thorough referencing, care with note-taking, skilled writing, and finding your 'voice'. They are very much interrelated, so mastering all four is important.

Referencing

In an essay or project, you will be presenting three different kinds of material: (1) general knowledge; (2) evidence and ideas from other people; (3) your own evidence and ideas.

1 General knowledge (e.g. *English is a Germanic language*) is not open to dispute, and there are many possible places that you could get that information, so it does not need to be referenced.
2 Evidence and ideas from other people include findings in work they have done and claims about what their findings, or those of others, mean for some wider question. This kind of material must be referenced clearly, both to give credit where it is due, and as a means of distancing yourself from it. Just because they say something, it doesn't make it true.

3 Your own evidence – from data you have collected, for example – and your own ideas, developed out of that evidence in conjunction with what you have read, cannot, of course, be referenced as such. However, you can certainly help the reader to see where your evidence lies (by presenting your data in tables, for example) and how you have got to your idea (by referring to your evidence, and also to ideas from others that you are drawing on).

Sometimes you will simply not be sure whether something needs referencing or not, because the boundaries between general knowledge, other's ideas, and your own ideas are not always clear. If in doubt, err on the side of *over*-referencing until you get the knack. Having too many references in a text breaks up the flow of your writing but that is the lesser of two evils. One problem can be the need repeatedly to reference the same work. For ideas on how to avoid this, see 'Skilled writing' below. Information on how to reference in the correct format is given in Chapter 21.

Taking notes

Good note-taking involves thinking. It is the time to develop your ideas, so get into the habit of asking more than just 'What does X say?'. You need to ask 'What does it mean that X says this?' and 'How can X say this when Y says that?' Rather than just summarizing what you are reading, make notes relevant to the task in hand and identify the major points that relate to your purpose. Make the notes under headings, so that similar ideas from different sources end up together. When you come to write, read through all the notes under that heading and try to work out how they relate. This is a productive and positive way to avoid any danger of plagiarism, because you will never simply transfer material from a source, via your notes, to your own work. You will quite naturally repackage ideas according to your own interpretations and priorities. You will also be keen to reference others' claims, because you will be taking issue with them (see 'Skilled writing' below).

When making notes, *never* copy anything out without putting it in inverted commas and putting a page reference next to it. Also write down the *full* reference details, as you will need them later and you will be frustrated if, a few hours before your deadline, you don't have all you need. *Never* copy and paste material from a website into your notes unless you mark it in some way as a quote: with highlight, perhaps. Always include, with material from the Internet, the full web address (that is, what you will need in your browser in order to get back to exactly that material). Also keep a note of the date that you accessed it, as you will need that for the reference (see Chapter 21).

As you read and take notes, try to think of examples of your own to match the ones provided. This is a good way of ensuring that you understand what you are writing about. However, if you are in doubt about whether your example is valid (e.g. where the examples have been drawn from a particular source that you cannot access), you can quote the ones you have been given provided you acknowledge them appropriately, i.e. as quotes. If there is any terminology you don't understand, look it up, don't just copy it out.

Skilled writing

Sometimes an assessor will incorrectly suspect that a student has plagiarized, because there is insufficient difference between the presentation of ideas from others and the student's own ideas. Clear referencing of others' ideas can be supplemented by the use of discourse markers that indicate where the student is expressing his/her own opinion. Consider the following passage:

> *Ji (2004) describes how Mao's Cultural Revolution affected the Chinese language. A number of politically charged linguistic formulas introduced during that period made it difficult for speakers to think in counter-revolutionary ways. The result was something similar to the linguistic control described in Orwell's novel* Nineteen-Eighty-Four. *The television-bound culture of modern Western life may have a similar effect. Because people are highly vulnerable to cultural influences, governments have a responsibility not to be too directive.*

It is not clear in this passage which ideas are Ji's and which are the writer's. However, a few simple markers can make it clear that the writer has developed two new ideas out of Ji's, leaving the reader confident that there has been no plagiarism:

> *Ji (2004) describes how Mao's Cultural Revolution affected the Chinese language.* **She proposes that a** *number of politically charged linguistic formulas introduced during that period made it difficult for speakers to think in counter-revolutionary ways.* **She argues that** *the result was something similar to the linguistic control described in Orwell's novel 1984.* **It is interesting to consider whether** *the television-bound culture of modern Western life may have a similar effect.* **It could be argued that,** *because people are highly vulnerable to cultural influences, governments have a responsibility not to be too directive.*

What should you do if you are referring for some time to just one work? How often should you mention the reference? The first trick is to avoid that situation. Why are you so reliant on one source? Perhaps you need to read some other works, and see if you can draw them in. We show you how to do this in 'Finding your voice' below. However, if you can't avoid repeated references, you may be able to say at the beginning of a section or paragraph: *The following is a summary of information given in Smith (2005).* Note, however, that it is *not* sufficient to give one vague reference to your source somewhere and then draw directly from it for page after page.

To get the knack of skilled writing and referencing, take note of how it is done in the books and papers you read.

Finding your voice: An exercise in using published sources, creating a sophisticated account, and avoiding plagiarism

Correct referencing, the avoidance of plagiarism, and the use of a variety of sources in your account are inextricably linked. The one most common reason why students end up accidentally plagiarizing is because they find it impossible to express the information they have read in a new way. There are two major causes of this problem. One is using only one source. Reading about something in only one place can beguile you into thinking that this is the only way to see the issue, and that there is nothing else to say and no other way to say it. In fact, it is a mistake to assume that all sources will tell you the same thing, so it is always a good idea to look up the same information in more than one place. The second cause is that you need the same quantity of information as the source provides you with. You are more likely to avoid plagiarism if the source has 20 pages and you only need five lines, or if you need to write 20 pages and the source only gives five lines.

In this exercise, Part 1 demonstrates the problems with drawing from only one source and suggests some ways of finding a new approach to the material. Part 2 challenges you to use two sources to create a tension, giving you an opportunity to take sides or act as referee. Part 3 shows how to add extra information and references to a text you have already drafted. Although this study will make sense if you just read the commentaries, it will make more impact on your skills if you do the exercises for each section before moving on.

The theme

For the purposes of this exercise, imagine you need to write a section of an essay on the way that English expresses comparatives (e.g. *faster*) and superlatives (*fastest*) and how it used to do this in the past. This is not a very complicated subject, and most books deal with it in a few sentences. So will you, but how do you avoid simply reproducing the sentences in a book word for word?

1 Using one source only

Exercise

Read the extract from Barber (2000: 274) given in Figure 22.1 and then write a paragraph on the subject, in your own words. Try to apply the guidelines on how to avoid plagiarism given in this chapter. When you have finished, read the commentary below.

Changes in grammar

In grammar we can see the continuation, in small ways, of the long-term historical trend in English from synthetic to analytic, from a system that relies on inflections to one that relies on word-order and grammatical words. An example is the comparison of adjectives, where *more* and *most* are spreading at the expense of the endings *-er* and *-est*. At one time, *-er* and *-est* were used much more widely than today, and in Early Modern English you meet forms like *ancientest, famousest, patienter, perfecter,* and *shamefuller*. In the first half of the twentieth century, adjectives of more than two syllables always had *more* and *most* ('more notorious, most notorious'), while adjectives of one syllable normally had *-er* and *-est* ('ruder, rudest'). Adjectives of two syllables varied, some being compared one way ('more famous, most famous') and some the other ('commoner, commonest'). In this group of two-syllabled adjectives there has been a tendency in recent years for *-er* and *-est* to be replaced by *more* and *most*, and it is now quite normal to say 'more common, most common', and similarly with *cloudy, cruel, fussy, pleasant, quiet,* and *simple*. Recently, moreover, *more* and *most* have been spreading to adjectives of one syllable, and it is not at all uncommon to hear expressions like 'John is more keen than Robert' and 'It was more crude than I expected'.

Figure 22.1 Barber, C. (2000). *The English language: a historical introduction.* Cambridge: Cambridge University Press, 274. Reproduced with permission of Cambridge University Press.

Commentary

This is actually an extremely difficult task, because using only one source gives you very little room for manoeuvre. The referencing can look rather silly if you are acknowledging the same page of the same work all the time. You may have felt under-confident about inventing your own examples, in case they were not valid ones. You may have found it very difficult to express things in your own words. Remember that it is still plagiarism if you change the odd word but leave the text effectively the same. Example 1 illustrates a 'rewrite' that would constitute plagiarism, because the underlined changes to the original are only superficial ones:

(1) <u>Once</u>, -*er* and -*est* were used much more <u>than they are</u> today, and in Early Modern English <u>forms could be found</u> like *ancientest, famousest, patienter, perfecter,* and *shamefuller.*

You need strategies that enable you to break out of the narrow restrictions imposed by the source text. One possibility is to approach the subject from a different direction:

(2) Within living memory the expression of some comparatives and superlatives has changed . . .

Another is to present some of the facts in list form, as in example 3, where you can also see how it helps to use phrases like 'according to' and 'X claims', to distance yourself from the author, making it clear that this is only one view and that others might exist:

(3) According to Barber (2000: 274), a study of the forms used in Early Modern English through to the present day indicates that a change has been in progress. He believes that there has been a decrease in the tolerance for -*er* (comparative) and -*est* (superlative), which were once acceptable endings on even polysyllabic words (e.g. *ancienter, ancientest; famouser, famousest*) but which have gradually been replaced by *more* and *most* (e.g. *more ancient, most ancient; more famous, most famous*). This change happened earliest on the longest words. By the early 20th century, the preferences were:
  - polysyllabic adjectives (more than two syllables): add *more* (comparative) and *most* (superlative), e.g. *more beautiful, most beautiful; more interesting, most interesting.*
  - monosyllabic adjectives: add -*er* (comparative) and -*est* (superlative), e.g. *richer, richest; bluer, bluest.*
  - disyllabic adjectives: either form, e.g. *most famous, commonest.*

Barber claims that the transition is now almost complete, with the -*er* and -*est* endings apparently being edged out of the picture entirely, as even monosyllabic words form their comparative and superlative with *more* and *most* (e.g. *The star is more bright than it was yesterday, but it will be most bright tomorrow*).

2 Using two sources and any arising

Exercise

Read the extracts from Strang (1970: 58 and 138) in Figures 22.2 and 22.3. Write a new account, incorporating the information from both Barber and Strang: note that the relevant extract from Barber (1964) has also been provided for you (Figure 22.4). When you have finished, read the commentary below.

§41 It is very much more difficult to show how synchronic variation in grammar provides a model for variation through time. A recent book on *Linguistic Change in Present-day English* (Barber, 1964) has substantial sections on pronunciation (33–76), and vocabulary and meaning (77–128), but a much shorter one on grammar (129–45). About the developments mentioned in the chapter on *Grammatical Changes* some people might have reservations – for instance, under the heading 'loss of inflections' Barber discusses the distribution of *who* and *whom*, though uncertainties in this area of usage can clearly be traced back to the time of Shakespeare, and sequences like *he gave it to my brother and I*, though many will feel this is non-standard (i.e., not a change in the variety of English under discussion). Barber thinks there is an increasing use of *more, most*, rather than *-er, -est*, in comparison, in keeping with a trend which again goes back at least four hundred years; he may be right, but we lack precise numerical information on the subject.

Figure 22.2 Strang, B. (1970) *A history of English*. London and New York: Routledge, 58. Reproduced with permission of Routledge.

The roles of adjectives and nouns were perhaps less sharply distinguished than now; such uses as *better than he* (= better men), *full of poor* (= poor people), and, with a determiner, *in many's eyes*, now require a nominal head. This is related to the growth of the prop-word as a noun-place filler, an aspect of the general sense that there are places that ought to be filled by certain form-classes or certain clause-elements.

Double comparatives and superlatives were perfectly acceptable at the beginning of the period (*more properer, most handsomest*), though they came under corrective treatment in the 18c. In certain cases where the forms of comparison had, for phonological reasons, come to be irregular, such as *late, latter, last*, new analogical forms, *later, latest*, had been developed before II, but they were quite recent, and were alternatives in free variation with the historic forms. It is only more recently that the two sets have been differentiated.

Figure 22.3 Strang, B. (1970) *A history of English*. London and New York: Routledge, 138. Reproduced with permission of Routledge.

The continued loss of inflexions, and their replacement by syntactic devices, is also seen in the comparative and superlative of adjectives, where forms with *-er* and *-est* are being replaced by forms with *more* and *most*. Here we see the continuation of a trend of long standing: Milton wrote *elegantest, famousest*, and *sheepishest*, and Archbishop Laud *notoriousest*, where we should write *most elegant*, and so on. To-day, adjectives with three or more syllables are normally compared with *more* and *most* (*beautiful, more beautiful, most beautiful*); monosyllabic adjectives, on the other hand, are normally compared with *-er* and *-est* (*bright, brighter, brightest*). The adjectives with two syllables are divided, some usually being compared one way, the others the other; and it is in this dissyllabic group that the change is most noticeable, adjectives formerly taking *-er* and *-est* tending to go over to *more* and *most*. A word where this is especially noticeable is *common*; twenty or thirty years ago, *commoner* and *commonest* were normal, but nowadays nearly everybody says *more common, most common*. Indeed, I recently borrowed from a university library a book written in the nineteen-thirties by a distinguished literary scholar: in one place, the word *commonest* occurred; this had been vigorously crossed out by some borrower (presumably a student), who had written in the margin "most common!!!" Another example is heard in B.B.C. weather-forecasts, which frequently say that it will be *more cloudy*, instead of *cloudier*. Other adjectives that I have heard with *more* or *most* include *fussy, quiet, cruel, subtle, clever, profound, simple*, and *pleasant*; all these, I think, were normally compared with *-er* and *-est* before the War. I have also been struck by the frequency of forms like *more well-informed* and *most well-dressed*, where people would formerly have said *better-informed* and *best-dressed*. Recently there have been many cases of *more* and *most* spreading even to monosyllabic adjectives; examples I have noticed in educated speech and writing include *more crude, more plain*, and *more keen*. In Miss Iris Murdoch's well-known novel, *The Bell*, occurs the remarkable phrase *one of the most good people that he knew*.

Figure 22.4 Barber, C. (1964) *Linguistic change in present-day English*. London: Oliver and Boyd, 131–2. Reproduced with permission of Pearson Education.

Commentary

The thing you should have noticed is that Strang (1970) and Barber (2000) do not hold entirely the same position. It is extremely good news for you when writers disagree. First, you can demonstrate that you noticed. Observe how much reservation Strang (1970: 58) expresses about Barber's claims. This can be highlighted by foregrounding the disagreement as a theme.

But, first, notice that Strang is referring to an earlier work by Barber, not to Barber (2000). So direct reference to Barber (1964) may be appropriate. In Barber (1964), the tone is very different from that in Barber (2000). In the former, he is much more personal. He lists examples that he has encountered. He refers (p. 131) to 'twenty or thirty years ago': remember that he is counting from *then*, not now, so he means the 1930s and 1940s. (The moral here is, always check when a book was written.) But is the *sentiment* the same in the two books? You must not assume that it is without checking. An author is at liberty to change his mind in the course of his/her career. In fact, it can be seen that Barber *does* still hold the same opinion in 2000 as in 1964. So that too can be incorporated, by giving both dates:

(4) Barber (1964, 2000) claims that the transition is now almost complete, with the
    -er and *-est* endings apparently being edged out of the picture entirely, as even

monosyllabic words form their comparative and superlative with *more* and *most* (e.g. *The star is more bright than it was yesterday, but it will be most bright tomorrow*). Barber (1964) cites examples that he has observed, including *more crude, more plain,* and *more keen* (p.132). Strang (1970), however, is more cautious about the final stages of this change: 'Barber thinks there is an increasing use of *more, most,* rather than *-er, -est,* in comparison, in keeping with a trend which . . . goes back at least 400 years; he may be right, but we lack precise numerical information on the subject' (p.58).

Once you have identified a disagreement, you can join in! Who do you think is right? Why? How could the conflict be resolved? Adding your views when you have explained those of others is a very good way to find your voice. You are able to speak with authority because you have clearly understood both sides of the argument. Here is one example of how you might develop a position:

(5) It is probably fair to say that there is no one correct solution to this conundrum. In the post-war period, English has diversified, as places other than Britain, particularly America and Australia, have become influential in setting trends. There is never any guarantee that a change, once begun, will continue in the same direction, as Aitchison (2001: 56ff.) illustrates with the case of postvocalic *r* in New York English, studied by Labov. It is perfectly conceivable that, in a hundred years, the changes in comparative and superlative forms will have reversed, so that *famousest* and *perfecter* (Barber 2000: 274) are as common as they were in Early Modern English.

Note that a reference to Aitchison (2001) has appeared in this example. This illustrates how, as you develop an argument, you may be reminded of something you read elsewhere, which turns out to be relevant to your point. We have not reproduced the text from Aitchison (2001) here, as it is rather long, but in essence she describes how postvocalic *r* disappeared from British and some east-coast American English by the end of the eighteenth century, with the *r*-less pronunciation continuing to spread into other parts of the USA well into the 1930s. But by the 1950s and 1960s the change had reversed, with postvocalic *r* considered higher status, a trend headed by the class-conscious lower middle class in New York, as Labov's research of the 1970s demonstrated.

3 Incorporating other information into what you've already written

Once you have written your draft, that doesn't mean that you can't incorporate other information and references at even quite a late stage.

Exercise

Read the extracts from Pyles and Algeo (2004: 181–2) and Crystal (2003b: 199) in Figures 22.5 and 22.6, and try to add references to them in relevant places. You can either add them to your own version or to one of the examples given above. Then read the commentary.

Adjectives and adverbs continued to form comparatives with *-er* and superlatives with *-est*, but increasingly they used **analytical comparison** with *mo(e)* (a semantic equivalent of *more*, though not comparative in form), *more*, and *most*, which had occurred as early as Old English times. ...

The present stylistic objection to affixing *-er* and *-est* to polysyllables had somewhat less force in the early Modern English period, when forms like *eminenter, impudentest*, and *beautifullest* are not particularly hard to find, nor, for that matter, are monosyllables with *more* and *most*, like *more near, more fast, most poor*, and *most foul*. As was true in earlier times also, a good many instances of **double comparison** like *more fitter, more better, more fairer, most worst, most stillest*, and (probably the best-known example) *most unkindest* occur in early Modern English. The general rule was that comparison could be made with the ending or with the modifying word or, for emphasis, with both.

Figure 22.5 Pyles, T. and Algeo, J. (2004) *The origins and development of the English language* (5th edition). Boston, MA: Thomson Wadsworth, 181–2. Reproduced with permission of Wadsworth Cengage.

THE LONG AND THE SHORT OF IT

The availability of two ways of expressing higher degree raises a usage question: which form should be used with any particular adjective? The answer is largely to do with how long the adjective is.

• Adjectives of one syllable usually take the inflectional form: *big, thin, small, long, fat, red*. But there are exceptions: *real, right,* and *wrong* do not allow **realler, *wrongest*, etc. Nor do participles (p. 204) allow an inflection when they are used as adjectives: *That's the most burnt piece of toast I've ever seen* (not **the burntest*).

• Adjectives of three syllables or more use only the periphrastic form: we do not say **beautifuller* or **interestingest*. But here too there are exceptions: for example, a few three-syllable adjectives which begin with *un-* do allow the inflection, as in the case of *unhealthier* and *unhappiest*.

• The chief problem arises with two-syllable adjectives, many of which permit both forms of comparison: *That's a quieter/more quiet place*. A few, such as *proper* and *eager*, are straightforward: they do not allow the inflection at all. Others, such as many adjectives ending in *-y, -er*, and *-le*, favour it: *happier, cleverer*, and *gentlest* are commoner than *more/most happy*, etc., but the choice is often made on stylistic grounds. In the previous sentence, for example, there is little to choose between *commoner* and *more common* except the rhythm and the immediate context (*commoner* avoids an inelegant clash with the use of *more* two words later).

Figure 22.6 Crystal, D. (2003b). *The Cambridge encyclopedia of the English language* (2nd edition). Cambridge: Cambridge University Press, 199. Reproduced with permission of Cambridge University Press.

Commentary

Neither of these extracts provides sufficient new material to justify a complete rewrite. But there are opportunities to indicate that you can see how their standpoint and/or illustrations relate to what you already have. Pyles and Algeo (2004) refer to the preference for avoiding *-er, -est* with polysyllabic words as a 'stylistic objection', which 'had somewhat less force in the early Modern English period' (p. 181). This way of putting things is quite elegant, so a quote might be in order. In the example below, we have underlined the passage that has been added:

> (6) According to Barber (2000: 274), a study of the forms used in Early Modern English through to the present day indicates that a change has been in progress. This <u>has entailed the development of a 'stylistic objection to affixing the endings [*-er* (comparative) and *-est* (superlative)] to polysyllables' (Pyles and Algeo 2004: 181), such that forms that used to be acceptable</u> (e.g. *ancienter, ancientest; famouser, famousest*) have gradually been replaced by forms with *more* and *most* (e.g. *more ancient, most ancient; more famous, most famous*) . . .

Note how a clarification of the forms under discussion has been added within the quote by enclosing it in square brackets. This indicates that it is not part of the original quote, where the immediate context made the focus clear.

Pyles and Algeo also say something else very interesting. They claim that, in Early Modern English, it was not unusual to find monosyllables with *more* and *most*! This is quite contrary to Barber's hypothesis that the trend towards these forms has taken 400 years. And in the light of this new evidence, Strang seems positively *timid* in her non-committal stance. This means you can make even more of a meal of the disagreements and, subsequently, of your own views on the matter. Rather than supporting any one opinion too wholeheartedly, treat everyone with scepticism! Example 7 demonstrates how this can be done, the new text slotting onto the end of that given in example 4.

> (7) Such prudence on Strang's part is certainly wise, if Pyles and Algeo's (2004: 181–2) claim that monosyllables with *more* and *most* were quite common in Early Modern English is to be believed. If they are right, then Barber may be mistaken when he says that there has been a change since Early Modern English *towards* these forms. On the other hand, such evidence may simply serve to remind us that no language changes either all at once or in only one direction, as Aitchison (2001: 56ff.) illustrates with the case of postvocalic *r* in New York English, studied by Labov. Perhaps trends are *only* trends, and it is not necessary to believe in a time when a form *never* existed in order to identify a shift towards its increasing popularity.

Now look at Crystal's (2003b) comments (p. 199). He is not being *prescriptive*, so we have no reason to doubt that he intends to simply describe English as it is today. His account of the rules for today looks very similar to Barber's for the first half of the twentieth century! What does that mean? There is potentially quite a lot of mileage in identifying all the possible interpretations of this correspondence. Does Crystal have an exceedingly old-fashioned view and/or has he not noticed the forms that Barber describes? Did the trend stop in the first half of the twentieth century, with Barber's later examples just 'noise'? Did Barber wrongly understand how things were then, but happen to predict how they would be now? Was Barber's basic idea right, but the speed of change much slower than he assumed? Does Crystal know about the forms that Barber describes but not think they're important? Have the trends that Barber reported in the 1960s reversed since (and he just reproduced his 1960s findings in his later book)? The point is, of course, we don't know which is right. We can't know. That means we are free to argue whichever one we like, provided we can justify our preference:

> (8) A different challenge to Barber's view comes from Crystal (2003: 199), who describes the *current* rules for the formation of comparative and superlative forms in virtually the same way as Barber gives for the first half of the 20th century. There are many possible explanations for this. One of the most plausible is that the speed of change is slower than Barber suggests. Another is that the system for expressing these forms has reached a steady state: perhaps the 'stylistic objection' (Pyles and Algeo 2004: 181) that has powered the change for so long has lost its momentum for some reason.

(On a technical note, you will see that in example 8, Crystal's work is referred to as '(2003)', not '(2003b)'. This is because, in the text constructed for the example, there is no other work by Crystal published in 2003. On the other hand, within this book as a whole, two works by Crystal from that year are referred to (see the reference list at the end of the book). As pointed out in Chapter 21, 'a' and 'b' do not *belong* to a work, and you will assign them to dates only if it is the only way to avoid confusion.)

Crystal says that, in disyllabic words, 'the choice is often made on stylistic grounds' (p. 199), which is reminiscent of what Pyles and Algeo said. That parallel can be highlighted. Example 9 could be added directly to the end of example 8.

> (9) Those very stylistic considerations might even be responsible for maintaining the steady state. Crystal (2003) suggests that it is our preferences in rhythm and lexical context that determine which form we choose in disyllabic words (2003: 19).

Summary

Having begun with one text which it was difficult to avoid simply copying or paraphrasing, we now have an account that draws together information from several sources, contrasts opposing views, and provides a forum for personal opinions that are not simply plucked out of the air, but are firmly based in the possibilities provided (explicitly or implicitly) in the literature. Here is one possible outcome, based on the examples given above. It ends with a list of references in the format described in Chapter 21. This list is an essential feature of academic writing and must be both complete and accurate.

> (10) According to Barber (2000: 274), study of the forms used in Early Modern English through to the present day indicates that a change has been in progress. This has entailed the development of a 'stylistic objection to affixing the endings [*-er* (comparative) and *-est* (superlative)] to polysyllables' (Pyles and Algeo 2004: 181), such that once-acceptable *forms* (e.g. *ancienter, ancientest; famouser, famousest*) have gradually been replaced by forms with *more* and *most* (e.g. *more ancient*,

most ancient; more famous, most famous). This change happened earliest on the longest words. By the early 20th century the preferences were:

- polysyllabic adjectives (more than two syllables): add *more* (comparative) and *most* (superlative), e.g. *more beautiful, most beautiful; more interesting, most interesting.*
- monosyllabic adjectives: add *-er* (comparative) and *-est* (superlative), e.g. *richer, richest; bluer, bluest.*
- disyllabic adjectives: either form, e.g. *most famous, commonest.*

According to Barber (1964, 2000), the transition is now nearing completion, with the *-er* and *-est* endings apparently being edged out of the picture entirely, as even monosyllabic words form their comparative and superlative forms with *more* and *most.* Barber (1964) cites examples that he has observed, including *more crude, more plain,* and *more keen* (p.132). Strang (1970), however, is more cautious about the final stages of this change:

> Barber thinks there is an increasing use of *more, most,* rather than *-er, -est,* in comparison, in keeping with a trend which . . . goes back at least 400 years; he may be right, but we lack precise numerical information on the subject. (p.58).

Such prudence on Strang's part is certainly wise, if Pyles and Algeo's (2004: 181–2) claim that monosyllables with *more* and *most* were quite common in Early Modern English is to be believed. If they are right, then Barber may be mistaken when he says that there has been a change since Early Modern English *towards* these forms. On the other hand, such evidence may simply serve to remind us that no language changes either all at once or in only one direction, as Aitchison (2001: 56 ff.) illustrates with the case of postvocalic *r* in New York English, studied by Labov. Perhaps trends are *only* trends, and it is not necessary to believe in a time when a form *never* existed in order to identify a shift towards its increasing popularity.

A different challenge to Barber's view comes from Crystal (2003: 199), who describes the *current* rules for the formation of comparative and superlative forms in virtually the same way as Barber gives for the first half of the 20th century. There are many possible explanations for this. One of the most plausible is that the speed of change is slower than Barber suggests. Another is that the system for expressing these forms has reached a steady state: perhaps the 'stylistic objections' (Pyles and Algeo 2004: 181) that have powered the change for so long have lost their momentum, for some reason. Those very stylistic considerations might even be responsible for maintaining the steady state. Crystal (2003) suggests that it is our preferences in rhythm and lexical context that determine which form we choose in disyllabic words (p. 199).

References

Aitchison, J. (2001) *Language change: progress or decay?* (3rd edition). Cambridge: Cambridge University Press.

Barber, C. (1964) *Linguistic change in present-day English.* London: Oliver & Boyd.

Barber, C. (2000) *The English language: a historical introduction*. Canto edition. Cambridge: Cambridge University Press.

Crystal, D. (2003) *The Cambridge encyclopaedia of the English language* (2nd edition). Cambridge: Cambridge University Press.

Pyles, T. and Algeo, J. (2004) *The origins and development of the English language* (5th edition). Boston, MA: Heinle & Heinle.

Strang, B. (1970). *A history of English*. London and New York: Routledge.

Of course, everyone's finished product will be different – indeed, that is the whole point. You can be sure, if you approach your work like this, that it will be individual as well as sophisticated and informative. Precisely because your own ideas, interpretations, and conclusions are integrated with the information from your sources – fully acknowledged, of course – you can be sure that no one will be able to accuse you of accidental plagiarism.

Handy hints on writing good academic English

Before you start to write

Model your style on what you read

A general awareness of what academic writing looks like will help you to adopt that style yourself. The best models are journal articles and subject-specialist books, but most introductory textbooks also use a suitable style.

Write a plan

A plan will keep your ideas organized. Start off by dividing the work into an introduction, between three and six major sections, and a conclusion. Then plan a breakdown of each section, itemizing what will go in it. If you allot to each section and sub-section an approximate number of words, you will have almost total control over keeping to your word limit. By using a plan you are much less likely to wander off the point or say something twice. For big pieces of work, keep a separate sheet of paper or electronic file for each chapter or section and jot down your ideas, references, and any other material on it. Then, when you come to write, your key information is already in the right place.

Know your weaknesses

Take a careful look at your previous marked work and write a list of the problems with structure or presentation that have been highlighted in it. If there are any criticisms that you don't understand, ask the tutor in question. Identify strategies for avoiding these problems in the future, such as keeping to hand a list of words that you tend to spell incorrectly. Most people have only a few words that they always get wrong. Write the correct spelling of each on a sheet of paper and stick it on the wall above your desk. Don't worry about memorizing the correct spelling but do try to remember which words are on the list, so that you look at it when you need to! Although electronic spellcheckers may seem to be a reasonable substitute for spelling with care when you write, they have some major shortcomings (e.g. they do not know whether you are intending to write the word *from* or *form*), and it will serve you well to develop an eye for spelling errors.

As you are writing

Develop and sustain a sense of audience

Be aware of who it is that you are writing for, and why. Remember that you are writing in order to explain your research, so you need to say *why* you did what you did (why it was an interesting research question, for example) and be explicit about the issues and your procedures. You are writing for assessment purposes, so make sure you demonstrate that you know what you are talking about. If in doubt, err on the side of being too explicit: assessors will tend to assume, if you explain something inadequately, that you do not understand it properly. Your work may be read by a second internal assessor and/or an external examiner, so do not make references to information that they are not party to (such as module names, residence halls, and local clubs, or activities or running jokes from within a lecture course) unless you clearly explain and contextualize them.

As your assessors are knowledgeable about the general field, you can make certain assumptions about what they will understand, particularly when it comes to peripheral information. For example, it is acceptable to make a passing reference to Chomsky when writing about something in which his ideas are not central. However, no one, including your assessors, knows about *everything,* so, if you are making reference to work or ideas that you judge not to be commonly known about, give all the details necessary to make your account comprehensible.

Use the technology

Most universities now expect you to word-process your assignments. By word-processing from the start, you can:

- make alterations and still have a clean copy;
- keep a back-up copy of earlier versions in an archive folder;
- keep a copy on a memory stick or CD as well as on the hard drive of your computer, in case the computer crashes;
- email yourself the latest version so that you can work on it wherever you have access to a computer;
- run spellchecks and use thesaurus and dictionary facilities at any stage.

Mark problems for later checking

You may feel that stopping to check a spelling or to rephrase an awkward sentence will break your flow when you are writing the first draft. If so, simply mark any problem by underlining or highlighting it. Then, later, you can easily return to the right place and find a better alternative. The same technique can be used if you have a fact or a reference to check: just highlight it and carry on, coming back to it when you have finished.

Use a dictionary and thesaurus

Do not be reticent about using a dictionary. Even the best writers have to do it. There is no shame in not knowing the meaning of, or how to spell, a word, providing you *know* that you don't know, and look it up. Where terminology is concerned, use a specialist dictionary or a subject textbook with a glossary. Use a thesaurus to widen your vocabulary: it will increase the accuracy with which you express yourself, as well as making your prose more stylish. However, take care not to assume that words are entirely interchangeable. Prefer words that, once you see them in the thesaurus, are immediately familiar and compelling alternatives. If you have not seen the word used by other writers in the way that you plan to use it, then it may be that your planned usage is not quite appropriate. For example, a thesaurus may mislead you into believing that *insinuate* means the same as *suggest*. In fact, *insinuate* is very loaded with negativity. As a result, it is rarely possible to interchange them (*the informants suggested that* … does not mean the same as *the informants insinuated that* …). One advantage of studying language is that you will have access to academic staff who have a good sense of what 'sounds right', so, if in doubt, ask.

Copy correctly

When quoting, citing, or otherwise taking information from another source, pay attention to the form. In a quote, copy the punctuation and spelling correctly. Take particular care with proper names.

Use headings

In keeping with your plan (see above), use headings. These can save words, and make it much easier for both you and your assessor to follow the structure of your work.

Write summaries

In a lengthy piece of work, and especially in data analysis, it is often helpful to provide a one- or two-sentence summary at the end of each section. Doing so helps both the writer and the reader to retain a focus and a sense of the structure of the whole piece of work.

Draft it and craft it

Don't be beguiled into thinking that everyone else gets it right first time. Drafting and re-writing are part and parcel of the process. The best writing is carefully crafted – in itself an absorbing and rewarding aspect of the work. Stand back from your draft and ask yourself whether you could make it flow better, say something more succinctly, or draw out the points in a more appropriate way.

After you have written

Proofread

Leave enough time to put your work aside and then come back to it with a fresh eye. Try to read it as someone would who was seeing it for the first time. Check that the argument and ideas are clear and that there are no problems with the grammar or spelling. If it is too late to change typed or word-processed work, make neat legible corrections by hand. Always allow plenty of time for proofreading – it can (and usually does) take far longer than you think it will.

The uses of apostrophes

Apostrophes are important because they contribute to the meaning in a written text. Most people who use apostrophes incorrectly do so because no one has ever explained the rules to them. So here they are. The apostrophe has *two* major functions. One is to indicate that one or more letters are missing. The other is to indicate possession.

Omission of one or more letters

The use of the apostrophe to indicate an omission accounts for examples like *can't, don't, won't,* for *ha'penny, o'clock*, and for abbreviations like *S'hampton*. It can also be used when depicting non-standard speech in dialogue as in *I s'pose so*. Importantly, it also accounts for the word *it's*, which therefore means *it is* or *it has* (**not** the possessive form of *it*).

Possession

There are several parts to the pattern:

- **Singular nouns that do not end in s already** take an apostrophe + s to form the possessive form. Examples include: *the dog's bone* and *Michael's concern*.
- **Singular nouns that end in s** either take an apostrophe at the end of the word, or apostrophe + s. Examples include: *the class' assignment* or *the class's assignment, Her Royal Highness' schedule* or *Her Royal Highness's schedule, Mr. Jones' complaint* or *Mr. Jones's complaint*.
- **Plural nouns that already have an s** (i.e. most of them) take an apostrophe at the end. Examples include: *three horses' heads* and *20 boys' results*.
- **Plural nouns that do not end in an s** take an apostrophe + s. Examples include: *the children's games* and *the women's semi-finals*.
- **Pronouns:** The possessives of pronouns do *not* take apostrophes. *His, hers* and *its* are all examples of possessives. Remember that *it's* means 'it is', while *its* means 'belonging to it'.

Using punctuation

Using punctuation correctly is important, not only on stylistic grounds, but because you may end up saying something you didn't mean otherwise. Truss (2009) is full of examples. Common problems include the following.

Commas where full stops should be

In speech, we tend to chain sentences together without stopping for breath, but in academic writing, sentences must be separated by full stops. For example, instead of *The participants sat at separate tables, they read the text for ten minutes*, it would be better to use a full stop: *The participants sat at separate tables. They read the text for ten minutes*. Alternatively, the two parts could be linked with *and*, particularly if the writer is implying a logical connection and sequence between the two facts.

Full stops where commas should be

In this case, only half a sentence has been written before the full stop comes. It tends to occur where a dependent clause (a clause that needs another one) has been stranded. An example is: *Although the subjects had several minutes to prepare themselves*. Here, *although* has been treated as if it means *however*, whereas it actually needs an answering clause: *although this . . . (nevertheless) that*. Example: *Although the participants had several minutes to prepare themselves, they seemed flustered when the stimulus presentation began*.

Another common cause of the incomplete sentence is using a verb in non-finite form, as in: *The reason being clear*. In academic writing, there needs to be a finite verb in the main clause of every sentence, as in: *The reason is clear*.

Semi-colons for colons

The **colon** (:) is little used these days, but it still has one important function: it introduces items (as in this sentence). When you write a list, a colon indicates that the list is about to begin. A list may define (e.g. *There are three primary colours: red, blue, and yellow*) or it may illustrate (e.g. *The stationery shop sold various things: pens, paper, diaries, etc.*). Avoid using the semi-colon for these purposes.

The **semi-colon** (;) is rarer in standard written English than it is in students' essays, where it is rather overused. Its purpose is to act as a weaker version of the full stop and the clause that follows it may contain a finite verb (e.g. *Eight subjects failed to complete the task; four others left early*), but need not (e.g. *He glanced round the room; what to do now?*). Pay particular attention to not using the semi-colon to introduce information (use the colon) or speech (use inverted commas around the speech).

Other common problems

Subjectivity

It is not customary in academic writing to use the first person or to make personal comments (e.g. *After interviewing my participants, I transcribed the recordings*, or *I found this book very interesting*). You might use a passive form (e.g. *After the interviews had been transcribed …*) or use a modifier (e.g. *This interesting book …*) as in these examples. There is always more than one way to say something and you should always try to find an impersonal formulation rather than a personal one. In particular, avoid undermining your case by self-deprecating comments such as *This was all I could find out about the subject* or *Here is one explanation for the phenomenon but, knowing me, it's probably wrong.*

Referencing

There are clear conventions for referencing, which are laid out in Chapter 21. Poor referencing will be interpreted as indicative of carelessness or ignorance, and can lead to charges of plagiarism (see Chapter 22).

Troublesome pairs

Use of 'i.e.' and 'e.g.'

The abbreviation, **i.e.** means *that is*, as in: *I filled him in on the situation, i.e. I explained what had happened*. The abbreviation **e.g.** means *for example*, as in: *If you have anything for the sale, e.g. old clothes or toys, please bring them*. Some people feel that *i.e.* and *e.g.* should not be used in prose writing at all, and your tutors may prefer that you avoid them. The important thing is that if you do use them, you know which is which.

Use of 'imply' and 'infer'

The words *imply* and *infer* are easily confused because they express two sides of the same coin. When you *imply* something, you attempt to place an idea of yours into the mind of your reader or hearer by indicating it indirectly. When you *infer* something, you figure out an idea that a writer or speaker has *implied* by providing indirect information about it. In our experience, students tend to use the word *infer* when they mean *imply*. If you find the distinction difficult, ask yourself the question: is the idea coming *into* the person's head (*infer*) or going *out of* their head (*imply*)?

Use of 'amount' and 'number' and of 'less' and 'fewer'

To use these words in the standard way, you need to be alert to the difference between count nouns (nouns you can sensibly put a number in front of and pluralize), such as *questionnaire*, and mass nouns (where you cannot), such as *information*.

Fewer is used with count nouns, and it pairs up with *number* or *quantity*. For example, *A small number (quantity) of questionnaires had to be discarded, but fewer than anticipated*. Avoid writing: **A small amount of questionnaires had to be discarded but less than anticipated*.

Amount and *less* are used with mass nouns. For example, *A small amount of information was gathered, but less than anticipated*.

For more detailed guidance on how to improve your writing skills, see the excellent *Student's Guide to Writing* (Peck and Coyle 2005a) and *Write it Right* (Peck and Coyle 2005b) or other similar study skills titles that your tutors may recommend.

Hints on giving a good oral presentation

Public speaking can be a frightening experience, but knowing you have planned and practised your presentation can help boost your confidence and even enable you to enjoy yourself.

Some general points

Oral presentations are an opportunity for students to share their work with a group of people rather than just one reader. An oral account – particularly if accompanied by a visual presentation and, if appropriate, audio or video examples – can be vibrant and interesting. You can put a lot across in a few words, and capture your audience's imagination.

It is good training to think about your work in a different way. An oral presentation is not just a spoken version of an essay. Different emphases and styles are required. Furthermore, outside the world of work, people often find themselves needing to making a case orally – perhaps in protest about something, or arguing a case on their own or someone else's behalf. To have some preparation for this, therefore, enhances opportunities for success later on.

There are some important advantages to doing an oral presentation, compared with writing an essay:

- You can be more 'yourself' – if you struggle with sounding 'academic' in your essays, it can be a relief to find that in an oral presentation it's actually a positive bonus to convey your own personality and style.
- A writer cannot change the reader's perceptions of what is being read as the reading progresses. But an oral presentation is assessed at the time it is being delivered and the presenter can monitor the audience's reaction and respond accordingly.
- Whilst an essay might include graphs and diagrams as visuals, there are still far fewer opportunities to communicate in different ways than there are with an oral presentation.

However, oral presentations also have limitations:

- As presenter, you need to gauge the best speed for delivering the information, so as neither to bore your audience nor lose them. In the written medium, it is the reader that chooses when to speed up and slow down, when to flick back and check something from earlier, when to sneak a look at what comes later, and so on.

• You cannot pack as much information into an oral presentation as an essay, and you should avoid trying to, because an audience just can't process oral input as fast as written input. So, be sparing with detail. To keep the main presentation slick, indicate where you could expand further at the end on request.

Because this is a book about writing projects, we assume in this chapter that if you are giving an oral presentation it is not instead of, but in addition to, a written report. That being so, you really can be selective about what you say, because you know there is another source of information for your audience to refer to.

A poorly planned presentation may hide good content (just as poor writing can hide it in an essay) so adequate planning is vital and can't be rushed. It may take longer than you anticipate.

Time management

In the same way that you need to know the word limit for an essay, you need to know how long your presentation is expected to last. Does the allotted slot include time for questions at the end? What will happen if you run over time? At academic conferences, presenters are often simply told to stop, mid-sentence, and if you are one of several people all occupying a session of presentations, the same draconian approach might be used on you, since otherwise you are compromising another speaker by reducing the time they have.

Once you know the time limit, think about the implications. There obviously is not time to present all the details of your study, so you need to prioritize a subset of themes and ideas.

When you rehearse your talk (see later section) notice what sort of speaker you are. Do you have difficulty formulating your ideas into coherent sentences? Do you tend to say the same thing three times? Are you tempted to elaborate with examples or comments that you hadn't planned to say? All three are very common characteristics of speakers and all three gobble up time. They are resolved by practising (for fluency) and being disciplined (to avoid embellishments). Also resist lengthy introductions, such as thanking lots of people or giving a long preamble about why you became interested in this topic. Your audience wants to hear about what you did and what you found, and it's better to spend your time on that.

If you are particularly worried that you will run out of time, consider presenting your talk 'backwards'. To do this, begin with the question that is driving your presentation, along with a very brief explanation of why the question is important (a sentence, no more). Then move immediately to presenting the answer. Next, explain what sort of evidence you have that this is the answer, using extracts from your data. Then explain where the data came from (method) and finally, if there is still time, present some of the more general context, perhaps focused on what your findings mean for the wider world or for current research. This approach means that if you run out of time, it's the detail of the method and context that is lost, not the findings. Do warn your audience what you are doing, and you might want to check with your supervisor if you risk going against the guidelines you were given.

It is remarkably difficult, even for experienced lecturers, calmly to handle the problem of having only three minutes left to present ten minutes' worth of information. Neither gabbling nor making off-the-cuff decisions about what to miss out is all that effective. So you might plan a 'false' ending that is five minutes earlier than your planned end.

Anything after that point will be bonus material. You might draw your conclusions and then say 'as I have a little time, I'd like to just mention a couple of small issues that I think are quite interesting/challenging'.

Talk, don't read

If you write an academic essay and then read it out loud, your audience will find it very hard to cope with the density of information (compare Project 193). But even a script of your talk needs handling carefully. By all means prepare a script, but don't just read it out. Either it will sound like an essay or, if you have made it more speech-like, it may sound artificial and non-spontaneous. Aim to memorize it, or use it as a guide for extemporizing. Although it is probably scarier to not be tied to a script, it will free you in many ways to be yourself and engage with your audience. It also removes the risk of stumbling over words – reading to an audience can make one very self-conscious. Alternatively, use simple cue cards containing a key word or phrase for each idea, so you remember the order of points, but then speak spontaneously.

The 'talk, don't read' advice has another aspect to it as well. If you use a presentation package such as PowerPoint or iWork Presentation, avoid just putting text on the slides and reading it out. It's true that your audience will understand your written script better by having it in front of their eyes, but it's still a written script. Think about how you can use the slides to better advantage, to complement rather than mimic your spoken words.

In Chapter 23 we suggest that you model your writing style on that of the authors you find most enjoyable to read. The same applies to oral presentations. In lectures and seminars, pay attention to how the information is delivered, as well as to the content. Which styles do you like most and why? How could you imitate that style? Think about what preparation different presenters must have done, to be in a position to deliver the material in the way they have.

Content

Assess how much you think your audience already knows about your topic. The project itself will be new to them, presumably, but they will have general background knowledge. It is not easy to gauge where to draw the line between things you do need to tell them and things you don't, and it may help to try out your judgements on your supervisor or some fellow students.

There are many similarities between the structuring of an oral presentation and an essay:

- Have a clear informative title.
- Introduce the topic at the beginning and indicate the main areas to be covered in the presentation.
- Structure the content for the audience, so they have a mental map of the talk.
- Be logical and progress clearly from one point to the next.
- Make each point *once*, at the appropriate place, and then move on.
- Explain each acronym when it first appears (either on a slide or orally).
- Avoid sweeping generalizations (e.g. 'boys are more disruptive in class than girls' or 'women object to swearing more than men'), as they can annoy, and thus distract, the audience.

There are some important differences, too, however. The most major regards the amount of literature review you should expect to cover. Unless you have been advised otherwise, keep the literature review part of an oral presentation to the minimum, because it is not possible to convey to listeners enough about other studies to make it worth the time it takes. Rather, use the literature strategically. For instance, you might:

- Use one quote as an anchor, to show why you have chosen to research what you have, and then one more quote each time the literature contributes to a decision you made (e.g. about methodology, your predictions, or the interpretation of your data).
- Construct a diagram to represent the relationship between the main positions held by other researchers, with one example reference for each position.

Slides (e.g. PowerPoint)

It is often expected that students will use a projected presentation of slides, but it might not be obligatory. It is worth asking:

- Is it going to be positively useful – that is, will visual presentation support and enhance your aims? If your talk is focused on data that won't fit easily on slides, you might be better using handouts instead.
- Do you have time to prepare a good-quality visual presentation? This question cuts both ways. Although it will take time, preparing slides is a good way to work out what is most important and to experiment with ways of organizing it.

Colour scheme and layout

Presentation packages offer ever more colour schemes and layouts. Think about which colours will be most visible under the lighting in the room that you are to present in. In general, light print on a dark background is more visible than the reverse. Avoid patterned backgrounds, which make it harder to read any superimposed text.

The preloaded layouts are not necessarily ideal for your purposes, as plain colours are often most effective, and design features tend to reduce the usable space on the slide.

Visual impression

Avoid slides becoming crowded, which makes them hard to follow, even if you introduce the text in stages (see 'Animation' later). Use headings to help your audience sustain a sense of the structure of your talk. If you find you need to split material onto several slides, consider whether you can reduce the detail instead.

Use a font size large enough for all members of the audience to read (including the back row) but not so large that you cannot get a coherent message on the slide. As a rough guide, avoid using a font smaller than 18 point, and use 24 point for most material.

Choose your font carefully, so it is not a distraction or impediment. Tempting as it might be to choose one of the so-called 'fun' fonts like Comic Sans or Papyrus it could backfire if you diverge too far from standard academic practice. On the other hand, you certainly can use fonts creatively to make a specific point.

Be very careful indeed when using phonetic fonts or non-roman alphabets, because they are not standard on all versions of the same program. You may find that your phonetic transcriptions turn into gobbledegook just when you need them most. There are several things you can do to minimize the risk of this happening:

- Check the computer in the room you will be using, by running sample material through the presentation program. (You don't need to project it, just look at it on the screen.)
- Bring your own laptop in (with the fonts on, of course) and connect it to the projector that you are using for your presentation. (Be sure you know how to connect it up success-fully as many a presenter has lost ten minutes trying to get the image onto the screen.)
- Save the file using the 'embed fonts' option. This is supposed to carry the images with it (at the cost of a lot more memory) – but check it really does do this because it doesn't always work.
- Create a pdf of what you want to show, and embed it as an image in your presentation. This is the surest way to ensure you have exactly what you want but, of course, it makes animating it more complicated.

Images

Because you share cultural and contextual knowledge with your audience, you can use images to convey complex ideas instantly. A logo, for example, carries information beyond just the name of the company or product. If you are giving your presentation to people beyond your own academic community, simply using your university's or college's logo on the title page can give your work a sense of authority as research, without your having to say anything.

Use images sparingly – make them work, rather than just being decoration. Clipart is a useful general resource for images, but nowadays is instantly recognizable for what it is, so you might want to range more widely, using Google images or other freely available image banks, or even taking your own photographs.

You can easily generate graphs, bar charts, pie charts, etc., from a table in your word-processing program or from a spreadsheet, and then copy them into your presentation. People can read and internalize information very quickly from graphs, so you don't need to then say everything again.

Animation

'Animation' is the term used for introducing, or removing, material from slides on demand or after a pre-set time interval. Most commonly it is used to introduce lines of text one at a time, which can help with following the development of the argument. Many experienced presenters, however, use animation only sparingly, knowing that when text dances round the page or arrives one letter at a time it can be irritating to the audience. The bottom line is that you want people to engage with and remember the *content* of your talk, not come away with a headache. Try things out, stand back and ask yourself 'Is this helping the pre-sentation or not?'.

Moving through the slides

If you are using notes or a script, it is a good idea to mark the places where you need to change to a new slide.

Ask if a remote slide changer (a handheld device that sends a wireless message to the computer) is available. It enables you to stand wherever you like and move around the room. If you do need to use a mouse or keyboard to change slides, try to set things up so that you don't have to turn your back on the audience to do so. If you are using a lectern or table for your presentation, you need the computer – or at least the mouse – in easy reaching distance for changing slides.

Get the details right

Proofread your slides carefully. A spelling error, or omitted word, will be staring your audience in the face for as long as the slide is on the screen.

Always indicate when words are being used as data. Use italics or a different colour, to avoid bizarre alternative readings, e.g. the statement that 'Some people chose to put avocados on their wordlist' is clearer if you write 'Some people chose to put *avocados* on their word list'.

Handouts

Unless you have been instructed to, don't assume you must provide a handout. You are most likely to need to use a handout if you are presenting data that won't fit on slides, or if you particularly want your audience to have something to take away (e.g. if your examiners need to be able to recall your presentation accurately). Ask yourself, 'How will I use this during the presentation?' and 'How will this be useful to people afterwards?' If the answer is not obvious, do the planet a favour and save the trees!

Self-presentation

How you present yourself plays a role in how you feel and how you and your work are perceived. What impression do you want to give? Will relatively smart and formal dress fit the occasion (as it would for a job interview), or is it safe to go for the casual or scruffy look? Should you remove adornments such as nose-rings and tongue studs? Smart and tidy is usually a safe option, though you might feel you will be least intimidated by the experience if you wear the clothes you are most comfortable in, and appear as 'yourself'.

Rehearsing

Rehearsing a presentation is vital, both for fluency and for editing. Each time you go through it, you will find more things to modify, until you are finally satisfied that it does the job just as you want, in the available time.

If you use a presentation software package like PowerPoint, you will find there is a rehearsal option that tracks the time taken on each slide and the overall total. This is very useful. **However**, *don't* click the option to save the timings, because it means the slides will change automatically at those times next time you go through it. The same problem (automatic slide transition) can also occur if that option is ticked in the program on the computer you use for the presentation (it is often ticked by default). So, take a moment to check and disable it if necessary.

Use your rehearsals to log in your notes or on a slide where you expect to be by, say, five minutes from the end of your time. During the presentation, ask someone to give you a five-minute warning. You can then easily judge if you are running out of time, while there is still an opportunity to do something elegant about it.

Will you become bored if you rehearse too much? That is for you to gauge. But the level of familiarity that comes about from rehearsing can give you a level of confidence that outweighs the disadvantages of repetition. If at all possible, rehearse in the room where you are to give your presentation. If that is not possible, find an equivalent space, or imagine yourself in one, so that you really present, rather than mumbling under your breath – the timings, and your entire engagement, will be quite different.

Before your presentation is due to start (even the day before, if possible), go to the room where you will be making your presentation and make some *in situ* preparations:

- Check that your memory stick works on the computer in the room (or, preferably, load the presentation directly onto the computer hard drive and access it from there).
- Work out how the equipment works, including any lighting controls, volume for audio, etc., and ask for help to be provided if you foresee a problem.
- If there is a remote control for changing slides or controlling the screen or projector, try it out.
- Look at the projected image on the screen and satisfy yourself that the font size you have chosen is appropriate.
- Stand where you will stand for the presentation and get a sense of how big or small the room feels. You might feel stupid talking to yourself, but try out the first few sentences of your presentation, to hear your own voice in that space.
- If you can, rehearse the entire presentation there, with particular attention to whether you feel you are speaking more slowly, or faster, than you anticipated (see 'Fluency, projection and speed' below).
- Look at the seating in the room. Is it as you want it, and if not, do you want to adjust it? You might not be able to move any chairs till the day, and you should ensure they are moved back afterwards, but it's your presentation, and if you want people sitting in a particular way, see if you can arrange for this to happen.

On the day

If you are using handouts, ask a friend to pass them round while you are setting up. This gives you one less thing to worry about. In all events, avoid having the handouts in circulation during your presentation, because this is distracting for everyone – you included. Have a few handouts next to the door for late-comers, and if they fail to pick one up, don't be tempted to solve their problem for them – they'll figure out what to do.

It is standard for a chairperson or a helper to signal to the speaker when they have, say, five minutes left, but you can choose what signals you want. So if you would prefer warning at ten minutes, or three, just ask. If you are shown a sign reading 'stop', you need to do so, especially if you are one of several people sharing a slot – it's only fair. See earlier in this chapter for suggestions on how to ensure you retain control of the overall presentation, even if you find the timing has gone wrong.

If you know you will be nervous, get a friend to sit somewhere prominently in the audience during the presentation and nod encouragingly. This really works, even when you know you've set it up! If you are more courageous, you can ask your friend to signal things like 'slow down', 'speed up', 'speak louder'.

However nervous you feel as you start your presentation, look at the audience, smile and make eye-contact. If you signal that you don't have confidence in what you are doing, they will pick that up and feel nervous for you. You will pick *that* up and may easily misinterpret it as negativity towards what you are doing.

The following features of performing as a public speaker need thought in advance, and also practice.

Posture and movement

- Stand squarely on both feet with your weight evenly distributed. When we are nervous, we often unconsciously stand off balance (e.g. on the side of a foot), and you might actually lose your balance. Standing in a confident way will feed your confidence.
- Avoid walking round too much as this can be very distracting to an audience.
- Watch out for any personal habits, such as putting your hands behind your head as you are speaking, folding your arms, scratching your nose, looking down too much. Not all such traits have to be expunged, but you need to have some control over them.

Fluency, projection and speed

- Energize your voice, as this feeds the tone and makes you sound more interesting. Make sure everybody can hear you, but avoid shouting, which will not only damage your voice but also tire your audience. The more confidence and energy you can put into your speech, the less of a problem volume is likely to be. However, if you know you have a quiet voice, ask if it is possible to use a microphone.
- Avoid making side comments in a lower volume. If something is worth saying, it is worth saying at a volume that everyone can hear. A witty remark can backfire if half your audience can't hear it.
- Avoid speaking in a monotone. Modulate your voice as a means of indicating that you yourself find what you are saying interesting.
- Avoid (over-)using fillers such as *like, er, um* or *you know*. You can do this by knowing what you want to say and having rehearsed ways of saying it.
- Look out for any linguistic 'tics', such as sighing between utterances, which can arise as an unconscious signal of your lack of confidence. Your audience will form their interpretation of what you do on the basis of what they see and hear. They don't have any idea what you are thinking, unless you give yourself away.
- Irrespective of your accent, you must work for clarity of speech. If your audience cannot understand what you are saying, they will lose interest very quickly. You do not need elocution lessons to give an oral presentation, but you do need to enunciate clearly. One of the most common causes of unclear speech is that it is delivered too fast for adequate enunciation.
- An audience breathes with a performer. This means that how you handle the pace of your speech may have a direct effect on the heart rate, breathlessness or relaxation of your listener.
- Avoid speaking to fast or too slowly. When nervous, people often speak faster, so make a concerted effort not to rush. On the other hand, waiting for signs of understanding from an audience, repeating points, and responding appropriately to the acoustics of a room, can slow us down.

Making it work for your audience

A presentation is for your audience, not for you, so do what you can to make it interesting and enjoyable.

- Don't take yourself too seriously. If you get tongue-tied, or something goes wrong, just laugh and move on. Don't carry with you anything that has happened earlier. Put it down and leave it behind or it will become a burden to both you and the audience.
- Present what you have in the best light possible. You may know there are a few gaps in your knowledge or problems with the detail, but your audience doesn't necessarily need to be told. Avoid self-deprecating comments, which signal that you do not believe your audience should be forming a positive view of what you have done. Comments like 'hopefully this diagram will make it clearer but it probably it won't', or 'if that makes sense' may seem disarming and informal – and they do have a very interesting socio-linguistic function – but they can backfire in a formal situation.
- Don't stand in front of the screen, or create a shadow on it. Stand well to one side, and notice if anyone is craning their neck to see something.
- If you are referring to things on the screen, don't turn round and talk to the screen. Either use the display on the computer screen as your reference point, or use a printout of your slides, so that you can look out towards your audience. If you have to look at the screen, stand well to one side, glance at it, and turn back to the audience.

Questions and answers

During your presentation, you have control. Although you can, if you wish, invite listeners to interrupt with questions, this will upset your timing and may require you to suddenly present your material in a different order. It is better to ask people to save their questions till the end.

The good thing about the questions section is that it enables you to display further knowledge in your answers, and to expand on points you covered more quickly earlier on. It's also a good way to connect with your audience as you gain insight into what has most captured their imagination or been most puzzling to them.

However, the question time can also be a little scary, because the questions can come from anywhere (literally and metaphorically) and are very difficult to predict. The main types of question and comment you may encounter are:

- Requests for clarification. Respond briefly, unless it's clearly of interest to everyone.
- Requests to expand on something you already described. Don't be afraid to say 'I'm sorry I can't give that information off the top of my head. But I could send it to you afterwards if you are interested.' But on topics you particularly want to expand on, prepare in advance, with extra slides if useful, and do signal during the presentation that you can add more details at the end.
- Personal observation or anecdote. Often there is nothing to say back, so just thank them and move on.
- Long-winded or incomprehensible questions. If you haven't followed it, ask the questioner (who has been thinking as they talk) to rephrase it. The incoherence is their problem, not yours.

- Three or more questions rolled into one. Jot down your ideas as you go. If you can answer one part of the question but not another, start with the easy bit and see if, by the time you have answered that, everyone has forgotten there was more.
- Aggressive questioning. It is often not intended that way, but indicates that the questioner feels insecure. To avoid feeling cornered, stay calm and don't get defensive. If there is a criticism in the question, it is remarkably effective to say 'Yes, you may be right about that' and, if necessary, 'I will think about that, thank you'. If you don't look fazed by a criticism, it will make it seem less important.
- The perfect question you hoped someone would ask. You don't have to live in hope. Set someone up to ask it!

Wait for the complete question to be asked (rather than jumping in and anticipating what you think is being asked). Waiting shows respect for the questioner (rather than indicating that any fool could have guessed where that question was going) and provides you with a few seconds of valuable thinking time.

References

21st Century China Daily (ed.) (2005) *Speaking for success*. Shanghai: Shanghai Foreign Languages Education Press.

Aarts, B. and McMahon, A. (eds) (2006) *The handbook of English linguistics*. Oxford: Wiley-Blackwell.

Aitchison, J. (2001) *Language change: progress or decay?* (3rd edition). Cambridge: Cambridge University Press.

Aitchison, J. (2003) *Glossary of language and mind*. Edinburgh: Edinburgh University Press.

Aitchison, J. (2011) *The articulate mammal* (5th edition). London: Routledge.

Aitchison, J. (2012) *Words in the mind: an introduction to the mental lexicon* (4th edition). Oxford: Blackwell.

Alderson, C. (1997) Models of language. Whose? What for? What use? In Ryan, A. and Wray, A. (eds) *Evolving models of language: papers from the annual meeting of the British Association for Applied Linguistics 1996*. Clevedon: Multilingual Matters, 1–22.

Algeo, J. (2010) *The origins and development of the English language* (6th edition). Boston, MA: Wadsworth Cengage.

Anderson, S. (1988) Morphological theory. In Newmeyer, F. (ed.) *Linguistics: the Cambridge survey, Vol. 1 Linguistic theory: foundations*. Cambridge: Cambridge University Press, 146–91.

Anderson, W. and Corbett, J. (2009) *Exploring English with online corpora: an introduction*. Basingstoke: Palgrave Macmillan.

Androutsopoulos, J. (2006a). Introduction: Sociolinguistics and computer-mediated communication. *Journal of Sociolinguistics* 10 (4): 419–438.

Androutsopoulos, J. (ed.) (2006b). Sociolinguistics and computer-mediated communication. Special issue of *Journal of Sociolinguistics* 10 (4).

Appel, R. and Muysken, P. (1987/2005) *Language contact and bilingualism*. Amsterdam: Amsterdam University Press.

Aronoff, M. and Rees-Miller, J. (eds) (2001) *The handbook of linguistics*. Oxford: Blackwell.

Atkinson, J.M. and Heritage, J. (eds) (1984) *Structures of social action*. Cambridge: Cambridge University Press.

Austin, J.L. (1961) Performative utterances. In Austin, J.L. *Philosophical papers* (ed. by Urmson, J.O. and Warnock, G.J., 3rd edition, 1979). Oxford: Oxford University Press. Reprinted in Martinich, A.P. (ed.) (1996) *The philosophy of language* (3rd edition). New York: Oxford University Press, 120–9.

Austin, J.L. (1962) *How to do things with words*. Oxford: Oxford University Press.

Ayers, D.M. (1986) *English words from Latin and Greek elements* (2nd edition). Tucson, AZ: University of Arizona Press.

Bachman, L. and Palmer, A. (2010). *Language assessment in practice*. Oxford: Oxford University Press.

Bailey, K.M. and Nunan, D. (eds) (1996) *Voices from the language classroom*. Cambridge: Cambridge University Press.

Baker, P. (2002) *Polari, the lost language of gay men*. London: Routledge.

Baker, P. (2005) *Public discourses of gay men: that's so gay*. London: Routledge.

Baker, P. (2010) *Sociolinguistics and corpus linguistics*. Edinburgh: Edinburgh University Press.

Baker, P., Hardie, A. and McEnery, T. (2006) *Glossary of corpus linguistics*. Edinburgh: Edinburgh University Press.

Baldick, C. (2009) *The Oxford dictionary of literary terms*. New York: Oxford University Press.

Barber, C. (1964) *Linguistic change in present-day English*. London: Oliver and Boyd.

Barber, C. (1997) *Early modern English* (2nd edition). Edinburgh: Edinburgh University Press.

Barber, C. (2000) *The English language: a historical introduction*. Cambridge: Cambridge University Press.

Barber, C., Beal, J. and Shaw, P. (2009) *The English language: a historical introduction* (2nd edition). Cambridge: Cambridge University Press.

Barfield, O. (2002) *History of English words* (2nd edition). Great Barrington, MA: Lindisfarne Books/ Steiner Books.

Barnes, S. (2002) *Computer-mediated communication: human to human communication across the Internet*. Boston, MA: Allyn & Bacon.

Baron, J. (1973) Phonemic stage not necessary for reading. *Quarterly Journal of Experimental Psychology* 25, 241–6.

Baron, N. (2008) *Always on: language in an online and mobile world*. Oxford: Oxford University Press.

Bauer, L. (2002) *An introduction to international varieties of English*. Edinburgh: Edinburgh University Press.

Baugh, T. and Cable, A.C. (2002) *A history of the English language* (5th edition). London: Routledge.

Bavin, E.L. (2006) Syntactic development. In Brown, K. (ed.) (2006) Vol. 12: 383–90.

Beal, J. (2006) Dialect representations in texts. In Brown, K. (ed.) (2006) Vol. 3: 531–7.

Bell, A. (2006) Speech accommodation. In Brown, K. (ed.) (2006) Vol. 11, p.648–51.

Berko-Gleason, J. (1975) Fathers and other strangers: men's speech to young children. In Dato, D. (ed.) *Developmental psycholinguistics: theory and applications*. Washington: Georgetown University Press.

Berlin, B. and Kay, P. (1969) *Basic color terms: their universality and evolution*. Berkeley and Los Angeles: University of California Press. (Republished 1999, Stanford, CA: CSLI Publications).

Bhatia, T. (2006) Bilingualism and second language learning. In Brown, K. (ed.) (2006) Vol. 2, 16–22.

Bhatia, T. and Ritchie W.C. (eds) (2012) *The handbook of bilingualism* (2nd edition). Oxford: Wiley-Blackwell.

Biber, D. and Reppen, R. (eds) (2011) *Corpus linguistics* (4 volumes). London: Sage.

Blake, B. J. (2007) *Playing with words*. London: Equinox.

Block, D. and Cameron, D. (eds) (2002) *Globalization and language teaching*. London: Routledge.

Bloomer, A.M., Griffiths, P.D. and Merrison, A.J. (2005) *Introducing language in use: a coursebook*. Abingdon: Routledge.

Bloor, T. and Bloor, M. (2004) *The functional analysis of English: a Hallidayan approach* (2nd edition). London: Arnold.

Bloor, T. and Bloor, M. (2007) *The practice of critical discourse analysis: an introduction*. London: Hodder Education.

Boardman, M. (2005) *The language of websites*. London: Routledge.

Booij, G. (2005) *The grammar of words*. New York: Oxford University Press.

Bousfield, D. (2008) *Impoliteness and interaction*. Amsterdam: John Benjamin Publishing.

Bousfield, D. and Locher, M. (2008) *Impoliteness in language: studies on its interplay with power in theory and practice*. Berlin: Mouton de Gruyter.

Brace, N., Kemp, R. and Snelgar, R. (2009) *SPSS for Psychologists: a guide to data analysis using SPSS for Windows* (4th edition). Basingstoke: Palgrave MacMillan.

Bradley, H. (1916) Shakespeare's English. In Bradley, H. *Shakespeare's England*. Oxford: Oxford University Press.

Bridges, R. (1913) *A tract on the present state of English pronunciation*. Oxford: Clarendon Press.

British Library (2010) *Voices of the UK: accents and dialects of English*. London: British Library Publishing. (Audio CD).

Brook, G.L. (1957) *English sound changes*. Manchester: Manchester University Press.

Brook, G.L. (1978) *English dialects* (3rd edition). London: André Deutsch.

Brouwer, D., Gerritsen, M. and de Haan, D. (1979) Speech differences between men and women: on the wrong track? *Language and Society* 8, 33–50.

Brown, A.S. (2008) Tip of the tongue experience. In Byrne, J.H. (ed.) *Learning and memory: a comprehensive reference, vol 2: cognitive psychology of memory*. Oxford: Elsevier, 378-87. Available at: http://www.cingulate.ibms.sinica.edu.tw/ftpshare/Protocol/Internet%20 Resources/E%20books/Learning%20and%20memory/Volume%202%20Cognitive%20 psychology%20of%20memory/022%20Tip%20of%20tongue%20experience.PDF (Last accessed 10 October 2011).

Brown, G. (1990) *Listening to spoken English* (2nd edition). London and New York: Longman.

Brown, H.D. and Abeywickrama, P. (2010) *Language assessment: principles and classroom practices* (2nd edition). Upper Saddle River, NJ: Pearson Education.

Brown, J.D. and Rodgers, T. (2002) *Doing second language research*. Oxford: Oxford University Press.

Brown, K. (ed.) (2006) *Encyclopaedia of language and linguistics* (2nd edition). Oxford: Elsevier.

Brown, R. (1973) *A first language: the early stages*. Cambridge, MA: Harvard University Press.

Brown, R. and McNeill, D. (1966) The 'tip of the tongue' phenomenon. *Journal of Verbal Learning and Verbal Behavior* 5, 325–37.

Bryman, A. (2012) *Social research methods* (4th edition). Oxford: Oxford University Press.

Bryson, B. (2009) *Mother tongue: the story of the English language*. London: Penguin.

Burchfield, R. (2002) *The English language*. Oxford: Oxford University Press.

Burke, P. and Porter, R. (eds) (1987) *The social history of language*. Cambridge: Cambridge University Press.

Burke, P. and Porter, R. (eds) (1994) *Language, self and society*. Cambridge: Polity Press.

Burnley, D. (2000) *The history of the English language: a source book* (2nd edition). London: Longman.

Burstall, C., Jamieson, M., Cohen, S. and Hargreaves, M. (1974) *Primary French in the balance.* Windsor: NFER.

Burton-Roberts, N. (2010) *Analysing sentences* (3rd edition). Harlow: Pearson Longman.

Caldas-Coulthard, C.M. and Coulthard, M. (1996) *Texts and practices: readings in critical discourse.* London: Routledge.

Cameron, D. (2001) *Working with spoken discourse.* London: Sage Publications.

Cameron, D. (2006) Gender. In Brown, K. (ed.) (2006) Vol. 4: 733–9.

Cameron, D. (2012) *Verbal hygiene* (2nd edition). Abingdon: Routledge.

Cameron, D. and Kulick, D. (2003) *Language and sexuality.* Cambridge: Cambridge University Press.

Cameron, K. (1965) *Scandinavian settlement in the territory of the five boroughs: the place-name evidence.* University of Nottingham, Inaugural Lecture, 4/3/65.

Cameron, K. (1996) *English place names* (6th edition). London: Batsford.

Cameron, L. and Low, G. (eds) (1999) *Researching and applying metaphor.* Cambridge: Cambridge University Press.

Caplan, D. (1987) *Neurolinguistics and linguistic aphasiology: an introduction.* Cambridge: Cambridge University Press.

Carey, J. (1997) *Eyewitness to history.* New York: Avon Books.

Carlson, N. (2011) Goldman to clients: Facebook has 600 million users. *Business Insider,* 5 January 2011.   Available at: http://www.msnbc.msn.com/id/40929239/ns/technology_and_science-tech_and_gadgets/ (Last accessed 10 October 2011).

Carr, P. (2008) *Glossary of phonology.* Edinburgh: Edinburgh University Press.

Carroll, D.W. (2008) *Psychology of language* (5th edition). Belmont, CA: Thomson Wadsworth.

Carroll, J.B. (ed.) (1956/2011) *Language, thought and reality: selected writings of Benjamin Lee Whorf.* Cambridge, MA: MIT Press. Reprinted 2011, Eastford, CT: Martino Fine Books.

Carroll, L. (1865/1971) *Alice through the looking glass.* London: Macmillan.

Carstairs-McCarthy, A. (2002) *An introduction to English morphology.* Edinburgh: Edinburgh University Press.

Carstairs-McCarthy, A. (2010) *The evolution of morphology.* Oxford: Oxford University Press.

Carter, R. (2004) *Language and creativity: the art of common talk.* London: Routledge.

Carter, R. (2012) *Vocabulary* (3rd edition). London: Routledge.

Carter, R., Bowring M., Goddard. A., Reah, D., Sanger, K., Swift. N. and Beard, A. (2007) *Working with texts* (3rd edition). London: Routledge.

Carter, R. and Nash, W. (1990) *Seeing through language.* Oxford: Blackwell.

Carter, R. and Nunan, D. (eds) (2001) *The Cambridge guide to teaching English to speakers of other languages.* Cambridge: Cambridge University Press.

Chambers, A. and Trudgill, P. (1998) *Dialectology* (2nd edition). Cambridge: Cambridge University Press.

Chaski, C. (2001) Empirical evaluations of language-based author identification techniques. *Forensic Linguistics: The International Journal of Speech Language and the Law* 8 (1): 1–65.

Cheng, W. (2011) *Exploring corpus linguistics: language in action.* Abingdon: Routledge.

Cherny, L. (1999) *Conversation and community: chat in a virtual world.* Stanford, CA: CSLI Publications.

Cheshire, J. (1978) Present tense verbs in Reading English. In Trudgill, P. (ed.) *Sociolinguistic patterns in British English.* London: Edward Arnold, 52–68.

Cheshire, J. (1982/2009) *Variation in an English dialect.* Cambridge: Cambridge University Press.

Chiaro, D. (1996) *The language of jokes: analysing verbal play.* London: Routledge.

Chilton, P. (ed.) (1985) *Language and the nuclear arms debate: nukespeak today.* London: Pinter/ Cassell Academic.

Chomsky, C. (1969) *The acquisition of syntax in children from 5 to 10.* Cambridge, MA: MIT Press.

Clark, E.V. (2009) *First language acquisition* (2nd edition). Cambridge: Cambridge University Press.

Clark, H.H. and Clark, E.V. (1977) *Psychology and language: an introduction to psycholinguistics.* New York: Harcourt Brace Jovanovitch.

Clark, J.L. (1987) *Curriculum renewal in school foreign language learning.* Oxford: Oxford University Press.

Clifton, C. Jr. and Ferreira, F. (1989) Ambiguity in context. *Language and Cognitive Processes* 4 (3/4), Special Issue (SI), 77–103.

Coates, J. (1996) *Women talk: conversation between women friends.* Oxford: Blackwell.

Coates, J. (2003) *Men talk: stories in the making of masculinities.* Oxford: Blackwell.

Coates, J. (2004) *Women, men and language* (3rd edition). Harlow: Longman.

Coates, J. (2011) Gossip revisited: language in all-female groups. In Coates, J. and Pichler, P. (eds) (2011) *Language and gender: a reader.* London: Routledge, 199–223.

Coates, J. and Cameron, D. (eds) (1989) *Women in their speech communities.* London: Longman.

Coates, J. and Pichler, P. (eds) (2011) *Language and gender: a reader* (2nd edition). Oxford: Wiley-Blackwell.

Collins Cobuild (1991) *English guides 1: prepositions.* London: HarperCollins.

Collins Cobuild (1996) *Grammar patterns 1: verbs.* London: HarperCollins.

Collins, B. and Mees, I.M. (2008) *Practical phonetics and phonology: a resource book for students* (2nd edition). Abingdon: Routledge.

Colman, A. and Pulford, B. (2008) *A crash course in SPSS for Windows: updated for versions 14, 15 and 16* (4th edition). Oxford: Blackwell.

Coltheart, M. (2005) Modelling reading: the dual-route approach. In Snowling, M.J. and Hulme, C. (eds) *The science of reading.* Oxford: Blackwell, 6–23.

Como, P. (2006) Elicitation techniques for spoken discourse. In Brown, K. (ed.) (2006) Vol. 4, p.105–9.

Conboy, M. (2007) *The Language of the news.* Abingdon: Routledge.

Cook, G. (2001) *The discourse of advertising* (2nd edition). London: Routledge.

Cook, V. (1993) *Linguistics and second language acquisition.* Basingstoke: Macmillan.

Cook, V. (1997) *Inside language.* London: Arnold.

Cook, V. (2008) *Second language learning and teaching* (4th edition). London: Hodder.

Coolican, H. (2006) *Introduction to research methods and statistics in psychology* (3rd edition). London: Hodder and Stoughton.

Coolican, H. (2009) *Research methods and statistics in psychology* (5th edition). London: Arnold.

Corbett, J., McClure, J.D. and Stuart-Smith, J. (eds) (2003) *The Edinburgh companion to Scots.* Edinburgh: Edinburgh University Press.

Coulmas, F. (ed.) (1998) *Handbook of sociolinguistics.* Oxford: Blackwell.

Coulmas, F. (2005) *Sociolinguistics: the study of speakers' choices.* Cambridge: Cambridge University Press.

Coulthard, M. and Johnson, A. (2010) *The Routledge handbook of forensic linguistics.* Abingdon: Routledge.

Coupland, N., Coupland, J. and Giles, H. (1991) *Language, society and the elderly.* Oxford: Blackwell.

Coupland, N. and Jaworski, A. (eds) (2009) *The new sociolinguistics reader* (2nd edition). London: Palgrave Macmillan.

Cox, B. (ed.) (1994) *The place-names of Rutland.* Nottingham: English Place-name Society.

Crichton, H. and Templeton, B. (2010) Curriculum for excellence: the way forward for primary languages in Scotland. *Language Learning Journal* 38, 2, 139–47.

Cruse, A. (2006) *Glossary of semantics and pragmatics.* Edinburgh: Edinburgh University Press.

Cruttenden, A. (1974) An experiment involving comprehension of intonation in children from 7 to 10. *Journal of Child Language* 1, 221–31.

Cruttenden, A. (ed.) (1979) *Language in infancy and childhood.* Manchester: Manchester University Press.

Crystal, D. (1989) *Listen to your child: a parent's guide to children's language.* Harmondsworth: Penguin.

Crystal, D. (2003a) *English as a global language* (2nd edition). Cambridge: Cambridge University Press.

Crystal, D. (2003b) *The Cambridge encyclopedia of the English language.* (2nd edition). Cambridge: Cambridge University Press.

Crystal, D. (2005) *Pronouncing Shakespeare: the Globe experiment.* Cambridge: Cambridge University Press.

Crystal, D. (2006) *Language and the Internet* (2nd edition). Cambridge: Cambridge University Press.

Crystal, D. (2008) *Dictionary of linguistics and phonetics* (6th edition). Oxford: Blackwell.

Crystal, D. (2010) *The Cambridge encyclopaedia of language* (3rd edition). Cambridge: Cambridge University Press.

Crystal, D. (2011) *Internet linguistics.* London: Routledge.

Culpeper, J. (2005) *History of English* (2nd edition). London: Routledge.

Cunliffe, D. and Herring, S.C. (eds) (2005) Minority languages, multimedia and the Web. Special issue of *New Review of Hypermedia and Multimedia* 11 (2).

Curzan, A. (2009) *Gender shifts in the history of English.* Cambridge: Cambridge University Press.

Cutler, A. (1982) *Slips of the tongue and language production.* Berlin: Mouton.

Dalzell, T. and Victor, T. (2006) *The new Partridge dictionary of slang and unconventional English.* London: Routledge.

Danet, B. and Herring, S.C. (eds) (2003) The multilingual internet. Special issue of *Journal of Computer-Mediated Communication* 9 (1).

Danet, B. and Herring, S.C. (eds) (2007) *The multilingual internet: language, culture and communication online.* New York: Oxford University Press.

Davenport, M. and Hannahs, S.J. (2010) *Introducing phonetics and phonology* (3rd edition). London: Hodder Arnold.

Davies, A. (2005) *Glossary of applied linguistics.* Edinburgh: Edinburgh University Press.

Davies, A. and Elder, C (eds) (2003) *The handbook of applied linguistics.* Oxford: Blackwell.

Deutscher, G. (2010). *Through the language looking-glass: why the world looks different in other languages.* London: Random House.

De Villiers, J.G. and de Villiers, P.A. (1973) A cross-sectional study of the acquisition of grammatical morphemes. *Journal of Psycholinguistic Research* 2, 267–78.

De Villiers, J.G. and de Villiers, P.A. (1978) *Language acquisition.* Cambridge, MA: Harvard University Press.

Dictionary of South African English (1996) Oxford: Oxford University Press.

Ding, Y. (2007) Text memorization and imitation: the practices of successful Chinese learners of English. *System, 35,* 271–80.

Dixon, R.M.W. (2005) *A semantic approach to English grammar* (2nd edition). Oxford: Oxford University Press.

Dörnyei, Z. (2002) *Questionnaires in second language research.* Mahwah, NJ: Erlbaum.

Dörnyei, Z. (2007) *Research methods in applied linguistics: quantitative, qualitative and mixed methods.* Oxford: Oxford University Press.

Dörnyei, Z. (2009) *Questionnaires in second language research* (2nd edition). Mahwah, NJ: Erlbaum.

Dörnyei, Z. and Murphey, T. (2003) *Group dynamics in the language classroom.* Cambridge: Cambridge University Press.

Dörnyei, Z. and Taguchi, T. (2009) *Questionnaires in second language research* (2nd edition). London: Routledge.

Dörnyei, Z. and Ushioda, E. (2010) *Teaching and researching motivation* (2nd edition). Harlow: Longman.

Dorian, N. C. (1981) *Language death: the life cycle of a Scottish Gaelic dialect.* Philadelphia, PA: University of Pennsylvania Press.

Doughty, C. and Long, M.H. (2003) *The handbook of second language acquisition.* Oxford: Blackwell.

Douglas, D. (2009) *Understanding language testing.* London: Hodder Education.

Drew, P. and Heritage, J. (eds) (1992) *Talk at work: interaction in institutional settings.* Cambridge: Cambridge University Press.

Eckert, P. and McConnell-Ginet, S. (2003) *Language and gender.* Cambridge: Cambridge University Press.

Eckert, P. and Rickford, R. (eds) (2002) *Style and sociolinguistic variation*. Cambridge: Cambridge University Press.

Edelsky, C. (1976) The acquisition of communicative competence: recognition of linguistic correlates of sex roles. *Merrill-Palmer Quarterly* 22, 47–59.

Edwards, J. (2006) Language attitudes. In Brown, K. (ed.) (2006) Vol. 6: 324–32.

Edwards, V. (2004) *Multilingualism in the English-speaking world*. Oxford: Blackwell.

Ekwall, E. (1923) *English place-names in* -ing. Lund: C.W.K. Gleerup; Oxford: Oxford University Press.

Ekwall, E. (1925) The Scandinavian element. In Mawer, A. and Stenton, F.M. (eds), *Introduction to the survey of English place-names*. Cambridge: Cambridge University Press, 55–92.

Ekwall, E. (1928) *English river-names*. Oxford: Clarendon Press.

Ellis, G. and Sinclair, B. (1989) *Learning to learn English*. Cambridge: Cambridge University Press.

Ellis, R. (2008) *The study of second language acquisition* (2nd edition). Oxford: Oxford University Press.

Ellis, R. and Barkhuizen, G. (2006) *Analysing learner language*. Oxford: Oxford University Press.

Elmes, S. (2005) *Talking for Britain: a journey through the nation's dialects*. London: Penguin.

European Communities (2003) *Promoting language learning and linguistic diversity: an action plan 2004–2006*. Available online at: http://ec.europa.eu/education/doc/official/keydoc/actlang/act_lang_en.pdf (Last accessed 10 October 2011).

Eysenck, M.W. and Keane, M.T. (2010) *Cognitive psychology: a student's handbook* (6th edition). Hove: Psychology Press.

Fairclough, N. (2001) *Language and power* (2nd edition). Harlow: Longman.

Fairclough, N. (2010) *Critical discourse analysis: the critical study of language*. Harlow: Longman.

Farb, P. (1973) *Word play*. Sevenoaks: Hodder and Stoughton.

Farringdon, J., Morton, A., Farringdon, M. and Baker, M.D. (eds) (1996) *Analysing for authorship: a guide to the CUSUM technique*. Cardiff: University of Wales Press.

Fasold, R. (1984) *The sociolinguistics of society*. Oxford: Blackwell.

Field, A. (2009) Discovering statistics using SPSS (3rd edition). London: Sage.

Field, J. (2003) *Psycholinguistics: a resource book for students*. London: Routledge.

Field, J. (2004) *Psycholinguistics: key concepts*. London: Routledge.

Field, J. (2005) *Language and the mind*. London: Routledge.

Firth, J.R. (1968) *Selected papers of J.R. Firth 1952–59*. F.R. Palmer (ed.). London: Longman.

Fisher, J.H. and Bornstein, D. (1984) *In forme of speche is chaunge: readings in the history of the English language* (2nd edition). Lanham, MD: University Press of America.

Fletcher, P. (1985) *A child's learning of English*. Oxford: Basil Blackwell.

Fletcher, P. and Garman, M. (eds) (1986) *Language acquisition* (2nd edition). Cambridge: Cambridge University Press.

Fodor, J.A. (1983) *The modularity of mind*. Cambridge, MA: MIT Press.

Foley, J. and Thompson, L. (2003) *Language learning: a lifelong process*. London: Hodder Arnold.

Foster, S.H. (1990) *The communicative competence of young children*. London: Longman.

Foulkes, P. and Docherty, G. (eds) (1999) *Urban voices: accent studies in the British Isles*. London: Arnold.

Fowles, B. and Glanz, M.E. (1977) Competence and talent in verbal riddle comprehension. *Journal of Child Language* 4, 433–52.

Freeborn, D. (1995) *A course book in English grammar: Standard English and the dialects*. Basingstoke: Macmillan.

Freeborn, D. (1996) *Style: text analysis and linguistic criticism*. Basingstoke: Macmillan.

Freeborn, D. (2006) *From Old English to standard English* (3rd edition). Basingstoke: Palgrave Macmillan.

Freeborn, D. with Langford, D. and French, P. (1993) *Varieties of English* (2nd edition). Basingstoke: Macmillan.

Fromkin, V. (1973) *Speech errors as linguistic evidence*. The Hague: Mouton.

Fromkin, V., Rodman, R. and Hyams, N. (2010) *An introduction to language* (9th edition). Boston, MA: Thomson Heinle/Wadworth.

Fulcher, G. (2010) *Practical language testing*. London: Hodder Education.

Garman, M. (1990) *Psycholinguistics*. Cambridge: Cambridge University Press.

Garnham, A. (1985) *Psycholinguistics: central topics*. London and New York: Routledge.

Garrett, M.F. (1976) Syntactic processes in sentence production. In Wales, R. and Walder, E. (eds) *New approaches to language mechanisms*. Amsterdam: North Holland, 231–55.

Garton, A. and Pratt, C. (1998) *Learning to be literate*. (2nd edition). Oxford: Blackwell.

Gaskell, M.G. (2009) *The Oxford handbook of psycholinguistics*. Oxford: Oxford University Press.

Gass, S. and Mackey, A. (eds) (2011) *The Routledge handbook of second language acquisition*. London: Routledge.

Gee, J. and Handford, M. (eds) (2011) *The Routledge handbook of discourse analysis.* Abingdon: Routledge

Gibbs, R. (2006) Metaphor: psychological aspects. In Brown, K. (ed.) (2006) Vol. 8: 43–50.

Giglioli, P.P. (ed.) (1972) *Language and social context*. Harmondsworth: Penguin.

Goddard, A. and Mean, L. (2008) *Language and gender* (2nd edition). London: Routledge.

Gordon, E., Campbell, L., Hay, J., Maclagan, M., Sudbury, A. and Trudgill, P. (2004) *New Zealand English*. Cambridge: Cambridge University Press.

Görlach, M. (1991a) *Introduction to early modern English*. Cambridge: Cambridge University Press.

Görlach, M. (1991b) *Englishes: Studies in Varieties of English 1984–1988*. Amsterdam: John Benjamins.

Görlach, M. (1995) *More Englishes: new studies in varieties of English 1988–1994*. Amsterdam: John Benjamins.

Görlach, M. (1998) *Even more Englishes: Studies 1996–1997.* Amsterdam: John Benjamins.

Görlach, M. (2002) *Still more Englishes*. Amsterdam: John Benjamins.

Graddol, D., Leith, D., Swann, J., Rhys, M. and Gillen, J. (2006) *Changing English* (2nd edition). London: Routledge.

Graddol, D. and Swann, J. (1989) *Gender voices*. Oxford: Blackwell.

Gramley, S. (2011) *The history of English: an introduction*. London: Routledge.

Grant, T. D., and Baker, K. L. (2001) Identifying reliable, valid markers of authorship: a response to Chaski. *Forensic Linguistics: The International Journal of Speech Language and the Law, 8* (1), 66–79.

Green, J. (2005) *Cassell's dictionary of slang* (2nd edition). London: Cassells.

Greenbaum, S. and Nelson, G. (2009) *An introduction to English grammar* (3rd edition). Harlow: Pearson Longman.

Greene, J. and Coulson, M. (1995) *Language understanding: current issues* (2nd edition). Buckingham: Open University Press.

Greene, J. and D'Oliveira, M. (2005) *Learning to use statistical tests in psychology* (2nd edition). Maidenhead: Open University Press.

Grice, H.P. (1975) Logic and conversation. In Cole, P. and Morgan, J.L. (eds) *Syntax and semantics*, Vol. 3. New York: Academic Press. Reprinted in A.P. Martinich (ed.) (1996) *The philosophy of language* (3rd edition), New York: Oxford University Press, 156–67.

Gries, S.Th. (2009) *Quantitative corpus linguistics with R: a practical guide*. Abingdon: Routledge.

Griffiths, P.D. (1986) Constituent structure in text-copying. *York Papers in Linguistics* 12, 75–116.

Griffiths, P.D., Merrison, A.J. and Bloomer, A. (2010) *Language in use: a reader*. Abingdon: Routledge.

Groom, B. (1934) *A short history of English words*. London: Macmillan.

Grundy, P. (2008) *Doing pragmatics* (3rd edition). London: Arnold.

Gruneberg, M. (2002a) *Instant recall Spanish vocabulary*. New York: McGraw-Hill Contemporary Books.

Gruneberg, M. (2002b) *Instant recall French vocabulary*. New York: McGraw-Hill Contemporary Books.

Guendouzi, J., Loncke, F. and Williams, M.J. (eds) (2011) *The handbook of psycholinguistic and cognitive processes: perspectives on communication disorders*. New York: Psychology Press.

Gumperz, J. (ed.) (1982) *Language and social identity*. Cambridge: Cambridge University Press.

Gumperz, J. and Jacquemet, M. (2006) *New ethnographies of communication*. Oxford: John Wiley and Sons.

Hall, C.J., Smith, P.H. and Wicaksono, R. (2011) *Mapping applied linguistics*. Abingdon: Routledge.

Halliday, M.A.K. (1975) *Learning how to mean*. London: Edward Arnold.

Halliday, M.A.K. and Matthiessen, C.M.I.M. (2004) *An introduction to functional grammar* (3rd edition). London: Arnold.

Halsall, E. (1968) *French as a second language: levels of attainment in three countries*. Hull: Institute of Education, University of Hull.

Hanks, P. (2006) Personal names. In Brown, K. (ed.) (2006) Vol. 9: 299–311.

Harley, T. (2007) *The psychology of language: from data to theory* (3rd edition). Hove: Psychology Press.

Harley, T. (2010) *Talking the talk*. Hove: Psychology Press.

Harley, T. (ed.) (2011) *Psycholinguistics* (6 volumes). London: Sage.

Hart, J. (1569/1969) *An orthographie.* Menston: The Scolar Press.

Hartmann, R. (ed.) (1996) *The English language in Europe.* Exeter: Intellect.

Hatch, E. and Lazaraton, A. (1991) *The research manual: design and statistics for applied linguistics.* Boston, MA: Heinle and Heinle.

Have, Paul ten (2007) *Doing conversational analysis* (2nd edition). London: Sage.

Hawischer, G.E. and Selfe, C.L. (eds) (2000) *Global literacies and the World-Wide-Web.* London and New York: Routledge.

Hawkins, E. (1987) *Modern languages in the curriculum* (revised edition). Cambridge: Cambridge University Press.

Hawkins, E. and Perren, G.E. (eds) (1978) *Intensive language teaching in schools.* London: CILT.

Hawkins, R. and Lozano, C. (2006) Second language acquisition of phonology, morphology and syntax. In Brown, K. (ed.) (2006) Vol. 11, 67–74.

Hay, J., Maclagan, M. and Gordon, E. (2008) *New Zealand English.* Edinburgh: Edinburgh University Press.

Heath, S.B. (1983) *Ways with words.* Cambridge: Cambridge University Press.

Herring, S.C (2003) Gender and power in online communication. In Holmes, J. and Meyerhoff, M. (eds) *The handbook of language and gender.* Oxford: Blackwell, 202–228.

Herring, S.C. (2004). Computer-mediated discourse analysis: an approach to researching online behavior. In Barab, S.A., Kling, R. and Gray, J.H. (eds) *Designing for virtual communities in the service of learning.* New York: Cambridge University Press, 338–76. Available at: http://ella.slis.indiana.edu/~herring/cmda.pdf (Last accessed 10 October 2011).

Hewings, A. and Hewings, M. (2005) *Grammar and context.* London: Routledge.

Hewings, M. (2007) *English pronunciation in use: advanced.* Cambridge: Cambridge University Press.

Hickey, R. (2004) *A sound atlas of Irish English.* Berlin: Mouton.

Hillier, H. (2005) *Analysing real texts: research studies into modern English language.* Basingstoke: Palgrave Macmillan.

Hillis, A.E. (2002) Models of the reading process. In Hillis, A.E. (ed.) *The handbook of adult language disorders.* New York: Psychology Press, 3–14.

Hinton, P.R. (2004) *Statistics explained: a guide for social science students* (2nd edition). London: Routledge.

Hinton, P.R., Brownlow, C., McMurray, I. and Cozens, B. (2004) *SPSS explained.* London: Routledge.

Hoey, M. (2005) *Lexical priming: a new theory of words and language.* London: Routledge.

Hogg, R. and Denison, D. (eds) (2008) *A history of the English language.* Cambridge: Cambridge University Press.

Hoff, E. (2009) *Language development* (4th edition). Belmont, CA: Wadsworth.

Hoff, E. (2011) *Research methods in child language: a practical guide.* Oxford: Wiley-Blackwell.

Holmes, J. (1995) *Women, men and politeness.* London: Longman.

Holmes, J. (2008) *An introduction to sociolinguistics* (3rd edition). Harlow: Pearson Education.

Holmes, J. and Meyerhoff, M. (eds) (2005) *The handbook of language and gender.* Oxford: Blackwell.

Hood, P. and Tobutt, K. (2009) *Modern languages in the primary school*. London: Sage.

Hotopf, W.N. (1983) Lexical slips of the pen and tongue: what they tell us about language production. In Butterworth, B. (ed.) *Language production*, Vol. 2: *Development, writing and other language processes*. London: Academic Press, 147–99.

Howatt, A.P.R. and Widdowson, H. (2004) *A history of English language teaching* (2nd edition). Oxford: Oxford University Press.

Huang, Y. (2006) *Pragmatics*. Oxford: Oxford University Press.

Huffaker, D.A. and Calvert, S.L. (2005) Gender, identity and language use in teenage blogs. *Journal of Computer-Mediated Communication* 10 (2), article 1.

Hughes, A., Trudgill, P. and Watt, D. (2012) *English accents and dialects: an introduction to social and regional varieties of English in the British Isles* (5th edition). London: Hodder Education.

Hunsinger, J., Klastrup, L. and Allen, M. (eds) (2010) *International handbook of internet research*. Berlin: Springer.

Hunston, S. (2006) Corpus linguistics. In Brown, K. (ed.) (2006) Vol. 3: 234–48.

Hutchby, I. (1996) Power in discourse: the case of arguments on a British talk radio show. *Discourse and Society* 7: 481–97. Reprinted in Jaworski, A. and Coupland, N. (eds) (1999) *The discourse reader* (2nd edition). London: Routledge, 521–31.

Hymes, D. (1971) On communicative competence. In Pride, J.B. and Holmes, J. (eds) (1972) *Sociolinguistics*. Harmondsworth: Penguin.

Jaeger, J.J. (2005) *Kids' slips: what young children's slips of the tongue reveal about language development*. Mahwah, NJ: Lawrence Erlbaum.

Jefferson, G. (1989) Preliminary notes on a possible metric which provides for a 'standard maximum' silence of approximately one second in conversation. In Roger, D. and Bull, P. (eds) *Conversation*. Clevedon: Multilingual Matters, 166–96.

Jenkins, J. (2009) *World Englishes: a resource book for students* (2nd edition). Abingdon: Routledge.

Ji, F. (2004) *Linguistic engineering: language and politics in Mao's China*. Honolulu, Hi: University of Hawai'i Press.

Johnson, S. and Meinhof, U. (eds) (1996) *Language and masculinity*. Oxford: Blackwell.

Jones, G. and Schieffelin, B. (2009) Talking text and talking back: 'My BFF Jill' from Boob Tube to YouTube. *Journal of Computer-Mediated Communication*, 14(4), 1050–79.

Joyce, P. (1994) The people's English: language and class in England, *c.* 1840–1920. In Burke, P. and Porter, R. (eds) *Language, self and society*. Cambridge: Polity Press, 154–90.

Kachru, B., Kachru Y. and Nelson, C.L. (eds) (2009) *The handbook of world Englishes*. Oxford: Blackwell.

Kaplan, R. (ed.) (2010) *The Oxford handbook of applied linguistics* (2nd edition). Oxford: Oxford University Press.

Kaufer, D., Hayes, J.R. and Flower, L.S. (1986) Composing written sentences. *Research in the teaching of English* 20, 121–40.

Kearns, K. (2011) *Semantics* (2nd edition). Basingstoke: Macmillan.

Kennedy, H., Evans, S. and Thomas, S. (2011) Can the Web be made accessible for people with intellectual disabilities? *The Information Society* 27(1) available from http://www.indiana.edu/~tisj/27/index.html (Last accessed 10 October 2011).

Kess, J.E. (1992) *Psycholinguistics*. Amsterdam: John Benjamins.

Kirkpatrick, A. (ed.) (2010) *The Routledge handbook of world Englishes*. Abingdon: Routledge.

Kirsch, C. (2008) *Teaching foreign languages in the primary school*. London: Continuum.

Knowles, M. and Moon, R. (2006) *Introducing metaphor*. London: Routledge.

Kökeritz, H. (1953) *Shakespeare's pronunciation*. New Haven: Yale University Press.

Koller, D. (2004) Origin of the name Google. http://graphics.stanford.edu/~dk/google_name_origin.html (Last accessed 10 October 2011).

Kortmann, B. and Schneider, E.W. (eds) (2005) *A handbook of varieties of English*. Berlin: Mouton.

Kramarae, C. (1981) *Women and men speaking*. Rowley, MA: Newbury House.

Kramer, C. (1974) Stereotypes of women's speech: the word from cartoons. *Journal of Popular Culture* 8, 624–30.

Krashen, S. and Terrell, T. (1983) *The natural approach*. Oxford: Pergamon.

Kreidler, C.W. (2004) *The pronunciation of English: a coursebook* (2nd edition). Oxford: Blackwell.

Kress, G. (1990) Critical discourse analysis. *Annual Review of Applied Linguistics* 11: 84–99.

Kress, G. (1997) *Before writing: rethinking paths to literacy*. London: Routledge.

Kress, G. (2000) *Children's early spellings: creativity and convention*. London: Routledge.

Kroll, J.F. and De Groot, A.M.B. (eds) (2005) *Handbook of bilingualism: psycholinguistic approaches*. New York: Oxford University Press.

Krueger, R.A. and Casey, M.A. (eds) (2000) *Focus groups: a practical guide for applied research*. Thousand Oaks, CA: Sage.

Kurath, H. (1949) *A word geography of the eastern United States*. Ann Arbor: University of Michigan.

Labov, W. (1966) *The social stratification of English in New York City*. Washington, DC: Georgetown University Press.

Labov, W. (1969) The logic of nonstandard English. *Georgetown Monographs on Language and Linguistics* 22, 1–31. Reprinted in Giglioli (1972), 179–215.

Labov, W. (1972) *Sociolinguistic patterns*. Philadelphia, PA: University of Pennsylvania Press.

Labov, W., Ash, S. and Boberg, C. (2006) *The atlas of North American English: phonetics, phonology and sound change*. Berlin: Mouton.

Lakoff, G. (1992) Metaphor and war: the metaphor system used to justify war in the Gulf. In Pütz, M. (ed.) *Thirty years of linguistic evolution*. Amsterdam: John Benjamins, 463–81.

Lakoff, G. and Johnson, M. (1980) *Metaphors we live by*. Chicago: University of Chicago Press.

Lakoff, R. (1975) *Language and woman's place*. New York: Harper and Row.

Larsen-Freeman, D. and Long, M.H. (1991) *An introduction to second language acquisition research*. Harlow: Longman.

Leap, W.L. and Boellstorff, T. (eds) (2003) *Speaking in queer tongues: globalization and gay language*. Chicago: University of Illinois Press.

Leech, G.N. (1973) *A linguistic guide to English poetry.* London: Longman.

Leech, G.N. (2006) *Glossary of English grammar.* Edinburgh: Edinburgh University Press.

Leech, G.N., Myers, G. and Thomas, J. (eds) (1995) *Spoken English on computer.* Harlow: Longman.

Leech, G.N., Rayson, P. and Wilson, A. (2001) *Word frequencies in written and spoken English.* Harlow: Pearson. Parts of the book available at http://ucrel.lancs.ac.uk/bncfreq/ (Last accessed 10 October 2011).

Leith, D. (1997) *A social history of English* (2nd edition). London: Routledge.

Levinson, S.C. (1983) *Pragmatics.* Cambridge: Cambridge University Press.

Lewis, T. (1991) *Pisspote's progress.* Lichfield: Leomansley Press.

Li Wei (2006a) Bilingualism. In Brown, K. (ed.) (2006) Vol. 2, 1–12.

Li Wei (ed.) (2006b) *The bilingualism reader* (2nd edition). London: Routledge.

Li Wei and Moyer, M. (eds) (2008) *Blackwell guide to research methods in bilingualism and multilingualism.* Oxford: Wiley-Blackwell.

Lieven, E. (2006a) Language development: overview. In Brown, K. (ed.) (2006) Vol. 6: 376–91.

Lieven, E. (2006b) Variation in first language acquisition. In Brown, K. (ed.) (2006) Vol. 13: 350–4.

Lightbown, P. and Spada, N. (2006) *How languages are learned* (3rd edition). Oxford: Oxford University Press.

Lindquist, H. (2009) *Corpus linguistics and the description of English.* Edinburgh: Edinburgh University Press.

Litosseliti, L. (2003) *Using focus groups in research.* London: Continuum.

Litosseliti, L. (2006) *Gender and language theory in practice.* London: Hodder Education.

Livia, A. and Hall, K. (eds) (1997) *Queerly phrased: language, gender and sexuality.* New York: Oxford University Press.

Long, D. and Preston, D.R. (eds) (2003) *Handbook of perceptual dialectology.* Vol. 2. Amsterdam: John Benjamins.

Lovegrove, J. (2001) *The foreigners.* London: Gollancz.

Lowie, W., Verspoor, M. and de Bot, K. (eds) (2005) *Second language acquisition.* London: Routledge.

Luzzatti, C. and Whitaker, H.A. (2006) Acquired impairments of written language. In Brown, K. (ed.) (2006) Vol. 1, 18–26.

Lynn, J. and Jay, A. (eds) (1987) *Yes, Prime Minister.* London: BBC Books.

Macaro, E. (ed.) (2010) *The Continuum companion to second language acquisition.* London: Continuum.

Macaro, E., Vanderplank, R. and Murphy, V.A. (2010) A compendium of key concepts in second language acquisition. In Macaro, E. (ed.) (2010): 29–106.

Mackey, A. and Gass, S. (eds) (2011) *Research methods in second language acquisition: a practical guide.* Oxford: Wiley-Blackwell.

MacWhinney, B. (2003) First language acquisition. In Aronoff, M. and Rees-Miller, J. (eds) *The handbook of linguistics.* Oxford: Blackwell, 467–87.

McCrum, R., MacNeil, R. and Cran, W. (2003) *The story of English* (3rd revised edition). London: Penguin.

McEnery, T. (2006) *Swearing in English: bad language, purity and power from 1586 to the present.* London: Routledge.

McEnery, T. and Hardie, A. (2011) *Corpus linguistics: method, theory and practice.* Cambridge: Cambridge University Press.

McEnery, T., Xiao, R. and Tono, Y. (2006) *Corpus based language studies.* London: Routledge.

McIntyre, D. (2008) *History of English: a resource book for students.* London: Routledge.

McTear, M. (1985) *Children's conversation.* Oxford: Blackwell

Malmkjaer, K. (ed.) (2010) *The Routledge linguistics encyclopedia.* Abingdon: Routledge.

Maltz, D. and Borker, R. (1982/2011) A cultural approach to male–female miscommunication. In Gumperz, J. (ed.) (1982) *Language and social identity.* Cambridge: Cambridge University Press, 196–216. Reprinted in Coates, J. and Pichler, P. (eds) (2011) *Language and gender: a reader* (2nd edition). London: Routledge, 417–34.

Marenbon, J. (1994) The new orthodoxy examined. In Brindley, S. (ed.) *Teaching English.* Milton Keynes: Open University, 16–24.

Marslen-Wilson, W. and Tyler, L. (1980) The temporal structure of spoken language understanding. *Cognition* 8, 1–71.

Martin, C. (2008) *Primary languages: effective learning and teaching.* Exeter: Learning Matters.

Mather, J.Y. and Speitel, H.H. (1975) *The linguistic atlas of Scotland.* London: Croom Helm.

Meier, P. (2009) *Accents and dialects for stage and screen* (19th edition). Lawrence, KS: Paul Meier Dialect Services.

Meinhof, U. and Richardson, K. (eds) (1994) *Text, discourse and context.* London: Longman.

Melchers, G. and Shaw, P. (2011) *World Englishes* (2nd edition). London: Hodder.

Merrison, A.J., Bloomer, A.M., Griffiths, P.D. and Hall, C.J. (forthcoming) *Introducing language in use: a coursebook* (2nd edition). Abingdon: Routledge.

Mey, J. (2001) *Pragmatics: an introduction* (2nd edition). Malden, MA: Blackwell.

Meyer, C. (2002) *English corpus linguistics.* Cambridge: Cambridge University Press.

Mills, A.D. (ed.) (1987) *The place-names of Dorset.* Nottingham: English Place-name Society.

Milroy, J. and Milroy, L. (1978) Belfast: change and variation in an urban vernacular. In Trudgill, P. (ed.) *Sociolinguistic patterns in British English.* London: Arnold, 19–36.

Milroy, L. (1987) *Language and social networks* (2nd edition). Oxford: Blackwell.

Milroy, L. and Gordon, M. (2003) *Sociolinguistics: method and interpretation.* Oxford: Blackwell.

Milton, J. and Meara, P. (1995) How periods abroad affect vocabulary growth in a foreign language. *ITL Review of Applied Linguistics* 107/108, 17–34.

Mitton, R. (1996) *English spelling and the computer.* London: Longman.

Molfese, V., Molfese, D., Molnar, A. and Beswick, J. (2006) Developmental dyslexia and dysgraphia. In Brown, K. (ed.) (2006) Vol. 3, 485–91.

Mooney, A., Peccei, J. S., Labelle, S., Henriksen, B.E., Eppler, E., Irwin, A., Pichler, P. and Soden, S. (eds) (2011) *The language, society and power reader.* Abingdon: Routledge.

Mugglestone, L. (ed.) (2008) *The Oxford history of English.* Oxford: Oxford University Press.

Mulcaster, R. (1582/1970) *The first part of the elementary.* Menston: The Scolar Press.

Myers, G. (2010) *The discourse of blogs and wikis.* London: Continuum.

Naiman, N., Fröhlich, M., Stern, H.H. and Todesco, A. (1978/1995) *The good language learner.* Toronto: Ontario Institute for Studies in Education 1978; Clevedon: Multilingual Matters 1995.

Nash, W. (1985) *The language of humour.* London: Longman.

Nation, I.S.P. (1990) *Teaching and learning vocabulary.* Boston, MA: Heinle and Heinle.

Nation, I.S.P. (2001) *Learning vocabulary in another language.* Cambridge: Cambridge University Press. Related software available online: http://www.victoria.ac.nz/lals/resources/ (Last accessed 10 October 2011).

Nation, I.S.P. (2009) *Teaching ESL/EFL reading and writing.* Abingdon: Routledge.

Nation, I.S.P. and Newton, J. (2009) *Teaching ESL/EFL listening and speaking.* Abingdon: Routledge.

Nattinger, J.R. and De Carrico, J.S. (1992) *Lexical phrases and language teaching.* Oxford: Oxford University Press.

Niedzielski, N.A. and Preston, D.R. (2003) *Folk linguistics.* Berlin: Mouton de Gruyter.

Nippold, M.A. (2006) Language development in school-age children, adolescents and adults. In Brown, K. (ed.) (2006) Vol. 6: 368–73.

Nussbaum, J. and Coupland, J. (eds) (2004) *Handbook of communication and aging research.* Mahwah, NJ: Lawrence Erlbaum.

O'Barr, W. and Atkins, B. (1980/2011) 'Women's language' or 'powerless language'? In McConnell-Ginnet, S., Borker, R. and Furman, N. (eds) (1980) *Women and language in literature and society.* New York: Praeger, 93–110. Reprinted in Coates, J. and Pichler, P. (eds) (2011) *Language and gender: a reader* (2nd edition). London: Routledge, 451–60.

O'Grady, W. (2005) *How children learn language.* Cambridge: Cambridge University Press.

O'Keeffe, A., Clancy, B. and Adolphs, S. (2011) *Introducing pragmatics in use.* Abingdon: Routledge.

O'Keeffe, A. and McCarthy, M. (eds) (2010) *The Routledge handbook of corpus linguistics.* Abingdon: Routledge.

Oakhill, J. and Cain, K. (2006) Reading processes in children. In Brown, K. (ed.) (2006) Vol. 10: 379–86.

Obelkevich, J. (1987) Proverbs and social history. In Burke, P. and Porter, R. (1987) 43–72.

Olsson, J. (2008) *Forensic linguistics: an introduction to language, crime and the law* (2nd edition). London: Continuum.

Onions, C.T. (ed.) (1966) *The Oxford dictionary of English etymology.* Oxford: Clarendon Press.

Orton, H. *et al.* (1962–1971) *Survey of English dialects: the basic material* (4 volumes). London: Arnold.

Orton, H., Sanderson, S. and Widdowson, J. (1978) *The linguistic atlas of England.* London: Croom Helm.

Pallant, J. (2010) *SPSS survival manual: a step by step guide to data analysis using SPSS* (4th edition). Milton Keynes: Open University.

Partridge, E. (1948) *Words at war, words at peace.* London: Frederick Muller.

Partridge, E. (2002) *A dictionary of slang and unconventional English* (8th edition). London: Routledge.

Partridge, E. (2008) *Origins: a short etymological dictionary of modern English* (4th edition). Abingdon: Routledge.

Paulston, C.B. and Tucker, G.R. (eds) (2003) *Sociolinguistics: the essential readings.* Oxford: Blackwell.

Pavlenko, A. (ed.) (2011). *Thinking and speaking in two languages.* Bristol: Multilingual Matters.

Pawley, A. and Syder, F.H. (1983) Two puzzles for linguistic theory: nativelike selection and nativelike fluency. In Richards, J.C. and Schmidt, R.W. (eds) *Language and communication.* New York: Longman, 191–225.

Pearson, B. and de Villiers, P. (2006) Discourse, narrative and pragmatic development. In Brown, K. (ed.) (2006) Vol. 3: 686–93.

Peccei, J.S. (2005) *Child language: a resource book for students.* London: Routledge.

Peck, J. and Coyle, M. (2005a) *The student's guide to writing* (2nd edition). Basingstoke: Palgrave.

Peck, J. and Coyle, M. (2005b) *Write it right.* Basingstoke: Palgrave.

Perera, K. (1979) Reading and writing. In Cruttenden, A. (ed.) (1979), 130–60.

Perera, K. (1984) *Children's writing and reading: analysing classroom language.* Oxford: Blackwell.

Perera, K. (1986) Language acquisition and writing. In Fletcher, P. and Garman, M. (eds) (1986) 494–518.

Phillipson, R. (2003) *English-only Europe?: language policy challenges.* London: Routledge.

Pinel, J.P.J. (2011) *Biopsychology* (8th edition). Boston, MA: Pearson Educational.

Pinker, S. (1994) *The language instinct.* London: Penguin.

Pratt, N. and Whitaker, H.A. (2006) Aphasia syndromes. In Brown, K. (ed.) (2006) Vol. 1, 321–7.

Preston, D.R. (ed.) (1999) *Handbook of perceptual dialectology.* Vol. 1. Amsterdam: John Benjamins.

Prideaux, G. (1990) *Psycholinguistics: experimental study of language* (2nd edition). London: Routledge.

Primary Languages (2011). *National languages strategy.* http://www.primarylanguages.org.uk/policy__research/policy_and_reform/national_languages_strategy.aspx (Last accessed 10 October 2011).

Psathas, G. (1995) *Conversation analysis: the study of talk-in-interaction.* Thousand Oaks, CA; London: Sage.

Pyles, T. and Algeo, J. (2004) *The origins and development of the English language* (5th edition). Boston, MA: Heinle and Heinle.

Quinlan, P. and Dyson, P. (2008) *Cognitive psychology.* Harlow: Pearson Education.

Rasinger, S.M (2008) *Quantitative research in linguistics: an introduction.* London: Continuum.

Rayner, K., Pollatsek, A., Ashby, J. and Clifton, C. (2011) *Psychology of reading* (2nd edition). Psychology Press.

Redmonds, G. (2007) *Names and history: people places and things* (2nd edition). London: Hambledon Continuum.

Rees, F. (1989) *Languages for a change: diversifying foreign language provision in schools*. Windsor: NFER-Nelson.

Reid, G. and Wearmouth, J. (eds) (2002) *Dyslexia and literacy*. Chichester: John Wiley.

Reisz, M. (2011) Year abroad study at risk, expert says. *Times Higher Education*, 7 April, available at http://www.timeshighereducation.co.uk/story.asp?storycode=415697 (Last accessed 10 October 2011).

Reitveld, T. and Van Hout, R. (2005) *Statistics in language research: analysis of variance*. Berlin: De Gruyter.

Richards, J.C. and Lockhart, C. (1994) *Reflective teaching in second language classrooms*. Cambridge: Cambridge University Press.

Richards, J.C. and Schmidt, R. (2010) *Longman dictionary of language teaching and applied linguistics* (4th edition). Harlow: Longman.

Ritchie, G. (2003) *The linguistic analysis of jokes*. London: Routledge.

Ritchie, W.C. and Bhatia, T. K. (eds) (1999) *Handbook of child language acquisition. London*: Academic Press.

Roach, P. (2009) *English phonetics and phonology: a practical course* (4th edition). Cambridge: Cambridge University Press.

Romaine, S. (1984) *The language of children and adolescents*. Oxford: Blackwell.

Romaine, S. (1995) *Bilingualism* (2nd edition). Oxford: Blackwell.

Romaine, S. (2000) *Language and society: an introduction to language and society* (2nd edition). Oxford: Oxford University Press.

Room, A. (ed.) (1999) *Brewer's dictionary of names* (revised edition). London: Hodder.

Rowe, B.M. and Levine, D.P. (2011) *Concise introduction to linguistics* (3rd edition). Upper Saddle River, NJ: Prentice Hall.

Sachs, J.S. (1967) Recognition memory for syntactic and semantic aspects of connected discourse. *Perception and psychophysics* 2: 437–42.

Sadock, J.M. (1979) Figurative speech and linguistics. In Ortony, A. (ed.) *Metaphor and thought*. Cambridge: Cambridge University Press, 46–64.

Saeed, J. (2009) *Semantics* (3rd edition). Oxford: Blackwell.

Sandred, K.I. (1963) *English placenames in -stead*. Uppsala: Almqvist and Wiksell.

Sarno, D. (2009). Twitter creator Jack Dorsey illuminates the site's founding document. Part 1. *Los Angeles Times*, 18 February, http://latimesblogs.latimes.com/technology/2009/02/twitter-creator.html (Last accessed 10 October 2011).

Saville-Troike, M. (2003) *The ethnography of communication* (3rd edition). Oxford: Blackwell.

Saxton, M. (2010) *Child language: acquisition and development*. London: Sage.

Schiffrin, D., Tannen, D. and Hamilton, H. (2003) *The handbook of discourse analysis*. Oxford: Blackwell.

Schmidt, H.A. (2011) *The White House blog: the national strategy for trusted identities in cyberspace and your privacy*. 24 April 2011. http://www.whitehouse.gov/blog/2011/04/26/national-strategy-trusted-identities-cyberspace-and-your-privacy?utm_source=related (Last accessed 10 October 2011).

Sealey, A. (2010) *Researching English language.* Abingdon: Routledge.

Searle, J.R. (1965) What is a speech act? In Black, M. (ed.) *Philosophy in America.* London: Allen and Unwin, 221–39. Reprinted in Martinich, A.P. (ed.) (1996) *The philosophy of language* (3rd edition). New York: Oxford University Press, 130–40.

Searle, J.R. (1975) Indirect speech acts. In Cole, P. and Morgan, J.L. (eds) *Syntax and semantics,* Vol. 3. New York: Academic Press. Reprinted in Martinich, A.P. (ed.) (1996) *The philosophy of language* (3rd edition). New York: Oxford University Press, 168–82.

Searle, J.R. (1979) A taxonomy of illocutionary acts. In Searle, J.R. *Expression and meaning.* New York: Cambridge University Press. Reprinted in Martinich, A.P. (ed.) (1996) *The philosophy of language* (3rd edition). New York: Oxford University Press, 141–55.

Selinker, L. (1972) Interlanguage. *International Review of Applied Linguistics* 10, 201–31.

Serjeantson, M.S. (1935) *A history of foreign words in English.* London: Routledge and Kegan Paul.

Short, M. and Leech, G.N. (2007) *Style in fiction: a linguistic guide to English fictional prose* (2nd edition). Harlow: Pearson Education Limited.

Shultz, T.R. and Horibe, F. (1974) Development of the appreciation of verbal jokes. *Developmental Psychobiology* 10, 13–20.

Shuy, R. (1993) *Language crimes: the use and abuse of language evidence in the courtroom.* Oxford: Blackwell.

Simpson, P. and Mayr, A. (2010) *Language and power.* Abingdon: Routledge.

Sinclair, J.McH. (1991) *Corpus, concordance, collocation.* Oxford: Oxford University Press.

Sinclair, J.McH. (2003) *Reading concordances.* London: Longman.

Singh, I. (2005) *The history of English: a student's guide.* London: Hodder Arnold.

Skeat, W.W. (1911) *English dialects from the eighth century to the present.* Cambridge: Cambridge University Press. (also Kraus Reprint Co., New York, 1973.)

Smith, N.V. (1973) *The acquisition of phonology: a case study.* Cambridge: Cambridge University Press.

Smith, P. (1985) *Language, the sexes and society.* Oxford: Blackwell.

Smith, P.T. (1986) The development of reading: acquisition of a cognitive skill. In Fletcher, P. and Garman, M. (eds) (1986), 475–93.

Snow, C. (1986) Conversations with children. In Fletcher, P. and Garman, M. (eds) (1986), 69–89.

Spada, N. and Fröhlich, M. (1995) *Communicative orientation of language teaching observation scheme: coding conventions and applications.* Sydney: National Centre for English Language Teaching and Research.

Spender, D. (1998) *Man made language* (4th edition). Rivers Oram: Pandora.

Sperber, D. and Wilson, D. (1987) Precis of 'Relevance: communication and cognition'. *Brain and Behavioral Sciences* 10, 697–754. Reprinted in Geirsson, H. and Losonsky, M. (1996) *Readings in language and mind.* Cambridge, MA: Blackwell, 460–86.

Sperber, D. and Wilson, D. (1995) *Relevance: communication and cognition* (2nd edition). Oxford: Blackwell.

Stark, R.E. (1986) Prespeech segmental feature development. In Fletcher, P. and Garman, M. (eds) (1986) 149–73.

Steinberg, D. and Sciarini, N.V. (2006) *An introduction to psycholinguistics* (2nd edition). Harlow: Longman.

Steinberg, D., Nagata, H. and Aline, D. (2001) *Psycholinguistics: language, mind and world* (2nd edition). Harlow: Longman.

Stevick, E. (1989) *Success with foreign languages.* Hemel Hempstead: Prentice Hall.

Stockwell, P. (2007) *Sociolinguistics: a resource book for students* (2nd edition). London: Routledge.

Stoel-Gammon, C. (2006) Infancy: phonological development. In Brown, K. (ed.) (2006) Vol. 5: 642–8.

Stoppard, T. (1979) *Dogg's our pet.* London: Fraser and Dunlop.

Strang, B. (1970) *A history of English.* London and New York: Routledge.

Stubbs, M. (1995) Collocations and cultural connotations of common words. *Linguistics and Education 7* (4), 379–90.

Stubbs, M. (1997) Whorf's children: critical comments on critical discourse analysis (CDA). In Ryan, A. and Wray, A. (eds) *Evolving models of language: papers from the annual meeting of the British Association for Applied Linguistics 1996.* Clevedon: Multilingual Matters, 100–16.

Stubbs, M. (2001) *Words and phrases.* Oxford: Blackwell.

Sullivan, K. and Lindgren, E. (eds) (2006) *Computer key-stroke logging and writing.* Oxford: Elsevier.

Sunderland, J. (2006) *Language and gender.* London: Routledge.

Swan, M. and Smith, B. (2001) *Learner English: a teacher's guide to interference and other problems* (2nd edition). Cambridge: Cambridge University Press.

Swann, J. (1992) *Girls, boys and language.* Oxford: Blackwell.

Tajfel, H. (2010) *Social identity and intergroup relations.* Cambridge: Cambridge University Press.

Tajfel, H., and Turner, J. C. (1986) The social identity theory of intergroup behavior. In Worchel, S. and Austin, W. (eds) *Psychology of intergroup relations.* Chicago: Nelson-Hall, 7–24.

Talbot, M.M. (2003) Gender stereotypes: reproduction and challenge. In Holmes, J. and Meyerhoff, M. (eds) *The handbook of language and gender.* Oxford: Blackwell, 468–86.

Talbot, M.M. (2010) *Language and gender: an introduction* (2nd edition). Cambridge: Polity Press.

Tarone, E. (2006) Interlanguage. In Brown, K. (ed.) (2006) Vol. 5, 747–52.

Teubert, W. and Cermakova, A. (2007) *Corpus linguistics: a short introduction.* London: Continuum.

Thomas, J. (1995) *Meaning in interaction.* London: Longman.

Thomas, L. (1993) *Beginning syntax.* Oxford: Blackwell.

Thomas, L. and Wareing, S. (2003) *Language, society and power* (2nd edition). London: Routledge.

Thornborrow, J. (2002) *Power talk: representation and interaction in discourse.* Harlow: Longman.

Thorne, B. and Henley, N. (eds) (1975) *Language and sex: difference and dominance.* Rowley, MA: Newbury House.

Thurlow, C. (2006) From statistical panic to moral panic: the metadiscursive construction and popular exaggeration of new media language in the print media. *Journal of Computer-Mediated Communication* 11 (3): 667–701.

Thurlow, C., Lengel, L. and Tomic, A. (2004) *Computer-mediated communication: social interaction and the internet*. London: Sage.

Thurlow, C. and Mroczek, K. (eds). (2011) *Digital discourse: language in the new media*. New York and London: Oxford University Press.

Tirkkonen-Condit, S. (2006) Think-aloud protocols. In Brown, K. (ed.) (2006) Vol. 12, 678–86.

Tognini-Bonelli, E. and Sinclair, J.McH. (2006) Corpora. In Brown, K. (ed.) (2006) Vol. 3: 206–19.

Tomasello, M. and Bates, E. (eds) (2001) *Language development: essential readings*. Malden, MA: Blackwell.

Trask, R.L. (1993) *A dictionary of grammatical terms in linguistics*. London: Routledge.

Trask, R.L. (1994) *Language change*. London: Routledge.

Trask, R.L. (1995) *Dictionary of phonetics and phonology*. London: Routledge.

Trask, R.L. (2007) *Historical linguistics* (2nd edition). London: Hodder.

Trask. R.L. and Stockwell, P. (2007) *Language and linguistics: the key concepts* (2nd edition). London: Routledge.

Traxler, M. and Gernsbacher, M.A. (eds) (2006) *Handbook of psycholinguistics* (2nd edition). London: Academic Press.

Trott, K. (1996) *'Pink for girls, blue for boys': aspects of lexical development in children aged 4 to 9*. Misterton: The Language Press.

Trott, K., Dobbinson, S. and Griffiths, P. (2003) *The child language reader*. London: Routledge.

Trudgill, P. (1972) Sex, covert prestige and linguistic change in urban British English of Norwich. *Language in Society* 1, 179–95.

Trudgill, P. (1974) *The social differentiation of English in Norwich*. Cambridge: Cambridge University Press.

Trudgill, P. (1999) *The dialects of England* (2nd edition). Oxford: Blackwell.

Trudgill, P. (2000) *Sociolinguistics* (4th edition). Harmondsworth: Penguin.

Trudgill, P. and Hannah, J. (2008) *International English* (5th edition). London: Arnold

Truss, L. (2009) *Eats, shoots and leaves*. London: Fourth Estate.

Tyler, L.K. and Marslen-Wilson, W.D. (1977) The on-line effects of semantic context on syntactic processing. *Journal of Verbal Learning and Verbal Behavior* 16, 683–92.

Upton, C. and Widdowson, J.D.A. (2006) *An atlas of English dialects*. Oxford: Oxford University Press.

Upward, C. and Davidson, G. (2011). *The history of English spelling*. Oxford: Wiley Blackwell.

Vallins, G.H. (1965) *Spelling* (revised edition). London: André Deutsch.

van Gelderen, E. (2006). *A history of the English language*. Amsterdam: John Benjamins.

Van Orden, G.C. (1987) A ROWS is a ROSE: spelling, sound and reading. *Memory and Cognition* 15, 181–98.

Veith, W.H. (2006). Dialect atlases. In Brown, K. (ed.) (2006) Vol. 3: 517–28.

Viëtor, W. (2007). *Shakespeare's pronunciation: a Shakespeare reader in the old spelling and with a phonetic transcription* (1909/2007). Whitefish, MT: Kessinger Publishing.

Wallace, M. and Wray, A. (2011) *Critical reading and writing for postgraduates* (2nd edition). London: Sage.

Waniek-Klimczak, E. (ed.) (2008) *Issues in accents of English.* Newcastle-upon-Tyne: Cambridge Scholars.

Waniek-Klimczak, E. (ed.) (2010) *Issues in accents of English: variability and norm 2.* Newcastle-upon-Tyne: Cambridge Scholars.

Wardhaugh, R. (1993) *Investigating language.* Oxford: Blackwell.

Wardhaugh, R. (2010) *An introduction to sociolinguistics* (7th edition). Oxford: Wiley-Blackwell.

Waseleski, C. (2006) Gender and the use of exclamation points in computer-mediated communication: an analysis of exclamations posted to two electronic discussion lists. *Journal of Computer-Mediated Communication,* 11(4), article 6. http://jcmc.indiana.edu/vol11/issue4/waseleski.html (Last accessed 10 October 2011).

Watts, R.J. and Trudgill, P. (eds) (2001) *Alternative histories of English.* London: Routledge.

Weber, J-J. and Horner, K. (2012) *Introducing multilingualism: a social approach.* London: Routledge.

Weigand, M. (2011). Internet and identity in South Korea's popular culture. *Asia & Pacific Business & Technology Report,* 4 April 2011. http://www.biztechreport.com/story/1189-internet-and-identity-south-korea%E2%80%99s-popular-culture (Last accessed 10 October 2011).

Wells, G. (1986a) *The meaning makers: children learning language and using language to learn.* London: Hodder and Stoughton.

Wells, G. (1986b) Variation in child language. In Fletcher, P. and Garman, M. (eds) (1986), 109–39.

Wells, J.C. (1982a) *Accents of English. Vol. 1: an introduction.* Cambridge: Cambridge University Press.

Wells, J.C. (1982b) *Accents of English. Vol. 2: the British Isles.* Cambridge: Cambridge University Press.

Wells, J.C. (1982c) *Accents of English. Vol. 3: beyond the British Isles.* Cambridge: Cambridge University Press.

White, J. (1986) The writing on the wall: beginning or end of a girl's career? *Women's Studies International Forum* 9 (5): 561–74.

White, L. (2003) *Second language acquisition and universal grammar.* Cambridge: Cambridge University Press.

Widdowson, H.G. (2004) *Text, context, pretext: critical discourse analysis: the critical study of language.* Oxford: Wiley-Blackwell.

Wikipedia (2011a) *IPod.* http://en.wikipedia.org/wiki/IPod (Last accessed 10 October 2011).

Wikipedia (2011b) *Twitter.* http://en.wikipedia.org/wiki/Twitter (Last accessed 10 October 2011).

Wikipedia (2011c) *Web scraping.* http://en.wikipedia.org/wiki/Web_scraping (Last accessed 10 October 2011).

Williams, J.M. (1986) *Origins of the English language: a social and linguistic history.* New York: Free Press.

Wood, C., Meachem, S., Bowyer, S., Jackson, E., Tarczynski-Bowles, M.L. and Plester, B. (2011). A longitudinal study of children's text messaging and literacy development. *British Journal of Psychology* 102, 3, 431–42.

Woods, A., Fletcher, P. and Hughes, A. (1986) *Statistics in language studies.* Cambridge: Cambridge University Press.

Wray, A. (1992a) Authentic pronunciation for early music. In Paynter, J., Howell, T., Orton, R. and Seymour, P. (eds) *Companion to contemporary musical thought*. London: Routledge, 1051–64.

Wray, A. (1992b) Restored pronunciation. In Knighton, T. and Fallows, D. (eds) *Companion to medieval and Renaissance music*. London: Dent, 292–9.

Wray, A. (1995) English pronunciation *c*.1500–*c*.1625. In Morehen, J. (ed.) *English choral practice 1400–1650*. Cambridge: Cambridge University Press, 90–108.

Wray, A. (1996) The occurrence of 'occurance' and 'alot' of other things 'aswell': patterns of errors in undergraduate English. In Blue, G. and Mitchell, R. (eds) *Language and education*. Clevedon: Multilingual Matters, 94–106.

Wray, A. (1999) Singers on the trail of 'authentic' Early Modern English: the puzzling case of /æː/ and /ɛː/. *Transactions of the Philological Society* 97 (2): 185–211.

Wray, A. (2002) *Formulaic language and the lexicon*. Cambridge: Cambridge University Press.

Wray, A. (2008) *Formulaic language: pushing the boundaries*. Oxford: Oxford University Press.

Wright, A., Betteridge, D. and Buckby, M. (2006) *Games for language learning* (3rd edition). Cambridge: Cambridge University Press.

Wright, S. (ed.) (2004) Multilingualism on the Internet. Special issue of *International Journal of Multicultural Societies* 6.

Yus, F. (2006) Relevance theory. In Brown, K. (ed.) (2006) Vol. 10, 512–19.

Zachrisson, R.E. (1909) *A contribution to the study of Anglo-Norman influence on English place-names*. Lund: Håkan Ohlsson.

Zachrisson, R.E. (1913) *Pronunciation of English vowels 1400–1700*. Gothenburg: Zachrisson.

Index

abbreviations, 136, 138

abstract, 18, 19, 20

abstracting journals, 19

academic writing style, 258, *Chapter 23*

accents, 92, 95, 96, 100, 106, 109, *Chapter 9,* 165, 169–71, 175, 176, 189, 195

acceptability, 73

accessibility, 145, 147

accommodation, 100

acquisition, *Chapter 3, Chapter 4,* 108–9, 118, 189
   of consonants, 37
   lexical, 52

acting, 118

active sentences, 23, 37

adjectives, 36, 80, 117, 168
   of dimension, 44

adverbs, 117

advertising, 69, 79, 81, 83

age, *Chapter 1, Chapter 3,* 55, 57, 86, *Chapter 7, Chapter 8,* 118, 121, 157, 160, 165, 166, 176, 179, 185

agrammatism, 24–5

agreeing and disagreeing, 9, 23, 41, 63, 69, 77, 87, 90, 121, 164, 168, 175, 254

algebraic symbols, 228–9

alliteration, 79

allophones, 190

alternative hypothesis, 21

Amazon, 7

ambiguity, 63, 71
   avoidance of, 63
   lexical, 22–3
   structural, 22–3, 66–7

analysis of variance (ANOVA), 224

anaphoric reference, 82

Anglo-Saxon, 81

Animal Farm, 80

animated tone, 201

anonymity, 166, 172, 174, 185

ANOVA *see* analysis of variance

answerphones *see* telephone answering machines

antonymy, 80

aphasia, 24–5, 29

aphorism, 83

apologies, 105

apostrophes, 71–2, 263–4

apps, 135

appendices, 2, 185

applause, 203

arguments, 9, 90, 154, 255, 263

aspiration, 124

assessment, 10–11, 55, 262

assessors, 13, 14, 126, 156, 180, 183, 185, 196, 204, 214, 233, 235, 248, 262

assimilation, 25, 37, 46

assonance, 79

asynchronous communication, 142

attention span, 33, 163

attitude scale *see* Likert Scale

attitudes, 49, 52, 56, 57, 71, 81, 87, 90, 92, 96, 99–100, 101, 103, 119, 164–70, 174–5

attribute, 81, 87, 97, 109, 158–9

audience, 63–4, 76, 83–4, 85, 89, 203, 262

audio data, 33, 115, *Chapter 12,* 204 *see also:* data: audio-recorded

Austin, J.L., 63

Australian slang, 115

authorship, 77, 88, 240–1

autism, 42

averages, 28, 40, 214–9, 221–2, 227, 228

babbling, 35

backchannel, 105

background noise, 19, 106, 154–5, 203

Bank of English, 210

BBC, 51, 84, 90, 100, 115, 154

Bede, 131

Belfast, 96, 113

bereavement, 176

Bible, 81, 82, 131

bibliographies, 5, 234

bilingualism. 17, 30, 46, 53, 55, 56, 59, 92–3, 98

Black Vernacular English, 72, 113

BNC *see* British National Corpus

blogs, 135, 136, 138

brackets, 197–200, 203, 226, 236–9, 243, 246
    angle, 202–3, 211
    double, 197, 198–201, 202–3
    slanted, 189, 192
    square, 189, 192, 200, 257

brain damage, 17, 20, 24

BRICLE *see* International Corpus of Learner English

Bristol Survey of Language Development, 40

British National Corpus, 210, 211–12

broad phonetic transcription, 190

Broca's aphasia *see* aphasia

Canterbury Tales, 79

carer language, 39–40, 49, 99, 181

carers, 25, 30, 33, 40, 42, 107, 181, 182, 184

Carroll, Lewis, 68

cartoons, 43, 104

case studies, 12, 34, 42, 53, 59, 109, *Chapter 15*, 181–3

cataphoric reference, 82

catch phrases, 97

CDA *see* Critical Discourse Analysis

ceiling effect, 161

ceremonies, 86

chance, 3, 117–18, 155, 163, 166, 222–4, 228

charities, 87

charts,
    bar, 214, 218–221
    paint, 39, 158
    pie, 214, 220

Chaucer, Geoffrey, 79, 131

Cheshire, Jenny, 95, 97, 104, 113

child language *see* first language acquisition, 7, 32, 34, 36, 37–8, 39–41

child-directed speech *see* carer language, 39

CHILDES database, 7, 32

children as subjects, *Chapter 3*, 33–4, 101, 104, 161, 163, 174, 176, 181

chi-square test, 224

Chomsky, Noam, 39, 93

chronologies, 125, 131

chunks, 21

citation, 234, 235, 244, 263

clause, 22, 81–2, 264–5

clinical studies, 10, 19

clipart, 271

closed questions, 167–8, 172–3

co-authored books, 239–40

Cobuild, 67, 68, 210

cockney, 120–22

code-mixing, 98

code-switching, 98

coefficient, 224, 228

cognitive development, 37–8

cohesion, 82

cohort theory, 20

coinages *see* neologisms, 70

collective nouns, 69

collocation, 67, 86–7, 206–9

colloquialisms, 94

colons, 200, 202, 237, 243, 265

colour terms, 38–9, 80, 158

comedy, 63–4, 83, 90–1, 101 *see also* jokes

comma, 201, 238, 240, 243, 246, 264

commercials, 101 *see also* advertising

communication-based teaching, 50

communication strategies, 54

communicative competence, 32, 34, 38, 50, 93, 105, 109

Community Language Learning, 51

comparative adjectives, 36, 252–60

compatibility, 166

competence, 32, 49, 52, 93

compliments, 99, 105

comprehension, 10, 21, 44, 49
  sentences, 23, 28, 37
  spoken word, 20, 28
  text, 28

computer analysis of text, 88, *Chapter 19*

computer-readable texts, 205

concepts, 38–9, 53, 96

conclusions, 4, 13

concordances, 206–11

confidentiality, 166, 172, 181, 185

connotation, 80–1, 86–7, 108, 207

conquest, 119, 131

consent, 106, 180, 182, 184–5

consonance, 79

constituent boundaries, 26

constructivist approach, 64

content words, 24–5

context, 17, 20, 22–3, 30, 51–2, 65, 92–3, 96, 107, 116, 121, 179, 191, 206

continuous variables, 95

contrastive analysis, 54

control group, 19, 29, 160

convergence, 100

conversation, 34, 40, 52, 63, 77, 89, 93–4, 98, 100, 101, 105, 108, 132, 154, 156, 158, 175–6, *Chapter 18*

conversational implicature, 63

cookery, 68

copying, 26–7, 247–8

copyright, 153–4, 212

copyright date, 242

corpus/corpora, 7, 68, 73, 86–7, 115, *Chapter 19*

'correctness', 72–3

correlation, 224, 228

coughs, 200

counselling, 27

courtesy bias, 167

courtroom language, 86–7, 107–8

co-variation, 94

Critical Discourse Analysis (CDA), 86–7

critical period, 30

critical value, 228

cross-cultural comparisons, 30

cross-linguistic comparisons, 30

cross-referencing questions, 171

cross-sectional study, 43, 182

cummings, e. e., 70

dactyl, 79

data *see* qualitative data; quantitative data
  audio-recorded, 14, *Chapter 12, see also* audio data; video data
  collecting, 113–5, 159, 167–71, 174–6, *Chapter 15, Chapter 16*
  data, backing up, 262
  interval, 215
  nominal, 215, 217
  numerical, 13
  non-numerical, 13
  ordinal, 215–217
  ratio, 215–7

databases, 5–7, 32

data-based research, 10–11

data protection laws, 186

date of publication, 10, 237, 241–3

Dead Parrot Sketch, Monty Python's, 74

deadlines, 3, 14, 172, 249

Dearing Report, 57

degrees of freedom, 228

denotation, 80

descriptivism, 72

determinism, 27

development, *Chapter 3*, 31, 108, 124, 131, 181
    conversation, 34, 39–40, 43
    lexical, 34, 36, 38–9
    literacy, 41, 133
    phonological, 34–6
    semantic, 34–5, 38
developmental sequences, 48
df *see* degrees of freedom
diachronic change, 94, 124
diacritics, 190
diagnostic tests, 181
diagrams, 10
dialect, 72, 92, 96, 100, 104, 106–7, *Chapter 9*, 124, 131, 154, 165, 167, 171, 176
dialect geography, 93
dialectology, 93, 103, 119, 165
dialogue, 77, 89, 108 *see also* conversation
dictionaries, 8, 43, 68–70, 73, 113, 126, 128, 132, 205, 242, 262
diglossia, 98
direct questions, 167, 175
directness, 64
disability, 31, 42, 179
discourse analysis, 76–7, 86, 93
dissertations, 1, 8
distracters, 167, 169
distractions, 143
distribution (statistical), 219–224
divergence, 96, 100
doctors' language, 50, 86–7, 182
domain, 98, 110
dominance, 107–8, 132
double brackets *see* brackets
double negative, 117
Down's syndrome, 42
drafting, 3, 86, 243, 251, 262–3
dysfluency, 49
dysgraphia, 26–7
dyslexia, 26–7, 42

e.g., 265
edited collections, 5, 237–8
education, 41, 55, 90, 109–10, 114, 118, 119, 122, 133, 157, 166, 225
EFL *see* English as a Foreign/Second Language
elicitation, 24–5, 36, 56–7, 95–7, 114, 155, 164–70, 173–7, 179, 182
ellipsis, 82
email, 85, 142, 172, 244, 262
emergencies, 162
emoticons, 139
emphasis, 66, 91, 97, 201–2
encyclopedia, 5, 7, 242
English as a Foreign/Second Language, 46, 82
English Place Name Society, 126
equipment, 11, 18, 32, 153, 159, 162, 180–1
ERIC, 6
error analysis, 54
errors, 22, 24–5, 36–7, 49, 54–5, 73, 181, 189, 261
ESL *see* English as a Foreign/Second Language
essay, 86, 247–8
estate agents' descriptions, 85
et al., 240
ethics, 11, 33, 106, 154, *Chapter 16*
ethnicity, 92
ethnographic research, 96–7, 165, 179
etymology, 65, 69, 70
euphemism, 100, 132
evolution of language, 10
exaggeration, 111, 120
exclamation mark, 202
experimental design, 13, 24, *Chapter 13*
experiments, 8, *Chapter 13*
explicit approach, 167
external events, 203
extralinguistic variables, 94, 96, 109
eye-witness accounts, 133

Facebook, 135, 138, 142
facial expressions, 99

falling tone, 201–2

fall-rise tone, 202

family history, 133

fathers, 40

fatigue effects, 162

Fawlty Towers, 100

feasibility of project, 180

fiction, 41, 75, 80, 110

first-language acquisition, *Chapter 3*, 45–6, 54, 77, 108

Flanders and Swann, 91

flash-cards, 159, 176

floor effects, 161

fluency, 46, 57, 58, 59

fly-on-the-wall documentary, 156

focus groups, *Chapter 14*

folk linguistics, 103, 105

fonts,
    phonetic, 13, *Chapter 17*, 191
    proportional, 196

football results, 36, 85

foreign-language learning, 30, 46, 53–4, 60, 118, 165

foreign language, 56–8, 114, 210

foreigner talk, 49, 99

forenames, 176

forensic linguistics, 63, 88

formal language, 85, 95, 99, 177

forms of address, 64, 83–4, 94, 99, 106, 108

formulaic language, 21, 83

forthcoming works, 244

French, 46, 56, 57, 122, 124, 127, 133

frequency (statistical), 97, 221–5

frequency tables, 206

friendliness, 169

function words, 24, 25

garden-path sentences, 22, 66–7

gay language, 101–2, 104, 106–7

gender, 30, 38–9, 87, 92, 99, *Chapter 8*, 159, 166, 189, 205

genre, 76, 85, 110, 205

Geordie, 72, 119, 122

German, 48, 53, 233

gestures, 35, 99, 199

glossaries, 8, 262

good language learner, 53

Google, 6, 135, 138, 210, 242

Google Books, 7

Google Translate, 145, 147

gossip, 85, 104–5

GPS navigation, 135, 136

grammar, 49, *Chapter 5*, 80–81, 111, 115–7, 124, 131, 263 *see also* syntax

grammar-based teaching, 50–51, 55

graphs, *Chapter 20*

grep, 138, 139

Grice, H. P., 63–4

group identity, 96–7

group membership, 94, 97, 166

handedness, 159

Hardy, Thomas, 120, 206f

Harvard referencing, 3, *Chapter 21*

headings, 4, 249, 263

head movements, 199

hearing impairment, 42

hedging, 105

heraldry, 67

hidden messages, 62–3

historical events, 133

historical linguistics, 10, *Chapter 10*

holiday brochures, 84

homophones, 21

honesty, 169

Hopkins, Gerard Manley, 70, 79

house-rules, 2, 14

humane referencing system, 3, 237, 245–6

humour, 38, 63, 74, 102, *see also* comedy; jokes

hypertext, 140

hyphens, 199

hyponymy, 80

hypotheses, 4, 8, 19, 21, 23, 25, 158, 162–3, 221–2, 224

i.e., 265

iamb, 79

ibid, 243

ICE *see International Corpus of English*

identity, 96, 100, 111, 118, 127, 136, 137, 143, 144, 174–5, 185, 197

Identity Ecosystem, 144, 145

ideological standpoint, 80

idioms, 17, 28, 43, 58, 68, 73, 74

illustrations in text, 77

immersion programmes, 45

immigration, 105, 119

in-breath, 198

indecipherable speech, 200

indexes, 5, 210

Indian English, 72

indirect approach, 167

indirect request, 76

individual differences, 53, 54

Indo-European, 124

inexplicit approach *see* indirect approach

infer, 265

informality, 85

informants, 4, 11, 114, 153, 155–6, 164, 167–8, 171, 176–7, 184

inhibitions, 153

in-house rules, 2

integration, 119

interference, 54–7

interlanguage, 54

inter-library loans, 6

International Corpus of English, 115, 210

International Corpus of Learners' English, 210

International English, 96

International Phonetic Alphabet, xii

Internet, 6–7, 154, 210, 244–5, 247, 249
  language, 135
  referencing, 244–5

interpersonal function, 83–5

interruption strategies, 88–90, 105

intertextuality, 79

interviews, 12, 83, 86, 90, 95, 103, 130, 154–5, *Chapter 14*

intonation, 17, 23, 32, 35, 36–7, 39–40, 49, 61, 79, 91, 99, 196, 201–2

intuitions, 68, 118, 175

IPA, 180 *see* also International Phonetic Alphabet

iPod, 138

Irish, 58

irregular verbs, 116

ISBN number, 241

i-Work Presentation, 269

Japanese, 139

jargon, 94, 113

jokes, 37–8, 43, 58, 61, 74, 83, 90

journals, 5, 6, 31–2, 47, 62, 78, 94–5, 102, 113–4, 126, 137, 238, 246

judgement sample, 166

Kafka, Franz, 81

keystrokes, 142

keywords, 6

Kindle, 147, 242

kinship terms, 69

knowing a language, 49

Krashen, Stephen, 46, 51

L1 *see* mother tongue, first language

L2 *see* second language

Labov, William, 72, 93–7, 104, 113

Lakoff, George, 64, 65

Lakoff, Robin, 105, 107

Lancaster-Oslo-Bergen (LOB) corpus, 211

language
  change *see* diachronic change
  choice, 100
  comprehension, 20–1, 28, 37, 43–4
  contact, 93
  games, 37, 122, 176
  learning, 22, *Chapter 3, Chapter 4,* 60
  planning, 93
  production, 28, 36,
  processing, 20, 22, 25, 28
  standards, 137
  surveys, 165
  transfer, 54
  variety, 98, 99–100, 122, 190

language and thought, 27

latching, 197

late submission, 2

Latin, 81, 132, 138

laughter, 64, 196

layout, 195ff

leading questions, 171

learner goals, 49, 52, 54

learning strategies, 53, 54

lemmatised text, 205, 212

lesbian language, 106

lexical choice, 76, 80

lexical phrases, 21

lexical retrieval, 25

libraries, 5–6, 84

Likert Scale, 168

linguistic atlases, 113

linguistic determinism, 27

linguistic judgements, 72

linguistic relativity, 27

linguistic variables, 93, 95

Linkword, 52

listening, 17, 46, 78, 88, 96

lists, 19, 25, 69, 85, 95, 115, 167, *Chapter 19,* 240

literacy, 30, 34, 37, 41, 48, 109, 133, 173

literary texts, 65, 76, 79, 120, 125, 211

literature review, 4, 8–9

liturgy, 82

loaded questions, 171

LOB *see* Lancaster Oslo Bergen corpus

Logogen model, 20

lol, 138, 139

longitudinal study, 25, 34, 181–2

Longman/Lancaster English Language
  Corpus, 211

macrolinguistic studies, 93

magazines, 70

male–female differences, 39, 86, *Chapter 8,* 121,
  160, 165

Mann-Whitney U test, 224

Martha's Vineyard, 95, 113

matched guise, 99, 169

matched pairs design, 160

maxims, 63, *see also* conversational
  implicature

mean (statistical), 217, 218–9, 227, 228

Mean Length of Utterance (MLU), 34

meaning groups, 68

meaning, 21, 23, 24, 30, 38–9, 53, *Chapter 5,* 81,
  107, 117, 126, 128

memories as data, 165, 175

memorization, 19, 24, 43, 44, 79, 160

memory, 19, 155, 169, 216, 218, 248, 262

mental lexicon, 26

metalanguage, 175

metalinguistic awareness, 37

metaphor, 43, 61, 64–5, 100

methodology, *Chapter 1*

metrical patterns, 79

micro linguistic studies, 93

microphones, 181

Middle English, 65, 71

minimal pairs, 95, 191, 192

minimal response tokens, 88, 105

mishearings, 20

mispronunciations, 36, 37

MLU *see* Mean Length of Utterance

mnemonics, 52

mode, 64

models, 10, 28
   bilingual storage, 53, 98
   foreign/second language
      learning, 46, 50, 137
   lexical processing, 20, 22
   lexical storage and retrieval, 23, 45
   memorizing, 19, 24, 43, 52, 53, 79, 160
   processing, 21, 22, 41
   reading, 20, 26, 27
   sentence processing, 19
   writing, 26

modern dialectology, 93

modularity, 19

monographs, 5

monolingualism, 46

monologues, 77

monomorphemic words, 70

monosyllables, 257

morphemes, 34, 70

morphological errors, 36

morphology, 36, 48, 61, 70, 81, 112, 115

mother tongue, 45, 57, 166,

mother tongue teaching, 166, 215–16

motherese, 49 *see also* carer language

motivation, 29, 47, 50, 56, 60, 69, 97, 103, 117,
   130, 165, 169

MP3, 115, 136, 156

MT *see* mother tongue

Mulcaster, 130

multilingualism, 10, 30, 46, 55, 92, 165

multiparty talk, 140

multiple choice, 169, 185

mumbling, 200

naming tasks, 19, 25, 38, 39

narrative, 43, 144, 206, 207, 208, 209

narrow phonetic transcription, 154, 190

National Sound Archive, 112

native national varieties, 50, 112, 113, 114, 192

native regional varieties, 92, 111, 112, 114

Natural Approach, 51

naturalness, 63, 89,

needs analysis, 165

negative, 80, 81, 117, 131, 169, 171, 224

negotiation, 97

neologisms, 24

netiquette, 143

network (social), 96, 97

New York English, 95, 96, 113, 119, 255, 259

news interviews, 86, 90, 112, 156,

newspapers, 52, 66, 80, 83, 84, 85, 87,
   88, 119, 242

newspeak, 27, 59

Nineteen Eighty-Four, 27, 59

nodding, transcription of, 199

noise, 35, 106, 153, 156, 203

nominal data *see* data

non-competitive overlap, 105

non-native speakers, 48, 49, 55, 56, 57, 59, 60,
   68, 73, 82, 99, 112, 118, 205, 206, 210, 215

non-proportional fonts, 196

non-rhotic varieties, 192, 194

nonsense sentences, 21, 71,

non-verbal communication, 198

non-words, 129

Norwich, 95, 113

note-taking, 110, 174, 248, 249

novels, 27, 59, 65, 67, 70, 75, 80, 104, 120, 206

null hypothesis, 158

nursery rhymes, 37, 79, 160, 220,

obituaries, 100

observation, 8, 12, 43, 50, 51, 59, 97, 105, 115,
   121, *Chapter 15*

observer effect, *see* observer's paradox

observer's paradox, 12

occupation, 34, 94, 99, 107, 126, 176,

The Office, 89

Old English, 65, 131

omission of data, 203, 235

one-tailed, 222

on-line communities, 142

on-line discussions, 141

onomatopoeia, 79

op.cit., 243

open questions, 167, 173, 174

oral presentations, *Chapter 24*

order effects, 161

order of acquisition *see* developmental sequences

ordinal data, *see* data

orthographic transcription, *Chapter 18*

Orwell, George, 27, 59, 80, 250

Oslo *see* London Bergen corpus

out-breath, 198–9,

Outnumbered, 89

over-extension, 35, 36, 38,

overgeneralization, 54

overlapping talk, 105

over-referencing, 249

page numbers, 10, 14, 233, 236, 237, 238, 242

papers in journals and books, 238

paralinguistic features, 76, 99, 179

parametric tests, 224

parents, 33, 34, 39, 40, 41, 43, 45, 57, 69, 98, 109, 118, 161, 176, 178, 180, 182, 184

parsing, 21

participant observation, 180

participant roles, 66, 97

participants, 11, 12, 157, 161, 167 *Chapter 13*, *Chapter 14*, *Chapter 15*, *Chapter 16*

passive sentences, 23, 32, 37, 81, 131

past participles, 22, 116

Paston Letters, 134

pauses, 26, 195, 198, 203

pdf files, 6

peer groups, 41, 96, 104, 109

pejorative language, 86–7, 207

percentages, *Chapter 20*

performatives, 63

personal information, 166, 186

phishing, 145

phoneme checklist/chart, 193–4

phonemes of English, 193–4

phonemes, 28, 37, 154, 190, 191, 192

phonemic transcription, 79, 112, 120, 134, 190, 191

phonetic spelling, 120, 129, 130

phonetic symbols, 112, 121, 122, 129

phonetic transcription, 79, 93–4, 134, 154, *Chapter 17*, 199–200

phonetics, 28

phonological errors, 24

phonology, 9, 30, 32, 34, 36, 50, 112, 118

phonotactics, 37

phrase structure analysis, 73, 74

pidgins, 92

pilot studies, 12, 159, 162, 170, 172, 174

pitch, 201, 202

place names, 127, 128, 129

plagiarism, 10, 14, 148, *Chapter 22*

planning, 3, 33, 158, 177

playground games, 122, 176

playground vocabulary, 70

plurals, 36, 48, 116, 264, 266

poetry, 79

pointing, 76, 199

politeness, 60, 64, 99, 100, 101, 105, 106, 116, 141

political correctness, 101, 108

political events, 46, 57, 58, 84, 119, 125, 127, 131, 133

political texts, 66, 80, 90, 97, 119

polyglots, 55–6

polysemy, 38

possessives, 48, 116, 264

post-vocalic *r*, 255

power, 57, 58, 86, 87, 93, 98, 99, 107

powerless language, 107

Powerpoint, 269, 270

practice effect, 160, 162

practice sessions, 162

pragmatics, 23, 31, 43, 44, 61, 62, 63, 74, 97, 140

predictions, 4, 8, 10, 19, 55–6, 118, 180, 190, 223

prefixes, 70

prehistoric language, 124

pre-linguistic development, 35

prepositions, 24, 25, 66, 72

prescriptivism, 72, 90, 257

presentation, 2, 14, 50, 77, 110, 154, 159, 168, 171–2, 185, 195, 215, 218, 249–50

prestige language, 95, 104, 107, 131

probability (statistical), 221–4

production of speech, 10, 17, 19, 21, 25, 28, 29, 36, 42

proficiency, 59, 68, 165

projects, feasibility, 10, 39, 111, 166, 180

pronouns, 73, 116, 264

pronunciation, 25, 36, 49, 54, 55, 95, 100, 104, 111, 115, 121, 122, 127, 129, 130, 164, 167, 189, 206, 199, 255

proof-reading, 212, 236, 263, 272

propaganda, 83, 84, 87

proper names. 125

Proto-Indo-European, 124

prototype, 68, 69

proto-words, 35

proverbs, 43, 132

pub names, 128

punch lines, 90

punctuation, 10, 61, 71, 110, 138, 243, 246, 264–5

puns, 38, 64, 81, 130

Quakers, 119

qualitative data, 8, 99, 167, 170, 179, 181

quantitative data, 8, 95, 99, 170, 179, 215, 216–7, 238

questionnaire fatigue, 173

questionnaires, 4, 12, 48, 103, 106, *Chapter 14*, 170

questions, 4, 7, 30, 45, 61, 76, 82, 92, 101, 103, 111, 124, 135–6, 157, 164, 167, 170, 173–4, 205

question and answers sessions, 275

quote, 2, 7, 10, 131, 203, 233, 234, 235, 249, 257, 263

race, 87

radio, 25, 27, 78, 83, 84, 86, 87, 90, 98, 104, 112, 115, 153, 156, 176, 180

random sample, 159, 166, 178

ranking schemes, 169, 216, 221

rating scales, 74, 168–9, 216, *see also* Likert Scale; semantic differential, ranking schemes

readers, 5

Reading (town), 95, 97, 104, 113

reading, 9–10, 17, 20, 26, 41, 42, 110, 216, 233
    lists, 11
        schemes, 41, 42, 82

Received Pronunciation (RP), 115, 206

reference lists, 234

referencing, 3, *Chapter 21*, 248, 249, 265

regionalisms, 94

register, 39, 43, 94, 98, 99

rehearsal, 12, 159–60

relative clauses, 32

Relevance Theory, 63

reliability, 6, 7, 9, 34, 158, 166, 170, 192, 214, 224

religion, 53, 94, 97, 98, 100

repairs, 25, 26

repetition, 39, 82

rephrasing, 248, 262

replications, 2, 18–9, 159, 160, 180

representativeness, 12, 105, 157, 166, 182, 184, 213

reprint dates, 242

requests, 64, 76, 145, 275

research assistants, 159

research expenses, 177

research questions, 4, 8

response rate, 170–1

results, 4, 12, 13, 157, 160, 183, 212, *Chapter 20*

revised editions, 242

rhotic varieties, 192, 194

rhyme, 79, 90–1, 130

rhymes, 25, 37, 79, 160

rhythm, 63, 79, 90–1

rising tone, 201

rogue results, 13, 191

Rossetti, Christina, 79

route of development, 30

Roy, Deb, 34

Royal Family, the British, 118

RP *see* Received Pronunciation

rural dialectology, 93

Russian, 58

Sachs, J.S., 23, 26

safety, 11–12

sample size, 181–2

Sapir, 27

SARA software, 210

satire, 67–8

scanners, 212

schemata, 21

schools, 34, 50–1, 56–7, 111, 154, 156, 178, 180

Scottish English, 113

Scouse, 119

scrape, 139

scripted conversation. 63, 64, 89, 143

secondary quotes, 234–5

second language, *Chapter 4*, 152, 201
    acquisition, (SLA), 45, 48, 49, 77, 94, 189
    learning, (SLL), 46, 182

Second Life, 143

secret observation, 155, 180

self-evaluation tests, 106

self-presentation, 272

self-report, 166

self-study, 11

semantic differential, 168–9

semantic errors, 24

semantic feature hypothesis, 35

semantic roles, 66

semantics, 25, 32, 50, 61, 80, 131, 140, 205

semi-colons, 265

sense of audience, 262

sentence builders, 21

sentence frames. 21

sentence structure, 65–6

Sermon on the Mount, 81

sex *see* gender

sexism, 101, 108

SGML (Standard Generalized Markup
    Language), 211

shaggy dog stories, 64

Shakespeare, 79, 88, 120, 124, 130, 211

siblings, 40, 118

sign language, 70

significance level, 217, 222–3

SIL *see* Summer Institute of Linguists

silence, 156, 198

simplified texts, 82

situation, 31, 94, 95, 99, 111, 157, 163,
    174–5, 176

situational variables, 94

Skype, 142

SLA *see* Second Language

slang, 113, 114, 125, 165

slanted brackets *see* brackets

slips of the ear, 20

slips of the pen, 26

slips of the tongue, 24, 67, 179, 199 *see also*
    speech errors

SLL *see* Second Language

slogans, 80

SMS, 136, 137

sneezes, 200

SNS, 136

soaps, 64, 89

sobbing, transcription of, 199

social background, 40–1, 92, 94, 95, 109, 112, 117–8, 165

social context, 30, 92, 93, 100

social group, 30, 96

social identity *see* identity

social judgements, 72

social networks, 96–7, 135, 138

social relationships, 92, 102–3

socialization, 109

society, 92, 99, 103, 104, 106, 108–9, 111, 128–9, 133

socio-economic background, 87

sound patterns, 79, 80

sound systems. 190

Spouth African English, 116

Speech Act theory, 63

speech and writing, 10–11, 19, 20, 48, 49, 50, 75–6

speech communities, 96

speech data, 153, 154, 167–8

speech errors, 22, 24, 25, 30–1, 32, 49, 119, 189

speech recognition software, 147

speech styles, 95, 98, 158, 189, 194

speech therapists, 29, 182

speech transcribing, *Chapter 17, Chapter 18*

speed of speech, 202–3

spellchecker, 261

spelling (as a topic of study), 21, 41, 73, 79, 110, 120, 127, 138

spelling (guidance), 9, 261, 262, 263

spelling reform, 130

split infinitives, 72

spoken questionnaires, 164

spontaneous speech, 25, 89, 96, 162, 180, 181

SPSS (Statistical Package for the Social Sciences software, 225

square brackets *see* brackets

standard deviation, 228

statistics, 12, *Chapter 20*

status, 46, 57, 64, 97, 107, 255

stereotypes, 101, 103, 108, 109, 160–1

stopwatches, 159

story-telling, 43, 154

strategies
    communication, 53, 54–5, 101
    conversation, 88, 97, 105, 106, 107, 108, 111, 112
    politeness, 99

streetnames, 128, 129

stress, 79, 201, 202

stretched sound, transcription of, 199, 200, 201

strong verbs, 116

stuttering, 42

style (as a topic of study), 70, *Chapter 6*, 93–4, 105, 131

style (guidance), *Chapter 23, Chapter 24*

style shifting, 100, 108, 109

styleless prose, 80

stylistics, 76, 79, 206, 207, 208, 209

subjective responses, 176

subjectivity, 265

subjunctive, 116, 131

subsections, 4

substitution, 24, 25, 37

sucker bias, 167

suffixes, 70

suggestopaedia, 51

summaries, 4, 5, 13, 263

Summer Institute of Linguists, 191

superlatives, 251

supervisors, 2, 11, 18, 34, 157, 184, 214

surnames, 113, 126, 127, 237, 239, 246

Survey of English Dialects, 103, 113, 121, 175

swearwords, 106, 132, 167, 185

syllable structure, 37

synchronous communication, 142

synonymy, 38, 80

syntactic theory, 10, 66

syntax, 21, 32, 37, 61, 65, 66, 73 *see also* grammar

systematic variation, 93

tables, 2, 12, 115–6, 161, 181, 185, 186

taboo words, 100, 101, 105, 106, 132

tagging (corpus annotation) *see* word class tagging

tags, 105, 117

talkativeness, 105

tape-recorders, 12, 106, 155, 180

Task-Based Learning, 51

teachers, 33, 41, 43, 48, 49, 50, 51, 52, 54, 55, 57, 64, 73, 98, 109, 130, 161, 176, 181

Teaching English as a Foreign Language, *Chapter 4, see also* second language

Teaching English as a Second Language, *Chapter 4 see also* second language

Teaching English to Speakers of Other Languages, *Chapter 4, see also* second language

teaching policy, 56–7

technical terms, 8, 51, 158, 222

technology, 130, 139, 159, *Chapter 19*, 262

TEFL *see* Teaching English as a Foreign Language 46

telephone,

answering machines, 100

conversations, 40, 100

voice, 100, 169–70

television, 78, 83, 84, 87, 88, 112, 154 *see also* TV

templates, 21

tenses, 22, 36, 70, 116

terminology (as a topic of study), 28, 38–9, 68

terminology (guidance), 31, 45–6, 79, 93, 101, 112, 262–3

TESL, 46 *see* Teaching English as a Second Language

TESOL, 46, *see* Teaching English to Speakers of another Language

test statistics, 228

testing, 10, 50, 55, 158, 161, 164

text,
analysis, 12, 62, 64, 65, *Chapter 6*, 99, *Chapter 19*
creation, 26, 44, 70, *Chapter 23*
references, (corpus annotation) *Chapter 19*

textbook, 5

texting (*see* txt language), 135

text-to-speech conversion, 147

thanking, 11, 173, 185

theory, 8, 59, 158, 223

theory-only projects, 10

therapy, 25, 29

thesaurus, 262–3

thinking aloud, 26, 48

Thomas, Dylan, 79

three-author publications, 239–40

threshold of activation, 20

timetable, creating, 3

'tip of the tongue' phenomenon, 17, 24, 25

topic management, 89, 105

topic shifting, 77, 154

Total Physical Response, 51

trade unions, 119, 131

traditional dialectology, 93, 103, 165

training, 6, 19, 160

transcribing machines, 195

transcription conventions, 197–204, *Chapter 18*

transfer of training, 54

transferability of skills, 19

transition relevance points, 88

translation, 52, 53, 79–80, 127

Trudgill, Peter, 92, 95, 96, 104, 113, 125

true/false questions, 168

t-test, 224

Turnitin plagiarism software, 248

turns, 58
   turn-taking strategies, 89, 105, 197–8

tutors, *see supervisors*, 11, 90, 99,
   162, 261, 265

TV, 52, 58, 63, 64, 89, 153, 156, 179 *see also*
   television

twin studies, 9, 40, 109

twitter, 135, 136, 137, 138

Two Ronnies, 63

two-author publications, 239–340

txt language, 138, 139

typing
   errors, 142
   speed, 142

under-extension, 35–36

under-fives, 36

underlining, 243, 253

underlying form, 114

unethical practice, 180

unfinished words, transcription 199

universal grammar, 49

unmarked structure, 82

unusual pronunciations, 199–200

up-date studies, 121

urban dialectology, 93, 103, 165

URL, 136

variability, 93–94, 96, 131

variables, 2, 93–94, 102, 103, 111, 117, 157, 163,
   179, 222

variation, 30, 34, 40, 49, 64, 65, 83, 93, 94, 96,
   113, 117, 136, 139, 210, 211, 228

verbs, 22, 24, 36, 48, 54, 68, 88, 115, 116, 175, 205

video data (*see also* data: tape-recorded), 12, 25,
   33, *Chapter 12*, 174, 175, 178, 185

Vikings, 128

virtual worlds, 143

vocabulary acquisition, 50, 52

vocabulary, 9, 38, 39, 42, 49, 54, 65, 67, 80, 97,
   108, 111, 124, 128, 132, 138, 158, 165, 175,
   262–3

volume (sound), 49, 202

weak verbs, 116

Webcorp, 211

webpages, referencing, 244–5

websites, 6, 74, 85

Welsh, 53, 58, 98

Wernicke's aphasia *see* aphasia

whispering, 202

Whorf, 27

Wikipedia, 7, 73, 74

Wilcoxon test, 224

Wittgenstein, 68

witticism, 58

women's language, 105, 107

word class tagging (corpus annotation), 211, 212

word classes, 36, 115

word distribution, 69, 86, 206, 209, 212

word endings, 24

word formation, *see* morphology,
   115, 206

word frequency lists, 206

word limit, 2, 4, 9, 183, 252

word order, 65

word recognition, 20, 130

wordbanks, 210

word-counting, 14, 238

word-finding difficulties, 24, 25

word-initial cohort, 20

word-processing, 2, 13, 14, 181, 219, 233,
   235, 262

word shape, 20

WordSmith, 206, 211

wordstring, 211

World Englishes, 114

world wide web, 210, *see also* internet
writing up, 9, 164
writing, 26, 41, 42, 48, 66, 76, 79, 85, 90, 110,
written questionnaires, 170, 171, 174
Wug study, 36

XML (Extensible Markup Language), 211

Yahoo! 211
year abroad 58
yes/no questions 168